The Greek Discovery of Politics

THE GREEK
DISCOVERY
OF POLITICS

CHRISTIAN MEIER

Translated by David McLintock

HARVARD UNIVERSITY PRESS

CAMBRIDGE, MASSACHUSETTS

LONDON, ENGLAND

1990

Copyright © 1990 by the President and Fellows
of Harvard College
All rights reserved
Printed in the United States of America
10 9 8 7 6 5 4 3 2 1

Originally published as *Die Entstehung des Politischen bei den Griechen*
© Suhrkamp Verlag Frankfurt am Main 1980

Translation of this volume has been aided by a grant
from Inter Nationes.

This book is printed on acid-free paper, and its binding
materials have been chosen for strength and durability.

Library of Congress Cataloging-in-Publication Data

Meier, Christian.
The Greek discovery of politics /
Christian Meier; translated by David McLintock.
p.   cm.
Translation of: Entstehung des Politischen bei den Griechen.
ISBN 0-674-36232-2 (alk. paper)
1. Political science—Greece—History.
2. Greece—Politics and government—To 146 B.C.
I. Title.
JC73.M3913   1990
320.938—dc20   89-48371
CIP

Contents

Preface to the English-Language Edition

NOT ALL THE questions that this book seeks to answer are immediately obvious, and some of the ways in which the answers are sought may appear strange, at least to students of ancient history. I should therefore perhaps briefly attempt to clarify my approach.

I believe that ancient historians do not work only for ancient historians. I also believe that, in seeking a wider public, they should not look solely to those with classical interests who are prepared to immerse themselves wholeheartedly in the world of antiquity. It seems to me rather that we should also join in a more general debate, viewing our subject, the history and societies of the Greeks and the Romans, from the outside and expressly relating it to others, if only to understand its special character.

In asking one of the big questions to which this book addresses itself, the question of how democracy arose, we should not simply take it for granted that the Greeks were a specially gifted people, predestined to achieve great things (so that it would be a matter of course for them to "invent" democracy). Nor should we confine ourselves to scanning their early history for this or that circumstance that might have prepared the way for democracy. Rather we should start from the "statistics" of world history, from which it appears to have been highly unlikely that democracy would evolve anywhere. The Greeks could have known nothing of such a possibility before they realized it themselves: they had no Greeks to emulate. We should therefore refrain from facile assumptions and make a critical, cautious, and strenuous effort to trace the path upon which such an extraordinary history became possible, and upon which, at some point, the Greeks presumably became what they subsequently were. About this the sources seldom tell us much, and the information they do vouchsafe is only fragmentary. Yet it should be possible, if we proceed with caution, to draw some inferences from the obvious facts they reveal, or from what can be reconstructed from them.

The same is true of the second big problem treated in this book: What constituted the special character, not only of democracy, but of the whole world of the Greeks during the classical period, in which politics played such a dominant and determining role? The first democracies of world history defied all the rules to such an extent that they can have arisen and survived only under quite extraordinary circumstances. A study of the sources and contemporary conditions certainly allows us to make this or that statement about the peculiarity of the Greek political world, but a more precise picture will emerge only from a comparison with other cultures. In this book the conditions of ancient Greece are compared chiefly with those of modern Europe. The questions that arise from such a comparison can be answered only by a student of ancient history, but the questions that must be asked become clear only from extending one's attention to other cultures, especially the older cultures of the East, and from viewing the object of one's study against a wider horizon. The chapters in this volume were originally written as essays for various readerships whose interests lay principally in modern history. Relying above all on the work of Reinhart Koselleck, I have tried, with the help of particular categories, to contrast some aspects of the Greek world with that of modern times. Much of the inspiration for this effort came from the experience of the post-1968 period in Germany, and from the brave hopes for the future that were revived then, especially among students, directing attention to the questions of how change comes about, in what areas it occurs, how events and change interrelate, what role is played by expectations, and much else besides.

Viewed from the outside, the preoccupations of one's own discipline appear in many ways puzzling and surprising, yet at the same time more clearly defined. This has many advantages. But I believe we also have an obligation to communicate our findings to the world outside, presenting them in such a way that they can be appreciated by scholars in other fields. It seems to me that the compartmentalization of the different historical disciplines is less and less justified, and that we should do all we can to create, as far as possible, a synopsis of different periods of history and to facilitate comparison between them. Indeed, we should try to promote a wider understanding of the nature of the societies that are the object of our study, so that the extraordinary period of classical antiquity may be more fully integrated into an interdisciplinary debate. The need to bring the remarkable achievements of the Greeks within the compass of a wider scholarly dialogue, and to the attention of a public that is not specifically concerned with *litterae humaniores,* is presumably not confined to Germany.

The chapters in this book are therefore addressed to a fairly broad interdisciplinary public (insofar as such a public exists). Yet it will have become clear by now that they are also intended to promote the study of ancient history itself. Concepts such as that of "civic identity" direct our attention to important prerequisites for a proper understanding of the functioning of democracy. Questions about configurations of action or the relation between events and change help us to recognize specific modes of thought which are unfamiliar to us today, but with which we must familiarize ourselves if we wish to comprehend the conceptual world of the Greeks, their historiography, and the very basis of democratic action and commitment. The attempt at a detailed contrast between what appear to be "ideas of progress" and the corresponding modern notion demonstrates clearly not only the absence of an ancient concept of progress, but also the specific nature of its Greek equivalent, the "consciousness of ability."

Despite its predominantly comparative approach, this book also deals with questions that belong to the mainstream of ancient history, such as the reform of Cleisthenes, the interpretation of Aeschylus' *Eumenides*, Greek political thought, the prehistory and practice of democracy, and the idiosyncrasy of the Greeks.

Finally I must mention one question that has engaged my attention from the beginning: whether the category of "the political" can help us understand essential elements of the Greek experience, and, if so, how. The question of the nature of the political was raised by Carl Schmitt in a particularly radical form on the basis of the changes that Germany underwent in the aftermath of the First World War. While it is true that some of the consequences that he or others drew from his answers are dubious or mistaken, his work provides us with a range of ideas that deserve to be brought into the scholarly debate. The topicality of such considerations in Germany may have to do with the way in which questions are apt to be posed there, as a consequence of the upheavals in the country's recent history and, not least, of its philosophical tradition. But the answers may stand up to scrutiny in a wider context.

I am very grateful to David McLintock for the care he has taken in translating this far from simple text. I have supervised the whole translation, which reproduces the original edition except for two chapters on Greek historiography.

Munich, June 1989   C. M.

The Greek Discovery of Politics

Introduction

The time is coming when we shall have
to rethink our views on politics.

—NIETZSCHE

THIS BOOK addresses itself fundamentally—and I hope not too single-mindedly—to two questions: How was it that Greek civilization, unlike all others preceding it or comparable with it, gave birth to democracies? And what was the nature of the political among the Greeks? What made it a distinctive and vital element in Greek society, by which it was fashioned and which it also helped fashion?

It is not easy to understand how a people that knew nothing about the possibility of democracy could create democratic systems of government. It cannot have been an altogether probable development, or the Greeks would not have been the exception to the rule among advanced civilizations. For, whatever else may be said in their favor, there is nothing to suggest that the Greeks were from the beginning more "gifted" than so many other peoples. Nor can the explanation lie in the special character of their culture, for this was itself clearly the outcome of the process that produced the conditions favorable to democracy. There was a two-way connection between this process and the development of democracy, the former supplying the requisite conditions for the latter and being in turn conditioned by it.

The first democracies in world history could arise only if the citizens lived together as citizens, and if this mode of living "politically" became a central feature of civic life. This depended on various preconditions and had various consequences. The result was that the Greeks came to occupy a unique position in the world, one in which the citizens exercised unprecedented control over their conditions of life. This involved a specific form of social identity, a particular way of experiencing time, a special relationship between stability and change, a particular mode of experiencing, perceiving, and understanding human potentialities, history, society, and change and—not least—a unique exposure to reality, special forms of poetry, of theological, philosophical, and scientific questioning, as well as

infinitely more besides, which we know—or perhaps do not (yet) know—
to have been connected with it. Even in such spheres as sculpture and
architecture, Greek culture received, at the very least, a strong impetus
from politics. What we are here seeking to understand as "the political"
is the ambience in which the Greek *polis* communities took shape and
underwent what were doubtless their most important experiences. This
is something far more comprehensive than the democracy in which it
culminated.

By developing the political, the Greeks became the eye of the needle
through which the whole of world history had to pass before it could
arrive at the modern European stage. What were the conditions that led
to the emergence of Greek society? Or, to put it in cruder terms, was
Greek history, together with the place it came to occupy in world history,
an inevitable outcome of prior developments, or was its development fortuitous? This is a question we are bound to ask if we hope to arrive at
anything more than a superficial historical understanding of our present
situation.

At this point, therefore, it is necessary to set a specifically historical
conception of long-term processes against the prevailing evolutionary
view of history. For the unique character of Greek cultural development
appears to confound those hypotheses that see social developments as
conforming to a regular, universal pattern. At all events, the emergence of
the political among the Greeks cannot be explained away by reference to
the well-attested human capacity for creating advanced civilizations, and
it must be strictly distinguished from the emergence of what are loosely
called the earliest "states." What is at issue, then, is the entire program of
"history as a social science."

Such an assessment of the role of the Greeks in history naturally presupposes that the importance of the political is realized in its own right
and in any contexts in which it may be involved. Running counter to this
view is the tendency, which has recurred repeatedly in recent decades (for
the most varied reasons and despite ample evidence to the contrary), to
play down the role of the political and to dismiss it as something merely
functional. And indeed, in a paradoxical though by no means unmean-
ingful way (one might perhaps say in a "cataparadoxical" way),[1] Germany has in recent years witnessed the progressive atrophy of any sense
of the political, yet at the same time the politicization of many areas of life
that were formerly unpolitical. As a result, the short-term upheavals of
our age tend increasingly to engender a kind of weary detachment, giving
a new topicality to Ecclesiastes' proposition that "there is nothing new
under the sun." The political may thus easily appear to be merely a function of the economic.

From this point of view Greek society may appear to have been basically one of the "ancient class societies" that evolved between Persia and
Italy in the first millennium B.C.[2]—as though the ability to visualize the
whole of an order without seeking to control it (or to identify oneself
with some human or divine ruler) were not something entirely new; as
though the emergence of an alternative (namely, whether the rulers alone
should have a decisive voice in the affairs of the community or whether
the ruled should also be involved—whether or not the citizens were
entitled to a say in the conduct of civic affairs) were not a phenomenon
quite unprecedented in world history.

While granting that individual strands in the development may have
evolved in the manner of autonomous processes, I suspect that the emergence of the political as a whole can be explained only in historical
terms.[3] We are dealing here with a development that was set in motion by
the contingent concurrence of a number of different forces under quite
specific conditions. This is true at least insofar as our sources admit of
any conclusions, and insofar as we have any knowledge—or can make
reasonable deductions—about historical connections. In this respect
even the astonishing phenomenon that great "advances" were simultaneously in train in different places during the "axial period"[4] only adds to
the puzzles confronting us, for—to repeat what we have said already—
the political arose only among the Greeks.

But what is "the political"? What is it in general, and what form did it
assume among the Greeks? In the wide and highly controversial area of
discussion that this question opens up, it is bound to seem at least somewhat risky to claim that the political was a Greek concept. True, *politics*
and *political* are words of Greek origin. However, the abstract term *the
political* (*le politique, das Politische*) is so very modern and so oriented to
the modern sense of the word that it may not be scientifically helpful at
present—however politically justified it may be—to invoke the Greek
notion of the political at this point without further ado.

The senses that the word *political* has taken on in the course of time are
not only very varied but also to some extent contradictory. Originally the
term related to the *polis*, which was identical with the civic community,
and to a particular constitution; later it related to the state, represented
by the monarch. To act "politically" was at first understood in the positive sense of acting in the general interest, the converse being to act out of
self-interest. Subsequently the term came to be understood rather in a technical sense and even to acquire pejorative connotations such as "shrewd,
cunning, crafty." Finally it ceased to be essentially linked with the state.
With the progressive socialization of the state (that is, the growing politicization of society) it has in recent times extended its semantic range to

embrace the most diverse elements in a world that is rapidly becoming politicized. This phase is represented by Carl Schmitt's attempt to redefine the "concept of the political."[5] The fact that in Schmitt's definition of the political an essential part is played by the distinction between friend and foe seems to produce a further contrast with the Greek meaning of the word, which implies the overcoming of such oppositions and the restriction of power.

However, in the intermediate, Janus-headed situation for which Carl Schmitt was trying to supply a theoretical framework, this criterion constitutes only that part of his insight which still relates to the state. Whatever may be said on this score, it is more important to note that Schmitt provided the impetus for a radical redefinition, if not for the discovery, of what is meant by the political in the world of today. Pursuing this idea, as we are bound to do in the present situation, we find that the political turns out to be a broadly uniform and universal phenomenon; the various meanings of the adjective—as well as the contradictions among them—merely reflect the different forms assumed by the political at different stages in history and denote merely differing aspects of a comprehensive whole. Herein lies the specific theoretical and practical value of the concept. We must not forfeit this by treating the *the political* and *politics* as though the terms were more or less synonymous.[6]

If we are to identify the political as a general phenomenon that exists both in history and in the present, it will not do to invest it either with the sum of all the senses contained in the adjective or with some element common to them all, let alone to stress certain of these senses at the expense of others. The great merit of the term *the political* lies in the fact that it is able, in tune with an essential strand of the modern meaning of the word, to capture something that is not identical with the multiplicity of meaning conveyed by the words *political* and *politics*. *The political* denotes a "field of association and dissociation,"[7] namely, the field or ambience in which people constitute orders within which they live together among themselves and set themselves apart from others. It is at the same time the field in which decisions are made about order and delimitation, as well as other questions of common interest, and in which there is contention for positions from which these decisions can be influenced.

In a theory of the political it would be possible to understand the various specific modes of association and dissociation, to establish a basis of comparison, and to incorporate them into a wider theory of social structure. Concomitant with the right of all the citizens of the democratic city-states of Greece to participate in public affairs were an extension of the area of political decision making to the center of government and a particular way of distinguishing between internal and external. This means that the citizens were "politicized," and this politicization defined the place of the political in Greek life: in the classical period at least, politics bore almost exclusively upon the relations between citizens *qua* citizens and the relations between the different city-states, and any changes that took place were in reality largely identical (and felt to be almost wholly identical) with political movements. The political order and politics (as the sphere in which it was consciously shaped) were thus, to an almost unique extent, wrested from the "self-moving" mechanism of processes (*automaton*)[8] and from the influences of other spheres of life. The result was an almost ideal model of the political: political events and political conditions became subject to the will of the participants and whatever was contingent upon their interaction. The conditions of political life were at the disposal of the citizens. To this extent the political was not only an important sphere of activity in many respects, but the central element in the life of Greek society, and of Athenian society in particular.

It is hardly necessary to expatiate on the differences between Greek conditions and those of the early modern period, when the monarch acquired a monopoly on power and political decision making. This monopolization of power was matched by an extension of the area of monarchical control to state organization and to social and economic affairs, and even (by virtue of the *ius reformationis*) to religious affairs. On the other hand, certain powerful forces were still ranged against the state—at first the churches, and later society. The boundaries between the state and what lay outside it were drawn more clearly. Yet at the same time differentiation led to the evolution of processes. Besides political movements, other forms of activity came increasingly to the fore—developments in science, technology, culture, society, economics, and in everything affected by them. Even in the period since the end of the eighteenth century, when citizens (by virtue of the *ius revolutionis*) acquired a say in political affairs, only a fraction of the changes that have taken place has been determined by politics, whose relation to them has remained fairly marginal. More important than the attempted politicization—which found expression, for instance, in the use of the word *citoyen* as a form of address during the French Revolution (and later in the understanding of political unity as a process of integration)—has been the "temporalization" of the social world. Our fate may in the short term be determined by politics, as we in the present century know only too well, but in the long term it is determined by processes of change resulting from infinite accumulations of disparate impulses. Today there is an unprecedented gulf between short-term sequences of individual events (of the most intense and often violent kind) and long-term processes of change.

Today this is becoming evident in new ways: problems arise not only from change—and its increasing rapidity—but also from the changed structure of the political, including the new position it occupies in our world and the part it plays in relation to the tasks that have to be performed. In the nineteenth century and until well into the twentieth, it was possible to see the various processes of change as running in one direction—to the benefit, first, of the bourgeoisie, then also of the proletariat. Today, however, one increasingly senses that they are running in contrary directions, to the benefit of scarcely anyone. Where there once seemed to be progress, we now have attempts to *compensate for the progressively negative side effects of progress.*[9] Walter Benjamin asks whether revolutions really are the "locomotives of world history," and not rather "mankind's attempts to grab the communication cord."[10] Attention is focused more and more on the state of emergency. Rather than allow everything to be decided by processes, we are told, we must ensure that present action becomes decisive.[11] Unprecedented demands are made of political action: it should work to remove the material constraints on individual freedom, that is, to counter the minor (and major) processes of change that, in the circumstances of our age, result from the unintended side effects of our actions. The political is becoming *all-pervasive.*[12] Almost everything is subject to political decision making—even the decision as to what should be exempt from it. All this threatens to engulf the very nature of man and the world he lives in (at least in the modern form of "preliminary decision making," whereby partial decisions are made that affect the whole).[13] At the same time, association and dissociation are changing to such an extent that power is becoming increasingly diffuse; on the one hand, areas of participation and scope for political action are being widened, yet, on the other, all sources of political authority are being weakened, at least where restricted procedures are concerned. *Potestates indirectae* are becoming so strong, interdependency so complex, and power so widely diffused, that one wonders whether what happens in the world, even in the sphere of the political, is not motivated by processes that result from the unintended side effects of action rather than from real decisions.[14] Not the least important of these processes is the vicious circle consisting of our excessive expectations of politics (deriving from the pretensions of the modern age), the ensuing disappointments, and the subsequent increase in expectations (together with the plea to be left out of politics).

What happened in ancient Greece was that the sphere of communal life was wrested from the control of self-motivating processes and made subject to political action. Today, by contrast, political action itself has become overlaid with processes by which we ourselves—and our identity—appear to be "motorized."

How this works in detail need not detain us here. We are not concerned with the present situation, with its anxieties and expectations, though they do seem to sharpen our perception of the issue. There are times when political association and dissociation crisscross in such complex ways as to create divisions even within individuals, when we feel powerless, beyond a certain point, in the face of what is happening around us. This feeling, which is due in part to the discrepancy between the high hopes that are placed in political action and what it can actually deliver, calls for at least some readjustment of our level of expectation. There are times when the fruitful link between the representation of interests and the settlement of structural problems within one and the same party system (a characteristic feature of modern times) no longer seems assured, when it is uncertain to what extent our conditions of life—supposing that we have reason to be dissatisfied with them—can still be brought into the arena of political controversy. It is at times like these that the significance of the political—its nature and the place it occupies—becomes clearer. At all events, one may suspect that the relation between political controversy and the possibility of change has passed a certain critical limit, or soon will; the modern debate about the ungovernability of our society is the clearest symptom of this suspicion.

Given this situation, it seems likely that a new concept of the political may at least supply a new orientation. Insofar as the Greek form of the political—viewed in the light of this modern concept—can be regarded almost as an ideal type, it may perform an important, though necessarily limited, function.

When the political detaches itself from the state (in accordance with the continuity and discontinuity of modern traditions), when not only the decisions become critical, but the very possibility of making political decisions that can in any way affect what is imposed upon us by our conditions of life, when our very identity is at stake [15]—at such times we are able to gain a fresh view of what was special about the Greeks and their achievements, a fresh view of the political, which was their creation (in the essential sense of the term—of citizens living together in freedom), of the civilization they represent, the one political civilization among all the others the world has known, and hence of the position they occupy in world history.

This is the complex of problems that we propose to discuss here—admittedly in an incomplete and somewhat fragmentary fashion. We are thus provided with a certain theoretical and methodical starting point. Since this may not at once be self-evident, a brief outline of the position will be necessary.

We have to start from the fact that the world of the Greek *polis*, viewed as a whole, differs fundamentally from our own, that it is alien to us [16] and made up of a specific combination of the most diverse factors. Much about it is of course familiar to us; many phenomena resemble or are identical with corresponding phenomena in our own age. Were this not so, we should not be able to understand it at all. Yet, taken as a whole, it is very different.[17]

The specific combination of factors cannot be elicited directly from the sources. All the essays presented here are, of course, based on source-study, and in parts they amount to nothing more. Yet what interests us here was for the most part unknown to the Greeks and therefore could not find expression in the sources, which often seem to be no more than indicators. But whether they really are indicators and, if so, of *what*— these are questions to which they cannot supply a direct answer. The answers, then, can be only indirectly inferred from the recorded tradition; they can supply interrelationships between various data (facts, institutions, modes of thought, conditions, and so on) that may be elicited from the sources in a variety of ways. Many of these data were brought to light by earlier scholarship; others became clear only in the course of my own research.

In every case my principal concern has been to reach an adequate understanding of the individual interrelationships; this involves establishing categories that will help us, first, to identify and register these interrelationships and then to correlate them with others. Since the interrelationships between different factors and different areas vary from society to society and rest upon varying preconditions, no modern theory could serve as a basis for research. The theoretical components of my investigation were primarily individual elements that might contribute to an understanding of the total structure. At the same time, of course, my investigation tends toward the construction of a theory of the period as a whole, within which the elements can be brought into relation with one another. Such a theory may supply a basis for comparisons with other periods. This is not, however, my immediate aim.

Historical writing should be couched in ordinary language;[18] it should be factual and adhere as closely as possible to what underlies all history—human action and the contexts in which such action takes place and becomes effective. In dealing with remote epochs, this everyday language must of course contain certain *points de repère,* certain concepts that will focus the reader's attention and point to distinctions and complexes that would otherwise be revealed only to the most minute and painstaking study. (In this way, ordinary language is enriched and adapted to historical purposes.) The historian cannot operate without immersing himself in such study, but he must also emerge from it from time to time, for his task is to mediate between the object of his study and his own age. For this purpose he needs certain concepts, and also certain theories that underlie the concepts and coalesce in such a way as to yield explicit and consistent conceptual systems. This is only part—but an essential part— of the historian's task.

We are concerned here with matters that have so far received scant attention, and for which our age sharpens our perception. Apart from the structure and place of the political, we also have to consider such questions as the specific contexts of action, the relations between them, change and time, the civic presence, and various forms of social affiliation and identity. We have to distinguish between different species of historical change, the relations between events and change, between politics and processes, between change and the perception of change, and between different perceptions of men's capacity to achieve significant improvements in their conditions. A particularly interesting and important problem is the one posed by the conceptual worlds of different periods. In the prehistory of democracy it has proved possible to discern a "social history of political thought" and then to attempt a reconstruction of the Greek experience of "politicization."

Needless to say, the assumption of a specific link between various factors and various areas does not imply that any one sector of society is to be credited with initiating particular historical trends. Unfortunately I was unable to complete my study of democracy, economics, and slaves in classical Athens in time to include it in this volume. That work would have made it clear that, under a radical democracy, the politicization of the widest possible sectors of society and the unprecedented involvement of the "common man" in practical politics went hand in hand with the discouragement of economic motives in the thinking of the poor. The satisfaction of domestic needs was largely transferred from the economic to the political sphere. The contrast that Plato and Aristotle observed between political and economic activity ultimately reflects a basic condition of life in the Greek city-state: that the political should assert itself against economic motives in the narrow sense of the term.

However, what is presented here is in any case somewhat fragmentary. This is to some extent unavoidable—in that the special features of an age inevitably transcend any theory.

PART I

The Concept of
the Political

ONE

From *Politikos* to the Modern Concept
of the Political

T
HE WORD *political* was used by the Greeks to designate what
pertained to the *polis*. It referred in a quite specific sense to
the city, which was identical with the civic community, being
grounded in and constituted by the whole of the body politic. The *polis*
provided the only significant link between citizens beyond the home. All
other affiliations were to a large extent related to the city (for instance,
the cult communities) or had little importance outside the private sphere
(for instance, economic relations).[1] To the Greeks, then, the opposite of
"political" was "private," "personal," "self-interested." "Political" meant
the same as "common" (*koinos, xynos*) and referred to what concerned
everybody. So closely was the word—in its specific sense—connected
with the *polis* of the free and equal that it denoted the opposite of "despotic," indeed of any form of rule by the few over the many. Thus, to
broaden an oligarchy was to make it "more political." Thucydides used
the term *political* to designate the proper form of a constitution founded
on equality.[2] "Political" rule, according to Aristotle, was government of
and by the free and equal. It appears to have been associated with a particular form of power and a particular exercise of power.[3] Within what
we would call political rule, then, the Greeks distinguished between the
constitutionally restricted sphere of the political order and the unre-
stricted sphere that did not conform with the *polis,* in which things were
not ordered politically and in which arbitrary tyranny prevailed or might
prevail. Relations between different *poleis* were not political in the Greek
sense. Political action was correct action within the *polis*.[4] In this way
the Greeks could view the life and activity of the *polis* with a certain
detachment, but not from the perspective of established norms belonging
to a different area of life.

In modern times, by contrast, the state has always had to be defined in
relation to powerful and relatively autonomous rival forces or *potestates*

indirectae, such as the churches, society, and the economy. The word *political* relates primarily to the state, which was built up in order to hold the contending parties in check during the wars of religion. In this context the state is simply an entity of a particular kind, one among others. At first it was embodied in the monarch, and nothing in the specifically modern meaning of *political* (which is, however, by no means its sole meaning) allows us to distinguish between states with different constitutions.[5] In its specific sense, the word relates to a special mode of action whose characteristics could be clearly recognized in the light of the claims of Christian revelation and on the basis of the extraordinary "technical" possibilities available to the modern state. These were first enunciated by Macchiavelli, and then practiced—and at the same time condemned (this being part of the exercise)—by his opponents. Such activity was concentrated in a relatively small and exclusive circle of politicians. As a result, it was not bound by certain obligations. The existence of powerful external forces such as the churches, and later of a society that was highly conscious of its own moral values, also served to make others distance themselves from politics. The term *political* thus came to be equated with "cunning," "crafty," "guileful," "insincere."

In its general and ethically neutral sense, politics may be defined, in the words of Frederick the Great, as "the science of always acting by suitable means in accordance with one's own interests."[6] The Greeks too, of course, practiced this art or science. They called it *politike techne* or *arete.*[7] But the entities to which it related were different: for the Greeks it was the civic community, whereas in early modern times it was the state, which was to a large extent set apart from society. Accordingly, there were different ways of viewing it (from within or without), different degrees of detachment, different horizons of expectation.

Ever since the Renaissance it has been possible to use the word *politics* to designate any action of which the state is capable. Political action may perhaps still be delimited against war, yet war too can be understood as politics, though pursued by different means. As the distinction between war and nonwar becomes obsolete, however, so too does the borderline between war and politics.[8] Being delimited against the church and society, the area occupied by the state was at first fairly clearly defined. The initiative in political affairs lay for the most part with the state; the nucleus of power concentrated at the center was so firmly institutionalized that access to it was limited and controllable. Relations with other areas were regulated largely by administrative means or "police" (in the older sense of the word)[9] and were hardly subject to politics. The state had "a monopoly on the political."[10]

However much the meaning of the word *political* may have been affected by the "temporalization" of the world of concepts around 1800, what determined its subsequent history was undoubtedly the radical change that took place in the position of the state, beginning with the growth of pluralism in the nineteenth century and the politicization of more and more areas of life. Only when the unity of the state had come under pressure from other forces was it possible for "political affairs" to be distinguished from "affairs of state," and for the term *political* to lose its unequivocal link with the state. In this situation it was theoretically possible, if one adopted a very radical and uncompromising approach, to be faced with the problem of, on the one hand, defining political units more rigorously (and so distinguishing between these and the growing number of political subjects) or, on the other, recognizing and understanding the political as a single comprehensive field of activity.

At this point Carl Schmitt's concept of the political becomes relevant. It is famous above all for the thesis that the criterion for the political is the possibility of distinguishing between friend and foe. Corresponding to this thesis is his observation that the political is not "a particular domain, but only the *degree of intensity* of an association or dissociation among people whose motives may be religious, national . . . economic, or of some other kind."[11]

Carl Schmitt never claimed, of course, to have supplied a basic definition of the political, let alone of politics. He was concerned only to establish a criterion. He clearly indicated the theoretical step he had taken.[12] I would wish to limit his thesis, however, and maintain that his criterion applies not to the political in general, but to the *political unit*. The term *political* applies to those human associations that have the potential, in extreme cases, to distinguish between friend and foe within the framework of the political field, in other words of being the *partie belligérante*.[13] This basic definition requires a criterion for distinguishing those friend-foe relations that are political from those that are not. According to Schmitt, the foe is "a body of people that, at least potentially—that is, in circumstances that could conceivably arise—might come into *conflict* with a similar body of people."[14] In modern times the bodies of people in question have been states. Given the clear distinction between war and peace that could exist between states, the term *conflict* is unequivocal.

At one time, then, the contenders in the political field were states, but today one can say that the term *political* applies to those decisions about who is a friend and who a foe that are made either by states or by other forces capable of entering into conflict with them. Other friend-foe distinctions are politically of no interest, though their consequences may fall within the competence of state authorities such as the police or the courts. In general—that is, in the perspective of world history—the other contenders in the political field are those autocephalic units in which (to put it in broad terms) supreme legitimate power and the *ius belli* (probably the surest criterion of such power) are vested;[15] in early societies these may have been family alliances, clans, city-states, or other units. Only with this qualification can Schmitt's definition hold good for periods other than that of the modern state.[16]

How far it can be maintained that the political has no special domain of its own is a question of definition. At all events, political relations are to a limited degree autonomous,[17] and dealings are conducted from political motives (whatever ulterior motives there may be). It is important to remember that the field of politics is open to the most varied problems arising in other areas; potentially it may encompass all these, thus politicizing them and drawing them into the process of association and dissociation. Even supposedly unpolitical issues are settled by political means. The ways in which this happens vary from period to period.[18]

Schmitt's definition of the political is theoretical; it cannot be affected by contemporary party positions such as may have been suggested to its author by the existential or existentialist premises of his thinking.[19] It relates to an obvious state of affairs and has an analytic potential that turns out to be extraordinarily fruitful in any number of contexts. A good example is provided by those periods of political history that consist largely of shifts in the form of political association and dissociation: one such period is that which saw the transition to the *polis,* which became a decisive political unit only at a fairly late stage; before this there had been a long period in which alliances between relatively independent noble families and tyrants, involving a number of cities, had at least competed with the *polis* in deciding who was a friend and who a foe.[20]

It was only the opponents of Carl Schmitt (or his foes perhaps?) who extended his thesis of the "concept of the political" to imply that politics (*sic!*) meant conflict or polarization between friend and foe. Hence, what he conceived as an extreme possibility was misconstrued as a general rule; what was intended as a theoretical definition of the political was mistaken for a practical norm of politics. With regard to foreign affairs this is belied by Schmitt's clear concept of the foe, which is taken from the age of limited war[21] (even though it was already becoming obsolete in view of the ideological polarizations of the period and the tendency to identify the enemy on ideological grounds: this, after all, proves that it was theoretical). In internal affairs there can be no enemy, if the political unit is defined as it is by Carl Schmitt, for "the essence of political units consists in the exclusion of such extreme oppositions from within the unit."[22]

It is true that the particular intensity of political oppositions led Schmitt to conclude that a "concrete opposition is all the more political, the more it approaches the extreme point, the division between friend and foe."[23] "Political" is here simply equated with "existential" and "intense." This is the parting of the ways.[24] In my view it is wrong to disregard all the other dimensions of the word to such an extent that it would be possible to restrict the term *political* to this one dimension. Nor will it do, where internal politics are concerned, to admit only one secondary "concept of the political";[25] this is out of the question, especially after the disappearance of any clear division between internal and external. True, these observations can be understood and discussed only within the wider context of Carl Schmitt's total theory, but this would be to digress too far. Here we are concerned essentially with the one particular insight that seems to me crucial to the definition of the political as a whole and toward which one should adopt a theoretical and not a political stance.[26]

I refer to the basic conception of the political as a definite "field of action" that potentially pervades the whole of life. In attempting to define the political, one must undoubtedly direct one's attention to the whole of the field and not just to parts of it—the political units, for instance.

Here one must distinguish clearly among the terms *political, politics,* and *the political*. The adjective *political* and the concept of *the political* do not simply mean the same thing at different levels of abstraction. Grammatically, *the political* is of a piece with those substantivizations of adjectives by which the Greeks were able to "postulate the general as something definite,"[27] as when they spoke of the concept of the beautiful or the just. But there is a logical distinction. The adjectives *beautiful* and *just* each denote the same quality, whatever nouns they qualify. What the Greeks tried to do was to define these qualities by inquiring about the beautiful or the just as qualities inherent in those things described as beautiful or just. The adjective *political*, by contrast, means quite different things, belonging to different dimensions, according to the nouns it qualifies—units or orders, groups, questions, processes, conflicts, modes of action, or modes of perception. Sometimes it relates to affairs that concern the state as a whole, at other times to matters that are determined by particular interests; sometimes to controversial matters, and then again to craft and cunning.[28] Certain of these senses can be substantivized, so that one can speak, for instance, of "the political" in a person's way of viewing things. In doing so, however, one does not capture the whole or even the central element of the wide semantic spectrum covered by the word. The term *the political* cannot therefore denote the essential element in all the meanings of the adjective *political*.[29] It can in fact relate to what all these have in common only if it is conceived as a definite plane, as a field or element in which—to put it in general terms—individuals or groups behave toward one another in a specific manner. Carl Schmitt speaks very appositely of a "field of relations and tensions."[30] As a result of decentralization, what was previously concentrated in the state has been increasingly diffused among a variety of forces and relations, and the concept of the political seeks to do justice to this state of affairs in much the same way as corresponding contemporary formations—such as "the religious" or "the moral"—seek to do justice to complementary phenomena in other areas.

Viewed as a whole in this way, the political is seen to be characterized by a certain "degree of intensity of association and dissociation."[31] In its extreme form (which is not necessarily its most political) this involves a grouping into friends and foes. At the same time it is important to bear in mind all the various forms of mutual opposition that can exist within an overall ambience of friendship or solidarity.

"The political" is thus the element in which political units interact and in which various forces, however motivated, gain—or try to gain—direct influence over them through political action. All forces acting in this way are *ipso facto* political, whether or not this is what they want to be or admit to being—unless of course, while intending to be political, they fail to make an impact on the other occupants of the field and either remain ineffectual or fall within the jurisdiction of the police or the courts.[32] By adopting certain positions and opposing others they are acting politically, and so the questions at issue also become political. Between them they thus constitute a political field, which necessarily interacts with others, right up to the level of world politics. The effective combination of these forces acquires a limited autonomy: within this combination of forces, nonpolitical power factors do not assert themselves directly, but only indirectly, inasmuch as they can be transferred into the political.

We have now reached a state of affairs in which the political world, once so neatly structured, with clear-cut divisions between states and between internal and external affairs, is crisscrossed by a plethora of purposeful and effective political forces that are not themselves states and whose activities are not obviously confined within individual states;[33] these include supranational organizations. In this transitional situation the political can be conceived only as a comprehensive element such as we have described.

This element is defined chiefly by reference to political units. For it is with these that the ultimate decisions lie (no matter how they are made, who instigates them, and how ineffectual they may be at times). The will to achieve anything politically must ultimately address itself to the political units. Only by reference to these can the other forces be called political.

Aristotle could not speak of a field of activity of this kind, whose limits are determined by the range of politicizable issues and groups from the most varied spheres of activity. The main reason for this is that the political, as the Greeks understood it, was not concerned with problems and opinions emanating from other areas, but concentrated solely on the civic community as such. On the other hand, such fields of activity do exist elsewhere, even among the Greeks. The elementary concept of the political would enable us to evolve a theory that embraced the most varied manifestations of this field throughout world history and made it possible to compare them; such a theory could at the same time provide the starting point for a new, up-to-date, and much-needed form of political history, namely a "history of the political," which would range from detailed examinations of limited developments to the broad sweep of world history.[34]

Within the horizon of what Reinhart Koselleck calls the "conditions of possible history," which have now been worked out, we are concerned with—among other things—the ways in which people live together politically and the ways in which these modes of life are safeguarded, the distribution of power and access to power, the range of areas that have been politicized and—within the various structural possibilities—are still accessible to politicization. We are concerned with the typical oppositions that can arise and the contexts of political action (different forms of participation, different ways of exerting influence and achieving aims), with fusions between the political and other areas, with the relations between politics and "autonomous processes," between tasks that have to be performed (urgent problems to which solutions are expected and which, if left unsolved, will have far-reaching repercussions) and the possibilities of decision making.[35] We are concerned with the place of the political within society and within the process of change that society is undergoing.

Hidden behind this range of relatively abstract categories lies a host of problems relating to the proper understanding of the political as it was manifested at different moments in history. These problems naturally relate to constitutions (of whatever kind) and to constitutional realities. If the questions are posed broadly and realistically enough, they will at the same time generate—within the framework of political science—a whole series of demands, inasmuch as a proper understanding of political reality always implies the need for particular measures to safeguard and improve constitutional and legal conditions, to ensure peace, to increase the capacity of political centers for action and decision making, to promote integration, and so on. Any number of aims may be involved. However, it is probably no longer possible to invest the concept of the political or politics with the kind of normative content it carried in an essential strand of the semantic history of the terms *politikos, politike techne, episteme,* or *arete.*

The concept of the political as a particular field of activity is basic to what follows. Here a mere outline of the concept must suffice. It would in any case be impossible to deal adequately, in such a limited compass, with all the problems that arise here. What follows should therefore be seen as a contribution to the understanding of a problem whose total dimensions can at present hardly be appreciated.

TWO

The Political in Ancient Greece

THE AIM of this book is to understand some of the essential features marking the emergence of the political in Greece, that is, the specific pattern assumed by this field of activity during the classical age, especially in the democracy of Athens. As ever-wider sections of the body politic—and finally the overwhelming majority—won the right to a regular and powerful role in politics, this field of activity underwent a radical transformation, ultimately taking in the opposite pole of what had in earlier civilizations been the sole sphere of "political" activity (in the general sense of the term). It was now occupied conjointly by the rulers and the ruled.

Within the perspective of world history, this meant a great advance in politicization. For the first time the very core of the political order became a real political issue. The question was who was to govern—the monarch, the nobles, or the people? In other words, should the governed (who were thus no longer merely the "ruled")[1] have a decisive voice in political affairs or not?

Constitutions could now be established, and the rights and freedoms of the middle and lower ranks of society constitutionally secured. A separate political order, in which the citizens collaborated as citizens, was split off from the social order and set over against it. In this artificially created order, quite different relations obtained among the members: all had equal rights, and the majority of the citizens gained supreme authority (with the help of those nobles who placed themselves in their service).

On the basis of certain conditions dating back to early times, the problems of the *poleis* were transferred into the political sphere, where the citizens met as citizens (*politai*). The *polis* became identical with its citizens; the term for the citizen body (*politeia*) came to denote a just constitution, and it was this use of the term that determined the strict sense of the word *political* (*politikos*), meaning "appropriate to the *polis*." This almost total orientation toward the *polis* also determined Aristotle's concept of politics, enabling him to declare that it was the science of the highest good attainable through human action, and hence the "most important and fundamental of the sciences."[2] From the viewpoint of both the individual and the community at large, politics, understood in this way, was concerned with the whole.

The citizen's political affiliation (that is, his affiliation to the *polis*) became so central and, being general, so untrammeled by competition from other affiliations that it produced a political identity unique in world history, weighted toward the middle and lower ranks of society. This was especially true in Athens, but also to a large extent elsewhere, though the social center of gravity varied from place to place.[3] Even though metics and slaves—and of course women—had no political rights, the result was that those who were actively engaged in politics were largely identical with those affected by them.

This meant that the unity of the *polis* had to be grounded in the community as a whole—and not just in an abstract sense. It was the citizens who constituted the real nucleus of the city, the source of authority for the increasing control if exercised over the activities of its members, including the nobility. There was no way in which anything resembling a state could establish centralized power or state institutions that were divorced from society.

This close identification of the *polis* with its citizens presupposed a high degree of solidarity, and this could take root only in a general civic interest that transcended all particularist interests. This general interest became so powerful that, on this new plane of citizenship, the citizens determined the conduct of politics just as much as politics determined the conduct of the citizens. Other interests, by contrast, were neglected—relatively speaking!—or at any rate largely excluded from politics. Having politicized themselves, the citizens were not able to politicize their domestic interests. Only the general supply of food and the allocation of certain imposts were subject to political decisions.

This new situation entailed a special form of association and dissociation, a particular distribution of power and access to power. At first, the movement toward isonomy and democracy put an end to—or at least attenuated—the specific divisions between friend and foe existing within the nobility, which could lead to violent feuds within the city-states and beyond them. Against these divisions the broad mass of the citizens established and consolidated the general interest of the community as a whole. Since political rights came to occupy a position of central importance, however, it became possible, somewhat surprisingly, for a relatively clear and deep-seated distinction between democracy and oligarchy to develop, though this did not generally manifest itself until the middle of the fifth century. According to Plato, rich and poor might often live side by side like two cities within one city wall.[4] This was an exaggeration (which shows that even in his day political thinking, with its high political pretensions, tended to proceed from the exception and could not easily do justice to the rule). It is nevertheless true to say that, in the absence of comprehensive institutional safeguards, internal unity was often highly precarious, internal oppositions often being linked to external oppositions (especially those between Athens and Sparta), and that civil war and banishment were common. The centrality of citizenship was concomitant with the absence of an autonomous "state."

The political field was thus as extensive, with regard to the number of its occupants, as it was restricted with regard to the issues pertaining to it; moreover, it harbored a potential for extreme tension. It lacked the numerous modern devices by which energy can be discharged into non-political activity, but which may at times serve to overcharge relations all the more—though usually under the aegis of the state.[5] The political was an area of life teeming with activity, yet belonging, not to a society in the modern sense of the term (for in modern societies the various areas of life tend to be set alongside the state or against it), but to civic communities that identified themselves with the state.

The political was thus at the center of all perceptible change, and especially perceived change. The only change that men could perceive was the sum of political actions and events, since everything outside politics was essentially static, or changing only slowly and for the better.

The Greeks enjoyed not only a civic (or, in their terms, political) *presence*, but also a civic (or political) *present*, which went hand in hand with political identity: a civic *presence* inasmuch as the citizens were able to assert their will by being present and participating in political affairs; a civic *present*, inasmuch as they had a special mode of experiencing present time. The present was for them not the "moving point of dust where past and future meet," but a broad and richly charged band of immediate experience.

There were special contexts of action, both within what took place in society and within contemporary modes of perception. One matter that has received scant attention—and is therefore perhaps all the more interesting—is the question of the kind of events a society confronts when it looks at what is taking place inside it and outside it, and how it is involved in them. We are concerned here not with the totality of events, but only with those that transcend day-to-day life or at least produce appreciable changes in existing conditions, events that not only are of general interest but actually affect people's lives, whatever their personal involvement. I refer to the universally relevant experiences that befall people, and the reactions they produce. For the Greeks such events could be equated in large measure with politics and warfare. And this was, in even larger measure, how they were perceived. The corollary is that the developments of the age (and above all the way in which it perceived them) were essentially produced by deliberate political actions and their contingent effects, and by the decisions made in the course of such actions. Political action was the central factor. It consisted of the many movements of political subjects in a world that was on the whole perceived as unchanging.

Hence everyone—especially the prominent members of society, but also, to an extraordinary extent, whole communities, and in Athens even the common man—acquired a certain stature in relation to whatever happened in the world, an ability to influence the course of events that is scarcely conceivable today. They had a fairly direct, concrete, and existential share in the making and execution of decisions (and could identify themselves with the decision makers—and not just in an abstract manner). Whatever happened was to some extent commensurable with the citizens. They were close to events and inextricably involved in them. The events took place in their midst, largely as a consequence of their own decisions. One might almost say that they were exposed less to events than to the actions of others. They probably had no control over what took place: only the powerful Athenians and their statesman Pericles had any real control, at least for a time. The whole of life was eventful. One might suffer defeat; not only individuals, but whole cities, might cease to exist. These were relatively dangerous times.[6] But this was inevitable in a world in which everything was determined by political action. Thus—not to put too fine a point on it—the Greeks came to occupy a political position in the world. This position is diametrically opposed to that in which men are at the mercy of processes and find themselves taken over by them, in which it is necessary to resort to complex identifications with various movements—as in the modern age, and even in very recent times—if the individual is to have any sense of belonging, if his identity is to be raised above all the fragmentation and isolation that afflict him and integrated into a larger whole. Relatively few Greeks of the fifth century can have felt the "need for fatalism" that O. Marquard describes.[7]

This position that the Greeks occupied in the world of the fifth century was matched by an acute consciousness of human abilities, which seems to have been especially intense in Athens, from which the rest of the Greek world took its lead. Increasing opportunities for action and creativity were observed in the most varied spheres. Yet such observations remained additive: they were not generalized and did not coalesce in the perception of a great, all-encompassing process in which change became independent of those who caused it. There was a growing consciousness of the abilities and accomplishments of individuals—of large numbers of

individuals—but not of a broad current in which everything moved irresistibly forward and became a function of time.

The special character of the political as a central element in Greek life
had many and varied effects, radiating out into the most diverse areas of
life and helping to shape them. Its influence can be discerned in literature
and art, philosophy and faith. We perceive it in all the questions—and in
many of the answers—that were generated by the shattering experiences
the Greeks underwent as they contemplated their new-won freedom. Particularly interesting is the high degree of tolerance to contingency they
developed, which was a basic element of their historiography. They were
clearly quite modest in their search for the total meaning of what happened to them. The unchanging conditions that prevailed in the world
outside politics had a stabilizing effect in this respect. Whatever happened could be clearly appreciated as having been initiated by identifiable
agents or acted out between them. The Greeks were unable to see themselves—either as a whole or even within their city-states—as a "world
unto themselves," nor did they feel any need to see what befell them as
being, in some metaphysical sense, tailored to themselves. This is consonant also with their view of the enemy. They did not regard their enemies,
Greek or non-Greek, as in any way inferior to themselves; they saw them
essentially as equals, and did not hesitate to describe them publicly as
such. Invoking the aid of the gods against the enemy did not introduce
any significant religious component into the struggle, for the enemy
simply had different gods—or perhaps even the same ones.

The Greeks thus lacked much of the institutional and ideological pan-
oply that protects men from the perception of reality, from taking it seriously and being affected by it. Their openness was matched by an unusual
degree of exposedness, their conviction of the importance of action by
their experience of the rigors of decision making, the freedom born of
self-reliance by a keen awareness of the enormity of human suffering.
Probably nowhere else in the whole of historiography has such striking
emphasis been placed on the sufferings (*algea, pathemata*)[8] of the participants. Thus, while proud of man's monstrous capacities, the Greeks
were aware of his terrible nature. "Humanity, in all its vulnerability and
exposure to danger, with all its problems"[9] and frailties, yet at the same
time with all its joy and greatness, was experienced in a way that was
both disturbing and utterly new.

All this erupted and assumed definitive shape in a situation that was to
a large extent dominated by the emergence of the political (in its specifically Greek form, that is, related to the *polis*). Greek civilization is
thus the one political civilization in the whole of world history. Because
the political came to occupy such a central and dominant position (not
being confined to particular centers or reduced to a function of time and

society), this not only signified a new departure: it also meant embarking upon a unique and unrepeatable course.[10] The new departure belongs to history; the special course is of interest in the context of a theory of politics. In describing the characteristic features of Greek civilization it is customary to invoke the concept of the "classical"—a model for many, the attraction of which lay in all that was achieved, experienced, and represented, within the narrow confines of the world of the *polis,* in terms of accomplishments, of intellectual questioning and matching up to the questioning, of human greatness and commensurability with events, and at least one notable point of orientation. What was achieved in the Greek city-states was a close approximation between participating in politics and being at the receiving end of politics, between subject and object in the syntax of politics. So close was this approximation that it resulted in what might be called total politics: politics became the dominant element in the life of the community (rather than an element of domination and potentially total disposition). Even if all this was unique and unrepeatable, the simultaneous efflorescence of the political and the human is nevertheless of concern to our own age, in which the political is, on the one hand, in danger of being engulfed by self-motivating processes, yet on the other supposedly on the point of opening up enormous new dimensions in the form of a legal world revolution[11] (while now and then giving rise to new problems connected with the desire to opt out of politics altogether).

PART II

The Prehistory and Emergence
of Greek Democracy

THREE

The Emergence of the Trend toward Isonomy

THE GREEKS had no Greeks to emulate. They were therefore unaware of the possibility of democratic government before they created it themselves. Yet if a people are to acquire a say in how they are governed and even take over the reins of government, they must somehow evolve aims and pretensions that will ultimately be conducive to these ends. Ways and means must be found—that is to say, institutions must be created—that will make political participation possible, indeed conceivable. Knowledge of public affairs and claims to participation must become so firmly rooted in the whole complex of common interests and attitudes that the relatively minor abstract interest in politics shared by many of the citizens can increase and, transcending all the obvious divisions among them, become a major interest shared by all. A usurper knows roughly what he wants and simply has to seek the power and opportunity he needs in order to realize his aims, but where the broad mass of the people is concerned it is necessary, at such an early stage of political evolution, first to awaken, and then to reinforce and perpetuate, the idea that they can win a regular and powerful position in the community. A new political role has to appear, not just a new player to take over an old role. This calls for social reasoning of a quite different and more abstract kind. Finally, since the first democracies in world history could presumably arise only as direct democracies, a readiness for serious commitment had to take shape among the citizens, and this meant nothing less than a transformation of social identity. All this takes time.

What could be realized only in the future had therefore to be repeatedly anticipated in the present. This segment of history brings us up against Vico's old problem: men alone created this order, and yet, for most of the time at least, their understanding and intentions were too limited and too selfish for them to be able to understand or intend what they were creating. Vico's answer to the problem—that they were guided by divine providence—cannot carry much conviction with us. So how did the Greeks arrive at democracy?

We will attempt here, on the basis of what can be gleaned from the meager sources available, to reconstruct that phase in the prehistory of democracy that saw the emergence of the trend toward isonomy, the stage of political evolution that preceded democracy proper, when broad sections of the citizenry won an effective political voice in competition with the ruling nobility. Isonomy was realized in Athens around the end of the sixth century B.C., with the reforms of Cleisthenes; elsewhere it may have come earlier.

To study the emergence of the trend toward isonomy is to study a historical process. We must therefore try to show the concrete interrelationships between actions that constituted this process in specific situations (which reproduced themselves in these actions in varying forms).

Such a train of development (which at some stage presumably became an autonomous process, though this need not be elaborated here)[1] is indicated by a number of inferences that can be drawn partly from the sources themselves and partly from a comparison between the starting point and the end point of this particular phase of history. We may therefore be fairly certain—as will be demonstrated—that the well-known outcome of this phase, namely isonomy, permits us to draw certain conclusions about the process that led up to it, fragmentary evidence of which is afforded by the recorded facts or by what we can infer from the sources. At all events, our aim is to give a historical account of this development. Anticipating our thesis, we may say that this development, following upon a fairly protracted period of increasing movement, amounted essentially to a "social history of political thought," which in due course affected the most diverse areas of Greek life, producing the movement that eventually led to isonomy and determining its direction.

Most of the factors that are now held to have caused the process leading to democracy were in fact no more than preconditions that either made the process possible or were themselves produced by it. This is, at all events, the most we can make out. It is true that the geography of the Aegean region favored the existence of numerous independent city-states, but it would scarcely have impeded the rise of larger political units. In Mycenean times the region appears to have been organized quite differently, in much larger kingdoms. And if Sparta could rule the broad lands of Messenia beyond the high Taygetus, while empires such as that of Polycrates proved short-lived and the larger political units proposed by Thales of Miletus and Bias of Priene[2] had no prospect of being realized, geographic reasons were certainly not decisive.

Nor does the whole complex of traits that have been thought to make up the Greek "character" bring us much nearer an explanation of what took place. If the inhabitants of the Greek city-states were indeed imbued with an exceptionally strong, exclusive, and tenacious sense of solidarity, we have no way of knowing how far this was the cause, and how far the effect, of the process under consideration. Even supposing that at the very beginning of the process (about 800 B.C.) the *polis* was felt to be a kind of extended family unit, we are bound to ask whether this conception was sufficiently strong to become a determining factor in the process, independent of specific configurations and the specific course of later history. We can by no means dismiss the idea that what has to be explained is not that such features were present at the beginning, but that they actually survived, contrary to all probability. The same applies to the retention of original forms of "primitive democracy"[3] such as communal assemblies, memories of erstwhile equality,[4] the system of land tenure, and certain forms of piety, worship, and "theology." It is perhaps less surprising that such things should have existed at the beginning than that they should have persisted and gone on developing as Greek culture evolved. Perhaps this was at first not so much the motive force behind the trend as the by-product of a highly idiosyncratic cultural development. It is, after all, a general rule that advanced civilizations arise through the development of powerful monarchies that radically transform the whole of society and leave their impress on it. It would in any case be wrong to equate the mere retention of archaic features with their tenacity and potential for development.

To maintain that these and similar Greek characteristics represent the actual causes of the trend toward isonomy would be to risk incurring all the difficulties associated with the question of the priority of the chicken or the egg. If, on the other hand, we were to adopt a gradualist approach,[5] we might suppose that at an early stage there were a modicum of chicken and a modicum of egg, and that from such small beginnings—supposing that the trend continued in the same direction—the ultimate outcome would be a full-fledged chicken and a fully formed egg.

We do not know when the process began. Nor is it the purpose of these observations to deny that the people who came together, at the beginning of the first millennium B.C., from various tribes and communities, both indigenous and immigrant, may have possessed certain characteristics that were ultimately conducive to the development of isonomies. Some of these characteristics were doubtless brought by the immigrants from their former homeland; others may have arisen under the conditions of migration, yet others during the period of conflict and learning to live together in the Aegean region after the destruction of the previous culture. On this subject it is difficult, if not impossible, to make any convincing assertions. We do not even know to what extent we are dealing with the emergence of specific and distinctive traits. It may even be that

when these small communities, living out their modest and uneventful
lives, were caught up in the movement of the archaic period, what distinguished them was precisely the fact that so little had taken shape, that so
much was still open to development—that their situation was, to use a
term from modern evolutionary theory, largely one of "evolutionary
openness."[6] It is certainly clear that Homer preserves some very ancient
notions, deriving partly from Mycenean times, but differing from those of
"primitive communities in general."[7] Homer's language too—or for that
matter the art of geometry—displays certain peculiarities that are characteristic of the Greeks of later times. But many of the features that seem to
point forward to the later period probably accrued during the eighth century, the beginning of the period of revolutionary change with which we
are concerned here.[8] The same is true of art.

Faced with these difficulties, we would do well to treat whatever Greek
"characteristics" had developed by about 800 B.C. as unknowns—or a
complex of unknowns. Whatever their nature and however marked they
may have been, we cannot derive the trend to democracy from them.
Even if a few elements can be discerned with special clarity amid the
obscurity of these sparsely recorded centuries, we are still not entitled to
extrapolate from the known effects and infer that these elements were the
causes. They alone cannot have set the process in motion and determined
its subsequent course: the isonomy that ultimately emerged can have been
produced only within a framework of changing circumstances, which
caused men to act in certain ways at certain times.

Our purpose here is to trace the process within which the trend toward
isonomy evolved. This can be done only in outline. Much about the
process remains unknown—and not only the precise role that was played
in its motivation by the complex of Greek "characteristics" present at the
outset. Nevertheless, we can roughly discern the circumstances under
which the Greeks entered upon a period of movement in the eighth
century, followed by a crisis that shattered the inherited order, the difficulties confronting them, and the gradual buildup of forces that gave the
final push toward isonomy—without anyone's being aware of what was
happening.

In studying this process, we must pay special heed to the manner in
which the political arose in Greek society. In other words, we must ask
how the Greeks came to embark upon their unique course. We must
therefore view the process in its entirety, and how it got underway in the
circumstances that arose after the Doric migration, that is, by about 800.
In this context, those other "causes" of democracy which are so often
invoked, but which crystallized only during the course of the process, can
be seen at best as particular concentrations of impulses that were at once
a product of the process and part of the motive force behind it. This

applies, for instance, to Delphic religion, to the potency of the Greek belief in justice, to the hoplite phalanx, and to much else that seems to stand out with special clarity from the general obscurity.

One of the most notable facts about the origins of Greek society is that monarchy played no significant role in it. Hence, the process we are describing lacked the dominant motive force that is found elsewhere. This also meant, however, that the aim of evolving a new political order could be attained only in a later phase of development and with the aid of new and different forces. First of all, the negative preconditions had to emerge, on the basis of which a new order could take shape.

The Emergence of the Opportunity to Work toward a Political Order Based on Broad Sections of the Population

In the late ninth and eighth centuries, the Greeks somehow entered quite suddenly upon a period of movement, having hitherto lived in fairly primitive conditions with little social stratification. Whereas the rise of other civilizations was motivated by the presence or the buildup of a central political authority, this was for the most part absent in Greece. The initial impetus was remarkably unpolitical; so too was the early phase of intense social and cultural change.

The Aegean region was a political vacuum in which the Greeks had until now led their uneventful lives in loose-knit political units, small and largely autonomous communities in which there was no great concentration of power in the hands of monarchs[9] and no notable economic and social differentiation between the nobles—however this term is understood—and the peasants.

An important feature of the life of the Greeks was that from early times they had been a seafaring people and that many of them owned ships. This was encouraged by the proximity of the islands to one another and to the mainland, where much of the terrain was impassable. Not surprisingly, therefore, the Greeks sailed beyond the Aegean and came into early contact with eastern civilizations.[10] The area of Greek settlement extended as far afield as Cyprus. This led to an unusual combination of distance and propinquity: the Greeks had easy access to the treasures, ambitions, and experiences of Middle Eastern civilizations without being exposed to political influences from this quarter. Until the sixth century, none of the eastern empires was interested in their region. There was thus no external pressure on the Greeks to concentrate their power, to build large empires, or to develop strong internal government—in other words, to bring society under central political control and so to determine its structure and its religious and spiritual life.

Instead, the Greeks became very active overseas. This activity was at first centered on trade, with both east and west. While they themselves had little to offer in return for the treasures of the east, they were able to supply raw materials from the west that were in demand in the east. To what extent they supplanted the Phoenicians as traders has recently become a matter of controversy,[11] but we cannot discuss the details here. Concomitant with trade was the growth of piracy;[12] and the Greeks traveled widely. A final consequence was colonization, which led to shifts of population on a scale that can scarcely be overestimated. This was favored by geography: the wide scope for settlements along the Mediterranean littoral gave the Greeks an ideal opportunity to solve their internal problems.

We cannot know what prompted such extensive activity among the early Greeks. The favorable geographic situation merely supplied the necessary conditions. Traits such as the spirit of adventure and the desire for wealth need not have been present from the start (except in a few individuals), and may just as well have been a product, rather than a prerequisite, of the movement, which was probably instigated by a fortuitous concatenation of circumstances and then reinforced by repeated successes, which encouraged further activity. Bad harvests, food shortages, and other contingencies may have furnished additional motives. Hence, although we may regard this enterprising spirit as characteristic of the Greeks, it may have developed in tandem with the extension of their area of activity and their growing success, or at least been promoted and perpetuated by them.

All the same, such enterprise gained extraordinary momentum when it offered a way out of the hardships caused by overpopulation.[13] For the interest of the merchants in acquiring important trading posts overseas seems somehow to have coincided with the interests of their landless compatriots at home. The link was not immediately self-evident, but, once established—for whatever reason—it led to the founding of countless colonies from 750 onward. Other remedies might have suggested themselves to a country afflicted by overpopulation, but these were less obvious or were simply not taken up. Whatever openings were available, either at home or in the east, to mercenaries and men with technical or commercial skills,[14] they held less attraction than the prospect of acquiring land and full civic rights in newly found Greek cities abroad. Above all, there was clearly no real chance of exploiting the growing population for the concentration of political power and territorial conquest in the immediate vicinity. No doubt there were attempts here and there; but in general the kings were clearly too weak (and too poor), and when once colonization had created an outlet—and with it (to anticipate the outcome for a moment) an extraordinary diffusion of power—this alternative ceased to exist. Only Sparta was successful in conquering new lands, Sparta being the exception that proves the rule.[15]

⌜Of crucial importance in the prehistory of isonomy was the fact that large numbers of people were engaged in the promotion of trade, piracy, and colonization. This involved so many cities and so many individuals, families, and groups (not all of them belonging to the nobility) that the accruing wealth, power, and prestige were widely distributed[16] and thus could not be monopolized by monarchs or exploited by a handful of magnates to extend their personal influence.⌟This combination of primitive and largely undifferentiated conditions at home with a high degree of mobility overseas at first had the effect of giving a fairly free rein, in favorable circumstances, to men of vigor and enterprise, whose energies were neither constrained within the limits of a primitive agrarian society nor tied down and exploited by central political authority. The freedom they enjoyed was consolidated in activity overseas, and such monarchies as still existed at the beginning of the colonial era were soon eliminated.

Leaving aside the details, we may say that everything we can observe or infer about the beginning of this intensive phase in the evolution of Greek civilization leads to the conclusion that it was marked by the weakness of all central political authority, especially monarchical authority. There was great scope for enterprise, and also freedom to pursue great ambitions in the knowledge that they were attainable, an enormous widening of the horizon, and an extraordinary growth of knowledge, resources, and opportunities for action. All this was seized upon and exploited by relatively large numbers throughout Greece.

This great movement not only accentuated the growing social differentiation and the increase in knowledge and opportunities; it also perpetuated the initial diffusion of power and resources both within the *poleis* and throughout the polypolitical Greek world.

The consolidation of this wide diffusion of power was of great importance for the subsequent course of Greek history. It made the practice of politics much easier. The pressure of excessive population was shifted outside the *poleis*, and energies were directed to a wider world. Numerous nonpolitical ideals gained ground, and a Panhellenic public took shape,[17] which for a long time set comparatively little store by political achievements. Victories in athletic contests (one of the areas in which this public manifested itself), wealth, fine living, and beauty were rated just as highly as political success and martial fame. Numerous avenues were opened up by which one could win renown outside the *polis* and political life. Hans Schaefer tried to epitomize all this when he described the Greeks as a nation that came together in social life.[18] These circumstances, together with climatic and geographic conditions and other factors (not least the absence of any threat from abroad), were responsible for the largely

unpolitical character of Greek cultural development in its early and decisive phases. Yet these very circumstances supplied the basis for the emergence of the political among the Greeks. For this could take place only
in a situation in which the existing political authorities had long been
powerless to deal with the crisis to which Greece was now more and more
exposed.[19]

The enormous opportunities generated commensurate demands, and,
owing to the small degree of social differentiation, these demands came
from fairly broad sections of the population—especially, though not
exclusively, from the nobility. This frequently resulted in debt, exploitation, and servitude for debt,[20] but also in new and often quite hazardous
enterprises. The great opportunities for gain and the high risk of failure
must have led to substantial restratification both within the nobility and
outside it.[21] Power and wealth began to be concentrated in a relatively
small circle of increasingly powerful families (though in Greece as a
whole this was still a fairly large circle). There must also have been fairly
many families who, through repeated failures, fell behind the successful
families and so became an additional source of unrest and discontent. In
the course of time many people who had lost their farms were forced to
sell their children into slavery and finally to pledge themselves to the service of others. Traditional relations between nobles and peasants were
undermined. Deep divisions arose, leading to unrest, insurgency, and civil
war. As a result of widespread emigration to the colonies and the unusual
degree of general mobility, individual affiliations were severed, or at least
loosened and relativized. Opportunity and hardship, gain and loss, gave
rise at once to a consciousness of extraordinary power and an oppressive
sense of impotence.[22]

Given this situation, it was almost inevitable that particularly ambitious politicians should exploit the opportunity to usurp the government
of the *polis* by enlisting the support of the discontented and the suffering.
From the mid-seventh century onward we constantly find tyrants in power
in various cities. It is a curious fact that these tyrannies never lasted more
than three generations—usually less—and that, despite all the power they
were able to muster, they failed to leave much of a mark on the society
of the *polis* or to extend their power far beyond its bounds.[23] Taking
a comparative view, one would have to say that the attempt to shape
Greek society through monarchical rule—if indeed any such attempt was
made—never succeeded. Such central authorities were clearly too weak
and the opposing forces too strong. Here we have two aspects of the same
situation: the relatively wide diffusion of power within and between the
city-states, and the relatively slight interest in the *polis* that was shown by
the nobles, and ultimately by the tyrants.[24] For it can hardly be presumed
that the failure of tyranny as an institution was the result of a contingent

accumulation of failures. The usurpers monopolized only the aristocratic possibilities; their rule amounted to no more than a redistribution of power within the nobility.[25] In many cases, new forms of methodical action were discovered; sometimes reasonable provision was made for the middle and lower classes, whose economic position was thus consolidated[26] and who were granted legal security. In a number of places, then, the economic aspect of the crisis was removed or significantly alleviated. In Athens the religious policy of the Peisistratids made an important contribution to the integration of the peasants and thus to the development of *polis* society. To this extent the prehistory of democracy is scarcely conceivable without them. Yet, apart from the effects they had on the economy and society, the tyrants generally failed to leave their mark on the communities—unlike the absolute monarchies of modern times, which left a profound and enduring impress on the modern state.

The weakness of tyranny may have resulted partly from the conviction that there was a just political order that precluded autocracy. At all events, this conviction later aggravated the suffering caused by tyranny and was in turn reinforced by it. Yet whatever interplay there may have been between the two, it is sufficient here to observe that tyranny on the whole did nothing to alter the wide diffusion of power. The new monarchies were unable to supply a political solution for existing difficulties.

Insofar as the tyrants found new ways of promoting agriculture, commerce, and trade—as well as religion and culture—they contributed to the intensification of Greek life as a whole, first in Greece itself and then in the colonies. There were numerous associated changes, one of the most important being the introduction of the hoplite phalanx. This was a new form of weaponry and tactics, but above all a new means of involving the middle ranks of the citizenry in military service. It enhanced the standing of this section of society and may have played a part in the usurpation of power by the first tyrants.[27] This military innovation is commonly accorded special prominence as a factor in the prehistory of democracy. This emphasis is justified as long as one is merely enumerating such factors, but the matter appears more complicated when one considers the whole range of interrelationships within the historical process between 800 and 500. What gave rise to this "factor" was again the prevailing situation, with wide diffusion of power, relatively little social differentiation, and no great concentration of financial resources in one place. There was presumably no money for the engagement of mercenaries. Whatever money the tyrants had at their disposal was generally insufficient for mounting sizable military enterprises, and tyranny was not widespread or influential enough to be able to dispense with the civic levy. In the long run, therefore, this situation favored the rise of wider sections of the citizenry.

The connection between political rights and military obligations was of course by no means as close as is commonly maintained on the basis of Aristotle's thesis, which was clearly suggested by the connection between the naval service performed by the Athenian *thetes* and their acquiring a regular role in politics.[28] In this case the link between the political and the military was actually established very quickly, but what was true in this instance need not have been true earlier. By the fifth century, popular participation in politics was institutionalized, and the *thetes* had only to strengthen their existing representation. Moreover, in a brief space of time they had made a signal contribution to the extraordinary successes of Athens: they owed their power to their direct and palpable importance to the city.

The role of the hoplites, by contrast, was much more limited, for their services were required far less often. The extent to which they were able to exploit this role in the political sphere was a function partly of their economic and social position, and partly of certain institutional conditions, which in turn presupposed the emergence of the idea that broad sections of the populace should be accorded a greater role in political affairs.

Here we face a whole series of problems. What we are told most often about the peasants of the archaic period—roughly from the middle of the seventh century to the end of the sixth—is that they suffered hardship, got into debt, and often lost their farms and their freedom. Hence the motive of economic hardship did not necessarily coincide with the political opportunities that might arise from military service. On the other hand, those recruited for hoplite service may well have found themselves in even greater economic difficulties as a result. Finally, there may have been times when the interests of the more prosperous peasants coincided with those of the less fortunate—when they had common grievances against the regime of the nobles. It is also possible, of course, that on occasion they joined with the nobles to combat unrest originating among the poorest inhabitants; they may often, at the very least, have deemed it prudent to keep out of politics. It may also be presumed that conditions varied greatly from place to place and from time to time, in ways we cannot know. It is thus hard to see what effect hoplite service may have had on the eventual political rise of the peasants. It probably served chiefly to ensure that the widely diffused power sometimes became concentrated in powerful impulses and so aggravated the crisis. On the other hand, the increased military importance of the peasants led to their first successes in the struggle for better guarantees of their rights (and probably of their economic position too, notably through the agency of the tyrants).[29] It was perhaps in consequence of this new military situation— and of what the hoplites achieved later—that hoplite service came to be linked with the growing force that was subsequently to work directly, though not consciously, toward isonomy.

Again we must leave aside many of the details. Taking an overall view of the great process of change that was in train in the Greek world during the one and a half to two centuries after 800, we find many factors that led to a growth of resources, insights, and opportunities for action; these had a shattering effect on the traditional order and combined to push matters toward a serious crisis. Even those measures that were in some way designed to solve the crisis often contained elements that served only to exacerbate it—through power struggles among the nobles, tyranny, and peasant revolts—because nobody had the power to establish a new and legitimate order. It may be presumed that for most of the individual *poleis* the effects of the many improvements due to trade and commerce, to new inventions and investments, to jurisdiction, and perhaps, even at this early stage, to the spread of a belief in justice[30] were still somewhat ambivalent.

As the crisis dragged on, there was a danger that the social and political order would be so profoundly shattered that a breakdown in the homogeneity of knowledge would ensue. Expectations of action proliferated and collided, both within the nobility and between the nobles and the ordinary citizens. The earlier order had been sustained by the traditional interlocking of expectations, fulfillment of expectations, and further expectations;[31] these had channeled and placed restrictions upon action, but traditional relations were now fundamentally disturbed. The nobles—at least in many of the more turbulent areas—no longer felt themselves bound by certain unequivocal and powerful expectations of action that recurred even within their own ranks.[32] Hence, in the long run the population at large also ceased to be so firmly tied to the existing order.

As a consequence, political thinking acquired new scope for development and was able to make headway, reinforcing doubts about the legitimacy of the status quo and, in the course of a long process, making common cause with the peasants (as well as with the minor nobility, and in some cases with representatives of trade and commerce) in various *poleis*. Such thinking eventually led to the development of a new force that was able to exert a strong influence in these communities.

As for the role of the Greek peasants in this early phase, we should recall a remark of Max Weber's: "Peasants become 'dumb' only where they are harnessed into and face a presumably strange bureaucratic, or liturgical urban machine of a great state or when they are abandoned as serfs to landlords."[33] The fact that these things did not happen in Greece at this period, or at least not generally, partly explains why—exceptionally—"the integration of the peasants as full members of the political community" was ultimately successful, and why they actually played a central part in the process.[34] Here too, of course, one must beware of presuming a simple causal link between sets of mutually conditioning factors. It seems to me entirely mistaken to say that the peasants' exemption from taxes was a precondition of their political advance.[35] It was, in at least equal measure, a consequence of the conditions under which this advance took place. For as soon as this exemption became important—in relation to the primitive conditions—it came under threat from the tyrants. Only with the collapse of tyranny were the peasants in general freed from imposts. This was a consequence of very complex conditions and of forces that were taking shape in them. We must now show how these conditions led to the crystallization of a new kind of change.

The Social History of Political Thought as the Engine of Change

The expansion of the Greeks into the wider Mediterranean world, the founding of colonies, the profound changes that were taking place everywhere, and the emergent problems of civic life—of living together in both the old and the newly founded cities—must have been matched by a growth of intellectual skills, insight, and experience. The founding of colonies in itself required devoting a great deal of thought to the practical question of how to set up a proper civic organization. Even when the aim was merely to copy the traditional order of the parent city, it was necessary not only to formulate a description of the customs prevailing there but also to extend and adapt it to suit the new conditions. All this had to be done at a great distance from the homeland, where the older citizens could doubtless have given advice on the proper way to set about the task. The need to invent general formulas to encapsulate rulings that had previously been tailored to individual cases led to fresh insights into the basic conditions of civic life. And there were many other problems that had to be worked out, especially when it was realized that certain things could and should be ordered better than they were at home.

In many places the middle and lower classes protested against existing laws, which were based on oral tradition and administered exclusively by the nobles. They demanded the appointment of lawgivers, who would not only formulate and write down the laws but also determine what was right; in making such demands they were relying on the existence of a wider intellectual expertise, which was now called upon to provide solutions to a host of problems. The many attempts to come to grips with the social crisis somehow presupposed the existence—and promoted the development—of an intellectual movement, extending throughout Greece and beyond, that could collect and exchange experiences and insights and devise, test, and develop appropriate ways of dealing with current difficulties, often by creating new institutions. In such endeavors, roughly the same course of action was pursued both by tyrants and by the *katartisteres* who were appointed by various civic communities to put things to rights or "bring things back into plumb."[36] The solutions that were arrived at are in many respects similar to the rules of wisdom then current in the east.[37] There must have been a lively exchange of ideas that was not confined to Greece.

It was from such beginnings that early Greek political thought evolved. It was by no means the exclusive achievement of an intellectual elite (or even of notable individuals, though such were not lacking). True, it was concentrated in an intellectual ambience that extended throughout Greece and for a long time had its center at Delphi, but it owed its vigor largely to the wider echo it evoked and to constant interaction with the real world, and its insights were in due course incorporated into the thinking and aspirations of large sections of the population. Reality was too close for the construction of grand, coherent systems. One had to grope one's way forward, seizing hold of one thing at a time, trying it out, and acquiring new experience in the process. The understanding that was gained and the plans that were devised were closely tied to specific situations and could aim only a short distance beyond them. It was scarcely possible to keep even one jump ahead of reality. In this way political thought, politics, and the reality of *polis* life—the insights of the few and the knowledge and aspirations of the many—influenced and promoted one another. This thinking was closely interwoven with political and social reality. To a large extent it represented a broad, anonymous process, a segment of social history, the intellectual advance of a whole society. It drew its sustenance from wide-spreading roots, even if prominent individuals such as Solon and others of the Seven Sages had a special share in it.

At this early stage, the evolution of political thought was due to the high degree of independence enjoyed by those engaged in it, to its wide scope, to the public manner in which it was pursued, and to the fact that it answered to a widespread demand. With power so widely diffused, the Greek intelligentsia and the impulses it generated could not be concentrated in royal courts or powerful hierarchies. There was "no caste that could have been at once the authoritative guardian of knowledge and belief and the proprietor of thought . . . no special class of bureaucratic families or the like, no 'education' that divided society. The men who were accounted wise by a kind of self-evident consensus, came from the most diverse backgrounds."[38] Thus, in a way that was quite unprecedented (except for certain parallels in Israel), the political order, like the gods and the universe, became a matter of private interest.

Yet precisely because this thinking was so independent, a special need was felt for it. If there was no political authority capable of solving the current crisis, men were repeatedly obliged to seek a way out of critical situations by turning for guidance to the "wise men," who thus became a considerable force in Greece, occupying a third position, between the contending parties. They were the source of a powerful pressure directed toward solving the crisis.

How this came about may be reconstructed in outline. A central role was played by the Delphic oracle.[39] In the era of colonization, Delphi became an important entrepôt for information and ideas.[40] Advice was constantly sought from the oracle, not only from the Pythia, but chiefly from the Delphic priests and nobles.

The oracle seems to have gained preeminence over all others in Greece—or to have consolidated an already existing preeminence—by giving much sound advice during the period of colonization,[41] and so earning the gratitude of the colonists, whose envoys are known to have brought countless precious gifts to Delphi. Far more important, however, was the fact that Delphi elicited from its visitors information that could then be used to advise other would-be settlers—by directing them to new places, warning them of dangers, and recommending new methods, different forms of organization, and the like. Delphi was not just a source of arcane oracular pronouncements, but a great repository of knowledge and expertise,[42] and in due course became a center from which a certain kind of "politics" was practiced. This development had practical repercussions throughout Greek life.

The oracle functioned, of course, only as a center for a broad current of intellectual activity. We hear of its having close links with the Seven Sages, who were themselves merely the most celebrated representatives of the contemporary intellectual movement.

Now, when one place had gained such preeminence as a source of knowledge in a world made up of countless *poleis,* people naturally repaired to it in increasing numbers in search of information and advice (especially as it was common practice to consult an oracle when founding a colony).[43] Whenever this happened, Delphi learned about new problems; the oracle could then question the next visitor to elicit further information and possible solutions to the problems. Information could be passed back and forth, and this led to a more intensive study of the problems and a livelier exchange of suggested solutions.

The Greeks were scattered throughout the world from Spain to Asia Minor, from Africa to the north coast of the Black Sea, though mainly round the Aegean and in Sicily, yet they had few important centers. Given this situation, the knowledge and expertise concentrated at Delphi clearly filled a universal need; moreover, knowledge grew in proportion to the need, the need in proportion to the knowledge. Hence Delphi became a kind of intellectual clearinghouse, with a catchment area extending far beyond Greece itself.[44]

In this way Delphi became an increasingly important center in the poly-political system of the Greeks, the one center that had a powerful and growing interest in supplying apposite advice on religious and politico-social matters (probably only a small fraction of it in the form of oracles). This was after all the basis of Delphi's reputation and prosperity. Delphi promoted itself in this role, as we know; it not only supplied a center for wide-ranging discussion, but in many respects determined the direction the discussion should take.

At the same time, prevailing circumstances ensured that this political clearinghouse did not become a seat of political power, but remained an intellectual center possessing great religious authority, whose function was restricted to mediation and the provision of advice (which meant that greater and greater intellectual achievements came to be expected of it).

This concentration of intellectual activity was called upon more and more. The many difficulties generated by the general crisis—disputes, famines, civil wars—caused the Greeks to turn repeatedly to Delphi. The result was inevitable: the intellectual supply grew in response to the general demand. Particular situations gave rise to requests for the appointment of lawgivers, and then of *katartisteres* and conciliators, who were called upon in desperate situations as third parties, by virtue of their wisdom and expertise, and charged with the task of setting things to rights. Even if this was a counsel of despair, it was no mean testimony to the confidence that was placed in the "wise men" of politics. A whole school grew up that was occupied with the invention, testing, and development of possible institutions. Some of its suggestions for solving the many political, economic, social, or religious problems appear to have proved successful. This cannot have happened in every case, but it must have happened in a good many, and there was, after all, no alternative to the hopes placed in political thought. The satisfaction of certain needs gave rise to others, and expectations were generated in all quarters.

The pressure of these expectations created, both at Delphi and in the wider circle of thinkers (many of whom were associated with the oracle), a strong incentive to ponder the many problems that beset the Greek political world. For what applied to Delphi applied also *mutatis mutandis* to the whole current of political thought in the archaic period, certainly by the time of Solon and probably earlier, that is, from about the middle of seventh century until at least the end of the sixth. Everywhere people were facing similar problems. An obvious result, given the short distance between *poleis,* was that people exchanged experiences, learned from one another, and built up mutual contacts.

Certain roles were created, and those who filled them were rewarded with material and nonmaterial benefits, wide public respect, and the knowledge that they were performing a highly useful service. There thus arose various relatively solid interests that gave substantial momentum to this current of political thought.

In due course political thought became institutionalized. A "third position" was established, and those who occupied it had the task of identifying all the problems and bringing their intellectual powers to bear on them. However the individual members of this circle may have thought or acted, it was not as a whole tied to any single power, let alone to a given political persuasion (even supposing that such a thing existed). What mattered were expertise, knowledge, and inventiveness, together with a profound insight into the connections between different phenomena and into what was seen as the divinely established order of the world and the *polis*.[45] The intellectual movement in which this all came together seems to have established itself as an independent force amid a multitude of expectations and the expectation of expectations. This generated the stability and self-confidence in which the movement had its roots.

Once this had happened, thinking was bound to be inspired and stimulated both by its successes and by its experience of the evils that called for redress, and indeed not least by its failures.

The movement embraced the most disparate elements. In certain respects the thinking of tyrants ran parallel to that of their opponents, and one of them was even numbered among the Seven Sages. Some of the interests of the movement—such as improving the economic structure, the food supply, and income; getting rid of unemployment; and creating legal security—were also features of the wisdom of the east. In time, however, more narrowly political problems came to the fore. There was a gradual strengthening of that strand in the movement that aimed to create a polity not controlled by one individual. The precondition of this, namely an intellectual position that did not correspond to any single powerful interest, but to a common interest, was already developing among the *poleis*, though it had yet to come into its own and was still somewhat academic, given the exigencies of everyday life; this produced advocates for the *polis* as a whole before there were any forces to support it. A focal point was thus emerging around which the solidarity and insight of broader sections of the citizenry could crystallize, as well as the political will to make the *polis* their own. A new *polis* order, based on broad sections of the body politic, was being anticipated step by step, thanks to an intellectual movement operating in a changing world.

A new standpoint was evolving and gaining strength in contemporary society, opening up and consolidating a new perspective that contributed significantly to political differentiation, extending the range of conceivable possibilities and putting an end to one-dimensional preoccupations. Different interests—interests in government and the prevention of arbitrary rule, the interests of the nobles and the ruled (a potential source of danger)—met and coalesced in a multidimensional view of the interest of the community at large, in which each particularist force would be seen as a part of the whole.

This third position corresponded to a species of philosophical and political thought that was able to view the order prevailing in the cosmos and the *polis* as something far too comprehensive to be represented by a single power[46]—a kind of abstract thinking that could extrapolate from reality and discern a more general pattern, an overriding regularity. This was precisely what was needed, in view of the wide diffusion of power and the shattering experiences to which it had given rise during the crisis of the archaic period. Jacob Burckhardt observes that the Greeks "appear original, spontaneous, and alert when all others seem imbued with a more or less stolid sense of compulsion."[47] The fact is that they could not have addressed themselves otherwise to the urgent problems of Greek life. They simply had to rely on their capacity for free thought, because they were unusually free from ties, unusually exposed, and deeply shattered by the fragmentation of their once-homogeneous knowledge of a just order.

It was in these circumstances that the Delphic doctrine of man's limitations and frailty evolved, epitomized by the injunction that man should know himself, be content with his lot, and limit himself to "mortal aspirations." This perception of the human condition, concentrating on man's needs and problems and relegating him to his proper sphere, was so radical that the consequence was hard to escape: one should try to devise moderate and effective remedies for the difficulties and of the individual and the *polis*. "We must seek what is fitting from the gods, using our human senses, knowing what lies before our feet—what is our lot. My soul, do not strive for eternal life! No, use to the full whatever lies within reach of action." Wolfgang Schadewaldt quotes this passage from Pindar to illustrate the influence of Delphic theology.[48]

The conviction was growing that there was no need to despair in the face of the many problems of contemporary life, because something could be done to combat them. (This phenomenon is exemplified by the doctrine of purification, which broke the spell of the most diverse apprehensions,[49] including those of political life.) A curious "religious realism" arose, which discerned a just order (eunomy) behind existing conditions, an order that was essentially immutable, since it was in accord with the will of the gods. According to Solon,[50] it was the citizens who were to blame for the ills of the age, but the just order could be restored, since the gods were fundamentally well disposed to the city. For the sake of the *polis* as a whole, the cycle of hubris and punishment must be broken.[51]

Clearly, what encouraged Solon in this optimism was his recognition of numerous causal connections, immanent in society, which produced the earthly calamities that his contemporaries saw as divine punishment, and in which—precisely because they were recognizable—he believed he could intervene. Here the belief in justice came into conjunction with a consciousness of the great possibilities for knowledge and action. Solon's vision of eunomy was derived from current conditions. The arbitrary actions of the nobles, the devices they used to exploit others, the hardships suffered by the peasants—everything that posed the threat of rebellion—could not possibly be right. On the other hand, the just order could not lie only in the future: it was something that had to be restored. Clues to the ideal were to be found in existing reality, even though it was not yet present. It must be attainable, because it was willed by the gods.

The real problem is how political thought allied itself with the interests of broad sections of the body politic. How was it possible that their political claims should even be considered, justified, and promoted? How could significant numbers of political thinkers back a section of society that for a long time had not been regarded, even remotely, as a regular and powerful factor in politics? And how could they succeed, when the victims of hardship had at first had quite different preoccupations, more immediate and pressing needs and anxieties? And—not least—how could the latter be induced, once their economic conditions had been stabilized, to commit themselves politically to the extent of assuming a leading role in what was to be the forerunner of direct democracy?

It is true that broad sections of the population from time to time demanded the appointment of lawgivers and *katartisteres*, who often advocated improvements in their situation—especially as they were otherwise liable to pose a threat—but in the present context this does not signify very much. The matters at issue were essentially economic grievances and the creation of private legal security. The degree of discontent is indicated by the occurrence of occasional demands for the redistribution of land (*isomoiria*). The political order was affected too, but only in a negative way, for the agitation seems to have been fomented by power-hungry nobles with a view to setting up tyrannies.[52] We have not the least reason to believe that democracy could have arisen at this time, about 600. And in any case we never hear of the implementation of a program of land redistribution.[53]

In due course, however, a particular strand of political thought must have developed that aimed at the establishment of a just, nontyrannical order. Even where attempts at reform were made, it must gradually have become clear from experience that neither oligarchies nor tyrannies could control the crisis in the long term. In the first place, they were unsuited to the task, being beneficiaries of the oppressive conditions that afflicted many of the citizens and provoked them to revolt. True, some tyrants tried to remedy these conditions—often out of deliberate self-interest— but whatever they achieved remained precarious: their mode of action and the nature of their rule were determined largely by their characters and the situation in which they found themselves.

This was why Solon deemed it desirable that a wider circle of citizens be given political rights (over and above the minimum right to participation in popular assemblies). In some measure they were to become politically self-reliant. This was to be achieved by his new census-division, by the provision that anyone might sue on behalf of the wronged, and perhaps by the creation of an annually elected council. For this purpose he appealed to the citizens' responsibility for the city, which could have been realized, at least in exceptional cases, within existing institutions, and introduced his *stasis* laws[54] and other measures. His poems too testify to his concern to foster a wider understanding of political affairs. We do not know the size of the circle in which Solon wished to encourage and facilitate a stronger commitment to politics.[55] It is clear, however, that political discussion took place among a wide public. Solon himself put his program to the citizens. Admittedly none of this produced a readiness for regular political commitment, and Athens subsequently succumbed to tyranny, which the great majority of its citizens apparently did not find unwelcome.

In various cities, however, a desire and a readiness for effective political participation were eventually aroused and sustained among a class of landowners that cannot be precisely defined,[56] and probably also among the more affluent merchants and traders. This is clear from numerous reforms attested for the sixth century, including the setting up of annually elected councils and new legal tribunals, possibly also the appointment of "opposition magistrates," the reorganization of the *phylai* on a local basis, and, finally, toward the end of the century, Cleisthenes' great scheme to institutionalize the "civic presence" through a comprehensive and complicated reform. Certain "democratic upheavals" that took place at the same period (or earlier) probably also point to a move to broaden the political base of the *polis*.[57]

Behind these changes there seems to have been a movement extending over large areas of Greece. In due course men were bound to realize that no true and lasting improvement of the civic order was possible, especially in the more important cities, unless fairly broad sections of the citizenry assumed a political role. The potent combination of the belief in justice and the opportunities for knowledge and action aroused aspira-

tions that were not easy to satisfy, and this led in due course to a certain
sensitivity to the abuses that prevailed under aristocratic regimes and
tyrannies. As a result, economic stabilization and improvements in legal
security only created fresh problems: they encouraged claims to political
participation and thus compounded existing difficulties arising from the
fact that certain nobles exploited civic discontent as a political weapon
against the majority of their own class, or that tyrannical regimes, being
insecure, tended to become increasingly severe. At some point it must
have become abundantly clear that, as long as it was a matter of course
for the nobles to determine the conduct of politics, there would be no end
to arbitrary rule, factional struggle, and usurpation, and that this state of
affairs would do grave damage to the whole community. There was now a
reversal of existing values in favor of an ethic directed to the good of the
polis. New criteria began to gain ground; wisdom and justice came to be
recognized as the salient virtues, and this recognition corresponded to the
popular demand for law and justice (*dike*).[58]

Various communities tried to bring the conduct of powerful nobles
under control because the cities were held responsible for the actions
of their citizens. This effort might take a religious form, through the
idea (propagated in the "guilt-culture") that the misdeeds of individuals
brought guilt upon the whole city, which was then obliged to atone for
them. It might also take the form of a threat: the city would be held to
account by other cities for crimes committed by certain of its citizens.[59]
The unbridled behavior of powerful nobles could simply no longer be tol-
erated. Wider circles of citizens had to show a greater interest and be
given the means to put an end to such conduct.

Since this aim appeared at the same time to be in the general interest of
the *polis,* the task of political thought came to be concentrated more and
more on trying to convert civic discontent into political demands. Some
part was played in this process by the frequent experience that those who
espoused the people's cause were usually intent upon tyranny. This was
an important consequence of the breakdown of social homogeneity (as is
demonstrated by a comparison with the conflict of the orders in Rome).[60]
Yet, in view of the great disparities of power and education, it was not
altogether easy to find champions for the political interests of the citizens
at large, so that for the most part the citizens had to champion their own
cause. Increasing numbers of citizens had to be not only persuaded of
their responsibility for the city, but also enabled to assume a direct and
effective role in politics. To this end, certain sections of the political intelligentsia allied themselves with the broad mass of the citizens to promote
a trend toward wider participation within the *polis*. Certain facts should
be borne in mind here. A process of this kind is made up of an accumulation of impulses, which need not always emanate from the same persons.

It may be promoted by different groups in turn, or even by activities that at first run counter to it but eventually work in its favor. The citizens of Athens, for instance, were quite capable of bringing Solon to power and then, moved by identical expectations, of succumbing to the tyranny of Peisistratus. Meanwhile, the kind of political thought that envisaged a nontyrannical eunomy could go on gaining ground elsewhere and ultimately win back the Athenians when they had been disillusioned by (and liberated from) tyranny. Their disillusion gave fresh momentum to the process, which may at the same time have been furthered by many Greeks belonging to cities that were not in the least democratic.

Moreover, a mechanism of gradual change developed as countless attempts were made, in different city-states, to solve basically similar but never identical problems. This or that solution might be tried and the effects carefully noted. Solutions would at times be simply copied, at others adopted with modifications. One thing led to another, and as soon as an interest in political participation arose, the process would be given a further impetus by the fact that certain nobles, wishing to ingratiate themselves with the people, were obliged to offer them political rights (and not just economic or other inducements).[61] In view of the unstable power relations, this must have occurred quite often. In this context, the role of the hoplites came to work in favor of isonomy.

The few glimpses we are vouchsafed of Athenian history in the age of Cleisthenes reveal, on the one hand, such sophistication in institutional thinking and, on the other, such a readiness on the part of large sections of the Attic citizenry (or peasantry) for serious commitment to the affairs of the *polis* as to lead us to postulate a long preparatory phase,[62] namely a social history of political thought that cannot have been confined to Athens. It is true that the Solonic tradition lived on in Athens, for instance in the notion of the citizens' responsibility for the city; but even this idea need not have been limited to Athens.

The ground was now laid—especially after the stabilization of the economic situation—for a general shift in the structure of interests. As Hume remarked, "though men be much governed by interest, yet even interest itself, and all human affairs, are entirely governed by opinion." We may also quote Max Weber, who observed that even if men were directly ruled by their interests, "the 'world views' generated by 'ideas' . . . would in many cases have set the points and thus determined the lines along which the train of action was driven by the dynamism of interests."[63] The citizens became more strongly aware of their political interests (which until now had perforce been only subsidiary interests), and these were consolidated through being shared. Above all, a new kind of insight was born. Reproaching the Athenians, Solon said (8.5 f): "Each of you follows the fox's trail, but together you all have little understanding." A common understanding now arose—a judgment binding upon all, maxims for action, basic lines of agreement, and communication between the citizens. This furnished a framework for the development of a common interest, which thus acquired strength and a prospect of realization.

The changed pattern of interests led to the politicization of broader sections of society; the citizens saw themselves more and more as citizens, aware of the interests they shared and motivated by a sense of civic solidarity that rested on a fundamental equality. The religious policy of the tyrants no doubt played some part in all this—in Athens at least—by creating a greater degree of civic cohesion.

The relatively abstract nature of the common interest that underlay this solidarity indicates the innovative power of political thought. On the other hand, the fact that large numbers of citizens involved themselves in politics, seeing themselves as citizens, meeting as citizens, and relying on one another as citizens, created a new area of public prestige and esteem, interest, and competition, into which it was only natural to venture. In this new public domain, a general affiliation to the *polis* gained ascendancy, for the first time, over the family affiliations and personal friend-foe relations that had hitherto predominated (among the nobles, who had so far commanded the field).

In a society made up largely of farmers, economic interests were not necessarily paramount—except in individual cases—when once the essentials of life were assured, and from now on they tended to stay in the background. Artisans and traders were of little consequence beside landowners and peasants. The original absence of social differentiation was transmuted into a solid political identity. One might say that the Greeks, not being *bourgeois,* were able to become *citoyens.* This formulation would correctly reflect one fact at least: as they acquired increasing prestige and sophistication, the Greeks took over the values prevailing among the nobility, in particular *time* (public rank and honor). The middle (and lower) orders in the Greek cities belonged to a mainly agrarian society, hardly touched by the growth of trade and commerce, and therefore had no choice but to embrace these values.[64] They could at most modify the aristocratic ideal by relating it to the *polis,* which came more and more to belong to them. But in order to do this they had to give reality to the ideal by committing themselves more strongly to politics. This was the beginning of a fundamental restructuring of social affiliations. A new chapter in the history of identity had opened; a decisive step had been taken in the politicization of *polis* life.

At this point isonomy became reality. Yet the isonomies that took shape toward the end of the sixth century—probably earlier in some places—started out as broad oligarchies, or at best as governments of hoplites, as later understood by Aristotle.[65] It is not clear when the term *isonomia* first came into use, but in its early (though not necessarily original) sense it probably implied a contrast with tyranny and restricted oligarchies[66] and was used to designate the new constitutions that were evolving in different places. We do not know how wide a circle of citizens was able to play a significant role in politics under these constitutions. We can only infer that it comprised rather more than the "leading nobles," who had formerly had exclusive control of political affairs. And there must in any case have been considerable regional variation.

Athens does not seem to have played a leading part in the process at first. It went over to isonomy at the time of Cleisthenes, but it did so in its own way. As the territory and its population were exceptionally large, special institutional provisions were needed, and it was necessary to proceed with unusual thoroughness, because certain groups, notably the nobles and their clients, were in a position to control the course of affairs. It was therefore especially difficult in Athens to mobilize individual citizens against the nobility and give effect to the general will. A radical constitutional change was called for—the reform of the *phylai*. This was no doubt the reason why isonomy, and the commitment that went with it, took such firm hold in Athens. And what happened in Athens may then have had a substantial influence elsewhere in Greece. To this extent, the Athens of Cleisthenes may have played an important part in the history of isonomy, but there is no way of knowing whether this was so.

At all events, we must remember that the next step, leading to democracy proper—as it later emerged in Athens with the involvement of the *thetes* and the democratization of the whole Athenian constitution after the Persian Wars—was determined so much by current events that it is questionable whether the same result would have been achieved without the fortuitous intervention of the Persians and their defeat by the Greeks, which, though it owed much to isonomy, was itself ultimately fortuitous.

The Greeks, then, eventually arrived at isonomy by way of what was for much of the time a "blind process." Disregarding whatever special traits the early Greeks may have possessed, we can say that the process began when the Greeks entered upon a period of movement about 800 B.C. During this period, power remained widely diffused (a fact that distinguished Greek civilization from others preceding it and independent of it); this diffusion of power could not be altered by later monarchies. As a result, the crisis that accompanied the onset of rapid changes in Greek life had such a shattering effect on the various civic communities that it could not be remedied by economic consolidation. The crisis led to a breakdown in the homogeneity of social knowledge; the political consequences were thus quite disproportionate to the causes. Right from the beginning, an important role was played by a broad, independent, and public movement of political thought, which continued in full vigor and became a highly influential authority, answering to a widespread demand, occupying a third position, and providing an institutional basis for an interest in the *polis* as a whole. It finally channeled the discontent and disaffection of the citizens (which it was partly instrumental in arousing) toward new, political goals. After the breakdown of social homogeneity, this could only mean ensuring that broader sections of the population committed themselves to the *polis* and strove to obtain a regular and effective voice in political affairs. This process, which acquired its unity from an awakening and increasingly political endeavor on the part of the peasants (for it was mainly peasants who were involved) to secure an improvement in their situation, and above all justice, was able to take advantage of religious, social, military, and economic conditions and press them into its service. Very gradually the goal of isonomy was conceived, and when this was achieved the process—presumably—came to an end, before continuing, under entirely new circumstances, in the direction of democracy.

FOUR

Cleisthenes and the Institutionalizing of the Civic Presence in Athens

THE FUNDAMENTAL PROBLEM facing the citizens of Attica toward the end of the sixth century was how to ensure that their collective will was regularly represented at the center of the *polis*—in other words, how to establish "a civic presence" (*une présence civique*).[1] For we may reasonably conclude that there was at this period a growing demand for political participation among broad sections of the population in many parts of Greece. Much had been done outside Athens to meet this demand. In Athens itself, which was by far the largest of the Greek city-states in area and population, the problem assumed a special form.

For a number of reasons the first democracies in world history could arise only as direct democracies. The Greeks knew nothing of the possibility of involving large sections of the people in politics before they realized it themselves, and this—together with other factors such as the size of the political units, the nature of the political issues, and the breakdown of social homogeneity during the archaic period—made it imperative that the communities themselves become seriously involved in political affairs if they wanted to bring their full weight to bear upon them.

To do this they had to change. They had to discover a new solidarity and set it on a firm foundation; they had to create a new sphere of communal life in which the citizens acted in their capacity as citizens. The citizens therefore had to concentrate their attention on this one capacity that they all shared but had hitherto neglected; they had to bring their affiliation to the city to the forefront of their consciousness. Having previously seen themselves as essentially different, they now saw themselves as essentially alike, as equals demanding equal political rights—whatever that might mean in practical terms. Society had to evolve a new identity. Here it is necessary to add a rider: in the isonomies that constituted the pre-forms or early forms of democracy, such politicization did not extend below the middle ranks of society.

To create a political identity—and a civic presence in which it could express itself—a large number of institutional preconditions had to be met. The area of arbitrary disposal over the political order had to be substantially broadened. Probably for the first time in history, it became possible to divorce the political from the social order and make it largely autonomous. For the new constitution conferred power on a whole class of citizens who, as individuals, were in no position to challenge the nobility. Thus, while still inferior to the upper classes socially, they would henceforth be able to prevail over them politically—or at least keep them in check.

The new disposal over the political order, the new institutions, and the new political identity—these are the three dimensions in which Athens was transformed in the age of Cleisthenes. We do not know how and to what extent the Athenians were aware of this transformation, but one thing at least must have been clear to them: a fairly large proportion of the body politic was staking a claim to a regular and effective say in the affairs of the *polis,* and ways had to be found to represent the general will of the citizens.

The representation of the will of the citizens, or a majority of them, in one place is a problem that has arisen repeatedly—among the Greeks, among the Romans, and subsequently in a great variety of historical situations right down to very recent times. In several important respects, however, the position of the Greeks was unique, for the possibilities, difficulties, and exigencies of their situation were different from those elsewhere.

It is only when we recognize this problem—or, more precisely, the particular way in which it was posed in Athens—that we can understand the great reform by which Cleisthenes gave practical reality to isonomy. It seems to me that, although earlier research has arrived at important results regarding the content of the reform and the conditions for its introduction,[2] it has failed to do full justice to the central problem that Cleisthenes confronted and attempted to solve—however he may have seen it and whatever personal interest he may have had in its solution. In certain essential respects this research has been determined too much by modern presuppositions and has failed to reach a sufficiently basic and concrete understanding of the reform.

The Starting Point and Method of the Present Investigation

The difficulty we have in understanding Cleisthenes' reform lies, first, in the fact that it is not easy to relate the known content of his work to its effects. Herodotus says that Cleisthenes "established the *phylai* and democracy among the Athenians" (6.131.1). Whether or not we fully accept this statement is a matter of definition. All that we know suggests that the concept of democracy was unknown to Cleisthenes and his contemporaries. It cannot therefore have been their intention to establish democracy.[3] Today one is more inclined to designate the constitution that was created at this time by the less anachronistic term *isonomy*. At all events, it seems certain that the change which Cleisthenes introduced went very deep and that his reform constituted the decisive step toward effective and regular participation in political affairs for broad sections of the Athenian population, and so to this extent it may have been a step in the direction of democracy.

Yet how could a reform of the *phylai*—together, perhaps, with the establishment of a new council—produce this effect? All we know for certain about Cleisthenes is, first, that he divided the citizens of Attica into new "constituencies" and allocated to these certain administrative functions, some of which were new; and, second, that he created a Council of 500 in which the new constituencies were proportionally represented. This may have amounted to no more than a reform of a council of 400 instituted by Solon.[4] Cleisthenes' council had at any rate an advisory role (*probouleusis*) in relation to the popular Assembly; there is no evidence that it had any other functions. It was reconstituted every year and existed side by side with the old council of the nobles on the Areopagus, of which the former archons, the most powerful and experienced politicians of Athens, were life members. There is no evidence of the relation between the two councils. We do not know what other new institutions Cleisthenes may have set up, nor is it certain whether the strange manner in which the Council of 500 was later said to have been constituted and to have functioned goes back to Cleisthenes.[5]

It is hard to see how a reform of the administrative structure of the community and the creation—or reconstitution—of an advisory body, in competition with the old council of nobles, can have been so significant as to furnish the necessary conditions for the emergence of democracy.

Before discussing this question, we should be clear about the aims of our investigation. The sources tell us about the political conflicts that preceded the Cleisthenian reform, about the matters in dispute, and about what happened subsequently. They offer certain explanations of Cleisthenes' intentions, though these are not based on tradition and we are therefore not bound to accept them. While adhering to the sources, we must not let them dictate our questions and our understanding of the situation. We are concerned here with the effect of the reform—insofar as its content can be discerned—on the concrete problems that Cleisthenes faced and set out to solve. This means that we must pay special regard to the position of the Athenian *demos* and the general aims of contemporary political thought. A study of parts of this complex in isolation can yield at most certain details. Only a comprehensive approach will allow us to begin to understand the sense of Cleisthenes' reform. Once we go beyond simple reconstruction of the actual institutions, we are no longer justified in making any statement without a knowledge of the situation in which they were set up. What they were meant to achieve emerges only from an examination of the conditions they were designed to meet.

It is important to emphasize this point, since previous research has largely ignored the concrete situation in which Cleisthenes was operating, and has tended to be more concerned with the idea behind the reform than with the actual situation in which it was realized—and without which it could not have been conceived. There are two aspects to the problem: we have to consider, in the first place, the opposition that Cleisthenes had to contend with and, in the second, the existing institutions that were susceptible of change.

I shall approach the interpretation of Cleisthenes' achievement from the concrete situation. Whatever ulterior motives there may have been for his reform are in the first instance unimportant. They were clearly not just "philanthropic" (or "philopolitical"). It is quite clear that, by winning over the people, he sought power for himself and no doubt for his family. Yet his interests must have been partly identical—or at least parallel—with those of the citizens to whom he appealed. It is this area of overlap that concerns us here.

But first we must ask: in what did Cleisthenes' principal achievement, the reform of the *phylai*, consist? What made the division of the Athenian body politic so important that it became the central feature of a momentous transformation of the political order?

The Old Order

The division of the community before Cleisthenes' reform can be reconstructed roughly as follows. The citizens of Attica were divided into four *phylai* (tribes), each consisting of several *phratriai* (brotherhoods), which in turn comprised various clans (*gene*) and cult communities (*thiasoi*).[6] The citizen thus belonged not only to his immediate family but also to a clan or cult community, through this to a *phratria*, and ultimately, through the *phyle*, to the civic community at large. In short, within the *polis* there were subdivisions at three different levels that took in all the citizens. Other free inhabitants stood outside this system; hence they were not citizens of Athens (or enjoyed only a limited affiliation to the city in the early period). How the citizen body came to be divided up in this way (not only in Athens, but similarly elsewhere) need not concern us here. In most cases the individual groups were based on lineage or family connections, provenance or geographic contiguity (which meant that other groups had to organize themselves in the same way). At a later date, intermediate levels were often created artificially. Obviously, this kind of division and its systematic organization were affected not only by the needs of the individual groups, deriving from the remote past, but also by the evolving needs of the community as a whole.

It is not easy to understand why it was necessary to divide the population of the Greek communities, which were in any case small, into smaller and smaller units. One may surmise that such a system was found to have practical mediating functions. Hence it was used for the allocation of rights and obligations, including the military levies,[7] the army being organized on a tribal basis.[8] Conversely, the citizen was able to attend to his interests within the community as a whole with the help of his fellows in the various groups to which he belonged. Undoubtedly much more important, however, was the function the system performed in providing the citizen with protection, status, and a sense of belonging—of belonging to a kind of family—both in the immediate sphere of his daily life and within the wider community. This has to be understood in a quite concrete sense: anyone who was *aphretor* (that is, who did not belong to a *phratria*)[9] stood outside the community and had no rights. There was also a tradition, clearly of great antiquity, that if a man was murdered and left no surviving relatives, the obligation to exact blood vengeance devolved upon ten members of the *phratria,* chosen from among the nobles.[10] In an age when open conflicts, self-help, and feuds were still widespread and when no adequate justice could be provided by the central organs of the *polis,* the members of these smaller groups were compelled to rely on one another; in particular, the common citizens had to rely on the powerful nobles who belonged to their *phratria.* The family-type ties that operated here manifested themselves above all in the fact that the various subdivisions of the community, especially the *phratriai* (which probably carried most weight), were cult communities, holding common sacrifices and sacrificial feasts.[11] The Greeks saw participation in common worship and sacrifice as the basis of close reciprocal ties.[12] When a man married, his bride was introduced to the other members of the *phratria* at a special sacrificial feast. When a son was born, he was ceremonially presented to them, to be accepted into their circle on reaching manhood.[13] Admission to the *phratria* entailed admission to Attic citizenship (in its early form): only a member of a *phratria* could be a citizen of Attica.[14] The *phratria* was thus the sphere in which the citizens met in a public capacity,[15] and at the same time the authority that legitimated the most important events in their private lives. There are good grounds for believing that at one time the "brotherhoods" also tended to live in contiguous areas, and that their centers and altars were located where large numbers of their members were concentrated.[16] At all events, everyone knew almost everyone else in the *phratria;* everyone had his place, and the cult community had a number of practical functions (in fact the *polis* as a whole was also seen as constituting a cult community).

What applies to the *phratriai* applies also to some extent to the divisions above and below it. In differing degrees they made up the "ambience" in which the citizen led his life. Through them he was bound to different forms of allegiance, some immediate, others more general. It was only by virtue of these allegiances that he belonged to the *polis* community. They ensured that he did not live in isolation. This was especially important in a *polis* such as Athens, which was exceptionally large and populous. Aristotle speaks at one point, with reference to the old divisions and subdivisions of the Attic community, of *synetheiai hai proteron,* "customary and familiar connections." [17]

Such connections within the various groups might coexist with differences and oppositions. We do not know to what extent this was true in Athens. The one thing that is clear is that while the divisions within the community might lead to conflict, they might also serve to counterbalance existing conflicts. By respecting certain differences and oppositions, they were able to foster a maximum degree of unity within the *polis.* Before the end of the sixth century a reform of the *phylai* along these lines was carried out in Cyrene.[18] Whatever differences and oppositions existed among the groups must be seen as a necessary complement to the solidarity that existed within them.[19]

Here it must be stressed that these groups of citizens—unlike, say, the medieval gilds—were not distinguished from one another by different economic or social interests. They were cult communities, essentially similar, though varying in size (here we may ignore the class differences between clans and *thiasoi*). They provided a framework within which the close family-type relationships existing within an originally homogeneous and largely agrarian society could manifest themselves.

Within this homogeneity, however, there was one overriding distinction, the distinction between high and low, noble and commoner. The noble families controlled the groups, and the other members were in many ways dependent on them.[20] The nobility supplied the headmen and priests, and the most important cults belonged to them; so too, in many cases, did the altars, on which sacrifices were also offered for the ordinary members.[21] Only the nobles could intervene effectively on behalf of the latter and safeguard their interests. The commoners were thus in a sense clients of the nobles, and such ties were particularly close and systematized within the individual groups.

Admittedly, the actual relations between nobles and commoners depended on the class relations prevailing within the community as a whole. No doubt they were often characterized by patriarchal severity. In the late seventh and early sixth centuries, however, Athens was affected by the profound social crisis that shattered and confused traditional social relations during the archaic period; this must have damaged the ties existing within the various groups in the city. The hardship suffered by peasants who ran into debt was often the result of pressure from the nobles in their own groups,[22] and when the impotent rage of the peasantry threatened to develop into open rebellion at the beginning of the sixth century,[23] relations within the groups must have been strained to breaking point. Finally, the tyranny of Peisistratus—under which the peasants benefited from the benevolence of the rulers, and which to some extent restricted the influence of the nobles and their earlier freedom of action—cannot have failed to affect the "customary and familiar connections."[24] Yet this does not necessarily mean that the old connections and the traditional dominance of the nobles within the *phratriai* had been rendered ineffective. They were no doubt weakened—so that less reliance could be placed on them in times of trouble[25]—but they seem on the whole to have survived as a traditional feature of Greek life, an established part of the "road network," as it were, within which the citizen normally made his way through life. The nobles retained their generally acknowledged intellectual (and economic) superiority until well into the fifth century; they were still "noble" (*esthlos*), still the "leaders of the people" (*hegemones tou demou*).

Here one should probably distinguish rigorously between the rule and the exception. In exceptional cases the citizens were able to speak up and take action against the nobles—in the Assembly, for instance. They did so when they succeeded in having Solon appointed as *katartister*[26] or when they resolved to provide a bodyguard for Peisistratus.[27] But in the normal run of politics they were not free citizens who made free decisions, but rather followers of the nobles, melting into the background of their cult communities and available to supply private retinues for the ruling families within them. These families thus retained a relatively firm hold on their power. This was finally demonstrated when the city was liberated from tyranny, and old-style clashes broke out between opposing noble factions, all supported by their retinues.[28]

One of these factions was now led by Cleisthenes, and there is nothing to suggest that he was at all dissatisfied with the old clan structure. Only when he had been worsted in the troubles, as Herodotus reports, did he seek to gain the support of the mass of the people[29] and to mobilize them against the nobility; only then did he announce his plans for reform.

Cleisthenes' New Order

It was not Cleisthenes' aim to destroy the existing structure. He left this virtually unchanged,[30] yet at the same time he completely reconstituted the *phylai*, transferring to the new *phylai* the most important political functions of the old and assigning some additional functions to them.[31] The new order was based on the demes, small local settlements, each consisting, as a rule, of a village or a small town. Some villages with few inhabitants were linked with others to form one deme; Athens itself, on the other hand, was divided into several demes, and the town of Brauron into two. Attica was thus divided, on a purely geographic basis, into 139 units (or thereabouts), each containing between about 100 and 1,200 adult male citizens.[32]

In rural areas the political organization of the demes was partly adapted to existing institutions.[33] They had their own officials, priests, and local assemblies charged with various tasks.[34] One of these tasks was to keep a roll of all inhabitants who enjoyed full citizenship, to which one was admitted by the *demotes* at the age of nineteen.[35] A particularly important function was to send a number of representatives, proportionate to the size of the deme, to serve on the Council of 500.[36]

Cleisthenes devised a curious way of grouping the demes into *phylai*. He divided Attica into three regions—the city of Athens and its environs (including the ports), the rest of the coastal area, and the hinterland. In each region he organized the demes into ten groups, known as *trittyes*, generally paying attention to neighborhood ties and geographic units.[37] This gave thirty groups of demes; from these Cleisthenes constituted ten *phylai* by combining three groups of demes (selected by lot), one from each region, into one *phyle*.[38] Each *phyle* had a hero assigned to it (as a "tribal ancestor"), chosen by the Delphic oracle from a list of 100 names.

The details of this extraordinary structure need not concern us here. At least the underlying principle is clear. Each *phyle* was to be a cross-section of all three regions, each region being represented in every *phyle*. Conversely, no *phyle* should represent particular local interests; each should simply represent one-tenth of the total community and had to be as homogeneous as possible. The members of each *phyle* were to have nothing in common but their shared citizenship, which was to be the basis of their solidarity; on this basis they were presumably meant to compete[39] and try to excel one another.

The reform of the *phylai* thus had two main elements: the organization of the civic community was based on the demes, while the *phylai* were artificial constructs comprising a mixture of the most diverse parts of the community.[40] Just as the demes took over many of the functions of the *phratriai*, so the new *phylai* assumed most of the functions of the old, such as providing military levies and distributing imposts.[41] Each *phyle* sent fifty deputies to the Council of 500, these being supplied by the demes in proportion to their size.[42] What did Cleisthenes seek to achieve by this reform?

Ancient and Modern Interpretations of the Aim of the Reform

Our sources offer three answers to this question, though these can hardly have been based on direct tradition. All three start from the observation that the most striking feature of the reform was the "mixing" of the citizens, though the purpose of this is variously interpreted. The author of the *Athenian Constitution* states that Cleisthenes wished to make it possible, by reorganizing the *phylai,* for new citizens to be admitted to the civic rolls.[43] In Aristotle's *Politics,* however, we are told that his aim was to break down the *synetheiai hai proteron,* the "customary and familiar connections" (1319b19ff). Plutarch writes (*Pericles* 3.2) that Cleisthenes' constitution, "by its admirable mixture of all the elements, guaranteed the concord and welfare of the community." This is basically another way of saying the same thing, though in a positive and admittedly more comprehensive way: the aim was to achieve uniformity by eliminating particular groupings. All three explanations seem plausible at first sight and have been accepted, singly or in combination, and with differences of emphasis, by modern historians.

The admission of new citizens was probably the least important reason for the reform of the *phylai.* Many immigrants from the rest of the Greek world lived in Athens, especially from Solon's time onward.[44] Cleisthenes seems to have taken care to see that they were admitted to citizenship. This increased his support in the Assembly,[45] though it is not known to what extent. Nevertheless, one wonders whether it was necessary, in order to achieve this end, to restructure the entire body politic. Possible objections to this view would involve us in an amount of detail that would be inappropriate here.[46] In any case this is unlikely to have been the true motive for the reform.

The destruction of the "customary and familiar connections," on the other hand, seems a much more obvious motive, especially as Cleisthenes was faced with the problem of asserting himself against a majority of the nobles. Hans Schaefer, for instance, writes that the reform of the *phylai* can be explained only by Cleisthenes' "endeavor to drive his internal rivals from the field by destroying the foundations of aristocratic influence that had previously been taken for granted and never interfered with."[47] Gustave Glotz puts it even more plainly: "The members of the great families, who had hitherto lived in gentilitial groups, surrounded by their clientele, now found themselves submerged in the mass of the people, dispersed in a whole system of constituencies based on geography."[48] In addition, the details of Cleisthenes' new order have often been studied, and much of what has been said might suggest that he sought to break up local connections based on religious cults, which could have constituted solid spheres of influence controlled by noble families. All these observations are of course susceptible of different explanations.[49]

Above all, one wonders how it was possible, in the absence of any police authority and without provoking open disturbances,[50] to destroy traditional religious links and affiliations—supposing that these were still strong—simply by an administrative reorganization. What Cleisthenes set out to achieve was after all not a scheme of resettlement, not a real mixing of the population, but simply an administrative reorganization of the body politic. It is of course possible that here and there, in the demes for instance, aristocratic influences were negligible or nonexistent, or that they canceled one another out; yet one also has to consider the possibility that the old connections based on dependency—if indeed they still had any force—could go on asserting themselves under the new constitution. For if the individual citizens were dependent on the leaders of their *phratriai*, this dependency could not be changed simply by the fact that the leaders now belonged to different demes. Despite all the changes in the administrative units, the old ties must have continued to be effective in the Assembly, or wherever else a retinue was required.[51] And this must in turn have affected the power relations within the new subgroups. However influential the ties within these subgroups may have been, a mere redistribution could certainly not countervail real existing dependencies. If, therefore, the old ties—and therefore the old noble factions—were still powerful, how were they to be prevented from continuing to make themselves felt, perhaps after some regrouping? When Hans Schaefer speaks of Cleisthenes' destroying the "foundations of aristocratic influence that were taken for granted and had never been interfered with," is he not presuming that Attic society could be manipulated to a degree that is quite inconceivable in the polities of the ancient world, which were rooted directly in their civic communities? And why did Cleisthenes allow the old order to go on existing beside the new? Was it too powerful simply to be removed? Or had it no longer any real significance? Might it even have been positively useful to him?

Conversely, if one supposes that the traditional connections had by now lost most of their potency, one must then ask what was the point of reforming the *phylai* at all.

On closer inspection, then, this explanation leads to an impasse. There may be some truth in it, but it cannot carry conviction in the form in which it is usually advanced. There is too great a gap between the measures taken by Cleisthenes and their alleged effect, or at least there are several missing links. Above all, the crucial question has not really been asked: What was the contemporary state of the Attic community? Until we can answer this question we cannot say whether or not it was possible or made sense to destroy the bond between the nobles and their followers.[52] Clearly, the situation has not been viewed in sufficiently concrete terms.

One arrives at the same conclusion if one considers the third explanation, namely that Cleisthenes sought to create uniformity within the civic community. This too sounds very plausible at first, especially when one remembers that the country had previously been rocked—even torn apart—by violent conflicts among various noble factions.[53] One might therefore say that in the traditional *phylai* the interests of certain families, and perhaps of certain social groups, had been paramount.[54] There is of course nothing to indicate that the attested formation of factions was in any way connected with the administrative division of the community,[55] but for want of a better explanation one can always surmise that this was so. One can say that in the artificially constituted new *phylai*, whose members had nothing in common but their Athenian citizenship, a new solidarity arose that led to a weakening of particularist interests and a strengthening of the civic element.

Yet all this presupposes that the citizens were willing to be absorbed into the new units and imbue them with fresh life. For this very reason, however, one has to ask how far the new forms of social cohesion (if indeed the new units did produce such cohesion) were able to supersede those that had existed hitherto. The mere creation of a new organization is at any rate not enough to produce solidarity and uniformity. A mere restructuring can be effective only if it creates a form that gives expression and force to a preexistent will. Was there any such preexistent will? And if not, would it not take some time before the new units could produce "customary and familiar connections"? Had Cleisthenes so much time at his disposal? He was not, after all, the reformist minister of a powerful monarch, able to make long-term plans, endowed with the modern capacity for looking into the future and acting accordingly,[56] but a self-reliant nobleman whose first priority was to assert himself in an internal struggle and whose plans had to be instantly convincing and effective.

Similar objections could be raised against all the other interpretations of the immediate aims of the reform of the *phylai*. When R. L. Wade-Gery and H. Schaefer write that Cleisthenes created a secular sphere of political life side by side with the religious sphere,[57] or when P. Lévêque and P. Vidal-Naquet maintain that he wished to establish a *temps civique* and an *espace civique*, corresponding to the geometrical thinking of the age,[58] one again wonders whether conditions in the Attic community were such as to enable Cleisthenes to give reality to such conceptions. Other interpretations, which concentrate on the upgrading of the demes (as the small areas of civic life) and at the same time neglect all the other organizational complexities, are clearly inadequate.[59] Given that there was one councilor for every sixty citizens and that the councilors were supposed to alternate, there must have been substantial numbers of people in Athens with a strong interest in politics; indeed, they must have been more numerous than the councilors themselves. Whatever sound observations are contained in the various theses that have been advanced, the true significance of these observations becomes clear only within a wider context. One cannot simply presume that Cleisthenes had the most favorable conditions for realizing his plans.

It appears, then, that the interpretations proposed so far cannot satisfactorily explain the reform. Some lead to an impasse, all are uncertain, and above all none is sufficiently concrete, because they all focus on Cleisthenes' supposed intention and ignore the most vital questions of all: What was the condition of the civic community, and what were the wishes of the citizens of Attica around the year 508, when Cleisthenes conceived his program? What do we know about the concrete situation and the task that Cleisthenes faced?

The Attic *Demos* at the Time of Cleisthenes' Reform

Herodotus tells us that after the tyrant had been driven out, Cleisthenes was defeated in a struggle with Isagoras, and that after his defeat he appealed to the people (*demos*) and thereupon gained the upper hand in Athens.[60] In all probability it was at this point that he at least proposed his reforms.[61] At all events, the majority of citizens seems to have been interested in his plans. His opponents reacted by resorting to a device that was familiar in the world of the archaic nobility: they appealed for outside help, from King Cleomenes of Sparta.[62] Cleisthenes fled, and most of his friends and supporters (said to have numbered 700 families) were banished. The victors now proceeded to change the constitution in order to set up a strictly oligarchic regime. From now on the *polis* was to be controlled by 300 citizens.[63] The rest were presumably to have few or no political rights. To this end, it was proposed to dissolve the Council (Herodotus unfortunately omits to say which council he is referring to). The Council resisted this move, and unrest broke out in the city; Cleomenes and his Athenian allies had to withdraw to the Acropolis and dig themselves in. Besieged by the populace, they were forced to capitulate after two days and agree to leave without offering further resistance, whereupon the exiles returned to Athens.[64]

The reaction of the Council and the citizens was unexpected. No one was prepared for such a turn of events. Cleomenes, Isagoras, and their followers had obviously calculated that the coup would be fairly easy to engineer: otherwise Cleomenes would not have come with such a small contingent,[65] and Isagoras would at least have made some preparations in order to be a match for his opponents. I believe one can draw the following inferences from the reports of these events:

Cleisthenes had a hard core of followers and friends on his side. He presumably enjoyed enthusiastic support among the rest of the citizens. Isagoras hoped that, after this hard core had been driven into exile, the citizens would submit to an oligarchy. He thus thought that the majority of the Athenians could be kept under control. He no doubt arrived at this conclusion on the basis of traditional aristocratic thinking (and short-sightedness), being unable to imagine that the citizens could find a way of escaping from aristocratic rule when they were no longer being "stirred up" by others. And what had happened up to then gave him good grounds for this assessment. However, he obviously feared that his future rule would not be entirely plain sailing, or he would scarcely have sought to alter the constitution.[66]

Yet if the people's initial response made Isagoras' calculations appear well founded, the subsequent opposition of the Council and the people must have come as a surprise: it was something quite novel at the time, not what one would normally have reckoned with. And what was even more curious was that the citizens' resolute opposition came in the absence of their leaders and those most committed to their support. It came, in other words, largely from the citizens themselves, who had not previously taken a prominent part in affairs, from men who were—to put it precisely—simply citizens, rather than politicians.[67] It was thus an uprising that had fairly extensive roots and was spontaneous in a way that only a popular uprising can be. Certain circumstances inherent in the situation may have played a part in these events. Those who were at first lukewarm in their support of Cleisthenes may have been incensed by the intervention of the king of Sparta and the threat to their political rights; they may have suddenly realized how important it was to put an end to old-style aristocratic rule. Be that as it may, we have here an expression of opposition to the aristocratic circles that had hitherto held sway, a mood of independence that was incompatible with the continuance of the old aristocratic regime. And the divisions went deep. Both sides distrusted each other and did not believe they could go on living together on the traditional basis: the balance had to be tipped one way or the other, in favor of either the nobles or the people. In broad sections of the citizenry there was thus at the very least a mood that Cleisthenes could exploit, a sense of discontent that had only to be aroused and pointed in the right direction.

Here we must attempt a more precise sociological description of the situation. Isagoras presumably had most of the powerful noble families on his side, and these must have enjoyed some popular support, especially within their *phratriai*. The majority of Cleisthenes' supporters, or at least a sizable minority, was no doubt drawn from the most varied sections of society, both from the city and from the country. Their ranks were probably swelled by recent citizens, or by residents whose civil rights were questionable. One must assume that the bulk of the movement was made up of the middle strata of society, consisting in the main of peasants and minor nobles.[68] For certain details of the reform show unequivocally that Cleisthenes had to rely on those segments of the population that enjoyed a measure of prosperity and were available to assume civic duties. Perhaps by this time even the lower classes had a strong interest in politics, though there is no evidence of this.

From all this it may be inferred that, though the old connections and customs had survived until the time of Cleisthenes, they no longer had any real force. The old social structure was thus considerably weakened. There must have been, by the time of Cleomenes' intervention if not before, at least a readiness, if not a strong desire or determination, on the part of the Athenians, to change existing power relations and substantially increase the role of the ordinary citizens in the affairs of the *polis*. Cleisthenes' reform must have seemed the appropriate means to achieve this goal.

The watchword of these broad sections of the citizenry, namely isonomy, is attested shortly afterward. Whether it is of Cleisthenian provenance or not—the sources do not make this clear—it is clearly an apposite designation for the goal toward which their efforts were directed.[69] They did not yet see their claim as a claim to government.[70] They understood it rather in quite concrete and general terms as relating to their shares in the city—and above all in determining its destiny.[71] These shares were now being reapportioned: the citizens were beginning to see themselves as equals (*homoioi*)[72] and could therefore lay claim to *isa* (equal shares) in the *polis*. To use the popular contemporary formula: the government of the city was to be placed in the middle (*es to meson*) of the citizens. As Lévêque and Vidal-Naquet put it,[73] "to establish isonomy is to place *arche es to meson*." It is questionable how far this was logically taken to mean that decisions about the city's affairs should pass out of the control of the few and into the hands of the many.[74] However, efforts were now being directed by broad sections of the citizenry toward genuine participation.

The precondition for such participation was a new conception of the *polis* and politics that had grown up during the sixth century.[75] Traditional aristocratic government had failed. Tyranny had not succeeded in winning over significant numbers of Greeks—or at least not for long. It was proving very difficult to set matters to rights. On the other hand, large sections of the population were becoming increasingly sensitive to injustice, exploitation, and lawlessness. The extraordinary opportunities the Greeks had opened up for themselves during the period of colonization generated increased expectations and demands. It was at this period that political thinking first began to evolve.[76] People began to understand the existing order, to reconstruct the norms on which it rested, and to envisage an ideal constitution that could serve as a criterion for political judgments. The idea arose that the citizens were responsible for the destiny of their city, and this idea gradually gained currency.[77] At first, of course, they had to rely on the help of a *katartister* in order to find solutions for the most difficult crises,[78] but later, thanks to new experiences and insights, they gained confidence in their own capacities. In Athens the tyranny of Peisistratus had brought a consolidation of the economic situation, and the broad mass of citizens had acquired a measure of legal security.

They now wished to protect themselves against a renewal of tyranny and oligarchic misrule, to act in their own right in ensuring that justice was safeguarded and the *polis* properly governed. They no longer needed a "figure qualified by certain exceptional gifts"; what they needed was a situation in which "the city resolved its problems through the normal functioning of its institutions."[79]

Finally, for the first time in the history of Athens, the citizens saw that basic reforms in the civic order not only made sense but also were attainable, that is, accessible to the general will. The time was past when superior insight was required to pronounce on the just order and discern it in existing conditions—when it could be realized only by expert authorities through the modification of existing conditions. It was now possible for a new order to be arbitrarily created by the decision of broad sections of the people. However much they may have been convinced that they were restoring time-honored law (see, for example, Herodotus 3.80.5 f), they nevertheless proceeded to breach the traditional order at one decisive point, namely where the mutual relations of the citizens were concerned. The problem no longer lay in the structure of society: what was at issue was the political order.

Such thinking generated new criteria. The nobles came to be seen in a different light. There had long been doubts about their natural superiority.[80] In Sparta the citizens had already begun to see themselves as equals (*homoioi*)—whatever that meant.[81] Now the fundamental distinction between nobles and commoners finally lost its legitimation. Above all, it now became possible to draw political consequences from equality. This cleared the way for the citizens to assert not only their equality before the law,[82] but the political equality of all citizens, and this meant, above all, equality between the middle classes and the nobility. This is what was meant by isonomy.

The claim to equality did not mean, of course, that the citizens were no longer willing to entrust offices, military commands, and diplomatic missions almost exclusively to members of the nobility. For years to come the nobles would—thanks to their intellectual and physical attributes, to their "breeding," in other words—have a distinct advantage over others, so that until well into the fifth century (and hence, we may presume, at the period in question) it was generally unthinkable to entrust offices and public functions to anyone else. Yet if this aspect of equality was absent, it is all the more important to emphasize the other: all citizens were deemed capable of judging what was in the interest of the community, and therefore all were responsible. Their claim to equality thus embraced the desire, if not the demand, for more effective participation, for control of the community, at least in all important matters, no matter how extensive such control might be.

It was at this period that the close link was established between equality and justice, a link that was to remain a vital element in the notion of isonomy.[83] Equality was seen as essential to any just order.[84] However, the chief ingredient and prime goal of this equality was "a new type of participation by the *démos* in the functioning of institutions."[85] This participation constituted the practical link between equality and the safeguarding of justice.

Yet if large numbers of the Attic citizenry sought equality and an effective voice in government, if they were so hostile to the nobles, why was it necessary to institute such a complicated reform of the *phylai?* What was to stop the citizens from asserting their will in the Assembly? What was to prevent their electing to the magistracy nobles who would be compliant to their will? Why was the Areopagus not abolished? Why was authority not redistributed among the officials, the Council, and the Assembly? Would it not have sufficed to give decisive powers to Solon's council of the *phylai* (if this in fact existed) or to constitute a new council from the existing *phylai?* For a broadly based popular will could surely have asserted itself in the old *phylai,* and annual elections would have enabled the people to maintain their influence in the Council. Or had the power relations not yet shifted decisively enough in favor of the citizenry at large? Was the balance between people and nobles still precarious?

We do not know to what extent a redistribution of authority or a restriction of the rights of the Areopagus would have been conceivable at this period. However, Cleisthenes and his supporters clearly did not believe that they could attain their objective by such measures—or, for that matter, by traditional constitutional means. They sought to reach it by a quite different route, one that to us seems somewhat strange. We will consider the reasons presently. In this context we can make only one more firm observation: whatever the current power relations may have been, it was only in exceptional cases that the will and authority of the people could make themselves felt in the prevailing circumstances. Only in exceptional cases were questions debated which concerned the citizen body as a whole and for which the broad masses could be mobilized. When it came down to day-to-day affairs, solidarity was soon bound to dissolve, and the pull of tradition, the old infrastructure of mutual relations, representation, and influence, was sure to reassert itself. In the limited sphere of everyday life, the superiority of the nobles was bound to prevail. The threshold beyond which the rule yielded to the exception—the threshold of tolerance, beyond which the people were capable of taking concerted action—was relatively high.

As we have said, Attica was unusually large and populous. Apart from Laconia, which was exceptional by any reckoning, it was almost twice as big as the next-largest city-state,[86] with between 25,000 and 30,000 adult male citizens.[87] The distance between the more remote townships and Athens itself was anything up to seventy kilometers—a good day's journey each way. Hence, citizens from these townships could hardly attend the Assembly without spending at least two nights in the city.[88] The distance between some of the outlying towns was even greater. It is evident that for the ordinary citizens—though not for the nobles, with their greater mobility—there was no scope for frequent contacts and a buildup of solidarity. Of the common citizens, only those who lived in the city and its immediate environs were in a position to exert any effective influence. As for the country-dwellers, who accounted for more than two-thirds of the population,[89] whatever political influence they had stemmed mainly from well-organized minorities—from the retinues of the nobles, who were intent upon promoting particularist interests. The door was thus wide open to private machinations and the influence of aristocratic cliques, to quarrels, divisions, and conflicts among aristocratic factions. This could mean a resurgence of lawlessness and exploitation. The resumption of the old habits in the struggle between Cleisthenes and Isagoras had revived memories of how things used to be.

Our analysis of the Attic community thus leads to our first conclusion: the old ties between the nobles and their followers had been substantially weakened and survived only *faute de mieux*. To destroy them was both unnecessary and impossible—unnecessary in exceptional situations and impossible in general. Instead, they had to be made superfluous: it was necessary to ensure that the citizens did not revert to the old ties in day-to-day affairs. The problem, therefore, was how to create an effective system in which the citizens would in future be able to conduct themselves as equals, rather than as supporters of the nobles—a system in which power relations were changed both in general and in particular areas. To free the citizens from their old dependencies, new forms of organization had to be created in which they could assert their freedom. Once this succeeded, the old system of the *phylai*, now substantially weakened, could safely—perhaps even usefully—be allowed to survive. Hence, if Cleisthenes wanted to help the people achieve greater participation in political affairs—and everything suggests that this was his intention—it was less important for him to destroy what already existed than to *establish something new*. Above all, he had to invent something that could coexist with the old and eventually replace it. What really mattered was the positive part of his reform; the negative part was an automatic side effect.[90] In the words of Napoleon, "On ne détruit que ce qu'on remplace."

To sum up: when the tyrant had been overthrown and there was a prospect of renewed factional conflict among the nobles, a new solidarity arose among the mass of the civic community; this solidarity had firm roots in the social history of political thought. This was something that Cleisthenes could build on. But the strength of this solidarity was evanescent. To become permanent, it had to be institutionalized. Aristotle states that one of the reasons why it was possible, in early times, for broad segments of the citizenry to be dominated was that they were "weak in organization and cohesion" (*kata ten syntaxin phauloi*).[91]

What was the positive element that Cleisthenes had to create? Why did he have to reorganize the whole civic community in order to make it better able to participate in politics?

The Problem of the Reform

There were various ways to secure regular participation in politics for broad sections of the civic community, whatever the extent of their participation and whatever the claims and ulterior motives of the citizens.

First, there was the Assembly. A wide range of decisions could be made dependent on its approval, although naturally this presupposed a precise definition of areas of competence. The influence of the *demos* could also be reinforced by requiring that the Assembly meet at least once within a given period. The great traveling distances naturally posed an insuperable problem. For this and other reasons there was a danger of the Assembly's being dominated by powerful magnates, supported by their retinues. Further conditions therefore had to be met if the community at large was to become a regular force in the Assembly.

In cases in which this body had only limited scope for action, the people had to be represented by deputies. These could strengthen the Assembly's capacity for action by holding preliminary deliberations on matters due for debate, supplying information, and putting forward proposals.[92] An annually elected council could be set up or popular control over its composition increased. According to Aristotle, the council was the most democratic organ in those communities in which the Assembly could not be frequently convened.[93] The electoral body that sent members to the council could be organized in such a way as to favor the broad mass of the community by providing that councilors be drawn from a relatively wide circle. There might for instance be a rule precluding them from serving for two or more successive years, or requiring them to be chosen by lot. This would ensure that the council gradually came to consist, not of particular "functionaries" or the most powerful and ambitious politicians, but of a wide range of ordinary citizens, and that there was a closer link between the representatives and those whom they represented. The problem here, however, was that the power of the council might thereby be reduced. In the age of Pericles this worked entirely to the benefit of democracy, by making it harder for him to override the Assembly.[94] In Cleisthenes' day, however, the chief aim was to counterbalance the power of the Areopagus and the aristocratic officials, and to assert the rights of the people against them. What seems to have been needed to achieve this aim was a strong council composed of men of skill and experience. For the power of the council could not depend solely on a definition of areas of competence (even supposing that this was at all feasible).

In any case, the composition of the council posed a peculiarly Greek problem. Between the nobility and the rest of the people there were great disparities of education, experience, wealth, and connections. The leading Athenian nobles, the former archons, sat in the Areopagus. It could hardly have accorded with the intentions of Cleisthenes and his supporters that these same men should also sit in the Council of 500.[95] It was therefore necessary to rely on a second set of nobles who had hitherto been less involved in politics, and on wealthy commoners who had time to spare for public office.[96] If, as seems likely, the main concern was to ensure that the people brought their weight to bear in Athens in defense of their vital interests, these men, though perhaps inferior to the leading nobles, were quite capable of doing whatever was necessary to limit the political influence of the magnates and above all their arbitrary exercise of power, by organizing opposition and establishing a degree of control over what took place in the community. The real problem was that in the long run a "popular council"[97] could be effective only if it had the backing of popular power—the interest and will of the people—and was capable of asserting this will should the need arise.

A third requirement was therefore that the people be to some extent politicized—and remain politicized. This necessitated, in the first place, a degree of political knowledge and political interest, and also a sense of political responsibility (all of which may be presumed to have existed in Athens at this time). A further requirement was that the citizens be freed from any ties binding them to the nobles, and that broad sections of the citizenry be able to form judgments and evolve a concerted political will in important matters. It was therefore necessary to create opportunities for extensive participation in politics. Politics had to be brought into the lives of the citizens. It was not enough for them to have the necessary information and an overall view of *polis* affairs: they must be able to exercise an effective influence, commensurate with the effort they invested in it.

In particular, communication had to be established between different parts of the community throughout the country. There had to be meeting points for the exchange of ideas, institutions that would create links among the citizens. It was not enough to "bring the citizens to the *polis*": they had to "come together" in new ways. Throughout the *polis* there had to be changes in the power relations that currently worked in favor of the nobility. Not only must politics ultimately become the affair of the citizens, but the affairs of the citizens must become the stuff of politics. The content of politics must change.

Once the crisis of the archaic period had been overcome, politics (as understood in the ancient world) were concerned essentially with the interests of the citizens *qua* citizens. What mattered now was, at the very least, to gain control over political events, and probably, in addition, to bring politics home to the citizens, to make them a topic of daily discussion, a new element in the life of the community. Most of the questions that affected the citizen in his domestic, economic, or professional life were exempt from political decision making. Hence, political participation was not colored by domestic interests to any great extent. One might almost say that the content of many of the political decisions that were made was of less interest to the citizens than the share they had in making them. The very fact that they were citizens brought them into a special sphere that they themselves created by their mutual interaction. This led—at first in the middle ranks of society—to the emergence of a political identity: the citizen's affiliation to the *polis* became more important than any other.[98]

It was therefore imperative that the citizens of Attica acquire a civic presence in Athens: directly in the Assembly, indirectly through the Council, and also metaphorically—in the sense that they should take a keen interest in the course of political events and that the Council should, as it were, become so embedded in the civic community and in the shaping of the common will that the one influenced the other. The competences pertaining to the various constitutional organs were of secondary importance. The problem of the reform was thus the creation of a civic presence involving as many of the citizens as possible.

This problem arose among the Greeks, especially in Athens, largely because the homogeneity of knowledge—and hence the reliability of expectations—had been seriously impaired during the great crisis of the archaic period. It was this homogeneity of knowledge, rather than any legal provisions, that had previously determined and limited the scope of action. Once lost, it could not be restored by monarchical or aristocratic rule. Even today there is little appreciation of the problems to which this state of affairs gave rise, yet unless we start from these problems we shall not be able to understand the special nature of the situation prevailing in

Greece at this time. What is involved may be briefly indicated by a comparison with Roman conditions. The Roman Republic made do, in the main, with rudimentary forms of a civic presence—relatively few meetings of the assembly, relatively few functions assigned to the *comitia*,[99] and permanent representation through the tribunes of the people.[100] For the rest, the "normal" functioning of countless ties and conventions guaranteed satisfactory and stable relations between the nobles and the rest of the citizens. There was an interlocking of conventional wisdom, reliable expectations, and—as a kind of emergency service—the tribunes of the people and the *comitia*. All this could be taken for granted. In Greece, by contrast, less and less could be taken for granted. Here and there the people may have had individual representatives (not unlike the tribunes of the people),[101] yet on the whole the experience of the Greeks was that successful popular leaders usually set up tyrannies. After the breakdown of social homogeneity, the opportunities for this were all too tempting, given the generally unstable conditions of the age. Moreover, the lawless conduct of the nobles caused more unrest in Greece than it did in Rome (for this there were both objective and subjective reasons). Hence, the influential intellectual movement of which we have spoken could in the end find only one solution for the crisis: responsibility for the *polis* should be assumed by the whole of the body politic. In Greece, the proper opponents of the nobles could not be individual magistrates or successful popular leaders, but the people at large. It was therefore necessary to create a far broader civic presence, with an overall view of everything that took place in the community. To a far greater extent than elsewhere it was necessary for wide sections of the citizen body to be somehow present, virtually every day, in order to keep public affairs under surveillance and to intervene if necessary.[102] To this extent the establishment of a civic presence was a matter of particular urgency in Greece; the *polis* had to be transformed so radically that one might even speak of its being "reconstituted." This was the only way to create a civic order that would be acceptable to those circles whose approval was all-important—the broad mass of the citizens.

With these problems in mind, we may arrive at a clear understanding of all the notable features of the reform of the *phylai*.

The Reform as a Means of Creating a Civic Presence

As far as we know, Cleisthenes did nothing to alter the rights of the Assembly though he may have decreed that it should be regularly convened and conferred the right of convention on the Council of 500.[103]

He established a close link between this Council and the community, first by giving it a fairly large membership, and second by reforming the *phylai,* each of which now returned fifty representatives to the Council. Presumably these were already supplied by the demes in proportion to their size.[104] There was one Council member to at most every sixty adult male citizens; thus even a medium-sized village sent three or four councilors. These men would travel to Athens to attend the Council and then return to their deme.[105] As for the mode of selection, Cleisthenes may have introduced various forms of election by lot and made other provisions to ensure that the same men were not returned year after year.[106]

The whole of the Attic community was thus ideally represented by a strong presence in Athens. At the same time, the political will that took shape in Athens was projected back into every deme. The Council could thus serve as a clearinghouse for the exchange of opinions and judgments and play an important role in linking the different parts of the community.

We know that at a later date the Athenian constitution provided that the councilors from the different *phylai* should be present at the Prytaneum in rotation for one-tenth of the year. If this provision dated from the time of Cleisthenes, the citizens must have enjoyed near-perfect representation, even at this early date. The difficulty of traveling to Athens and the comparatively small number of citizens who could spare the time to serve on the Council suggest that it did go back to Cleisthenes. This would give added point to the organization of the *phylai,* each of which comprised one-tenth of the citizenry, chosen at random. The widespread solidarity of the citizens would also serve to make the *prytaniai* appear representative.[107]

Not the least important aim of the reform of the *phylai* was to provide, as far as possible, the necessary basis for the shaping of a popular political will, which could then be given purposeful expression, both indirectly and to some extent directly. The fact that the civic community was from now on organized on the basis of the demes meant that citizenship already carried a certain democratic implication. It was possible for everyone to gain an overall view of conditions at this local level and to know what was happening. The individual was able to assert himself, and the excessive influence of a handful of nobles could be counterbalanced by a majority among the citizens. There were, moreover, age-old neighborhood ties: a certain solidarity already existed within the demes, competing with the units of the traditional order.[108] This popular solidarity was now reinforced by the fact that several new functions were assigned to the demes and their "democratically" appointed officials.[109] The communal life of a village or a small town now embodied a part of public life.[110] As a result the individual citizen was less isolated politically, less reliant on members of the nobility, and could now settle local affairs in collaboration with his peers. At the same time, the group in which he lived and enjoyed a certain standing became the basis of his political existence. Here were the beginnings of "grass-roots democracy."[111] It is hardly possible to overrate the importance of all this for the citizens of Attica.[112]

Of special importance, moreover, was the fact that everyone in the demes had access, through the Council, to the political life of Athens. The individual thus had the opportunity to promote his own interests without the help of nobles. This opportunity might arise through membership on the Council, through personal acquaintance with its members, and especially through the mediation of the *trittys* and the *phyle*. It is noteworthy that the *phylai* supported the individual in the courts; this too was a function that had previously been performed by the old communal divisions.[113] The individual thus became more independent. Whatever influence the nobles still exercised in individual demes could be neutralized within the *trittys* and the *phyle*. Any noble who wished to be held in esteem now had to put himself in good standing with his fellow citizens.[114] He might be taken into their service. This led to a change in relations within the demes too, no matter what personal influence he still enjoyed. Hence, by this stage at the latest, the close dependency of the citizens on the nobles had become the exception rather than the rule; at all events, many citizens were being freed from the close ties that had previously bound them to the nobles. The nobility was thus losing more and more of its control over the individual citizens, while the power of the citizenry as a whole was increasing.

Thanks to the principle of "mixing" the population, the new organization of the *phylai* could make a very practical contribution to the integration of the community. It is uncertain how soon new ties and a new solidarity began to evolve in the *phylai* as a result, for instance, of shared military service or the need to collaborate in allocating rights and obligations.[115] But this is of no great importance. Another form of solidarity already existed in wide sections of the community, and on this basis it was possible for *trittyes* and *phylai* to perform important mediating functions. Because a host of matters had to be settled by discussion in the course of establishing the new order, numerous contacts and acquaintanceships grew up among citizens from all over Attica, and further connections were to be added subsequently. To put it in simple terms: while the citizens of *trittys* AI were collaborating with those of AII and AIII in different parts of the country, their neighbors from *trittyes* BI and CI could be in contact with the citizens of BII, BIII, CII, and CIII, which were likewise located in different regions. The contacts of the neighbors of AII and AIII ran in yet other directions. There was thus a whole network of connections covering the entire country, and over time this network was bound to become increasingly dense.

The most significant increase in the number of personal connections came of course from common membership on the Council of 500 and from collaboration in the different areas of politics.

Various aspects of Cleisthenes' reform thus served to produce, among the middle ranks of society, what the nobility had long enjoyed—personal connections within the leading circles, which in this new context meant the fairly wide circles of those who would in future guarantee, in practical terms, the effective participation of the mass of the citizens in political life. Such simple, practical considerations hardly ever occur to modern scholars, who tend to take a far too detached view of their subject. Yet there can be little doubt that, if wide sections of the population (made up, broadly speaking, of peasants) in a relatively large city-state were to pursue a common policy, they had to have not only common aims but also mutual contacts.[116] Otherwise they could do little more than take part in short-lived uprisings or lend support to a popular leader, with the inevitable result that politics remained in the hands of professional politicians.

On the basis of the existing solidarity, collaboration among large numbers of people who had previously been strangers inevitably led them to act in a capacity which had so far been of minor importance and of which they had scarcely been conscious—their capacity as citizens. For it was as citizens that they now came together, getting to know one another and laying claim to one another's good offices. The common political will thus gained strength and durability, manifesting itself in concrete form and taking root in a shared political identity. For it is hardly an adequate description of what was created at this time to say that a large number of citizens took it into their heads—or suddenly felt an obligation—to engage in politics. Such a state of affairs can after all arise—and be perpetuated—only if the activity it involves carries special and lasting prestige, that is to say, if it is institutionalized in mutual expectations that, when fulfilled, will create further expectations. Only in this way can the necessary social dynamism be generated and sustained. A vital step in this direction was taken at the time of Cleisthenes, and what it led to could subsequently be reproduced.[117]

From our analysis of the Attic *demos* it was inferred that Cleisthenes' intention was not so much to negate or destroy the old order as to establish something positive. This inference now seems to be corroborated by practical considerations, provided that we are willing to take a sufficiently basic view of the problem. The aim was not so much to eliminate the old complex of influences, but to perpetuate an already-existing and relatively spontaneous solidarity, and to this end the body politic had to be mixed. And the fact that Cleisthenes divided up into different *trittyes* areas whose inhabitants owed their cohesion to common cult activities does not mean that he wanted to destroy their "organic ties." How could he have done so without building walls?[118] He could at best have counter-balanced or supplanted them with new and competing ties. The likeli-hood is that he consciously made use of them, since this would enable him to draw the network of associations even tighter. For even the "cus-tomary and familiar connections" must have shifted to some extent as soon as the middle ranks of society gained power and solidarity. Cleis-thenes' designs were thus presumably helped rather than hindered by allowing the old order of the *phylai* to continue in being, and in par-ticular by letting the *phratriai* continue to receive newborn children and so make the initial decision on their membership in the community.

Our analysis thus leads us to the thesis that Cleisthenes' reform has to be understood in more concrete and fundamental terms than hitherto. Its aim was to make broad sections of the Attic citizenry more autonomous, better acquainted with one another, and more powerful in perpetuity. This is best summed up by saying that they were to be given a political presence in Athens. This is the decisive point as regards the concrete effect of the reform, the power relations within the *polis,* and the formation of a political will. Only in this way could the power of the whole body politic be concentrated in one place, constantly regenerated, and pointed in an appropriate direction through linking the far-flung parts of the community with the central seat of power. Only in this way was it possible to establish, on a permanent basis, effective participation and control over the commu-nity. It seems to me wrong to say that Cleisthenes put the city of Athens in a "position of command."[119] It had long occupied such a position, though the command it enjoyed had so far been subject to many particu-larist influences. Rather, access to this commanding position was now substantially broadened: greater power flowed into it, and greater influ-ence radiated from it. Governing and being governed were converging.

Without this restructuring of the civic community there would have been no point in changing the competences of the constitutional organs. What had to be transformed first was the community, not the constitu-tion. The problems involved in trying to give broad sections of the citi-zenry a voice in political affairs were different from those that had to be addressed in the revolutionary period of modern history. It is doubtful, indeed, whether a precise reallocation of competences would have been conceivable; it would probably have been beyond the intellectual capac-ity of the age. Above all, it was probably clear that affairs would have to remain for the most part in the hands of those already in office—who perforce belonged to the upper class[120]—and of the Areopagus.[121] At first, then, the Council of 500 had to act as an opposition.[122] It had to make itself heard when the rights and interests of the community were clearly affected, and in particular when the Assembly had to be involved. The position that the citizen body as a whole ultimately came to occupy in the interplay of constitutional organs depended not so much on the areas of competence pertaining to the Council as on the frequency of its meetings and the power behind it. What mattered ultimately was the civic community; the Assembly and the Council mattered only insofar as they could serve as its organs.

We must now consider to what extent the reform of the *phylai* was designed to achieve other objectives. What can be said about the other intentions that modern scholars have attributed to Cleisthenes?

Other Aims of the Reform

Cleisthenes' personal motives for the reform of the *phylai* are not recorded. There can be little doubt, however, that he was concerned to find a new way of acquiring political influence. He acted as many nobles had before him, trying to win the people over to his side in order to gain an ascendancy that he could then exploit against the majority of his own class. However, he had clearly learned that to do this one had to offer the people not only economic benefits but also political reforms—that one should no longer aim to set up a tyranny, but seek a new form of collaboration with the citizens, whose status the reforms were designed to enhance. Hence, his interests were largely identical—or at least ran in parallel— with that strand of opinion in the Athenian civic community that was pressing for isonomy.

Consequently, having won the people over to his side, so Herodotus tells us (5.66.2), he saw to it that his supporters were given more freedom, independence, and power than any other group of supporters had enjoyed before.

Cleisthenes appreciated all this. He knew how to exploit and direct the wishes and aspirations of the citizens, and he tailored his plans so skillfully to current conditions that he was able to devise a bold and rational reorganization of civic community [123] while paying due regard to the realities of the situation. Herein lies his greatness. It was not a matter of putting a theory into practice, but of pursuing an eminently practical policy. This presupposed a high degree of openness to institutional thinking and contemporary reality. It is natural that Cleisthenes himself should have won high esteem. And the fact that his family were outsiders may be presumed to have contributed to a certain lack of prejudice. [124]

Cleisthenes probably took it for granted that the leadership of the community would remain with the nobles. The most he can have envisaged was a shift of emphasis in the power structure—certain changes in the rules of the game. Henceforth influence was not to be won and retained— politics was not to be pursued (or at least not to the same extent)—by means of the traditional retinues that the nobles had at their disposal, but much more through the power of persuasion and personal achievement, and through new forms of civic collaboration. What this amounted to was the institutionalization of a reality for which the ground was already laid in the claims and capabilities of large numbers of citizens. At the same time it opened the door to a freer kind of politics.[125]

We do not know precisely how Cleisthenes envisaged the future role of the *demos*. We must presume that his initial concerns were simply to enhance its status within the complex of existing institutions and to allow it to assert itself as a whole on a regular basis.

Several other effects with which Cleisthenes has been credited—insofar as they can be taken seriously—merely represent different aspects of the same fundamental change. It seems to me that they can be understood in concrete terms only on the basis of the reconstruction presented here, and that they were possible only after the successful establishment of a civic presence. Among these is the new position that is variously said to have been won by the ordinary citizen. Participation in politics was now no longer confined to the upper classes, but was accessible to everyone; this meant in practice that participation was extended to the middle ranks of society. Politics now demanded a very large part (relatively speaking!) of the thinking, planning, and activity of a fairly wide circle of citizens. To the obvious ties arising from family life, work, friendship, neighborhood contacts, economic relations, and religious affiliations was added direct involvement in the newly constituted life of the *polis*. On the other hand, the citizens came to be seen much more as citizens and no longer simply as town-dwellers or country-dwellers, nobles, peasants, artisans, members of local communities, and the like.[126] Supreme importance came to be attached to the one capacity in which they were all equal.[127] For the goal was not social equality, but purely political or "civic" equality, conferred by membership in the *polis*.

To be a citizen (*polites*) was now understood in a new sense deriving from the *polis*, while at the same time the *polis* began to be constituted by the citizens. Hence, the criteria to which the citizens subscribed had to prevail, at least in the long term—the criteria of men whose highest priority was law and order, not victory in aristocratic feuds, not the assertion of powerful personal claims, not a code of conduct determined by the dichotomy of friend and foe.[128] It is interesting—and characteristic of ancient conditions—that, according to the unanimous testimony of the sources, there were no contending factions within the *demos*, but only oppositions between the *demos* and the nobles or the rich, or between different groups within the upper class.[129] Archaic patterns of behavior, geared to personal relations, to relations between friend and foe, could never assert themselves among the broad ranks of the citizenry, unless they were directed outside the city; when they were, the individual *polis* would close ranks and act in an "archaic" fashion.[130] None of the preconditions existed that might have given rise to modern-style political groupings. However, the fact that the criteria prevailing in isonomies and democracies were those of the citizenry at large showed that the *polis* could often attain stability only as a peasant community, that the necessary safeguards for unity and justice could be provided only by the peasantry.

To this extent isonomy was a means of restoring the old law. When the first democracies were founded, there could be no possibility of establishing equality and liberty within the existing order; equality had to be created at the same time as law and order. This was the outcome of the wide diffusion of power that had characterized earlier times; it was also the chief feature distinguishing the Greek communities from the modern state.[131]

The fact that this also led to the unifying of the citizenry (which is often said to have been Cleisthenes' aim) can now be understood in clear and concrete terms. Contrary to the prevalent view, however, this uniformity was achieved less through overcoming oppositions based on geography than through the emergence of a lively interest in political affairs and of a regular political will that was broadly rooted in the body politic. This uniformity was not created by Cleisthenes: he simply ensured the continuance of a solidarity that was present at a given moment. In this solidarity his new *phylai* could discover an already-existing unity; all that remained to be done was to go on renewing and consolidating it.

Cleisthenes thus produced substantial changes in different spheres: in the sphere of constitutional history, by creating certain institutions; in that of political thought and action, by making central areas of the civic order subject to popular decision making; and, finally, in the sphere of identity, by transforming the pattern of affiliations within the body politic. This last change represented an important advance in the history of identity. That all this could happen so quickly was due to the fact that the ground had been prepared by long-standing predispositions; all that was needed was to give them institutional expression.

How far Cleisthenes' reform inaugurated the later move to democracy is an open question. As has been mentioned,[132] the special problems posed by the creation of a civic presence in Athens—and Cleisthenes' ingenious solution—may have produced a particularly robust and tenacious form of political identity. Yet what was decisive for the powerful shift to democracy in fifth-century Athens was the victory over the Persians and its subsequent effects in the early history of the Delian League. However, as Herodotus remarks, once the Athenians had their isonomy, everyone believed himself to be acting for his own personal advantage.[133] Hence, shortly after the reform, the Athenians won great military successes in their immediate vicinity. There seem to be many indications that the decision to wage war on the Persians, the growth in military power to which it led, and—not least—the intellectual and political room for maneuver that Themistocles gained in order to build up the fleet—were all conditioned by the Cleisthenian reform. The Athenians were determined to defend their isonomy, and so, to this extent at least, isonomy was the positive precondition for democracy.

It thus emerges that the real problem of the reform was how to establish a civic presence.[134] This was far too basic a question to be compassed by the abstract concepts of the later period. Aristotle at one point makes an oblique reference to it,[135] but it does not greatly interest him. Basically, Cleisthenes' solution must have seemed too obvious to him; hence his interpretation remained peripheral. And so, even today, it is true to say that the real problem concerning the reform of the *phylai* is the fact that it is so hard to see what is problematic about it.

FIVE

The *Eumenides* of Aeschylus and the Rise of the Political

ALL GENUINE historical records are at first tedious, because and insofar as they are alien. They express the views and interests *of their time*, and do not come a single step to meet us . . . For the ordinary half-educated man, all poetry (except political verse) . . . is incomprehensible and tedious."[1] This judgment of Jacob Burkhardt may explain why the political message of the *Eumenides* has aroused relatively little interest.[2] Yet the play occupies a special and significant place in the history of Greek political thought, being perhaps its most grandiose manifestation in the fifth century. It gave expression to the political at the very moment when it first burst upon Athens, and did so, moreover, in a manner that was wholly adequate to the theme and is still relevant today. This becomes clear, however, only when one considers the political problems posed by the situation to which the play addresses itself, the situation that prevailed in Athens around 458 B.C., or, more generally, in the period that saw the rise of the political among the Greeks.

This focus on a temporally restricted and "at first tedious" dimension of the *Eumenides* does not detract from the many other respects in which the play, taken in the context of the trilogy to which it belongs, makes an impact as direct and timeless as any classical work can.[3] Algernon Swinburne called the *Oresteia* "perhaps the greatest achievement of the human mind."[4] Yet however one reads the three dramas, the political is unquestionably a central aspect, and there are good reasons for saying that the *Oresteia* owes all its seriousness and greatness to its political theme. For the emergence of the political was the decisive, significant, and exciting human experience of the age.

The Situation around 458 B.C.: Politicization of the Civic Order

When the *Oresteia* was written and first performed (in the spring of 458), Athens lay in the shadow of a momentous event—the abolition of the political power of the Areopagus in 462/61.[5] This body had already been deprived of its character as a purely aristocratic council, but its membership probably still included the city's most experienced and influential politicians.[6] It is obvious, given the intense activity that had been going on in the field of war and foreign affairs since the Persian Wars, that the Areopagus had had an important role to play.[7] Cimon, the leading statesman and general of the period before 462/61, had relied on its support. It seems to have adhered to a definite policy, the main features of which were a reluctance to press ahead with the expansion of Athenian power and a desire to maintain good relations with Sparta. In internal affairs too the Areopagus must have exercised a significant influence, and it had the right to call the magistrates to account. It was thus a substantial force in Athenian politics.[8]

Then, in 462/61, a group of politicians led by Ephialtes persuaded the Assembly to forbid the Areopagus to involve itself in politics, leaving it with only a few juridical functions in cases of homicide.[9] The "reformers" were no doubt concerned chiefly with foreign affairs and wished to pursue a plainly expansionist policy regardless of relations with Sparta (and probably against Sparta). The Areopagus stood in the way and therefore had to be eliminated as a political organ.[10] But however much Ephialtes may have been motivated by these immediate aims, the supporters of the Areopagus must have made it clear that the Assembly's decision represented a serious violation of ancient rights, hallowed tradition, and the ancestral order.[11] The fundamental implications for the Athenian constitution must therefore have been pointed out at least by those who opposed the change.

The elimination of the power of the Areopagus changed the whole political horizon. The Assembly was relieved of an important competitor. Plutarch writes that Ephialtes filled the citizens' cup of freedom so full that they became intoxicated.[12] New men, new methods, and new political aims came to the fore, and hence opportunities for new excesses. The move against Sparta and the building of the Long Walls to the Piraeus were designed to enable the city to engage in a kind of power politics that was at variance with Greek tradition.[13] The lowest strata of society seem to have asserted themselves to a greater extent in the Assembly. The way was now open for a new kind of politics, based solely on the Assembly and the Council of 500.[14] The Assembly was emancipated, as it were. The political roof provided by the Areopagus suddenly caved in; the decisive step into a wider world had been taken.

It may be assumed that the removal of the political power of the Areopagus was an event of far greater consequence than Cleisthenes' reform of the *phylai*. The latter had given the citizens new power and influence within the framework of the existing order, enabling them to operate as a kind of official opposition and to defend themselves against the Areopagus and the administrators, restricting the power of the nobility, and obliging the nobles to pay more heed to the wishes of the people. It had changed the rules of the game, but still left the nobility as the superior ruling class.[15] Now, however, the nobility lost its leading position. Whereas the earlier reform had produced a stronger opposition, this later one destroyed an existing form of government. It represented a far more profound change and no doubt had far more opponents. Those whose interests were adversely affected were at least a fairly powerful minority. Attempts were made to repeal the new law. Ephialtes was murdered, and there were growing fears in Athens that civil war was about to break out and that various nobles were conspiring with Sparta to overthrow democracy.[16] This is the background for the *Eumenides*. The fact that Aeschylus implores the Athenians so earnestly to preserve concord and a just order shows that all the questions and conflicts that had been stirred up by the removal of the power of the Areopagus had by no means died down by 458.

Behind the immediate complications there must have been a disturbing awareness that the *polis* itself and its order had been called into question. For the first time in Greek history—and world history—the civic order as a whole was placed at the disposal of the citizens: it had become a matter of controversy, hence a political issue. For the first time in history men were presented with a clear alternative, the starkest alternative that is possible within civic communities (if one disregards the presence of non-citizens and slaves): Should the governed (that is, those who were not professionally engaged in political life) be granted a decisive voice in civic affairs *et de iure et de facto*, or should they not? It was no longer simply a question of whether or not there should be some kind of public order or of who should have the right to govern (either a monarch or an aristocracy); it was not a question of how government should be conducted or what its precise structure should be.[17] The question was now: Given alternative constitutions that differed fundamentally, which should be chosen? Should government be in the hands of the nobles or of the people? Should the governed be entitled to a decisive share in the governance of the *polis?* The distinction between the rulers and the ruled thus became a matter of political choice. Institutional alternatives emerged in respect of the public order. Moreover, it was recognized for the first time that there was such a thing as a political order in the narrower sense of the term; the clearest indication of this is the discovery that constitutions could be defined according to whether government was exercised by one person, by a few, or by the people. It was perhaps at this time, or at least not long afterward, that constitutional concepts such as "democracy" first arose.[18]

This development may be understood as the "politicizing" of the civic order, or—to put it more precisely—the completion of the process of

politicization; it may also be understood as the stage at which people suddenly became aware of the process. This is true above all in the modern
sense of the word *political:* the civic order became entirely subject to politics. This is the central insight of the *Eumenides*. However, it is true also
in a way that accords with the ancient sense of the term. For the order
that now became possible involved a decisive step toward the establishment of the *polis* as an entity that stood above all particularist forces—
toward the realization of an ideal of justice that was "political" in the
Greek sense of "relating to the *polis*," toward the containment of arbitrary action and the restriction of power.[19] This too finds clear expression
in the *Eumenides*. Finally, democracy (being the only form of government
that offered an institutional alternative to traditional forms of rule) had to
be direct democracy,[20] the precondition of which was that the citizens be
politicized, that they become citizens *(politai)* in the ancient political
sense of the word. This was of course something that Aeschylus was
unable to comprehend: it was on the one hand too obvious (though there
was some blurring at the edges), and on the other hand too novel.

Ever since the days of Cleisthenes the Athenians had seen themselves
largely as citizens. Yet at first they probably continued to think in terms
of interaction with the Areopagus, sharing in deliberations about civic
affairs and often in decision making, but always within the framework of
the traditional order, in which rulers and ruled were distinct. Moreover,
only a limited circle of citizens was involved. Now, however, all power
passed into the hands of the Assembly and the Council of 500 (and their
ancillary organs). As a result political life was played out to a vastly
greater extent among the citizens themselves, among the middle ranks of
the citizenry, and not least among its lower ranks, whose members therefore had to become citizens in a quite new and radical sense. This is true
in particular of the lowest class of all, the *thetes,* who, unlike the peasants, traditionally counted for nothing as a class, and whose status as citizens depended wholly on the services they performed for the city. Hence
it was at this level of society that the most thoroughgoing politicization
took place.

When the Areopagus was stripped of its power, politics became, to an
unprecedented degree, the concern of the citizens, and, conversely, the
concerns of the citizens became the stuff of politics. That is, the citizens
not only determined the conduct of politics, but at the same time politics determined the conduct of the citizens at this new level of shared
public life. Civic cohesion became so great that the citizen's affiliation to
the *polis* took precedence over all others and over all domestic interests.
Among his fellow citizens the Athenian was first and foremost a citizen.
This accorded with a feature of Athenian life that had its origins in the
age of Cleisthenes—the splitting off of the political from the social order.

The social differences remained intact, but against them was set a new, artificial order in which quite different relations prevailed—in which all had equal rights, and real authority lay with the majority.[21] Hence, there now existed a political order in the restricted sense of the term, an order in which the citizens related to one another as citizens. To this extent politics became the central element of Athenian life.

In many respects the politicization of the civic order involved venturing into a wider world where one was no longer protected, exposing oneself to new existential risks. It involved a new set of attitudes deriving from the relative weakness of primary institutions.[22] It engendered a new openness, but the corollary of this openness was a special kind of exposure. Men acquired greater scope for action but were at the same time brought face to face with the immense difficulty of decision making. Thrown upon their own resources, they became conscious of the full measure of human suffering. Pride in man's enormous capacities was matched by a sense of the enormity *(deinon)* of his nature.[23] Even enmity was taken extremely seriously and seen in purely political and military terms: the enemy was simply the other man, who threatened one's own existence; he was not in any way ideologically disqualified.[24] And with all this went a special form of generally relevant change. To a probably unprecedented degree, events were commensurable with human action; that is, the individual acquired a greatness and importance in relation to events that was unique in world history. The Greeks occupied a specifically "political" position in the world, above all in Athens, but also, to a degree that is not easy to estimate, in other places too.[25]

To arrive at this political destination, the Greeks had to make a long journey, in the course of which political thought had a special role to play, at first in a very primitive form; it had to grope its way forward, step by step, in a broadly based process.

The extent to which, in the course of this journey, the Greeks had to free themselves from tradition can be most clearly appreciated when one considers the two major steps that political thought had to take in its progress toward democracy. The first, which was taken in the age of Solon, led to the early notion of a constitution. This required defining the proper order of the *polis*. The definition was admittedly couched in conservative terms, but it did provide a means of distinguishing between the status quo and the ideal from which it differed. An ideal—or at least the outlines of an ideal—had been discovered and the first step taken toward liberating political thought from its attachment to immediate reality. But the ideal could develop the necessary force only if it represented the authentic, divinely enjoined civic order, beside which anything that differed from it was *ipso facto* inauthentic.[26]

Yet if the process was to continue and democratic systems were ultimately to emerge, the *demos* had to assert itself against the nobility and build up a quite distinct order in opposition to it. This required a further step—the abandonment of the notion that there could be only one just order. The result was that the citizens gained control over the constitution as a whole. This step was taken in Athens when the Areopagus was deprived of its power.

Whatever motives may have lain behind this move, and however little those involved in it may have been aware of what they were setting in train, it led to the sudden overthrow of the old order. This was plain for all to see; the prospect was exciting, but no doubt also alarming. Government by the people was now truly established.[27] At this point the many strands of political development were gathered together in one decisive event.

It is hard for us to appreciate the shattering nature of this experience, its existential profundity and explosiveness. We can scarcely imagine the fascination with which the Greeks contemplated the possibilities that now appeared on the new political horizon, ready to be usurped, as it were—together with all the questions and uncertainties they entailed. All this is reflected in the Greek culture of the classical period, on which it left an indelible imprint. However, the greatest expression of the political in the fifth century is probably to be found in the *Eumenides*. But before we can gauge the political importance of Aeschylus' work, we must be clear about the kind of political statements we can expect to find in a tragedy.

The Possibility of Political Statements in Tragedy

Tragedy could hardly be a medium for partisan pronouncements on matters of day-to-day politics. Its political function lay at a deeper level. The Attic theater formed part of the festivities in honor of Dionysus,[28] and the tragedies that were staged had to obey certain formal rules. Every year saw the performance of three plays (together with a satyr play) by each of three authors. The three authors were selected by the *archon eponymos* from a number of candidates who had "applied for a chorus" and also submitted their plays. We do not know whether the choice was his alone, or by what criteria it was guided. The archon also had to choose the three *choregoi* to supply the chorus for each author. They were all highly ambitious. No expense was spared, and there were enormous preparations: there was, after all, a prize to be won. The winner was chosen by a jury of ten citizens, selected by lot from the various *phylai* on the basis of a list drawn up by the Council of 500. This guaranteed a fairly discriminating jury, but it also ensured that the prize would not be awarded by specialists, and certainly not by champions of particular persuasions. Moreover, the jurors could only to a limited extent disregard the audience's applause or disapproval.[29] And the plays aroused great interest, both among the Athenians and among visitors to the city. The audiences may be estimated at 15,000 or more.[30] When Pericles introduced subventions for the plays, his aim was presumably to make it easier for the poor to attend.[31] The interest of the broad masses could, however, be relied upon in any case.

All this meant that the poets could hardly take sides on current political questions. Only exceptionally, and with great circumspection, could they risk doing so—if the seriousness of a particular issue seemed to warrant a limited breach of the rules. The *Eumenides* may have been such an exception.[32] However, this is by no means the most important aspect of the play. The question of the poet's political stance [33] is generally of minor interest, if only because it is difficult to identify what may have been his personal views with those voiced by individual characters or the chorus.

On the other hand, it was possible—and often quite natural—for the poet to allude to topical themes. We know of many instances. In the *Eumenides,* for example, there are unmistakable references to a recent treaty with Argos, to the involvement of Athens in the Egyptian uprising and in the Chalcidice, and to its claims to the Scamandrian plain.[34] The treaty with Argos was so central to the new foreign policy of Athens that its mythical prefiguration may be taken to imply that the author supported the treaty—though not necessarily the new policy in its entirety.[35] However, overt expressions of political opinion are rare. As a rule, such allusions probably do no more than echo what was being said at the time.

Of much greater interest is a third possibility for political statements. These could relate to a realm in which the poet was able, indeed expected, to allow himself greater freedom—the realm of political reflection, which transcended all factional groupings and related to the *polis* and political life in general. The poet might choose to treat a certain myth and interpret it in a new and essentially political manner, drawing upon political experience and reflecting current political problems. The myth could then be used as a vehicle for a rehearsal of these problems; these might sometimes be central to the work, sometimes peripheral. It could illustrate new political problems, insights, and experiences. Tragedy might thus mirror aspects of current political thinking; in doing so it fulfilled its intended educative function [36] by creating an awareness of the achievements of the *polis* or the problems it faced, or by reflecting the nature of politics, while presenting them in a largely nonpartisan manner; it might also incorporate certain general admonitions.

When a society's identity is largely political, political problems assume a particularly existential character. The unprecedented political changes that were taking place in Athens—the move into a wider world, the citizens' new disposal over the constitution—brought in their train extraordinarily difficult and fundamental problems of orientation. These find expression in Attic tragedy to an extent that has not been sufficiently appreciated. The real political content of tragedy, its message to the community, belonged to an area of political thought that transcended temporary factional groupings.

There was as yet hardly any distinction between poetry and thought.[37] Tragedy reached the widest sections of the public, making it possible for the long tradition of political thought to continue into the age of Athenian democracy. Presumably the tragic poets were strongly influenced by the "third position" in which Greek political thought was by now institutionalized.[38] This ensured a degree of realism, yet no doubt inhibited partisan attitudes.[39] It was of course a feature of this tradition that everything was still at a very primitive stage. The political emerged with surprising suddenness. It may be that certain norms were perceived behind some of the realities, and that individual demands were anticipated, but men had no general awareness of the full implications of their practical aims—until democracy was suddenly upon them. And even then the implications of democracy for the whole new order that came into being with it were not immediately self-evident. In consequence, men were all the more aware of the enormity of what was happening. What Aeschylus attempted to do was to evolve new concepts by means of which the whole of this new experience could be articulated and brought into equilibrium.

The Structure and Themes of the *Oresteia*

The *Eumenides* is the last part of the *Oresteia*, a trilogy that deals with the murder of Agamemnon by Clytemnestra *(Agamemnon)*, the vengeance of his son Orestes *(Choephoroi)*, and Orestes' eventual acquittal. It thus enacts a piece of family history.

The real theme of this family history, however, is the ancient chain of revenge and counterrevenge,[40] which reaches its climax in the aporia of Orestes. This consists in the fact that he can avenge his father only by murdering his mother. Right is pitted against right: a worse dilemma cannot be imagined.[41] How is a man to act in such a situation? Aeschylus leaves the question open. The decision is made not by Orestes, but by Apollo: the duty of revenge is paramount.[42] The old law of retribution has to be obeyed unconditionally; otherwise Orestes must reckon with unspeakable punishment. But what will happen to him if he murders his mother? According to Apollo he will be cleared of all guilt.[43] Yet can murder really go unpunished? Must not the law of retribution be enforced, equally unconditionally, against Orestes too?

Apollo's answer is that it must not, but the Erinyes, the spirits of vengeance, vehemently declare that it must.[44] They alone have assumed the task of avenging Clytemnestra, since no mortal avenger is left.[45] This leads to a dispute between Apollo and the Erinyes. The gods themselves are divided: Zeus and his dynasty find themselves in conflict with the spirits of vengeance, whom they have formerly employed as helpers to uphold the law.[46] Aeschylus presents this as a struggle between a younger and an older generation of gods, for to the Greeks the dynasty of Zeus was relatively recent, having succeeded those of Uranus and Cronos. The Erinyes, however, belong to the oldest stratum: Aeschylus makes them the daughters of the Night.[47] They are terrible, weird, and implacable; they are primitive powers, whereas the new gods represent a more humane and enlightened regime, at least in the *Eumenides*.

The conflict between the divine powers is now only superficially concerned with Orestes. Both sides approach the matter in such fundamental terms that the question at issue is now: What is law? In other words, which law—or, more precisely, whose law—shall be applied: the new law of Zeus and his dynasty or the old law of the Erinyes? According to how this question is answered, Orestes will be either doomed or acquitted. This dispute and its ultimate resolution constitute the central theme of the *Eumenides*.

The Erinyes pursue Orestes. Although Apollo has ritually purged him of his guilt, this does not prevent them from vehemently insisting on their claim to the matricide. We may find a "theological" interpretation for this and suppose that in fifth-century Athens the old purification ritual no longer carried conviction.[48] We may also see it in the context of the drama: with the gods divided, an act of purification performed by one side can no longer be binding upon the other. These explanations are not mutually exclusive.[49] At all events, the limited effectiveness of the purification is an essential part of the dramatic conflict. Orestes has to set out on a long period of wandering. This proves to him that he has been effectively purged of his guilt, for nothing has happened to those with whom he has associated (235 ff, 297 ff, 445 ff); yet the Erinyes continue in pursuit. Finally, in obedience to Apollo's command, he repairs to Athens, in order to be saved by Athene. This means that the case has to be decided. The goddess refers it to a tribunal: the verdict must be pronounced by the Areopagus (482 ff). In a regular court scene, the Erinyes present their claim; Orestes defends himself and is defended by Apollo (585 ff). The Areopagus finds him not guilty (709 ff).

As a consequence, the Erinyes no longer pursue him. But now a new danger looms:[50] the spirits of vengeance threaten to punish Athens for a verdict that seems to them a mockery of justice. In the course of a lengthy exchange, the goddess succeeds in appeasing them. By way of compensation she offers them a permanent home and cult honors in Athens, where they will henceforth be responsible for safeguarding the law, while Athens leads the city from success to success in war. The Erinyes are transformed into beneficent deities—the Eumenides, the "well-disposed." Thus a new, just, and all-embracing order is established both within the *polis* and among the gods.

In his tragedy, Aeschylus has in large measure reshaped and expanded the traditional myth—probably not so much by linking it with Athens as by making the Areopagus the instrument for breaking the ancient chain of vengeance and countervengeance, the curse that lies upon the house of Atreus. The conduct of the trial, the acquittal of Orestes, the appeasement of the Erinyes, their acceptance in Athens—and presumably their identification with the Eumenides—are all invented by the poet.[51] It appears, then, that a significant political message was grafted onto the legend in Athens shortly after 460.

What Aeschylus depicts in the *Oresteia* represents a great advance in the history of civilization: the ineluctable sequence of self-perpetuating revenge[52] yields to the law of the *polis,* self-help to citizenship, and the high-handed power of the house or the individual to the sovereignty of the city. What is involved here is nothing less than the establishment of the *polis* as an entity that transcends all particularist forces.[53] This is, at all events, a fundamental aspect of the trilogy. Indeed, in the last quarter of the *Eumenides* the action is concerned solely with the city of Athens and its newly established civic order. The breaking of the fateful chain of revenge and counterrevenge appears as part of a train of events that also involves the gods, and hence as a transformation of the universal order.

Especially interesting is the fact that this transformation comes about, not through the replacement of one race of gods by another, but through a rift within the already-established authority of Zeus: the "new party" carries the day, and the losers are subsequently reconciled.

This vision of the emergence of the new civic order is undoubtedly connected with the event in whose immediate shadow it took shape, the abolition of the power of the Areopagus. It was undoubtedly this event that placed the whole civic order, quite suddenly and for the very first time, at the disposal of the citizens. We are faced with the question of how the problem posed by political conflicts and the revolution in the civic order is depicted in the *Eumenides*—how it is thought out, reflected, and embodied in the drama.

The political dimension cannot of course be considered in isolation. In contemporary Athens, the sudden impact of politics was so central and overwhelming that a revolution such as the one that took place in 462/61 could not possibly be experienced in narrowly political terms. For a long time, and especially since the days of Solon, men had seen a mutual correspondence between the order of the *polis* and the order of the universe.[54]

Changing notions of the one generated fresh perceptions of the other. Accordingly, when confronted by such momentous political changes, the more thoughtful among them were bound to reflect anew on the universal order. Such shattering events called for a profound rethinking of everything, including the relations among the gods. Hence, although the following interpretation concentrates on the political configurations, it cannot disregard the universal order, with which they were held to be intimately related.

This leads us to ask, first, how the political configurations of the *Eumenides* fit into the wider context of the trilogy. What part does the conflict between the gods play within the action of the *Oresteia*? In other words, can it be incorporated into the broad historical perspective that is perhaps revealed in the trilogy as a whole, and, if so, how? How, in the context of the drama, is the decisive step taken from the primitive system of vengeance and feuding to the stability of the *polis*? Is it possible, as is often asserted, that behind the *Oresteia* there lies some kind of philosophy of history or theology of history, to which the *Eumenides* supplies the key? This raises above all the question of the role played by Zeus: does he undergo a development, and, if so, can this be construed as a kind of progress? [55]

The hypothesis runs roughly as follows. In the *Agamemnon* Zeus is conspicuously identified with various acts of retribution, especially the vengeance against Troy and Clytemnestra's vengeance against Agamemnon. In every case, just punishment brings guilt upon his mortal helpers, for which they then have to atone. All these events appear highly questionable. The Trojan War, in which so many men have to die because of an unfaithful wife and the need to punish her abductor, is publicly criticized by the citizens of Argos. [56] But the law of Zeus, which requires that whoever acts has to suffer *(pathein ton erxanta)*, is implacably enforced. Disgrace leads to disgrace, blow to blow, murder to murder. It is for this reason that Zeus is said to reveal himself as the "causer of everything" *(panaitios)* and the "doer of everything" *(panergetes)*. In accordance with this tradition, Dike, the goddess of justice, and the Erinyes, who repay like with like, appear as his helpers. [57]

When subsequently, in the *Eumenides*, Zeus abrogates the law of vengeance and countervengeance, we are inclined to assume that he has undergone a "development." It is worth noting here that, in *Prometheus*, Aeschylus shows quite clearly that Zeus progresses from the tyrannical cruelty and immoderation of the usurper to a wisdom and moderation that ensures universal justice. [58] The notion of development has been rejected on the ground that it runs counter to the Greek conception of the gods. In Aeschylus, it is said, the gods merely show different faces; at any one time certain aspects become visible while others remain hidden.

They may be seen from different angles, but this does not mean that they develop.[59] It is curious, however, that the varying aspects of the gods in *Prometheus* and, in a somewhat different way, in the *Oresteia* appear in a particular order, the more severe, cruel, and primitive aspect being succeeded by the humane and civilized—by the aspect that is in keeping with the *polis,* so to speak. As John Ferguson puts it, Zeus "politicizes" himself in the *Oresteia* from "Zeus Xenios" (who severely punishes the breach of hospitality) to "Zeus Agoraios" (who favors peaceful compromise).[60] The transition from self-help to the jurisdiction of the *polis* also runs parallel in some way with the last phase of the emergence of culture, as it was conceived by contemporaries. The doctrines of the emergence of culture played an important part in Aeschylus' thinking, and he understood them in religious terms.[61] Hence, it seems by no means improbable that the new recognition of the emergence of the *polis* was paralleled by the assumption of a transformation (though not a "development") in the regime of Zeus. Having once been a usurper, he finally brought stability (which was then reckoned to his credit, though it may have represented a compromise with preexistent powers rather than a facet of his own nature).[62] This seems to apply at least in the *Prometheia.* In the *Oresteia,* on the other hand, certain surmises regarding the historicity of all rule may have been at work, together with others involving parallels between the founding of terrestrial and celestial rule.[63] If they were, they can have been only tentative; we are dealing here only with the initial stage of the questioning which reaches its conclusion in the *Prometheia.*[64] If Zeus was once young, then his rule was also once young, and in the world of the fifth century there was little warrant for the assumption that it was perfect from the beginning. Admittedly, when once it reached perfection, it was bound to be enduring and changeless.[65]

Of course Aeschylus nowhere states that the new attitude and orientation of Zeus in the *Eumenides* are due to his having "developed" or reached "maturity," or even to a change of mind or a new understanding. Nothing is stated explicitly about his having undergone an inward transformation or his having a twofold aspect. If one traces the contours of the action, one discovers, somewhat remarkably, that the change of direction takes place in two stages.

The first stage is when Apollo, replying to Orestes, says that he must certainly take vengeance, but will nevertheless be freed from the guilt he thereby incurs. The Erinyes therefore call him the "all-causer of the mother's murder" (200). In the *Eumenides,* Apollo expressly states that all his oracles come from Zeus.[66] It therefore seems that Zeus is responsible for driving Orestes, willy-nilly, to the ultimate abomination that results from his obeying the unconditional command to take vengeance on his mother. The younger gods apply the old law consistently. Did they desire the ultimate climax of revenge in order to be able to destroy its fateful mechanism? It looks very much as though they did, although this is nowhere stated. But if they did desire it, then they achieved it only because the upholders of the ancient law saw themselves challenged by the execution of the ancient imperative.

For the Erinyes now take the second step by assuming the task of avenging Clytemnestra. They probably have no choice, but in seeking to avenge her they are acting in a partisan spirit, since they did not pursue her for the murder of Agamemnon (219 ff, 604 f). This seems to demonstrate that they are not simply fulfilling their obligations, but taking the murder of the mother more seriously than the mother's murder of her husband. This new one-sidedness of the Erinyes is explicitly stated (219 ff) to be the reason why Apollo is equally one-sided in defending Orestes. Had it not been for the resistance of the Erinyes—so one is led to believe—the purification of Orestes would have been the end of the matter. As it is, a conflict develops that ultimately gives rise to a fundamentally new law.

The action of the play thus presents a situation of extreme crisis, leading to further crises and ultimately to a revolution.[67] This is exactly how things can happen in politics: somehow a conflict arises, and if the opposing forces then become polarized, it may become so fundamental that not only the positions of the contending parties, but the very basis on which they have hitherto coexisted, are called in question. A chain reaction develops in which blow succeeds blow, and intensifies until eventually it gives rise to innovation. The old chain reaction continues, though now in the form of an opposition between old and new. Aeschylus obviously knew that fundamental change does not put an end to politics: it merely changes them—and quite often exacerbates them. We have to ask whether the change in Zeus's attitude results simply from the new situation or whether it has a more remote origin.

According to H. D. F. Kitto,[68] Zeus becomes involved because the rule of Aegisthus and Clytemnestra has suppressed the legitimate order of the *polis*. The command to Orestes to avenge his father is therefore to be understood politically. Argos has to be liberated. The fact that Zeus turns against the Erinyes is thus simply a consequence of this policy and shifts the problems to Athens.

This is true insofar as Aeschylus is at pains to show how sorely the city of Argos is afflicted by Agamemnon's murder. In the first part of the trilogy it is clear that his rule was legitimate and benign. Despite the complaints directed against the Trojan campaign and the king's conduct as commander of the fleet and the army, it did not bring slavery upon the people.[69] The rule of his murderers, by contrast, proves intolerable to the whole house and the whole city, as we hear not only from the Argive elders in the *Agamemnon,* but also from the Trojan slave women who form the chorus in the *Choephoroi*.[70] This is a powerful reason for Orestes' vengeance: liberty and legitimacy must be restored.[71] There is thus something of a shift of theme: the race of the Atrides is increasingly linked with the destiny of Argos. Accordingly, there is hardly any further mention of Agamemnon's guilt, but only of his greatness and justice, and the terrible manner of his death.[72] In the *Agamemnon* the gods, as custodians of the law, are implicated in the whole chain of revenge and counterrevenge stretching back into the past and on into the future, but in the *Choephoroi* they are repeatedly called upon for virtually one purpose only: that they may grant success to Orestes' revenge.[73] To this extent there is much to be said for Kitto's interpretation. It links the terrestrial changes with the will of Zeus in a plausible and revealing manner and elicits from the play an interesting conception of the history of the *polis*. One point must be added, however: Aeschylus is extremely reticent in hinting at such ideas. Above all, the question of why the fate of the city became so important to Zeus remains entirely open.

Kitto admittedly broadens the connection.[74] He believes he can observe a transformation in Zeus throughout the trilogy, parallel to the progress occurring on the human plane, so that the two constitute a single process on two levels. Zeus has established a law, so we are told in the *Agamemnon*, that man learns through suffering *(pathei mathos)*. Instead of sleep, the memory of past pain drops into men's hearts, so that, without their desiring it, thought and wise judgment *([so]phronein)* come to them. The gods bestow violent favor *(charis biaios)*.[75] This, according to Kitto, is how Aeschylus portrays the law of vengeance and traces the path that leads to its supersession.

This observation too has much to commend it, though it does not explain why Zeus should have set such events in train. One can indeed see a certain "progress" in the successive protagonists in Argos. Agamemnon learns nothing. Clytemnestra gains some insight after her crime. Orestes and Electra, who do not at first thirst for vengeance, gain insight even before their deed, though it does not release them from the necessity of matricide.[76] The real turning point in the drama thus arises only from the conflict between the gods and the intervention of Athene, who owes her wisdom to Zeus (850).

Yet here too we have some indication that earthly events are viewed in a historical perspective. Athene's wisdom stands for that of her city. This is not stated explicitly with regard to the mythical situation, but the drama does oscillate between the mythical situation and the present of 458 B.C. The Eumenides pray that the Athenians, as confidants of the virgin Athene, may acquire "wise judgment in time" *(sophronein en chronoi)*;[77] this "learning process," which still lies in the future, has to be accommodated in the interval between the mythical past and the political present.

This process, however, takes place outside the play—as indeed it must, since it extends over a long period. This becomes clear from the striking contrast between this and other ways of producing "moderate and considered thought." At the end of the *Agamemnon* Clytemnestra and Aegisthus twice threaten the Argive elders, telling them that they must submit to their tyranny; otherwise force, chains, and hunger will—as we might put it—bring them to their senses. The word Aeschylus used here is *sophrosyne*.[78] The Athenians, however, do not need such tyrants to teach them reason. The citizens will learn by themselves, in freedom—in time, in other words. Athene, appearing here instead of a king as the ruler of the (free) community, gives them the possibility of doing so.[79]

The goal of true *sophrosyne* is, however, attained not only by a gradual process. It is also stated that both man and *polis* learn it "under duress" (*hypo stenei,* 521), which may of course also mean that they learn it through the tribulations of their history, but in any case—and this applies up to and beyond 458 B.C.—they learn it through the presence of authorities such as the Eumenides and the Areopagus, acting as "watchers over their senses."[80]

Aeschylus may have considered that in 458 the Athenians were better able to understand this than they had been before. This would be a significant improvement (which might be connected with the emergent consciousness of human abilities). It would not of course be part of a comprehensive movement of progress. On the contrary, it quite clearly places constraints on the forward-striving political forces,[81] just as in the *Prometheia* constraints are finally placed on the forward-striving Zeus. In this sense it represents a kind of progress—but only in this sense. To be more precise: advances over time, at least up to the present, consist in men's ability, as individuals and as communities, to overcome such problems *politically,* but they do not amount to a universal improvement, which would make it possible to regard whatever was forward-striving, younger, and newer as necessarily better. Yet it is impossible to decide whether this—together with the long-term process preceding it—corresponds only to the will of Zeus or also to a change in his nature.

We may therefore say that the overall structure of the *Oresteia* reflects improvements in the history of human civilization, that these are matched by a change in the policy of Zeus, but that it remains unclear whether this change is a result of his becoming maturer and wiser. It could equally be construed as a continuation of the old policy under new circumstances.

In the *Prometheus* the situation changes. There, as has been said already, the change to a just order does not come with the rule of Zeus, as in Hesiod. On the contrary, Aeschylus draws the extremely bold consequence that it results from a transformation of Zeus and his regime over time. At first his dynasty was new and young, and men were well aware at the time what that could mean; only later did it acquire permanence and perfection, unlike all earlier regimes.

In the *Oresteia*, on the other hand, the change in the regime of Zeus is treated as an isolated historical event.[82] Here Aeschylus—by contrast with Hesiod and his own *Prometheia*—takes a particularly short-term view, locating the process merely within human history (at the time of the Trojan War), not within the history of divine dynasties. The dynasty of Zeus is not young, as in the *Prometheus*, but merely younger than the one that preceded it. The sequence of revenge and counterrevenge in Argos leads only to the restoration of legitimate rule. It is only because a conflict between the gods ensues that a new *polis* order is founded in Athens. In short, the theme is politics;[83] that of long-term historical processes (on which the politics rest) remains in the background.

However, the conflict is conducted, for part of the time, as a struggle between male and female. This has led to assertions that the *Oresteia* can be interpreted in terms not only of the philosophy of history, but also of anthropology. Aeschylus, it is said, depicts the great transition from a matriarchal to a patriarchal society. Clytemnestra embodies the sexual independence of woman and her (rather masculine) craving to dominate; Athene, the motherless daughter of Zeus, symbolizes the old male dream of being able to bear one's own children; while the Erinyes, as the (perhaps!) fatherless daughters of the Night, represent the exact opposite.[84] The ultimate purpose of the *Oresteia*, according to recent interpretations, is that women should accept the marriage bond, and hence male domination, as necessary, natural, and just.[85] These interpretations are in some ways interesting. However, it is not clear how much they tell us about Aeschylus (as distinct from the ancient and long-forgotten meanings of the myths he drew upon).[86] There was no reason for him to know what modern ethnological research and structuralist theory can discover about, say, the birth of Athene. Moreover, the transition from a matriarchal to a patriarchal society cannot be the theme of the work, if only because it is nowhere mentioned. The hierarchical order, with Zeus at its head and the Erinyes as his servants, is present not only at the end but also at the beginning. Apollo even threatens to set the Erinyes on Orestes if he does not kill Clytemnestra.[87] Similarly the rule of the Atrides is already established at the beginning. Clytemnestra's revenge temporarily interrupts it, just as the conflict between Apollo and the Erinyes interrupts the already established divine order. And if the new order in Athens and the universe represents progress, it is not progress along the female-male axis.

True, there remain strands in the play in which the sometimes fateful role of terrible women is dwelt upon. When Clytemnestra threatens all order, the chorus of libation bearers associates this with various cases of female independence, lust for domination, cruelty, and insatiable love

(585 ff). But this does not mean that Aeschylus necessarily knew about feminist aspirations. He may simply have been taking up old mythical conceptions of a victory of male over female domination. These would then be at most historical allusions.

Hence, all we can say with certainty is that the dramas depict the great step from self-help and feuding to the *polis*. To this extent the *Oresteia* treats of the "gift of justice," as the later *Prometheia* treats of the "gift of reason."[88] Anything beyond this—whether, for instance, Aeschylus was somehow trying to set the present or future of Athens, or the emergence of democracy, in a historical context—can emerge at best from an interpretation of the *Eumenides*. As for the trilogy as a whole, the only thing that is clear is the concentration on the political conflict on the isolated events.

It is in this connection that a central role is accorded to the fundamental division between man and woman, which is so starkly emphasized in certain passages in the first part of the *Eumenides*. The only question is: What is its significance in the play? Is the mention of the enormities of terrible women really anything more than a generalization of the deed of Clytemnestra? And above all: Is Aeschylus primarily concerned to represent a conflict between male and female as such, or does the basic natural difference of the sexes, which divides one half of humanity from the other, stand for something more general? In view of the fact that the problem of man versus woman was not one that much exercised the Greeks,[89] it is hardly likely to have constituted a central theme of the play. At all events one misses the sense of the drama by applying the feminist yardstick, for this is to jettison most of its rich content. And it would mean reading into it issues that either were topical a good deal earlier or were to become topical a bare two and a half thousand years later.[90] On the other hand, the division between the sexes— together with other profound divisions—is very well suited to the presentation of something that obviously did interest Aeschylus: the history of an existential conflict and its settlement in a just and political order. This brings us to the real theme: the conflict of the *Eumenides* and its resolution as an expression of political thought.

The *Eumenides* as Evidence of Early Political Thought

The whole design of the *Eumenides* is informed by political thought. Its dominant theme is the conflict between the Olympians and the Erinyes and their ultimate reconciliation. In the first half of the play Aeschylus sees this conflict as a confrontation between two fundamentally different concepts of law.[91] The starting point was provided by the traditional myth according to which one dynasty of gods was succeeded by another.[92] The Erinyes belonged to the older order, which was conquered by the dynasty of Zeus. Curiously, however, Aeschylus places the outbreak of the conflict during the reign of Zeus. The new regime is thus no longer young, though younger than the powers that it had defeated and overthrown. And precisely because it consistently applies the old law and the old rules, there comes a point when it is forced to proclaim and establish a new law. This extraordinary construct was presumably necessary in the context of the play. If freedom and legitimacy were to be restored in Argos, Agamemnon's murderers had to be eliminated. If Zeus was committed to the *polis*, this meant that he was bound to adhere to the law of vengeance. But is this the sole rationale of the construct? Might it not also have a bearing upon the problems connected with the opposition between the old and the new? It does, after all, reflect a segment of Athenian history. Like the Olympians and the Erinyes, the various forces in Athens had once lived together in peace under the rule of the *demos* (which was recognized by 463 at the latest).[93] When the conflict was over and the new political force, the *demos*, had carried the day, civic life was reestablished—or due to be reestablished—in a new form, just as it was among the gods under the rule of Zeus. To this extent the *Eumenides* seems to reflect exactly the relations between the old and the new in Athens—so exactly that one wonders whether the factor that precipitates change in the play, namely the radical application of the old rules by the new forces, was also paralleled in Athens—perhaps by the uncompromising severity with which the innovators sought to settle conflicts that arose in the city, leading to resistance by the nobles and the consequent abolition of the power of the Areopagus.[94] We cannot know, however, whether there was a political point to this paradoxical construct whereby the new forces act in accordance with the old rules. If there was, this would have been anything but a trite allusion—as can easily be the case with poetic treatments of political themes—in view of the close mutual connection between the political and divine orders.

At all events, in the first part of the tragedy, Aeschylus creates a rift within the divine order, traditionally conceived as unified and cohesive.[95] The dynasty of Zeus turns against the helpers upon whom it has formerly been obliged to rely. Out of a difference in the ages of the various divine powers—which is hardly likely to have exercised the minds of many contemporary Greeks[96]—Aeschylus makes a significant opposition. What was novel about his handling of the theme was his acknowledgment that the old powers had legitimate rights, which were in no way invalidated a priori. The Erinyes insist on these rights with the utmost vehemence.[97] They are opposed by Apollo and Athene, who represent the new rights of the dynasty of Zeus. Apollo asserts these with self-confidence and assurance of victory. Athene too refers occasionally to the power possessed by her father, though what she seeks is reconciliation, not victory.[98]

Aeschylus depicts the contrasts between the parties in the sharpest possible terms. In particular he shows Apollo and the Erinyes confronting one another in attitudes of extreme one-sidedness,[99] and to do this he brings the most varied contrasts into play.

The old law, being grounded in immemorial tradition, is something preexistent. The new law is the outcome of a recent dispensation, the creation of Zeus. Whatever else it may have to commend it in an age that was dominated by the cult of Zeus, its newness is not a point in its favor. In the *Eumenides* the terms *new* and *young* are nowhere used as proud watchwords to characterize the young gods, but only as reproaches leveled at them by the Erinyes.[100] True, Athene once refers to her youth, but she does so out of modesty, to show her respect for age (847 ff). The argument in favor of the old[101] has thus not lost its force. Hence, the young gods never state that they have a new law. Only the Erinyes make a fundamental point of this, reproaching the young gods for destroying the old law.[102] The Olympians, by contrast, advance practical arguments for new principles of law and a new form of justice. This cannot have been very different, *mutatis mutandis,* from what happened in political life.[103]

The old law, with its implacable insistence on punishment, is severe and terrible.[104] It affords no prospect of breaking the curse that hangs over the house of Atreus and obliges Orestes to avenge his father by killing his mother. The consequence is an endless chain of crime and punishment—or crime and revenge. The Erinyes do all in their power to ensure that the law is enforced, seeing this as their essential function. They insist on the oath for which they are responsible as ancient oath-goddesses; this oath now appears as the central point and symbol of their plea.[105] It can be used to establish the simple facts of the murder, which are all that concerns them (and which Orestes does not deny).[106]

Athene, on the other hand, maintains that it is a *quaestio juris:* the question she asks is whether or not Orestes' deed was just (426, 468), and to answer this question a court of law is needed to assess the facts of the case.[107] Yet the very institution of such a court imperils the old law (490). By acquitting Orestes, it breaks the chain of vengeance and counter-vengeance once and for all (779 f, 808 f). The new law is clearly more liberal than the old: in certain circumstances it can even permit the acquittal of a murderer. It offers Orestes an escape from the aporia into which the demands of the old law had driven him (82). A parallel to Athene's setting up of the court is the introduction of rational court procedures in Athens about the year 458, which was further proof of the great potential that lay in man's capacity for judgment.[108] The play contains allusions to this too. Aeschylus brings together very old and very recent achievements in order to stress the contrast between the old and the new as forcefully as possible. The law of the Olympians is thus new in three respects: in its content, in the fact that it makes certain problems subject to court proceedings, and in the way in which evidence is presented.

At one point Athene reproaches the Erinyes, saying, "You would rather be called just than act justly" (430). A new and genuine justice, associated with the *polis* and its institutions, is to replace the old.[109]

The dilemma of Orestes, who is forced to let his father go unavenged or kill his mother, is not considered in the *Eumenides*. Once the conflict has erupted, the issue between the contending parties is not the general question of the law of vengeance or the victim's claim to be avenged, but the differences between the various claims. Apollo maintains that the murder of Clytemnestra differs radically from that of Agamemnon. He was a victorious king who was slain, not on the field of battle, but treacherously in his bath. Such a killing bears no comparison with that of a "woman of monstrous infamy."[110] To the Erinyes, however, the truly heinous crime is matricide (210 ff, 604 f). For them the question can be narrowed to the relative status of father (or husband) and mother (640). Apollo responds by arguing that the marriage bond has the superior claim, while the Erinyes assert the priority of blood relationship (211 ff). Thus, both parties are biased in favor of one side or the other—male or female, marriage or blood tie.[111] Hence the Erinyes insist, at the start of the conflict, that they seek vengeance only for the mother and not—as in the rest of the *Oresteia* and elsewhere in Greek tradition—for all who are killed, and in respect of all injustice.[112] Conversely, Apollo finally asserts that the mother has little to do with her child, being simply the guardian of the male seed during a brief phase of its development. It is true that this corresponds to a theory that was emerging at the time, but it is by no means clear that Aeschylus endorsed the theory. At all events, the public cannot have regarded such a notion as anything but monstrous. In the words of Karl Reinhardt, it was an extreme argument, intended to shock the unsuspecting spectator.[113]

The contrast between young and old—between the new law and the old—is thus brought into parallel with the contrast between man and woman, between the bond of marriage and the ties of blood.[114] However, since the argument relating to age could favor only the old, a forensic symmetry could be created only by concentrating the advocacy on the opposition between the sexes and between different human ties. This made it possible for each side to argue a particular case. And the contrasts upon which the arguments focus are of the most natural and elemental kind. Moreover, they were already contained in the myth of Agamemnon, Clytemnestra, and Orestes. And although the institution of marriage could not be linked with the formation of the *polis*, it was nevertheless a man-made bond, and therefore well suited to serve as the antithesis of the natural and preexistent tie of blood.[115] It was thus obvious that Aeschylus should make the contending parties concentrate on the contrasts between the sexes and between different human relationships. The dispute is conducted with archaic vigor, though it is not really typical of the factional alignments of archaic times, which were usually dictated by personal considerations.

A situation of extreme conflict could not have been treated more starkly than by presenting it as a struggle between the sexes, the two halves of humanity that, though different, cannot live without each other. For this very reason one cannot take the dispute too literally or see the passages in which it is conducted as holding the key to the whole work. Had Aeschylus really been concerned with the opposition between male and female he would have been proceeding somewhat inconsistently. For what he presents in the drama is not an elemental conflict or opposition, but a temporary confrontation.[116] Whatever views he may have had about the relations between the sexes, the factional groupings within the drama are essentially symbolic: he needed two elemental causes that could be pursued by their advocates in an outrageously partisan fashion. The result is a highly interesting construct. The decision in favor of the male party is a triumph of the new law, yet it appears to be merely a by-product (just as the triumph of democracy in 462/61 was probably a by-product of the move against Sparta). The new law, as represented by Apollo, is not so much a legal as a party matter. It is the right of the male that triumphs, rather than the one that is supported by the better arguments.

Both parties take an extremely one-sided view of Orestes' killing of his mother, which they see in quite clear and simple terms, in partisan terms— one might say in party terms (219 ff, 426 ff). Neither side is conscious of any problem, and this is precisely where the problem lies. This is why there appears to be no solution, and why it is all so reminiscent of politics.

It is not change (and action directed toward change) that characterizes the course of events, but the victory of one side over the other (which then produces change). It is to this that our attention is directed.

Aeschylus introduces a further contrast—between Greek and barbarian. The behavior of the Erinyes is horrifying; they perform an eerie magic dance, and are so hideous and savage that the sight of them is almost unbearable. Aeschylus is said to have decked out the chorus in such strange and horrendous guise that during the performance women miscarried or went into premature labor.[117] Apollo says that the Erinyes are an abomination to the gods and should join the barbarians. They seem to him alien to the Greeks and the world of Zeus (186 ff). He calls them the powers of darkness, whereas his own Delphic world is presented as one of clarity and light.[118]

Apollo and the Erinyes obviously represent numerous contrasts—between man and woman, marriage and relationship, light and darkness, Greek and barbarian, the new law and the old, the Olympians and the primeval powers. Whether further contrasts exist beside and behind these[119] is a matter for surmise.

What proves decisive in the drama is the extreme partiality on all sides. This arises from the fact that the question is at first not which law should triumph, but whose. What matters is not who has the better case, but who is the more skilled in advocacy, who can deploy the most telling arguments. It is only through this confrontation of two points of view, both equally one-sided, that a new law emerges that finally breaks the mechanism of self-perpetuating vengeance and ensures that the murder committed by Orestes will be the last in the chain. The conflict goes so deep as to destroy the very basis upon which coexistence has hitherto been possible. Yet Apollo seems unaware of this. On the surface—and in the minds of the litigants—all that matters is the vindication of their own claims. The essential issue, the conflict about the legal order, remains in the background. Only the Erinyes are able to articulate it, because only they have the advantage of the argument regarding age. We may surmise that this is just how affairs were conducted in political life.

Finally, while the court is voting on their respective claims, Aeschylus makes Apollo and the Erinyes engage in mutual threats and promises of rewards.[120] The dispute is, in short, a "masterpiece of partiality and injustice."[121] Given the extreme positions taken by the two sides, each must be both right and wrong. Obviously both were meant to behave at first like political factions.

From Homer we learn that such behavior is not unknown among the gods, who are often all too eager to take sides, either in their own cause or on behalf of those whom they protect in war and tribulation—though of course not with arguments, and not before a tribunal. Perhaps one should speak of differences of attitude rather than of deliberate one-sidedness. It is striking that even the noble Apollo takes sides in this way. This is somewhat alarming, since what is involved is a struggle between two legal orders. Most important, the dispute clearly points to the doctrine that any new regime is bound to be highly partisan and prone to arbitrary action. The doctrine is not presented as starkly here as it is in the *Prometheus,* but it seems reasonably clear that the play incorporates certain experiences of how a new regime behaves—probably the new regime of the *demos* or that of Ephialtes and his associates (is there perhaps an allusion here to the ostracism of Cimon, who was an able and widely respected statesman and general?). At all events, what we have here is a surprisingly profound insight into the nature of political conflict, especially where it involves the legal order.

For Aeschylus, then, there seems at first to be not just *one* law, before which any contrary assertion about what is lawful is *ipso facto* wrong and unjust. He seems rather to adopt a neutral position, from which each of the disputants appears merely partisan, defending something that is vitally important to society, yet failing to recognize something else that is equally important.[122] This makes the alternative concepts of law seem fundamentally alike, and it will presently be shown how hard it is to choose between them.

In this confrontation between two legal orders and between the old and the new the audience must have perceived an allusion to the contemporary opposition between two political orders, and presumably also between the nobles and the people. That this is an intentional allusion becomes clear later in the play.

What is quite clearly recognized and presented here is the thorough politicization of the *polis* order, which is now brought into the field of political action and disposal. There was no longer one legitimate order, inherited from the past and sanctioned by the gods, to which the constitution of this or that city might approximate to a greater or lesser degree. It was no longer a question of finding one's rightful place in the inherited order. The civic communities were now free to choose among different constitutions. An individual might go on believing that this or that constitution was the only true one; he might postulate a new ideal of order—as Aeschylus does later in the play. Yet what really mattered was the fact that the civic order as a whole was now at the disposal of the citizens— and hence subject to controversy. The old distinction between the rule of the nobles and the rule of a tyrant involved only different distributions of power within the upper class, only one element among several within the total structure, which alone could be regarded as the *polis* order. For the broad mass of the populace the distribution of power was of no importance. What mattered to them was *how* they were governed, and this depended solely on the personalities of the rulers. The civic order as a whole could not become a matter for debate until "order" was construed in a more limited sense—as political organization, as the relationship between the citizens as citizens—and until the question of how the city was governed became dependent on its institutions. This was not possible until the *demos* had won a direct say in the city's affairs, that is, when the early isonomies had come into being. And even then people seem to have been content merely to introduce modifications into the system, such as Cleisthenes' reform of the *phylai*. Isonomy itself was understood not as a form of government, but as the establishment of a just order—an ideal to which was now added the concept of equality.[123]

As late as 472, in the *Persians*, Aeschylus had been able to give only a negative answer to the question "Who rules in Athens?" His answer was, "They are not slaves or subject to any man" (242). Then, in the *Supplices* (probably composed in 463,[124] a year before the overthrow of the Areopagus), he proudly extolled the rule of the *demos*. Admittedly he was describing the conditions prevailing in Argos, but the allusion applies equally, if not principally, to Athens. The realization that, under the new constitutions, government was actually exercised by the people seems to have been comparatively new at the time. The alternative to government by the people, however, was absolute monarchy; the only other possibility was restricted oligarchy.

Then in 462/61 a new opposition emerged within the existing framework of isonomy—between a form government controlled largely by the nobility and one based essentially on the people; between what was later called democracy (in the narrower sense) and what was called oligarchy (in the wider sense)[125] or, as Aeschylus indicates, between a relatively free democracy and one that is subject to certain constraints. It was no longer a matter of representing, more or less faithfully, the totality of the civic community, for this now comprised two powerful opposing groups— broadly speaking, the nobles and their supporters on the one hand and the people on the other. Which of the two should prevail became a matter of conscious decision making, hence of political controversy.[126] It was probably this deep division within the city that made the notion of the one just order hard to sustain and largely obsolete. Having once been part of the received social wisdom, it became merely a matter of personal conviction. Individuals or groups might continue to regard a certain form of government as the only legitimate one, but from now on there were bound to be conflicting opinions and competing interests—even if Aeschylus in the end refused to accept this.

In all probability it was this fundamental rift in the body politic that made it possible and meaningful to depict the Erinyes and the Olympians, the old order and the new, as mutually opposed, for the notion of such a division was at variance with traditional religious ideas. What is reflected here is clearly the experience of the new antagonisms that now permeated the entire civic order.

The intensity of this experience and the extent to which it seemed to lead to various kinds of impasse has its counterpart in the resolution of the dramatic conflict, which perfectly reflects the monstrous situation in Athens. Each side is prepared to leave the final decision to Athene; this is acceptable to Apollo because she belongs to the dynasty of Zeus, and to the Erinyes because she has shown them respect.[127] Each side, moreover, is convinced of the rightness of its cause. Athene declares that the case is too difficult to be tried by any single mortal, and it would be improper for her to be involved in judging cases of homicide. She therefore refers the matter to a tribunal, the Areopagus, which she now calls into being (470 ff).

The fact that the court is established by Athene confers divine authority on the legal system of the *polis,* and on the Areopagus in particular. As Friedrich Solmsen writes, it shows that "civic ways of administering justice are worthy to serve as symbols and manifestations of the divine government." This provides the Archimedean point from which the curse of self-perpetuating vengeance can be overcome.[128]

If the Areopagus is competent to decide the matter, it has to reach its decision by voting. Problems of decision making received a good deal of attention at the time, as is evident especially in Aeschylus' early dramas.[129] There, however, the decisions have to be made by individuals, for instance by King Pelasgus in the *Supplices,* who has to choose between the duty to take in those who seek asylum, and fear of their pursuers. True, the matter is subsequently laid before the people, but they decide unanimously and unhesitatingly. In the *Eumenides,* however, the decision is made by a committee,[130] since no one person is qualified to decide. Moreover, it is made much more difficult by the fact that it concerns the legal order; this had once been a matter of truth, but now it is a matter to be decided by ballot. The point of interest here is how a decision is reached by a large number of people.

What actually happens is not only extraordinary but positively absurd. Not only is there no unanimity, but the result is a tie. Athene has earlier decreed that in the event of a tie Orestes will be acquitted. Yet the tie arises solely because Athene casts her ballot in favor of acquittal.[131] The decision against the old law is thus reached not only on the basis of the least possible number of votes, but against the majority of the Areopagites. A disturbing construct: no objective decision, no majority, and not even a tie among the Areopagites. This is how decisions regarding the legal order are made! It is impossible for us to gauge the contemporary significance of such a construct. Whatever specific function this result has in the drama—a tied vote frees Orestes without bringing disgrace upon the Erinyes, who will later have to be conciliated[132]—and however reasonable it appears, given the nature of the case, the decision is nevertheless significant in its own right: it means that all the problems and difficulties generated by the new political situation, after the citizens had gained control over the legal order (and—most important—over the *polis* order), were deliberately being set before the citizens in a form that they were likely to find disturbing. The indecisiveness that we normally find in an individual was being quantified and shared out among the citizens, and the result was an almost equal balance—not of arguments, but of numbers.

It may be that this construct, whereby the decision in favor of the new order is reached despite the opposition of the majority of the Areopagites, was connected with the fact that the decision to remove the powers of the Areopagus was made in the absence of a contingent of 4,000 hoplites—which may mean that it was arrived at by a minority of those who were expected to attend the Assembly.[133] The fact that the vote comes just short of an absolute majority need not unduly disturb us: in the context of the play, a tie is all that is required for Orestes' acquittal. If this interpretation is correct, we are still left with the intriguing question of how the goddess's deciding vote (the *calculus Minervae*) is to be understood in the context of the play.

We are bound to ask whether Athene's vote is merely an extraneous factor that reverses the outcome, or whether it indicates that the final decision is sanctified by the dynasty of Zeus, which favors the new order. Only one thing is certain: Athene's decision is partial, for she expressly states that, having no mother herself, she is bound to side with the male—which means that she is obliged to side with the new order, and hence with Orestes. This is the only occasion in the play when the goddess takes sides so obviously and—as Reinhardt remarks—in such a way as almost to outdo the partiality of Apollo.[134] It is clear, then, that for Aeschylus Athene's deciding vote is simply part of the decision-making process. It cannot be taken to guarantee the rightness of the decision or the infallibility of her judgment.

However outrageous this hairbreadth decision of the Areopagus may be, with the *calculus Minervae* tipping the balance the other way, the tribunal she institutes seems to open up enormous possibilities. It can function undisturbed as a court of highest instance in cases that urgently need to be settled.[135] The case in question, seen politically, is a feud within the nobility. Such feuds were one of the gravest perils facing the Greek communities in the archaic period. Orestes' acquittal is a victory for the *polis* as a whole over particularist forces that are threatening to tear it apart—a triumph of justice over retribution, of freedom of decision over involvement in the vicious circle of vengeance.

What is presented here is, in a nutshell, the "decisionist" insight that emerged from radical reflection on the controversial law of 462/61. Aeschylus' presentation of the vote in the Areopagus is a bold construct, showing his awareness that in political decision making a distinction must be made between validity and truth. However sound the reasons that persuade the individual to vote in a particular way, the ultimate decision lies with the majority and this decision is binding, even though it may not necessarily rest on compelling arguments. As Aeschylus sees it, not even the daughter of Zeus can guarantee the correctness of a particular judgment: it may well be partial, and the best she can do is to try subsequently to enshrine this unquestionably partial judgment in a comprehensive "true order." Hermann Lübbe rightly calls this insight a precondition of any liberal political order.[136]

The establishing of the Areopagus and the decision it reaches may be taken to represent, in general terms, the great civilizing potential of the *polis:* the Athens of the *Eumenides* not only stood above the curse that hung over the individual house (as Thebes did over the children of Oedipus): it could also put an end to the curse before it had destroyed everything.[137] But this civilizing potential was accompanied by grave new problems threatening the city.

Despite the validity of such a decision, which also bears upon the legal order, it did not necessarily carry universal conviction; it might be overturned, especially if it had been passed by so small a majority. What is more, its consequences might be so far-reaching as to threaten the whole destiny of the city. This brings us to the next theme of the drama.

A fresh danger now looms. Orestes has been freed and gratefully departs, but the Erinyes, having been "downridden,"[138] threaten to punish Athens for the judgment that has just been passed—an intention they have already announced in advance. Now they intend to spread poison and pestilence, and Aeschylus dwells at length on the havoc their anger can wreak and the power they have at their command.

Having been defeated in Athens, they turn against the city. Now that their conflict with the Olympians has intensified to the point where the only alternative is between their law and that of their opponents, the defeated Erinyes threaten the city from without: having been opponents of Orestes, they will now become enemies of Athens. Here again there is a political parallel.[139]

Having been hitherto dominated by the contrast between Orestes and Apollo on the one hand and the Erinyes on the other, the scene is now dominated by the contrast between the spirits of vengeance and the city, together with its goddess, Athene, who seeks reconciliation, not war. Although she has the power to protect her city with lightning, she is reluctant to resort to such means (826 f), being intent upon compromise— upon a political solution. She offers the Erinyes a favorable settlement. They shall have a home, cult honours, and high office in Athens; no house shall prosper against their will. In return they shall obey Zeus—which means conforming with his order and his law. Given such an offer, their threats against the city are unlawful (*ou dikaios,* 888). It sounds as though there were a duty to preserve the peace: when a reasonable compromise is offered, the threat of force would be a violation of justice.

Yet the Erinyes are not easily won over. The goddess makes four attempts. Three times the spirits of vengeance reject her overtures, snorting with fury. Only at the fourth attempt are they prepared to enter into negotiations. Athene succeeds only by patience and by deploying all her powers of persuasion. Twice she appeals to Peitho, the personification of persuasion.[140] Finally she asks: "Is it not proper that fair words should point the way to those who have understanding?"[141] What is effective here, in deliberate contrast with the archaic dispute that the Erinyes have conducted with Apollo and their primitive insistence on upholding their honor and their office, is peaceful conciliation and the winning power of words,[142] which the Greeks saw as the antithesis of violence.[143] The suspicion of "manipulation" had not yet arisen.[144] The success of persuasion brought peaceful solution of a problem, the political solution, which was in any case preferable to settling it by force. The prerequisite was that the citizens be taken seriously in their civic presence. This was an essential element in Greek politics.

According to Athene, the success of Peitho represents a triumph of Zeus as the divine patron of the Agora: "Yet here Zeus Agoraios has triumphed. Victorious is our rivalry in doing good for evermore."[145] The Agora, which provides the citizens with a place and an opportunity to treat and argue with one another as citizens (that is, politically), is presented here as instituted by Zeus; political controversy is presented as *agathon eris*, which ends in compromise.

Reconciliation with the dangerous defeated opponents not only brings peace; it also guarantees lasting blessings for the city, since the Erinyes, by performing their new office, will be able to ensure internal order. By assuming this task they become the Eumenides (the "well-disposed"). It is clear that the Eumenides were identified with certain divinities who inhabited a cave not far from the Areopagus and were worshiped as the *Semnai*.[146] In lengthy hymns at the end of the drama the chorus invokes the activity of the Eumenides as bringers of justice and prosperity.

Thus the old law is transformed and incorporated into the *polis*. This interpretation has been disputed.[147] It has been maintained that, even after the reconciliation, the Erinyes remain what they have always been—helpers of Zeus and of Dike, the goddess of justice. Even toward the end of the play (930 ff) they still assert their claim to punish murder and breaches of the unwritten laws. On the other hand, the blessings they can bring upon the city are already mentioned in the *stasimon* before the legal proceedings begin (517 ff); they are described, moreover, in terms that are repeated almost word for word by Athene in her speech on the setting up of the Areopagus (690 ff). These observations are correct, but we must be careful not to draw the wrong conclusions from them. The crucial question is not what authority the Erinyes/Eumenides possess, but how *the relations between the dramatis personae have changed*. For it is these relations that determine the manner in which their authority will be exercised. Aeschylus has produced a construct that is not only remarkably bold, but utterly clear in all its essentials. At first the Erinyes, like their opponent Apollo, appear totally one-sided. They are cruel, terrifying, implacable, and bloodthirsty.[148] As such they fail in their claim before the tribunal, even though—according to Athene—this brings no disgrace upon them. Once conciliated, they cease to be the enemies of the city and become its friends, servants of the regime of Zeus. This means that they now occupy an entirely new position. It also means that their activity changes, for they begin to speak in a quite different tone. The office they will henceforth hold in Athens, and the honors (*timai*)[149] that go with it, are conferred by Athene, and they are astonished to hear how wide their authority will be (896 ff, 930 f). They are assured of an honorable role in the new and transformed regime of Zeus; under this regime a different position is also allotted to the city of Athens, upon which their activity will henceforth be concentrated.[150] No function outside Athens is mentioned: there is something almost naively self-centered about all this.[151]

This change of configuration is decisive within the drama. After it the Eumenides are no longer the same as before, though not as the result of some magical transformation,[152] but of their opting, somewhat abruptly,[153] for the new role they are offered. This role, however, must be viewed in its entirety. They will continue to punish murder and violent crime; indeed, this is to be a substantial part of their beneficent activity.[154] The old powers are needed precisely for what they are. They must not change. Even their terrible appearance can hardly have altered. On the other hand they now behave differently: having submitted to the new order, they cannot remain as cruel and implacable as they have been hitherto.[155]

At all events, the emphasis now shifts to the positive aspect of their activity: if justice reigns in the city, fields, trees, and cattle will flourish, houses and mines will prosper.[156] Even marriage, for which—according to Apollo—they once cared nothing (213 ff), is now placed under their protection (835), and Athene, to whom they once seemed neither divine nor human (410 ff), now addresses the leader of the chorus as a goddess (883; cf. 929).[157] "It is their appointed task to govern all things human" (930 f). This formulation clearly shows that the domain of the Erinyes is not to be limited—like that of women—to the household; it is to embrace relations between houses, hence the whole of the city.[158] By watching over the houses they will in future prevent revenge and feuding. Finally, cases of murder will from now on be dealt with by a court of law (682, 708), to which Aeschylus assigns functions very similar to those of the Eumenides, the court that broke the cycle of vengeance by acquitting Orestes (808 f). Athene is well disposed to the city, Zeus is close to it, and in time (1000) Sophrosyne will come to the citizens. This, then, is the Athens of the new order. Here the Erinyes/Eumenides must also change their nature. Just as Peitho can persuade men to commit good or evil deeds; just as an oath may appear now in a positive, now in a negative light; just as war may be senseless at one time and beneficial at another; just as Sophrosyne can mean submission to tyranny, but also enlightened government in the *polis*[159]—so too the activity of the Erinyes/Eumenides can be terrible or beneficent (and in some measure both at once), depending on the circumstances. Thus the very powers that once promoted feuds can now ensure internal peace.

Yet how do we explain the fact that as early as the *stasimon*, while the court is assembling (490 ff), the Erinyes speak of the blessings they can bring? At first they depict in somber colors what would happen if they ceased to punish misdeeds. They warn against vain and foolish (or, as we might say, starry-eyed) reliance on uncertain remedies that clearly command little respect (*akea ou bebaia*, 506 ff). This is a clear echo of the anxieties aroused by the removal of the power of the Areopagus. They now declare that the terrible (*to deinon*) (which they themselves personify) also brings benefits. Without the terrible there is no justice (517). This leads on to the statement that life should be neither ungoverned nor governed by force, and to their praise of the mean (*to meson*).[160] They thus take up the same position as Athene (696 f), a position between the two extremes. Finally they dwell on the advantages of the mean: echoing old doctrines about ill-gotten gains that bring no blessing, they rehearse in didactic form the workings of Dike, who at once punishes and rewards.

It has been observed that this second *stasimon* is largely addressed to the audience.[161] It is as though the Erinyes, suddenly becoming aware that in Athens men are free and unconstrained by force, now wish to emphasize the importance of the terrible only insofar as it appears necessary as a counterpoise to excessive freedom. This can be explained by saying that they feel secure in their power after showing that the threat of the terrible must always be present. In any case one would have to add that here, as in their first reply to Athene (336 f, 354, 359 ff, 421), they are describing their role in general terms, and this is how it is meant to be understood (514 f, 546). They may seem to be acting out of character, but only to the extent that they have briefly departed from the extreme one-sidedness that they employ against the equally one-sided Apollo. This momentary shift of position marks the point at which Athene can subsequently begin her attempt at conciliation. One might even say that they show themselves to be essentially far more moderate than the impetuous Apollo.[162] But none of this quite explains the function of the passage in the play. For Aeschylus this exhortation to moderation clearly was so important that he chose to introduce it at this early stage, as a teaching delivered by the chorus, in anticipation of Athene's inauguration speech and the concluding hymns. This is the one occasion when he puts the same words into the mouths of different characters: [163] the city must be neither ungoverned nor governed by force! These words would have been relatively ineffective had they been uttered only after Athene and the Erinyes had reached agreement. The idea had to be enunciated by two different sides. This does not alter the fact that there is a real change of positions in the play, which can result only from reconciliation. [164]

This interpretation is corroborated by Athene's curious shift in the opposite direction during the latter part of the play, in which she proves to be considerably more severe than the Erinyes. [165] This too is not to be explained by the requirements of the plot: it is part of the political message addressed to the audience. The need for severity is a *leitmotiv* that is taken up by different instruments during the course of the work, a political motto-theme that pervades the whole of the orchestration.

The new regime of the Olympians, once it is reconciled with the Erinyes, loses its one-sided, partisan character. The rule of Zeus remains, though transformed through the conclusion of an honorable alliance with its defeated opponents. To maintain law and justice it needs the help of these powers, which were at first forced into opposition by the fierce antagonisms between the parties. In view of the theme of the later *Prometheus,* we may add that in due course the order of Zeus achieves permanence. [166] Aeschylus was clearly much exercised by the question of how a new order, originally established on a "party" basis, could become permanent. Linking the experience of 462/61 with the doctrine of the succession of divine dynasties, he was led to speculate about the basis upon which the regime of Zeus was founded. In the *Eumenides* he arrives at a preliminary answer: the new regime acquires permanence by becoming all-embracing, by observing moderation, and by showing respect for the old. As always in Greek thinking, a close link is made between the earthly and divine polities.

The punitive goddesses are incorporated (or reincorporated) into the order of Zeus, as the Areopagus and the nobility were to be incorporated (or reincorporated) into the new democratic order of the city. The powerful warning that the city must be neither ungoverned nor too strictly governed (neither *anarchon* nor *despotoumenon*) refers to the possible extremes of tyranny and lack of leadership. What lies between these— even if Aeschylus could not see it in this way—is "political" government, a form of government appropriate to the *polis.* [167] The Erinyes add that the god confers strength (*kratos*)—that is, superiority, success, and victory—on all forms of the mean (*to meson*). [168] Since the government (*kratein*) of the *demos*—"democracy"—has just been recognized, this seems to imply that *kratos* should not reside with the broad mass of the *demos*. The word *anarchon* recalls the anarchic fury of the people (*demothrous anarchia*), to which reference is made in the *Agamemnon* (883). But the present passage is couched in very general terms; when Athene becomes more precise, she makes no mention of the mean. This may of course simply indicate restraint on her part, but the sense of the passage is clear: as Athene says (698), the terrible (*deinon*) is necessary, among mortals and among the gods.[169] She is referring to the Areopagus (690 ff, 704 ff). In her inauguration speech she refers expressly only to the court's judicial functions, yet this too seems to proceed from cautious restraint. For the reconciling of government and freedom presupposes that the Areopagus should have more than a merely judicial function, that it should act rather as a counterpoise within the newly established democracy—if not in foreign policy, then at least in the general conduct of civic affairs.[170]

It seems obvious to me that any impartial reading of the play is bound to arrive at this interpretation, and that no attempt to avoid it can be convincing or even plausible.[171] Such attempts are of course superfluous, for what they aim at can be achieved in other ways. Their aim is to emphasize that the play cannot be taken to indicate the poet's rejection of Ephialtes and his reforms—which would be to relegate the message of the Eumenides to the plane of current party politics, to which it patently does not belong. Aeschylus is addressing himself to a much more general theme, the order and unity of the city within its newly established framework. Perhaps one should say rather that while Aeschylus starts from the new political reality, he balances it with what he sees as right and necessary, namely the universal order—that he presents contemporary reality as an integral part of the cosmic order. One might say that the ideas enunciated so fervently both here and at later stages of the play are designed to establish a new synthesis that will supersede the current antitheses. Translated into political terms, they would amount not to a demand for the repeal of the reform of 462, but rather to a plea for a rethinking of the role of the nobility—and of the Areopagus, the organ through which it can bring its influence to bear. It is impossible to say how Aeschylus envisaged this in practical terms—even supposing that he did—especially as we know so little about Ephialtes' reforms and the powers that the Areopagus lost as a result of them. It is not even clear to what extent this body's judicial functions could be divorced from its political functions.

At all events, Aeschylus sought to understand the conditions and requirements of political order within a perspective that was both political and religious; such an understanding was for him far more important than any institutional consequences one might draw from them.[172] Moreover, the play could not reflect such institutional consequences, but only general insights. One should not seek to elicit from the drama more information than it can yield: one should not be so intent upon discovering the poet's concrete political opinions as to miss the crucial statements he has to make on the more abstract plane of political thought. This applies equally to one of the most enigmatic passages in the play—the passage in the inauguration speech in which Athene declares that the respect of the citizens (*sebas aston*) and the fear (*phobos*) that goes with it will henceforth have their place on the Areopagus, warding off injustice day and night, unless the citizens themselves poison the laws by some noxious "contamination." "If you foul the clear water with mud you will not be able to enjoy it" (690 ff). The text here is not entirely certain, but the context makes it clear that such poisoning must imply some reduction of the salutary power of the Areopagus to inspire fear and respect. We do not know whether this amounts to a criticism of Ephialtes' law or a warning against the enactment of further laws.[173] Even the poet's contemporaries may have been uncertain. Yet even if the hint remained obscure, it no doubt served its purpose: the warning against change, uttered by the moderate goddess, was sufficient to impress.

Given the striking parallel between the Erinyes and the Areopagus,[174] it is obvious that what is at issue here is the relationship between the classes in Athenian society. In earthly affairs too it was important to conciliate one's defeated opponents; otherwise there was a danger of civil war. Similarly the Erinyes, had they not been conciliated, would have spread plague and pestilence. Aeschylus makes Athene draw attention to this danger,[175] even though the Erinyes have so far uttered no such threat. Is she equating them with the nobles? Is the mention of their possible fury to be taken to mean that the nobles might be provoked into fighting (858 ff)? At all events, the warnings were topical and plain for all to understand. There was no mistaking what the poet was saying: the defeated should accept defeat, and the victors should accord them functions in the new order that partly corresponded to those they had performed in the old.

All this points to the new problems that arise from the fact that the citizens now had the whole of the political order at their disposal; for all political rights now derived from the community as a whole. This was something new. Solon had regarded the nobles as the natural leaders,[176] and even Cleisthenes sought to do no more than enhance the status of the citizens and make them independent of the nobles. Now the very role of the nobility was being called in question. Aeschylus, taking a comprehensive view of *polis* society, provides a new justification for this role by stressing the necessity of the *deinon*.

At this point the parallel between myth and reality appears to become problematic. For feuding, which was to be overcome in the myth, was in reality the preserve of the nobility. Was the fox now to be set to keep the geese? In reply to this it must first be said that the archaic feuding in the drama develops into an extremely one-sided and potentially dangerous antagonism between the old and the new. It is this antagonism that in the end constitutes the real problem in the Athenian part of the play. Second, it must be observed that the nobles had actually had little opportunity for feuding in the few decades before 462, so that the problem scarcely existed any longer, at least in its archaic form. We should therefore not interpret the feuding too literally. It had coalesced with the new factional divisions to produce a general condition of *stasis*. Aeschylus probably considered that, within this framework, the possibility of civil war fomented by the nobility constituted no more of a threat than a rigid refusal of the *demos* to enter into a compromise. To this extent the old was not necessarily any worse than the new. Finally it must be said that complete parallelism in the dramatic construction was impossible to achieve if the one institution that was particularly old in 462/61 was newly established in the play. Thus, by appearing new, while at the same time corresponding to the old powers, the Areopagus has two aspects—like Athene herself, who helps the new to victory, effects a reconciliation with the old, and then adopts the sterner role. The fact is that when once the extreme partisan attitudes had been overcome, the simple dichotomy of old and new became superannuated. The scene was now dominated by other problems, posed by the whole configuration of contemporary forces. These had to be realigned, and the realignment produced a new situation in which the old powers were different from what they had previously been.

The compromise that was achieved led to the disappearance of the fierce, one-sided, and almost irreconcilable partisanship that we find in the first half of the play; it also removed the dangerous consequences of the court's verdict. The full extent of the conflict, which had made the political order into a subject for conflicting opinions and party interests, is thus miraculously taken up into a new and all-embracing unity, into a new concept of a just order under which the *polis* can prosper.

The establishment of this new, comprehensive order on the basis of compromise is attributed by Aeschylus to Athene's *phronein*—her insight and judgment, or, as J. G. Droysen renders it, her "power of thought." Aeschylus puts into her mouth the remark that the Erinyes are older and therefore wiser (*sophoterai*) than she. "Yet to me too Zeus has given the power of thought in no small measure" (848 ff). The *phronesis* of the young goddess is thus not only a match for the Erinyes' superior wisdom deriving from age and experience; she is also wise enough to be able to involve these old powers in the new order.

After the one-sided verdict of the court, Athene's *phronesis* brings divine truth into play, as it were: this consists in the compromise that guarantees everyone his proper place in the *polis*. This is probably how Aeschylus' thinking is to be understood. It has its terrestrial equivalent in the expectation that the Athenians, as confidants of the goddess, will in time attain to moderate understanding (*sophrosyne,* 1000). We will presently try to discover the political, religious, and philosophical roots of this idea of compromise as the basis of the one just order. The connotations of *phronesis* need not detain us now. We must first discuss, in the context of this political interpretation, one final and particularly interesting turn of phrase.

The new relations between the classes resulted in a new form of association and dissociation, a realignment of friend and foe. This insight emerges from the prayers uttered by the Eumenides after Athene has demanded that no civil war break out—that war remain "outside the gate" (862 ff). The Eumenides pray that civil war (*stasis*) may never rage through the city and that the citizens' blood may not be shed through feuds in which men take fierce vengeance and "murder one another," thus bringing disaster upon the city.[177] They pray that "men may give joy to one another in a spirit of common friendship that loves the generality"—Droysen translates "at one in love of the whole"—and that they may "hate with one mind. This is the cure for many ills among mortals."[178] To this Athene responds by once more expressing her joy at the reconciliation, beginning with the words we have already quoted: "Is it not proper that fair words should point the way to those who have understanding?"

So here we have friendship (*philia*) within the city, and united hostility directed outside it.[179] Mutual murder (*poinai antiphonoi*) is to be replaced by the mutual giving (*antididonai*) of joy. Enmity is no longer to be directed inward, but outward, in a spirit of solidarity. There is to be a new, *polis*-oriented distinction between friend and foe, a shift in the friend-foe relationship. In this way the *polis* will attain unity.

Here, for the first time, we encounter the requirement that friendship prevail among the citizens. Friendship was formerly a matter of interpersonal relations, especially within the nobility. In the archaic period the friend-foe distinction was of central importance in relations among the nobles, for if one was to assure oneself of help and protection and secure one's rights and power, one had to identify one's friends and one's enemies and act accordingly. Against this background it was very difficult for the *polis* as such to assert its common interests.[180] After Cleisthenes had created a firm institutional basis for civic solidarity, a new situation arose in which the weight of the whole community could regularly be brought to bear against the excessive ambitions of the nobles. Various institutional means were later devised in order to limit the effectiveness of aristocratic groupings. Even so, the nobles continued to think in terms of

friendship and enmity.[181] This was the situation to which Aeschylus now addressed himself.

In 478 the formula "to have the same friend and enemy," which probably originated in the world of aristocratic factions, was applied to the Attic maritime league.[182] Now we find it applied to the city.

This was preceded, in the movement up to Cleisthenes' reform, by the formation of a fairly broad civic solidarity. This solidarity furnished the basis for the various attempts to secure participation in civic affairs and was itself reinforced by such participation. It is not clear, however, whether it was understood as friendship.

At all events, what is new in Aeschylus is the idea that the members of the different classes should be united by friendship, an idea that acquired topical importance only when the city was faced with the threat of civil war arising from the struggle for control of the political order. To what extent differences could exist within such friendship remains an open question, though clearly the *deinon* could not operate under an unclouded sky. With the emergence of the alternative of lack of restraint, that is, of excessive popular freedom—whatever that means—it became inevitable that the program epitomized in the words "neither ungoverned nor governed by force" should imply certain internal differences."[183] Yet the whole must be spanned by friendship.

Such friendship was possible only if there was sufficient solidarity to keep the existing factions in check, and, however strange it may seem to us, this ultimately presupposed common hostility to the world outside.

Yet this was not all. When the Eumenides express surprise at the extent of their future authority (even though they have previously claimed that the maintenance of law throughout the world depends on them), this clearly implies an inevitable growth of the power of the city over its citizens. It is clear that what is being stressed here is the connection between power over the civic order and power over the houses, and also between protection and obedience. Only in this way can the new law of the *polis* triumph.

If this aspiration was to have any real content, however, the power of the *polis* had to be rooted in a strong civic solidarity. For there was no strong state power of the kind that exists in modern times and was originally concentrated in the monarch and his governmental apparatus. The ambiguity of the expression *koinophiles dianoia*—love directed to the whole (the *koinon*) and mutual friendship within the community—aptly illustrates the fact that the city as a whole had its roots in the citizenry.

The idea of friendship among citizens could combine with the strong sense of family community, with its internal solidarity, the common hearth, common sacrifice, and much else besides, which had already been transferred to the *polis*.[184] Yet within this extended civic family there might

still be serious strife, and the notion of civic friendship might easily have remained an abstract ideal.

This is why it was so important to link it firmly with a common hostility to the world beyond the city. Aeschylus saw that there must be a realignment of friendship *and* enmity to cement the new civic solidarity. The practical situation afforded a chance to achieve this, for after the Areopagus had been stripped of its power, Athens embarked upon a remarkably extensive policy of conquest (or at least sought to extend its power).

We now see why Aeschylus lays such emphasis on the alliance between Athens and Argos. Whereas in the *Agamemnon* war is seen in a negative light, it is here shown to have a beneficial function.[185] It was not, after all, being waged for the sake of a woman. To this extent Aeschylus—for whatever reasons—ranges himself beside the impetuous champions of change.[186] But this is the necessary complement of his quite contrary views on internal politics. And in the very next year Cimon was to take up a similar position.[187]

Quite independently of this, however, Aeschylus' linking of friendship and enmity touches upon an important feature of the ancient *polis:* the fact that it was fairly directly rooted in the community as a whole meant that in large measure the citizens were purely and simply citizens. The *polis* and its *politai* had a reciprocal commitment. As a result there was little scope for the development of the numerous diversions into non-political activity that the modern state enables—indeed encourages—its citizens to pursue. In the words of Marx, "the political state as such" was "the true and exclusive content of their lives and desires."[188] Quite powerful energies were thus concentrated in the political sphere, especially in a *polis* as large and ambitious as Athens. It was of course quite possible for the citizens to live together without external enemies, yet all the same it was obvious that the achievement of a more general friendship was closely linked with a more general hostility, that it was part and parcel of a general shift of association and dissociation, or—to borrow the words of Empedocles—of *neikos* and *philia*.[189] In this context a clear—and, for that matter, quite formal—concept of the enemy could be accommodated.

The prayers of the Eumenides therefore express not just pious hopes, but a clear appreciation of reality. The new civic friendship was expected to proceed not simply from the realization that it was necessary: the hostilities that could no longer be allowed to rage within the city must be diverted outside it.

For Aeschylus, internal friendship and external enmity correspond to the division of labor proposed by Athene: while the Eumenides are to uphold law and prosperity within the city, she herself will direct her activity outside it and bring victories to the Athenians (903–915).

Here, then, we find an anticipation of the concept of *koinonia politike,* though not the term itself. However much was later said about the need for friendship among the citizens and among different parts of the city,[190] what is presented here, with a degree of realism that the Greeks seldom achieved again, is the whole range of problems posed by new modes of association *and* dissociation, by the concentration or diffusion of power, and by the distinction between friend and foe.

Even if the Eumenides ultimately reach a positive and harmonious compromise within a perspective that is concentrated solely on Athens, they continue to give vivid expression to the enormous and unforeseen problems that were concomitant with the revolutionary change to democracy. They thus articulate a part of the city's experience that was unique and unrepeatable. Never again were the Greeks to be so profoundly conscious of what it meant for the legal and political order to be at the free disposal of the citizens. The situation was unprecedented, the experience utterly new; later they were to grow accustomed to it.[191]

The Citizens of Attica in 458 and the *Eumenides*

One may wonder how transparent and comprehensible this political conception was to the Athenians of 458. There was clearly a lively interest in tragedy, but of course this may have had more to do with the performance than with the content of the plays. Nevertheless, it would not have been possible to ascribe to tragedy the function of "educating the adults" had it not been largely comprehensible to many members of the audience. As there were prizes to be won, and as public acclaim played an important part in their award, the poets are hardly likely to have composed their plays without an eye to the audience. Hence, the tragedies that have come down to us show what the poets felt the public would accept. True, only the best works have been preserved, and the decision as to which of them deserved to survive lay with later experts. But however much the plays may have varied in quality, those that survived are hardly likely to have been harder to understand than those that did not.

One particular consideration seems to me important: we know from various periods of history that if a whole society is strongly committed to a certain cause, even the "common man" can develop a high degree of receptiveness and sophistication. We have clear evidence that many of the citizens of Attica were interested in rhetoric and constantly demanded to hear something new; this implies that they were also capable of understanding and appreciating the problems of rhetoric.[192] The broad mass of the Athenians thus did not have to be particularly "educated" or "intellectually inclined" (as today's theater buffs may be suspected of being) in order to develop extreme interest and considerable understanding.[193] To produce this effect, tragedy simply had to occupy a different place in their lives. However, we may presume that it did. The festival of Dionysus was one of the high points of the Attic year. The mythical subjects were relatively familiar,[194] and over time they were treated in different ways by different poets. The Athenians of 458 had to a large extent witnessed the development of tragedy; they had grown up with it, as it were, and could discuss it in a fairly sophisticated manner. (They lived, after all, in a culture that did not have many distractions and concentrated on the few things that were interesting, relying largely on the spoken word and taking pleasure in discussion.) We may therefore conclude that many people must have understood, directly or indirectly, a great deal of what they saw on the stage.

This applies not least to whatever political statements the plays contained. The citizens of Attica had for years been engaged in political action, deliberation, and decision making.[195] Politics was a relatively concrete activity that took place among the citizens and before their eyes. Whatever happened was to a large extent commensurable with the citizens. They were certainly aware of how the political system worked and alert to anything pertaining to politics. It was precisely the political content of a play that was bound to appeal to them and capture their attention, and they must have read a political meaning into much that was susceptible of other constructions.[196] Moreover, their political identity presupposed a close link between politics and religion.

All this must presumably have been true in even greater measure in the years immediately following the reforms of 462/61. Admittedly we have no evidence of the extent to which the citizens of Attica were exercised by the political situation during these years, but as a majority had voted to remove the powers of the Areopagus, such a step cannot have been altogether inconceivable. Yet there was also considerable resistance to it; the objections did not die down, and many who had at first supported it on grounds of foreign policy may later have had misgivings. At all events, there is good reason to believe that the changed circumstances gave rise to a widespread feeling that a fresh orientation was needed; this meant finding a way of balancing the new political conditions with traditional knowledge about the gods and men, and matching the divine order with the human. This is what Aeschylus tried to do for the Athenians in the *Oresteia*. He focused on the political situation in Athens. Yet it is hardly conceivable that he could have produced such a subtle, comprehensive, incisive, and topical analysis unless many of the ideas expressed in the play had already been widely current. And where would they have gained such currency, if not in discussions among large numbers of citizens? We shall presently have to ask to what extent this was linked with a historical understanding. How much assent Aeschylus found for his thesis concerning the necessity, strength, and superiority of the *meson* is a question we cannot answer.

It should of course be noted that this demand is adumbrated in the first two parts of the trilogy. When Clytemnestra receives Agamemnon, she explains to him why Orestes is absent: she has sent him away because of her uncertainty about the outcome of the Trojan War and her fear that "the lawlessness of popular clamor might overthrow the council" (or "reject the counsel").[197] These words have no function in the play. They are an unmistakable allusion to what happened in Cimon's absence. The formulation, however, is clearly characteristic of the queen, who will soon be seen as a criminal and a tyrant. After the murder of Agamemnon, the chorus reproaches Aegisthus and threatens him with the people's curse. He reacts with some asperity: "This is how you speak, sitting on the lower bench of the oarsmen, while those who hold the tiller have all the power" (1617 f). This is an expression of the aristocratic pride that goes before a fall, and of contempt for the very class that gained political prominence in 462/61. These utterances by a pair of murderous tyrants are clearly meant to vindicate the political rights of the humblest class of Athenian citizens. In the wider context of what is said about Athens, these lines are balanced by those in which the Eumenides speak of the vital role of the Areopagus. The balance is not especially striking, as the two passages are widely separated, but it does document the view that the desirable mean should also concede to the *thetes* what is properly their due.

Summary: The Political Insight of the *Eumenides*

What Aeschylus treats politically in the *Eumenides* and in some way understands is:

1. The overcoming of the self-perpetuating feud (or, more generally, the menacing political conflicts) by means of a new legal (and civic) order. The whole of this order is at issue and "placed in the midst of the citizens." The result is:
2. The emergence of a fundamental antagonism of a highly partisan character that extends virtually to the entire political order. This leads to:
3. The new problems of decision making concerning central questions that were previously subject to the criterion of truth. This also means:
4. The establishment of a new civic authority over the houses. The united *polis* gains ascendancy over all particularist forces. It also involves:

5. The shifting of the friend-foe dichotomy from within the city to outside it. And not least:
6. The need for reconciliation and peaceful compromise among all the existing forces within an all-embracing order (which Aeschylus sees prevailing also between the mythical powers of different origins).

This understanding is embodied in the form of the myth:

How the chain of revenge and counterrevenge culminates in the aporia of Orestes;

how, because of this, various divine powers come into conflict with one another;

how their antagonism intensifies to such a pitch of partisanship that it becomes a fundamental confrontation between new and old;

how the aporia is then resolved by means of a verdict that is magnificent in its very absurdity—but only at a price: the basic consequences of the resolution cannot convince the opponents and cannot bind them;

how, as a result, those who have been defeated threaten the city from without, and the conflict is on the point of leading to war or civil war;

how finally the resolution itself, insofar as it has set the seal on the triumph of the new law, is incorporated into the exemplary order of Zeus, which, though new, shows itself to be just by embracing the old (and so gains additional power through preserving an element of the terrible)—

this is unquestionably the transmutation of a complex of burning political problems into a myth concerning the gods, the myth of the political, the mythical resolution of the problems of living together in a political order that has been called into question. Within this myth the archaic past is intimately linked with the present and future of 458.

The myth is precisely located, since the city of Athens plays a central role in it, both actively and passively. What takes place between the supernatural powers, however general it may be, is kept within bounds: the compromise relates to Athens, where the citizens join forces against the enemies outside the gates. At this point too the action on the mythical plane is linked with the present and future, as experienced and envisaged in the year 458: Athene will secure victories for her city. Aeschylus is thus also creating a *polis* myth.

The citizens could hardly have been given a more adequate account of how the political order passed from a state of affairs in which existing conditions reproduced themselves automatically (in all essentials) to one in which it became subject to political decision making.[198]

Aeschylus operates with quite basic categories: conflict and decision, internal and external, friend and foe, and—above all—reconciliation and compromise. This mirrors the profundity of the change, the completely new basis of decision making, and above all the fact that at this point the opposing forces were roughly equally balanced and civil war threatening to erupt. These existential problems bore so heavily upon the community as to call for a rethinking and realignment of the association and dissociation of the political forces. It can therefore hardly be coincidental that Aeschylus, in his "analysis," attached importance to the same categories as Carl Schmitt when he contemplated the dangers facing the modern state. On both occasions there was a great advance in politicization; fundamentally new groupings, themes, and dimensions were emerging in political life. And on both occasions the change was so incisive and all-embracing that it could be conceived in elemental terms. It was in the nature of the situation that the *polis* could not be seen to exist on its own, but only in the context of the immediate political situation, internal and external.

It was of course obvious that Aeschylus should see things in this perspective, because the city's internal conflicts resulted from its external successes and led in turn to increased activity abroad.[199]

Moreover, what Aeschylus expected did in fact come about in all essentials The external policy of Athens and the wars waged by the city played a decisive part in producing compromise within the civic community, even without any strengthening of the power of the Areopagus. This precondition for the stability of the most radical of the Greek democracies was later overlooked by Aristotle in his much more narrowly based political theory (so that his statements about extreme democracy prove untrue in relation to the very city from which they are derived—to the detriment of his whole theory).[200]

Aeschylus' close adherence to reality also obliged him to make reconciliation and compromise the prime goals of internal political action. There was no other way to secure internal peace. It is in this context that we should see the demand for the *meson* and a "political" form of government, such as we find later in Aristotle.[201] It seems a somewhat utopian postulate in view of the realistic presentation of the conflicting political forces. How far it initially articulated only a desperate hope is a question we shall have to discuss presently.

At all events, Aeschylus seems to have found an interesting way of combining analysis and postulate. The postulate of the one just order, based on compromise, derives from the normative Greek notion of what is proper to the *polis*.[202] Yet Aeschylus, in his analysis, comes close to the modern concept of the political, which is concerned primarily with the concrete situation, embraces both internal and external politics, and pays attention to partisan positions and decision making. Only in this way can

Aeschylus understand the whole new context of association and dissociation—a change that was for him so revolutionary that, paradoxically, the
increasing power of the democratic *polis* over internal affairs could be
understood as the power of the Areopagus, though with the proviso that
this body should take its place in the new political unity, which had its
counterpart in the order of Zeus.

However, Aeschylus did not evolve his categories in order to reach a
basic understanding of the political (in any sense of the word) or whatever
may have corresponded to it in his day. He employed them only to interpret
and come to grips with a real situation—an exceptional development that
was taking place in the exceptional city of Athens. The Eumenides myth is
concerned not with political life as such, but with the last act of politicization, in which the order of the *polis* itself becomes subject to politics. It
addresses itself to the new situation and the consequences that flow from it.
What is presented here is of course a Greek conception of what is proper to
the *polis*. The basic nature of the remaining categories accords with the
topical treatment of the myth in an exceptional situation.

Various questions now arise. The juxtaposition of extreme partisanship
and reconciliation, of profoundly differing conceptions of the political
order on the one hand and the postulation of a single just order on the
other, raises the question of continuity and discontinuity. Which of the two
is the greater? How does Aeschylus understand the new departure historically? To what extent does he grasp the fact that the turning point is indeed
a turning point?

This raises the question of the relation between factual analysis and
postulate, and also, in a sense, between the two "concepts of the political"
(to employ our own terms). As far as the myth is concerned, we must ask
how the mythical pattern of political compromise is to be understood.
Is it merely a metaphor, a construct born of wishful thinking, or does it
derive from a religious faith that lent force and certainty to the myth?
What was the source of Aeschylus' confidence in the benevolent influence
of the gods? It seems to us as though he was combining an extremely realistic analysis with a utopian demand (which in the end could be met only
thanks to successes in external policy). But perhaps this is mistaken.

These questions will be treated here within the wider context of Greek
political thought, which supplied the more general basis for Aeschylus'
construct. Only by drawing upon this background is it possible to reconstruct and understand the view of the *polis* and politics that informs his
thinking. This contention is supported not only by the isolation of those
passages within the drama on which we have had to rely, but above all
by the fact that we are dealing with an early, primitive, and fairly inex-
plicit understanding of the problems. It is only with difficulty that we, as
readers of Plato and Aristotle and as children of an age abounding in the-

ories, can grasp the essential features of this understanding. (Nor is it at all clear that, faced with the problems of our own age, we are at a less primitive stage of political thinking than the Greeks were when confronted with the formation of the *polis*.) It may be that we should take the indications as constituting the whole. At the same time, we are bound to ask how far the *Eumenides* of Aeschylus embodies elements of political thinking that were new at the time. Can we in fact discern in the play a turning point in the history of political thought corresponding to the one that occurred in political history in 462/61?

"Theological Politics": The *Eumenides* of Aeschylus in the Tradition of Greek Political Thought

Aeschylus' concept of the *polis* and the political derives from theological politics, an interesting counterpart to the political theology of modern times.[203] It was primarily concerned with the affairs of the *polis;* it also involved speculations about the will of the gods and played an important part in such speculations. Aeschylus too believed that the proper order of the *polis* was divinely ordained, for Zeus always conferred victory (*kratos*) on the mean (*meson*), which lay midway between anarchy and despotism—what Aristotle was later to call *politike arche* ("political rule" or a "political form of government"). This entailed some form of collaboration between the nobles and the people, which was clearly a precondition for a politically limited government and an effective legal order. Very similar notions are found in the poems of Solon (5, 24). Yet the situation had changed since Solon's day. For him the nobles were the natural leaders, but their leadership had meanwhile been swept aside, and one could at best plead for its restoration.

Aeschylus' advocacy of the mean can be understood only as the product of an idiosyncratic tradition of political thought that evolved among the Greeks under the exceptional conditions of the archaic period. Corresponding to the extraordinary nature of this process and of its outcome, democracy, this was a very specific intellectual movement that has so far received inadequate attention.[204]

Given the multiplicity of city-states and the absence of strong monarchical and hieratic authority, this tradition of political thought adopted a "third position" between the contending forces and provided an institutional focus for a widespread interest in proposals for solving concrete problems, and later in the conception of a just order, fostering expectations and the expectation of expectations[205] and so serving to consolidate this interest, which may have brought some material reward to those who catered to it. From this vantage point the political thinkers could become advocates for the whole of the *polis* at a time when it had not yet attracted enough champions to its cause. They were able to devise institutions, recognize connections, formulate demands, and finally anticipate the role that would gradually be taken over by ever wider sections of the body politic.

Occupying a relatively neutral position—in fact a position of weakness—the political thinkers could at best combat the more dangerous extremes—excessive use of power, dire hardship, extremes of wealth or poverty—by mediating between the parties, for there was no other means of solving the many serious crises and conflicts of the age. More often than not they had to side with the disadvantaged and rely on their support. In these circumstances the idea developed that some measure of political participation should be granted to wider sections of the citizenry, because their rights could not otherwise be safeguarded, and hence internal peace and order would be repeatedly threatened by rebellion.

This activity presupposed certain notions of a just order that could serve as *points de repère* for the political thinkers—and subsequently for wider sections of the citizenry. We can see how such notions arose, and how theology and politics came to be intimately linked in them, if we study the writings of Solon, whose thinking can probably be taken to represent a fairly broad and ultimately successful current of political thinking.[206] Solon identified the mechanism whose workings produced the crisis afflicting the Athens of his day: it was the logical consequence of the way affairs were conducted in the *polis* and not, as had previously been thought, a punishment sent by the gods. It was a process in which various causes—exploitation, hardship, and the threat of peasant uprisings—tended to generate civil war and tyranny. This realistic insight led Solon to surmise that behind the intolerable status quo lay the outlines of a just order, which necessarily contained none of these causes. He started from the conviction that a just order must be one that was sanctioned by the gods. If the status quo was at variance with it, the fault lay with men. Nevertheless, they could escape the consequences of processes that would otherwise inevitably lead to disaster by removing their causes at the last minute with the help of a righter of wrongs (*katartister*).

Solon thus discovers the just order, personified as the goddess Eunomia, by proceeding in a conservative and essentially realistic manner: the just order is the ideal pattern that lies behind the status quo; the different forces all have their allotted place in it, and there can be no conflict between just claims. Solon's activity as a political righter of wrongs was directed less to a search for compromise than to an equitable distribution of rights.

Against the background of the growing possibilities immanent in the age, this recognition of a divine order that meted out punishment in accordance with discoverable laws led to the rapid spread of a belief in justice, combined with a new confidence in man's capacity for understanding and action. This general belief in justice was strengthened by the conviction that it was possible to discern the workings of divine justice on earth; it thus provided a firm foundation for the concept of eunomy. And although the laws discovered by Solon were severe, their discovery was welcome, for it enabled men to halt the processes that they would otherwise have set in train. This may seem paradoxical. But to recognize political connections was at that time to recognize trends or processes whose outcome was virtually inevitable; on the other hand it was possible, at the moment of greatest danger, to convince others of the need to intervene, and there were potential majorities in favor of such intervention. In this respect, as in others, the recognition of these severe laws enhanced men's capacity for action. They were led to believe that the gods were benevolently disposed to the city. The gods were not only just, but merciful, in that they allowed the citizens a last-minute chance to escape the calamity that they had almost brought upon themselves. This was something denied to individuals and their families. Different laws applied to the *polis,* which was thus seen to enjoy a special dispensation.[207] The communal life of the city was privileged. Solon thus discovered a new dimension of justice that was directly linked to the *polis.* This must have been closely connected with his confidence in men's capacity for understanding and action, which generated a solid realism, or, to be more precise, a faith in reality that was rooted in religion. The favor of the gods was bound to appear all the greater because insight was the greatest power of the political thinkers—and because it combined in the long run with the powerful interests of the middle and lower ranks of society.

The wider framework of this intellectual movement was shaped by an interesting feature of Greek theology[208] that was determined principally by the political situation of the archaic period. There were no strong monarchical or priestly authorities who could convincingly relate the workings of the gods to themselves. Whatever claims kings and tyrants might make about their relations with the higher powers, they had to contend with strong competition from the widespread belief in justice, which in these unsettled times[209] increasingly determined the general conception of Zeus, and from the conviction of their opponents—above all the leading political thinkers[210]—that autocracy was wrong. The polytheistic and polypolitical world of the Greeks thus remained for the most part immune to monarchical pretensions and hieratic interference.

It remained open and receptive to a species of thought that was concerned ultimately with the whole—which was greater than any single political entity and depended on balancing the claims of the parts—and to a concept of justice that was not vested exclusively in particular earthly authorities. This justice was at first thought to be dispensed by the father of the gods. Later it was perceived as a universal law, for the whole world must be governed by one supreme law. And since not even the gods stood outside the world, they too were subject to a more general law.[211] Insofar as Zeus was credited with particular responsibility for this law, he had either to guarantee its execution or to become a kind of symbol for the universal order. The affairs of the *polis* could therefore be governed by divine justice only if this was realized in the *polis* as a whole; it could not be represented by any individual. The just order thus had to manifest itself in more abstract relations, in the interplay of the different forces within the *polis*. Earthly reality had to be transparent if it was to make sense.[212] This was especially true of politics, where the workings of divine punishment were discerned in terrestrial processes. This notion was sustained by the extremely frequent rise and fall of powerful magnates and their families.[213] Thus even the justice of Zeus occupied a "third position," as it were: again and again it was possible to observe its workings from a distance, for the polypolitical world in which the Greeks lived inclined them to view things from the outside; and the viewpoint of the broad masses, who were not actively involved, came to be linked with the third position adopted by political thinking. It was not enough to make sense of one's own lot;[214] one also had to pay attention to a general law that affected great and small alike, and was so all-embracing—and often so tardy in its operation—that belief in it was proof against almost any disappointment.[215]

This led to the postulate that a meaning could be discerned in all that happened in the world, the idea of the world as a "cosmos" (a word that, significantly, was used first in the sense of "order," and then as a designation for the world), and to the grand philosophical speculations that saw an immutable divine law at work in the very variety and mutability of earthly affairs. The Erinyes were responsible not only for maintaining the law on earth, but also—so Heraclitus has it—for maintaining the sun's course through the heavens.[216]

Cosmology and political thought thus drew sustenance from the same roots,[217] developing in tandem and corroborating each other. No small part in all this was played by theological speculation, operating from a neutral position that was not tied to particular authorities with pretensions to universality.

Theological politics, which sought proof of the workings of divine justice in the practical world of the *polis* and tried to arrive at a postulate for a just civic order, was presumably still a potent force at the time of Aeschylus. The gods were believed to dispense justice. The concept of the whole implied concern for the disadvantaged (who might otherwise rebel). After the Cleisthenian reform, an alternative to the traditional order had been realized in Athens. Broad sections of the population—those whom

Aristotle was to describe as "always striving for justice and equality"[218]—won the right to political participation. Only individuals suffered disadvantage—tyrants who were overthrown and nobles who were unable to assert themselves under the new rules of the game. Belief in the possibility of a just order must have been strengthened; it was then confirmed by the victory over the Persians, which the Greeks saw as proof of divine justice.[219] Subsequent Athenian successes proved that the city enjoyed the favor of the gods.

We thus find, both in the *Eumenides* and in the writings of Solon, the notion that the gods are responsible for the just order of the city, which can be perverted only if it is contaminated by the citizens themselves (693 f).[220] We also find the notion that divine justice is not implacable. For Aeschylus too the *polis*—whether Argos or Athens—is privileged. Its justice, he says (and here he goes further than Solon), is guaranteed by its institutions.[221] The great confidence that was placed in men's capacity for knowledge and action is expressed in the reference to the rational procedure of hearing evidence, but it also finds expression in other aspects of the emergent consciousness of human abilities, which was of great significance for Aeschylus. One of the most impressive passages in the *Agamemnon* is the detailed description of the path of the beacon fires that bring news of victory from Troy to Argos; this is no doubt a proud allusion to one of the strategic achievements of the Delian League.[222] The encomia on the power of persuasion, on Zeus Agoraios, and above all on Athene's "power of thought," together with the conviction that the Athenians would in time attain to *sophrosyne*, point in the same direction.

The power of thought that Athene has received from Zeus (850) is clearly contrasted with the ancient knowledge of the Erinyes, which rests upon experience. Even if this were not already indicated by the terms Aeschylus uses (*sophos* and *phronein*), it would be clear from the context that he is alluding to new modes of thought. The lively, incisive thinking of the fifth century was beginning to come into its own—a kind of thinking that broke free of tradition and, relying on its own capacity for cognition, dared to go to the heart of things and reconstitute—or at least rethink—the whole of the *polis* order (or of a work of art).[223] *Phronein* could also denote the "technical" aspect of human intelligence, which made success possible through the use of methodical procedures.[224] Aeschylus of course did not understand it solely in this sense. For him it meant primarily the ability to recognize the all-embracing divine order. Yet it also had practical consequences. Cognition was bound to spur men to action. The divine order that encompassed the whole was the source of wise action, and this worked in favor of compromise and conciliation. *Phronesis*, we are told, is the greatest gift that can be conferred on men.[225] Presumably, for Aeschylus such insight was still associated with the many new opportunities for "technical" knowledge and action as a manifestation of the new intellectual ability, which was at once theoretical and practical.[226]

In tracing the *sophrosyne* of the Athenians back to Athene, he finds fresh confirmation—in the long-drawn-out process of learning through suffering—for Solon's belief that the hand of the goddess shields the city. Even the notion that the turn for the better, toward the overcoming of pernicious processes (that is, the constantly renewed feuding), comes at the moment of extreme aporia, is anticipated by Solon. It is at precisely this moment that Aeschylus makes Zeus commit himself to the *polis,* thus implying that insight (and the remembrance of "past suffering") can become effective in just such a situation—that insight upon which political thought had long relied, whose power it had institutionalized, and in which the benevolence of the gods was revealed.

Yet there is one difference. Solon believed that such insight would become immediately effective through the dissemination of his teachings.[227] In his day it was enough—or so it seemed—to appoint a righter of wrongs to restore order in the city's affairs. Aeschylus, by contrast, believed that the whole community had to possess the requisite insight. This was why the doctrine of the gradual improvement of human abilities over time was so important to him.

We see here that the doctrine of the emergence of culture could flourish in a theological context too—presumably in connection with the "double causality" whereby divine and human causes were conceived as running in parallel.[228] We also see that the habit of viewing the development of culture in terms of historical processes could be extended to the gradual emergence of *sophrosyne* within the *polis.* The other references we have to it relate mainly to the period leading up to the formation of the *polis* (or to the increase in its power and size).[229] It was obviously necessary, given the quite unprecedented power now enjoyed by the citizens at large, to be assured of their moderation and reasonableness, which had evolved with time.[230] At first, the surest foundation for such insight was faith in the gods and their goodwill toward the city. The demands made on the citizens' virtue were not as great as those made by Plato and Aristotle at a later date.[231] Moreover, it was possible to believe that a process of development had led up to a state of enlightenment that was later conceived—in somewhat utopian fashion—to be at best a product of education (for the few).

The belief in the steady growth of moderate understanding, attained with the help of Athene, is nevertheless accompanied in the *Eumenides* by a note of urgent supplication. Had it been otherwise, the threat of civil war could not have been serious. Nevertheless, there were strong grounds for hope.

The greatness of *phronesis* was proved by the goddess's moderation. The order became all-embracing when the victors accorded the defeated an honorable place and appropriate functions within it. In this way the antithesis of old and new was resolved in the synchrony of a stable whole.

Aeschylus thus provides a fresh vindication, under new circumstances, for the religious realism of Solon, who made current reality the starting point for his search for the just order, taking all existing forces into account yet always distinguishing between the just order and the status quo. Justice now required that the *thetes* be included as a class; Aeschylus believed that it also required the inclusion of the nobles. To all appearances—unless one took a very superficial view—it was probably still quite difficult to imagine the *polis* without any leading organ of an essentially aristocratic character.[232] Expectations could not be pitched too far ahead of what was empirically feasible; one could not expect something totally new to emerge. And, given the background of traditional theological politics, there must have been many who were not prepared to endorse the stark "cratistic" alternative of democracy or oligarchy.[233]

A divinely ordained order, postulated from a third position on the basis of contemporary reality (which was now becoming better understood and easier to control), could be conceived and realized only under conditions of political compromise in the spirit of the *meson*. Political thought could have held out no prospect of improvement without reliance on given facts and careful attention to all existing forces. Moreover, any improvement necessarily involved the creation of an order that was in keeping with the will of the gods, that was always just and grounded in reality. This static conception of the true order actually outlived the age of theological politics. For, given the essentially static conditions of life— before the notion of progress was discovered or even possible—the principles of a just order could be conceived only in static terms. With greater insight it might in time be better understood; it might be defined in more abstract terms—indeed it had to be—but it could never be fundamentally changed. The nobility could not appear "superannuated."[234] It was not possible to cross the threshold into the realm of "temporalization" and "progress." To this extent there were still good grounds for believing that God "gave victory to moderation in every form."

This formula did not of course mean that it was impossible to envisage a great variety of change—or rather a great many individual changes. This becomes clear when we consider the whole sentence: "To moderation in every form God giveth the victory, but his other dispensations he directeth in varying wise.[235] The eternally valid principle is thus delimited against contingent change: the experience of change is embedded in a concept of changelessness. This leaves room for many variations in detail but precludes any relativization in crucial areas. Here we may observe an interesting divergence between Aeschylus and Pindar. In a poem composed by Pindar some ten years earlier we find the first attestation of the notion that there are three types of constitution: "tyranny, when the reckless populace rules the city, and when it is ruled by the wise." The poet immediately goes on to say that it is impossible to contend against God, who gives strength now to some and now to others.[236] If Pindar is referring, as seems likely, to the change of rulers under the constitution, it follows that this is the only change he envisages. Aeschylus, by contrast, emphasizes the norm that transcends all change and rules in accordance with the divine will. It follows that *kratos* should rest, not with any single authority, but with the mean. One should no doubt add that this is what ultimately happens again and again, though always under different conditions; this was ensured by divine justice. And whatever corresponded to this norm must be regarded as "normal" even if it was repeatedly threatened. The whole of the *polis* should be controlled by the norm, that is, by the commonalty (which was deduced from the mean), and not by one of its parts—as was customary at the time. The postulate of the mean was thus set against the new extreme of excessive democracy.

Thus once again the terrestrial and celestial orders could be mutually related under the umbrella of traditional religious attitudes, despite the deep divisions that pervaded the whole. Realistic analysis and the postulate of compromise could be brought close together in an ambience of political realism informed by religion. After the city had lived through so many changes, the belief in a predestined order had to be formulated in more abstract terms. Central to this belief was the ideal of compromise, whereby everyone was accorded his due (and what was necessary within the framework of the whole). This was the way to heal the divisions that threatened to intensify to the pitch of civil war. This was the political solution enjoined upon the *polis* by the gods. The notion of the mean, which was later sought mainly in sociological terms or in concepts of mixed constitutions, is here encountered for the last time within the old horizon of theological politics.

If such moderate and comprehensive insight was conferred by the gods, it had also to be applied to myth. A fresh understanding of the story of Orestes was now possible. Aeschylus saw the myth in political terms, as he was bound to do in the immediate present of 458. He incorporated this present into his vision of the world of the gods, which he interpreted in the light of changes taking place in the world of the *polis*. At the same time he conceived the new as something old—or, more precisely, as something that had existed before, and so discovered a divine model for the problem of his age.[237]

This new understanding was reached not simply by the construction of mythical models on the basis of wishful thinking, but by theological reflection on the myth, informed by political experience. The recognition of extreme partisanship raised the question of permanence, even in relation to the rule of Zeus. By resolving this question through compromise on the basis of contemporary reality, Aeschylus found a continuity that was proof against radical change—and indeed comprehended it. He could not understand the turning point in Attic democracy as a turning point. He neutralized change by conceiving the changeless order in more abstract terms.

The *Eumenides* is nevertheless dominated by a long-term historical perspective. For the consciousness of continuity was reinforced by the assumption that suffering would in time lead to a growth of moderate understanding.

However much Aeschylus may have endorsed the optimistic temporal perspective contained in the doctrines of cultural development, this did not mean that he readily embraced all that was new and radically forward-looking. The mean also had to stand between the old and the new. The reason of Athene had to prevail against those who were bent on innovation. In this context the curious difference between Athene and Apollo, in both demeanor and intellectual stature, becomes comprehensible and significant. Power of thought is ascribed only to the goddess—not to the god, the belligerent champion of the cause that gives birth to the new law. The contrast is not fortuitous.

It is pointless to seek to explain it by reference to a supposed rivalry between Athenian and Delphic religiosity, or to suggest that Apollo is being criticized because of the oracle concerning the Persian Wars (which was unfavorable to Athens and belied by subsequent events). If criticism was intended, it was aimed in a quite different direction. It is striking that Apollo appears as a friend of man.[238] Certain of his traits are not unlike those exhibited by Prometheus in championing man's cause against a different adversary, namely Zeus.[239] Apollo, like Prometheus, is fiery, partial, and given to exaggeration. It is impossible to see where this image of Apollo could have originated or how it could have served to focus criticism on Delphi, whose oracle appears in a not unfavorable light in the play (1 ff, 614 ff, 797 ff). It may be that Aeschylus intends a contrast with the views of the politicians associated with Ephialtes. One might regard the passionate, impetuous conduct of Apollo, and above all of Prometheus, as a reflection of the spirit of Athens, of its youthful intrepidity, its urge for expansion, and its reckless audacity (*tolmeron*), as a result of which the Spartans had sent the Athenians home after the Messenian War.[240] If so, the portrayal of Apollo would represent a criticism of those who were currently in power in Athens.[241] However, we are concerned here primarily with the relations between the dramatis personae. Both elements—the new and radically progressive on the one hand, the enlightened and conciliatory on the other—had to be accommodated in the play, and this necessity naturally determined the distribution of roles. In the myth Apollo was allied with Orestes, while Athene and her city stood between the parties.

A similar configuration is found in the *Prometheia*, though there the roles are reversed: the figure to whom the great increase in human potentialities is due belongs to the old dynasty, which is opposed by the tyrannical usurpers of the new. Given the situation in the *Oresteia*, we may find it strange that in the *Prometheia* the new forces should be so implacably opposed to the civilizing power of innovation. Yet this in itself makes it plain that for Aeschylus no particular values attached to the old and the new as such; the new was not always synchronized with the new in such a way as to imply progress. What is significant in both works is the gross one-sidedness of the contending parties and the way in which they are finally reconciled within a total order; in this order the new is able to assert itself, while the immoderation that enables it to do so is stripped of much of its power.[242]

According to Karl Reinhardt, the conflicting roles are distributed among the dramatis personae in a manner "determined by the nature of the myth and the idea that it either embodies or has imposed upon it."[243] Within this framework, the gods can be treated fairly freely in accordance with the exigencies of the dramatic structure. Apollo and Athene, Zeus and Prometheus—sometimes male and female—represent temporary attitudes within the drama. The only constant is the ultimate outcome—an all-embracing order established by Zeus or in his name.

We can thus ascribe the triumph of the new law in the mythical Areopagus (which may be seen as parallel to the earthly triumph of democracy in 462/61) entirely to the partisan positions prevailing among the Olympians. The crucial point is that the defeated are conciliated and a new and all-embracing polity inaugurated. Herein lies the real triumph of Zeus. What matters is the whole, within which all else is relative. This is what guarantees permanence.

In the whole of the *Oresteia*, starting with the *Agamemnon*, we find a striving for a definitive outcome and the recurrent illusion that it has been reached.[244] The goal is finally attained, at least for the time being, though further hopes may be projected beyond it.

It has been noted that Aeschylus' conception of Zeus resembles that of Heraclitus. When Aeschylus speaks of "Zeus, whoever he may be,"[245] we are reminded of the words of Heraclitus: "The one wise thing will not and will be called by the name of Zeus" (32). As Walther Kraus writes, this is not what men call their god, yet it is what they sense when they name him.[246] "God is day-night, winter-summer, war-peace, satiety-hunger," writes Heraclitus (67). Similarly Aeschylus writes, "Zeus is the air, Zeus is the earth, Zeus is the sky. Zeus is all things and what lies beyond them." Zeus has two aspects, of which men often see only the one, because they construe for themselves a false, one-sided, "private" image of him.[247] In reality both aspects are visible. There is of course at least one remaining difference: in the *Oresteia* the regime of Zeus undergoes a change, and (more important) in the *Prometheus* it is not old and new simultaneously, but first the one and then the other. Yet even the bold perspective of this play, according to which the rule of Zeus only gradually becomes moderate and just, is presumably no more than a device to combine the experience of change with the belief in a just and lasting order: either change belongs to a remote epoch or it is an interruption.[248] This means that change is haphazard.

We later encounter an analogous view in Herodotus. As far as we can tell, his ability to trace a sequence of events spanning many generations and involving many historical agents was linked with a conviction that whatever happens is governed by an underlying law. This law ensures that the political world as a whole remains constant: no power rules everyone or forever; whoever rises is destined to fall. This conviction no doubt conditioned Herodotus' skill as a historiographer and was at the same time conditioned by it; such mutual conditioning, together with the concomitant detachment of his approach to history,[249] was probably a vital factor in the emergence of historiography. Time was the dimension in which changelessness constantly reasserted itself in the midst of change: just as day alternated with night and summer with winter, so too domination alternated with subjection.[250] This metaphysical certainty produced a tolerance to contingency that made it possible for historical events and sequences of events to be observed realistically.

Aeschylus too had a clear perception of the profound factional divisions of his age and all the changes that were taking place in it. This was because they not only did not contradict the imperative of the mean, but actually supplied fresh arguments in its favor. The fact that Aeschylus had such a clear understanding of the political (in the modern sense)[251] was due to his faith in the just order, a faith that was grounded in religious realism.

The political synthesis of oppositions within the *polis* and the philosophical synthesis of oppositions within the cosmos were thus matched by the synthesis of historical change within the concept of a changeless order that manifested itself in countless individual changes. All this was governed by one idea—the idea of a great and all-pervasive law that was not concentrated in specific authorities, but operated through all authorities. In the absence of primary institutions and strong monarchical authority, this idea gave the Greeks the orientation and the certainty they needed, enabling them to conceive an order that transcended all authorities.

The consequence was the development of nomology, which paved the way to democracy. What now emerged was something of immense consequence for world history—a power of reasoning that could comprehend the whole of an order yet not necessarily seek to dominate it, and could take up the cause of the oppressed or defeated (at least insofar as they might prove dangerous) in the interest of the whole.

The ideal corresponded in all essentials to reality. There was little long-term change—far too little for it to be recognized as such (if one disregards the doctrines of the emergence of culture, which in any case related to the past). Moreover, the universal concentration of energy and interest on the political was a further impediment to developments in other areas of life and to the growth of a "processual dynamism" in them. The outcome was not a new fluidity in conditions and characters, but rather a new solidity. Dependency on processes was, it seemed, being overcome. Society took control of the civic order and brought it "into the midst" of the citizens.[252]

A political identity took shape. Politics became the concern of the citizens, and likewise the concerns of the citizens became politics. The problems of the civic communities were transferred to that area in which citizens met and treated with one another as citizens. No great comprehensive process of change emerged, such as we witness in modern times— no "progress," no claim (familiar to us from different philosophies of history) that the whole of the future is prefigured by certain groups in present society,[253] no division between church and state or between state and society (which might have generated claims and expectations that made it possible to conceive a totally different order unparalleled in previous experience).

This meant that the citizens were unable to politicize those of their interests that belonged to quite different spheres. There were none of the countless hopes or possibilities of relief that now originate in other areas and can either exacerbate political conflicts (if certain groups are oppressed in the name of a better future) or alleviate them (if certain groups are deflected from pursuing their aims or place their hopes in a future reconciliation). Nor was there anything resembling the modern state, which is able to assert its authority in so many matters outside the political sphere. Hence there was no illusion of a future end to politics.

Instead, the citizens politicized themselves. What we observe is not a society engaging in politics in order to realize objectives that belong to other areas, but a civic community asserting its identity as a political unit. The political sphere thus became a comprehensive whole that had no significant competition to contend with from any other quarter and was charged, moreover, with extraordinary energy. On the one hand the content of politics was limited; on the other it became possible, for the first time in world history, for politics to embrace the whole political order. The moment in which all this was consummated supplies the concrete situation of the *Oresteia*.

The Culmination and Turning Point of the History of Political Thought

The *Oresteia* marks the culmination of archaic political thinking, a culmination that would have been unattainable had such thinking not been able to draw renewed strength from the "modern" consciousness of human abilities. It also marks a turning point. For the first time, the center of the political order was at issue. Yet a compromise between the contending forces could be attained only by political means, since there was no way of defusing the situation outside the political sphere. Compromise had to be sought through a middle course, by involving all the parties. Victory had to go to the *polis* as a whole; in other words, there had to be a reconciliation, initiated by the victors (represented in the drama by the wise daughter of Zeus). At the same time there had to be a new form of association and dissociation. One could, of course, hope to educate the contending forces to accept this middle course, to draw them into a new comprehensive conception of the *polis*, but there was no question of their changing their nature or becoming superannuated. The old had to be accommodated, just as it was, in the new order. Given the contemporary situation, in which the whole of the civic order was being politicized, this inevitably produced a tendency to conservatism, which was nevertheless largely realistic and favored a political solution.[254]

On the other hand, the political problems of the classical period were already recognized in all essentials: stalemates resulting from excessively partisan attitudes, decisions that bordered on the absurd, the tendency of the new forces to go on acting in accordance with the old rules (with the result that the old one-sided attitudes were perpetuated in new conflicts of a fundamental nature), the haphazard and unsystematic way in which change was brought about. Men already realized how difficult it was to make judgments and to orient themselves against the new horizon of political possibilities (not necessarily of politics as such, which for the most part were not concerned with the order of the *polis*).

There is good reason to believe that the transition to democracy in Attica was never perceived as clearly as it was by Aeschylus. At least we have no other document that evinces such a clear appreciation of what was taking place. The moment was propitious. Only around the year 460 could the struggle for control of the city be understood as a conflict between the old and the new (even if this was not how it started). There had previously been no conflicts about government,[255] and later conflicts did not center upon differences between the old and the new (except when both sides invoked the *patrios politeia*). It was probably only at this moment, when nomistic determinism gave way to cratistic disposal, that a clear perception of the divisions within the body politic could produce such a clear appreciation of the change that was taking place.

In the drama, the move from the "processual" to the "political" is reflected not only by the transition from self-perpetuating feuding to formal litigation, but also by the dramatist's interpretation of the succession of divine dynasties (hitherto understood in mythical terms) as a conflict concerning the political order.[256] The *Eumenides* finally signals a "new relationship between man and god. Man is thrown upon his own resources; he sees with his own eyes, and judges according to his own lights; he can no longer, like Orestes, adhere blindly to the pronouncement of the god, but must decide for himself how to act."[257] This is the independence that came with the emergence of the political and was realized primarily through politicization. "And yet it is the goddess who places [man] in this position of freedom and danger."[258] This points to the fact—taken for granted by Aeschylus but not immediately obvious to us—that democracy had its origin in theological politics. What Aeschylus did not realize was that this kind of politics was coming to an end. The political order was being placed at the disposal of the citizens, with whom it was increasingly identified; whatever happened in the city was becoming commensurable with the citizens. The present permanence of the *polis*, which Aeschylus hoped was now established, would in future be matched by the permanent presence of the citizens.

According to Walter Benjamin the subject matter of Greek tragedy is myth;[259] in this respect it contrasts with baroque tragedy, whose subject matter is history. The dramatis personae owe their tragic position not to status (absolute monarchy) but to the place they occupy among the ancient heroes. In the baroque, the interest in the action of the sovereign, in the "art of government" (which we may equate with politics in the modern sense of the term) corresponds to the idea that the sovereign is the representative of history. Aeschylean tragedy, on the other hand, is concerned with the order that exists between and above the parts of the whole—in other words, with the political in the Greek sense. History as such has no representative—unless it is "Zeus, whoever he may be." The combination of heroic myth with theological speculation about the succession of divine dynasties is such that even change ultimately takes its place within a static scheme of things. In Greek tragedy, then, the subject matter is myth; in baroque tragedy the theme is "history": in the former the protagonists are the heroes of antiquity, in the latter sovereign princes; Greek tragedy is concerned with politics in the Greek sense, baroque tragedy with the "art of government"—politics in the modern sense. This comparison leads to a further juxtaposition: on the one hand we have the Greek concepts of *polis* and cosmos, on the other the modern concepts of the state and monotheism—on the one hand theological politics, on the other political theology.

It is to this wealth of meaning that Aeschylean tragedy owes its central role in Attic democracy, giving "integral expression to the religious, metaphysical, political, and economic tendencies of the age, an expression that cannot be restricted to any one of these fields." [260] Moreover, the recognition of the political depends essentially on the concrete political situation.

The Political Identity of the Athenians and the Workings of Periclean Democracy

I T IS CALLED government of the people [*demokratia*], because we live in consideration not of the few, but of the majority" (2.37.1). This, according to Thucydides, is how Pericles defined the Athenian constitution in his Funeral Oration. A little later, in his assessment of Pericles, he writes: "In name it was a government of the people, but in fact it was government by the first man" (2.65.9). Both statements are true, and the difference between them is not that the one relates to the theory and the other to the reality. Rather, the leadership of Pericles accorded with the will of the people, who enjoyed substantial participation in public affairs. It rested partly on the fact that it was he who had created, improved, and facilitated this participation. His leadership was deliberately limited to the broad lines of policy, for Pericles was generally careful to remain in the background.[1] This was no doubt essential to his power. Just as his power resulted from the "radicalization" of democracy, so it was one of the conditions of its preservation that Pericles allow the democratic institutions for the most part to work independently. The political course he set himself could after all be identified with the interest of the citizens at large, their long-term interest in Athenian power and greatness. Admittedly their understanding of this interest may at times have differed from his, and conflicts arose in which the first man had to assert his authority. Nor can we entirely dismiss the suspicion that the granting of substantial popular participation and the admission of the "common man" to various offices (the number of which had been deliberately increased), to membership on the Council and the people's court, was designed partly to create a false impression: if the citizens felt that policy was made by them, it was all the easier for Pericles to direct it. At all events, if an individual was possessed of great superiority, democracy afforded him a good prospect of occupying a prominent position.[2]

Moreover, if the interests of the first man had to coincide largely with those of the people, and if the middle and especially the lower ranks of society had a powerful and practical role to play in politics, these conditions ensured that in large measure they lived "in consideration of the majority." We must give a brief account of how this was achieved. First we have to bring together a number of factors relating to the concept of political identity. For Attic democracy in the fifth century was shaped and sustained by a particular structure of affiliations, which must have largely determined the self-image, the will, and the needs of the citizens. We must then briefly consider the workings of Attic democracy and try to understand how far and in what areas broad sections of the body politic were able to promote their interests through political action.

Identity is not confined to individuals: it exists also in societies,[3] representing as it were a nucleus in the social field that somehow tries to ensure that a society remains essentially true to itself. It generates autonomous processes in which certain attitudes, expectations, and values are reproduced and consolidated in further expectations, so that they become independent of the presence of whatever motives originally prompted them. In this way a power center is institutionalized that not only transcends all personal opinions and feelings of obligation, but actually produces and perpetuates them.

"Only among us," says Pericles in his Funeral Oration, "is a man who takes no part [in political affairs] called, not a quiet citizen, but a bad citizen" (2.40.2). This was meant to describe the very special conditions that obtained in contemporary Athens, but at the same time it is a clear indication of the social pressure that was brought to bear upon the citizens—and subsequently internalized—to ensure that they took an active part in politics.

The identity of a society is rooted in various aspects of reality. It depends on the different ways in which its members "relate to one another and activate and support one another in the pursuit of common objectives."[4] Ample opportunities and incentives for this were provided by the city's politics and military enterprises.

It is worth remarking here that the identity of societies may comprehend a variety of affiliations. Its individual members have affiliations deriving not only from society as a whole, but also from the various circles to which they belong—narrow circles such as house, family, and neighborhood, and wider ones represented by shared religious beliefs and philosophical attitudes, or connected with their role in the work process or their adherence to a political ideology. In a pluralist society[5] this can lead to a multiplicity of affiliations based on class, religion, and party, and these may be embraced by a national identity.

The identity of the Athenians was determined by the fact that the only significant affiliation that transcended the narrow ties of house and neighborhood was their political affiliation, that is, their affiliation to the *polis*. This had been so ever since Cleisthenes institutionalized a solidarity that united broad sections of the citizenry. In his day, however, the circle of those who were able to feel a strong sense of citizenship was much more restricted; matters pertaining to politics were far fewer, and political activity accordingly more limited, than they were after the Persian Wars, and especially after the reforms of Ephialtes and Pericles.

It is of course true that the identity of the Athenians rested on common religious observances,[6] but these were themselves politicized, religion being essentially an affair of the *polis*. The subdivisions within the body politic, though also cult communities, were first and foremost parts of the *polis*. This was true especially of those created by Cleisthenes. The *phylai*, for instance, were systematically designed to serve the interests of the city as a whole, by creating closer ties of solidarity, conducive to the optimal realization of citizenship. Moreover, no significant solidarity could arise from shared work. The political affiliation of the citizens was thus immune to competition from other affiliations—at least among the mass of the people (the picture was somewhat different among the nobility). The social identity of the Athenian *polis* was thus wholly and exclusively political, and so we may properly speak of a political identity.

It is important to stress that this conclusion does not proceed from an idealizing view of Attic society. We have no reason to believe that the Athenians were peculiarly virtuous, unselfish, or worthy of emulation. Nor need we assume that their lives were dominated more by Homeric epics, temples, and festivals than by bread and work. Quite the contrary: it must be presumed that they suffered great hardship and oppression in the archaic period and that their concerns were extremely basic; without this presumption no understanding is possible. It so happened, however, that in the special circumstances of early Greek history, broad sections of the population were given the chance—indeed, presented with the challenge—to find relief from many of their hardships by political means. Only when they were able to transfer their communal problems to the political sphere did they succeed in fully overcoming the crisis of the archaic period. There is no denying that they did succeed, and this had enormous consequences for world history that only modern political theorists have found it possible to underrate. Nor can it be denied that their behavior as citizens was just as "human, all too human" as anyone else's, though of course it was dictated by the possibilities and constraints that attached to their particular institutions.

This identity was informed only partly by "values." For the most part it resulted from certain social and political configurations affording scope for action, from political thought, and so on. It did of course go on to evolve its own values, but, as we have said, it was shaped by a wide range of factors, in particular by the actual situations which determined what interests were paramount at a given time, which resulted from the perception of these interests, and in which the political identity of the Athenians constantly reproduced itself.[7]

Here it should be added, in order to avoid misunderstanding, that this political identity was particularly marked among the broad mass of the people and affected very many members of Athenian society, though by no means all. The majority may have taken only a casual interest in political affairs, but a relatively large number were sufficiently committed and carried sufficient weight to determine the complexion of the whole; among these were nobles and more well-to-do citizens who applied *political* (that is, civic) criteria and set themselves their own objectives.

The concept of identity is invoked here in an attempt to understand a state of affairs that is little short of astonishing. How did such a relatively large number of citizens come to devote so much time, thought, and energy to politics, always acting in concert and not asserting themselves conspicuously as individuals?[8] One can suggest a number of motives: they may have been concerned with legal security or attracted by the prestige that attached to involvement in public affairs (a motive taken over from the nobility). At the practical level, participation in politics was facilitated by the defrayment of expenses. Moreover, political life in fifth-century Athens offered many sources of personal fulfillment—successes; booty; ownership of land; public esteem (even for the common man); wide experience; pride in the greatness, beauty, and fame of the city; the excitement of being at the center of political and commercial activity; and all the prestige that one enjoyed among the Athenians (and as an Athenian among other Greeks) through being an official, a member of the Council or the Assembly or the people's court.[9] Yet the defrayment of expenses—which, apart from military pay, was the only regular emolument to be derived from politics—was not enough to make politics a gainful occupation.[10] Before the end of the fifth century there was no compensation whatever for attendance at the numerous assemblies.[11] Moreover, domestic concerns such as the economic problems of artisans and tradesmen were not generally a matter for politics. Politics really became a matter of economic interest to the individual only at times of food shortage or when public revenues and land were distributed.

Without going into detail, one may say that a surprisingly large number of Athenians neglected their domestic interests to a quite surprising extent in order to play their part as citizens. And whatever motives may be suggested to account for this, they cannot adequately explain why so many citizens were regularly prepared to engage in such activity; the true explanation must lie in the permanent power center in which such motives, along with various other factors, were institutionalized,[12] namely political identity. For many citizens their commitment to politics, entered into for particular reasons, must have proved so compelling—and fulfilling—that politics became a way of life. They discovered their identity in politics and found "self-realization" in political action.[13]

This was closely linked with the fact that to the Greeks "the men were the *polis*."[14] The city was grounded in its citizens, not in an autonomous state apparatus. The citizens constituted the state. Hence the task of educating one another and the coming generation to the ideals of the *polis* was placed "in the midst" of them; in other words, it depended very largely on their practical collaboration. It was not without reason that political theory was later to associate each constitution with a particular type of person and particular virtues—so great was the effect of the constitution, especially in a democracy.[15]

Again we must recall the initial situation as it was in Cleisthenes' day. The separate interests generated by the needs and concerns of ordinary citizens and directed to the community at large could coalesce in a powerful common interest only within an abstract framework of common citizenship. Whatever solidarity existed among those who sought to secure justice and order by involving themselves in politics could hardly proceed from their immediate personal interests; it had to proceed from the general interest of the entire community. Only in this way could the general civic interest gain strength. This meant that the overwhelming majority of the members of the *polis,* having previously known one another as neighbors, farmers, artisans, and fellow worshipers, now rediscovered one another as citizens[16] and began to act, treat, and collaborate on a new level, with a new mutual respect and new mutual expectations. Obviously they did not become indifferent to their families, livelihoods, possessions, and work. In the lives and thinking of those who are not professional politicians, the political is just one interest among several and inevitably plays a subsidiary role. Yet for many citizens of Athens this subsidiary role came to be their chief role outside the house or family, the only significant one they played, even if its importance varied according to the stage on which they played it—in the local community or in the *polis* as a whole. Hence, for many ambitious and influential members of Athenian society, citizenship became all-important, challenging them to devote a significant proportion of their time, thought, and activity to "political" affairs. Their involvement in politics changed their lives. And this led to mutual commitment. Isonomies and democracies made demands on the citizens that could be met only by a transformation of social identity. The political form of the city-state (in the Greek sense of "political") was not to be had at a lower price.

What happened to a lesser extent, and with less intensity, at the time of

Cleisthenes was basically much more surprising than the wide-ranging civic activity that took place in the years following the Persian Wars.

A rift opened up between the social order and the political order.[17] While society, with all its inequalities, remained essentially unchanged, there grew up beside it, separated from it and secured by its own institutions, the new political sphere in which all were equal. There were, it is true, important respects in which personal inequalities continued to make themselves felt in politics, but these were now largely canceled out by the fact that the middle strata of society (and later the lower strata) combined to throw their weight into the political scale, so establishing new criteria and actually taking the nobles into their service. This must have been matched by a powerful group consciousness, a special awareness of belonging to the broad mass of the citizenry. The "common people," as a body, gained significantly in influence, with the result that the personal superiority of individual nobles no longer carried as much weight.

The consciousness of political equality[18] was all the stronger because one could not reckon with other forms of equality, and because it related to the public domain, involvement in which traditionally carried special prestige. The aristocratic system of values, which set great store by public service, remained paramount, for although the *demos* established new political norms that were at variance with the practices of the nobility, it was unable to supply a substantially different ethic[19] (unlike the bourgeoisie in modern times). To all intents and purposes everyone endorsed the same values, dictated for the most part by the aristocracy (and the Homeric epics) and merely modified by the new criteria adopted by the people. Thus no complete alternative to the nobility had arisen. The *demos,* in making the public sphere its own, took over certain aristocratic ideals. To be a citizen was thus a source of pride, contrasting with the unprestigious banausic existence one had to make do with at home.

Hence, in the later Athenian democracy of the *thetes,* "Cousin Glover"[20] was simply a citizen and not also a glover. This demonstrates the profound significance for the Greeks of the separation of house and *polis.* Hannah Arendt speaks of "the gulf that the ancients had to cross daily to transcend the narrow realm of the household and 'rise' into the realm of politics." Here the citizen was among equals.[21] This was the realm of freedom. The realm of necessity (*ananke*), on the other hand, was looked upon with comparative disdain, because it was merely necessary.[22] One had to be concerned about one's domestic affairs, as Pericles (according to Thucydides) later stressed—perhaps because they were being increasingly neglected.[23] The Attic *demos* was undoubtedly hardworking. The citizens could not afford the contempt for work that one finds later in affluent circles (expressed, for instance, by Aristotle), but it inspired no specially high regard, and it was scarcely a source of pride. It would hardly have occurred to them to bring any preoccupations connected with work into the sphere of politics. The *thetes*, who owed their enhanced status solely to their political and military services to the city, were probably particularly reticent in this regard and took exceptional pride in their identity as citizens.[24] Consequently, a good deal of the work was done by noncitizens and slaves. There was a clear dividing line between work and politics, between the house and the *polis*. One's civic affiliation thus remained the only important one beyond the home. Herein lies, to a large extent, the explanatory potential of the concept of identity.

Political identity was realized in its purest form in fifth-century Athens. Many citizens spent a good deal of their lives performing their duties as citizens (and soldiers). This was possible only because much of the economic activity in Athens was carried on by metics and slaves, and because they—and above all the cities allied to Athens—provided the economic basis capable of sustaining this kind of civic life.[25]

The concept of political identity thus seems appropriate when it comes to defining the position that citizenship occupied within the contemporary structure of affiliations. Identity is admittedly not something that can survive and assert itself against all interests, needs, and exigencies, but it is a particularly basic, significant, and central element in the makeup of both individuals and societies, and it can develop a certain resistance even to interests and needs, and to some extent determine their importance.

Politics were thus so much a way of life that they could not become a means to an end and cater to interests pertaining to other spheres. M. I. Finley cannot be right when he says that most of the citizens saw political rights simply as a means to attain nonpolitical objectives.[26] Applying Max Weber's simple and largely apposite distinction,[27] we may say that the Athenians, as *homines politici*, were less concerned with their economic needs and hardships than we *homines oeconomici*. They did not enter politics from the outside, as it were, in order to promote their extrapolitical interests. They had quite different priorities, for, given a structure of affiliations whose center of gravity is political, economic affairs are differently "embedded" within the whole complex of what is considered important. This emerges quite clearly from the fact that basic material needs did not inevitably relegate the citizen of Periclean Athens to the sphere of the economy (the house). In a restricted and subsidiary but far from unimportant sense, the "system of needs" can also be politicized, as Karl Marx recognized.[28]

In this connection it is noteworthy that the old connection between the right of citizenship and landowner or hoplite status seems to have corresponded to a close link between civic virtue, practical political activity, and—as an expression of this—entitlement to expenses for performing public functions.[29]

Because the citizens came to see themselves exclusively as citizens, they could not form political pressure groups. This determined the content of politics, which was about the concerns of the citizens *qua* citizens and the concerns of the city, about relations on the political plane and relations between the various city-states. This is what determined internal and external policy, as well as numerous wars.

It also determined the basic concepts of democracy, namely liberty and equality, both of which were understood in a wholly political sense. Only from Sicily, at a later period, do we hear of a demand that, for the sake of liberty, there should be equality of land tenure. Equality generally meant equality of political rights and no more; but that, as we have said, was already a great deal. And freedom was understood above all as the freedom of equals, precisely because the freedom of these equals was guaranteed only when they were strongly involved in the civic presence,[30] because there were no "rights to freedom" such as can be "granted" by a state (in the modern sense of the term) and guaranteed by special organs. The freedom "to live as one chose" went beyond this and impinged upon social life.

Democratic institutions were tailored precisely to the body politic, which was in a very real sense identical with the *polis*. The central organ of the constitution[31] was the Assembly. This met as frequently and as regularly as possible, and was expected to decide as many issues as possible. Some matters, however, also had to be deliberated in advance. Moreover, supervision of the whole executive was supposed to be exercised by as many citizens as possible, but it could scarcely be exercised by all. To this end it was necessary to employ the Council of 500, which was a relatively large body. However, as a means of ensuring that it had as few rights of its own as possible and that its membership did not include the most influential and experienced men (who might have outshone the others and so to some extent monopolized politics), its members were chosen by lot (at least from the middle of the fifth century onward),[32] expenses were paid so that all the citizens could take part,[33] and it was laid down that no one might serve for more than two terms. The Council was reconstituted annually, which meant that in the course of one generation at least 7,500 citizens had to serve on it; this amounted to between one-fifth and one quarter of the body politic. The Council was thus little more than a committee of the whole citizen body, chosen at random. A tenth of the councillors, the so-called *prytaneis*, had to be in constant attendance in the marketplace; some even had to sleep there.[34] This is a particularly striking illustration of the very concrete sense in which the "civic presence" was understood. Other committees of the citizens were the jury courts, which also had a large membership and often made political decisions. As Karl Reinhardt puts it, the citizenry of Attica was "notionally . . . a substance of which any quantity, taken at random, would exhibit the same character and mixture as the whole."[35] This result too was achieved by lot. The offices were strictly accountable. They were filled partly by election and partly by lot. Those requiring special expertise (and in some cases wealth), namely the military and financial offices, were elective, and thus were controlled by a small group of political experts. Beside them was a multiplicity of minor offices all of which were filled by lot. They were held by a number of men, and their competences were often closely linked. They afforded scope for frequent political activity of many kinds. The rotation of officers was so rapid that one could speak of the citizens' alternately ruling and being ruled.[36] Euripides saw this as an essential feature of democracy: "The people rules by turns, year by year." This concept of rule or government must be understood in a quite concrete sense, for rulers and ruled were equals.[37]

In the famous constitutional debate reported by Herodotus, it is urged in favor of democracy that "it fills offices by lot and holds the government to account, and all decisions are made by the generality" (3.80.6). Its advocate recommends its introduction "because in the majority is the whole." "Majority" here implies the greatest number, that is, the majority of the people. The argument for democracy thus relies on the principle that the majority is a valid representation of the whole. This is the most important consequence to be drawn from what was known at the time as "placing power or rule in the midst of the citizens." Euripides says on one occasion that power or government has been "socialized" (*dedemeutai kratos*). In this democratic order, all citizens had equal shares and worked for themselves. This too has to be understood in a very concrete sense. Under democracy the citizens were their own masters (*autokratores*).[38] The restriction of power achieved in this way finds its clearest expression in the distinction that was made between power within a framework of equality and laws, and power deriving from and directed toward the unbridled quest for advantage.[39] The former might be called "political" power (in the Greek sense of the term).

It will be asked how these democracies functioned, how power was actually exercised and political aims determined, and what role the ordinary citizen really played in politics. Did the democratic constitution really ensure that the broad mass of the people had a decisive voice and could successfully assert its interests? How is this to be seen in practical terms? How does it square, for instance, with the fact that until the Peloponnesian War all the leading politicians belonged to the nobility, and that even after it many still did?

At least one thing can be asserted with confidence: care was obviously taken—through the widespread use of selection by lot (and partly through the arrangements that were made for the few real elections),[40] through the annual change in the membership of the Council, and through the all-important role of the frequently convened Assembly—that a relatively large number of citizens had a share in important political functions and decisions. It is more difficult to see how these could be mobilized. At all events, it would hardly be wrong to say that the prime qualification for access to these centers of decision making was the ability to carry conviction in public speaking and debate. Personal authority and a gift for rhetoric were crucially important. There was thus only limited scope for the formation of aristocratic factions, with their specific form of power organization. However, it could probably not be ruled out: politicians belonging to the nobility probably supported one another, and important magnates doubtless relied upon a circle of friends and entered into alliances with them.[41] Moreover, in the early days of democracy aristocratic norms and objectives continued to hold good. Nonetheless, whatever power the nobles possessed was relatively insignificant. On the whole, retinues no longer counted for much, the citizens having largely freed themselves from their ties with the nobility. Insofar as such ties still existed, they were probably of subsidiary or merely temporary importance, relating to matters that in the main affected only individuals or small groups, as well as to money and connections of all kinds.[42] A group of politicians might occasionally manage, by mobilizing their supporters and campaigning assiduously, to influence the composition and decisions of the Assembly, or even of the Council of 500.[43] This was characteristic of the way in which at that time—and in the classical world generally—party divisions were determined by the issues under consideration. Hence, such situations could hardly be the rule or continue for very long. Factions could not become the constitutive factors in policymaking and settle affairs between themselves.

The formation of factions was probably also discouraged by ostracism, by which unduly powerful politicians could be forced into exile for ten years.[44] It is true that, in most of the cases we know of, ostracism was used to decide between two politicians who were contending for ascendancy. One of them had to go; this would probably be the weaker, but the measure of such weakness was the people's favor. It is quite possible—and in the early period even probable—that this led to the fall of politicians whose power derived from extraneous sources such as retinues and personal influence. At all events, ostracism as a rule placed permanent restrictions on the exploitation of such sources of power.

However, if power was only marginally dependent on factions and retinues, this did not mean that it was constantly shifting, according to who happened to be able to sway the Assembly. Rather, there was, as we have said, the possibility of winning a special authority with the people. In a certain sense, democracy tended to make it easy for individual personalities to win significant influence. Contentious cases were then resolved by ostracism. Yet there was not always somebody waiting in the wings who had sufficient authority to lead the people. Thucydides records that after the death of Pericles several men tried in vain to become first man,[45] seeking to outdo one another in suing for the people's favor.

It is therefore likely that many of the Assembly's decisions were actually reached on the basis of argument and counterargument and the judgment of large numbers of citizens. It is true that there was never more than a fraction of the citizenry present. The quorum laid down for certain issues was 6,000, that is, at most one-fifth of those entitled to attend.[46] There was therefore some room for manipulation. Certainly the agenda, and the alternatives put to the members, were determined largely by politicians. And many of the citizens who voted were often in no position to know precisely what was at issue, what some of the resolutions meant, and what consequences they entailed. It would be wrong, however, to underrate the competence of the citizens of Attica.[47] Moreover, all parts of the territory were optimally represented, at least in the Council; and it was the Council that decided upon the order of business and deliberated on most matters in advance.[48]

Above all, thanks especially to Athenian democracy, a field of political possibilities and alternatives had taken shape in several stages, and within this field it was fairly easy to see what would be beneficial or detrimental to Athens (and to the broad mass of the citizens, who decided matters in case of doubt). We have the testimony of Pseudo-Xenophon, one of the sharpest and most clear-sighted critics of Athenian democracy, that it knew exactly what it was about and how to take appropriate action. The alternatives were relatively concrete—opposing Persia and later Sparta, controlling the Delian League, and establishing the requisite conditions for such control. Here, as in internal politics, what was at issue was the clear and palpable interest of the *demos* as a whole and a relatively large proportion of its members. Control over the city's allies, together with the existence and extensive use of the navy, was clearly of benefit to the lowest class, and the farmers do not appear, on the whole, to have taken a different view of the city's advantage.[49] There thus arose a clear frame of reference against which to measure any proposals that were put forward. It was more important that a common cause and a broad line of policy should emerge than that the ordinary citizens should in every case know precisely what was in train. From this starting point it is possible to reconstruct the outlines of Athenian politics and the manner in which policy was formulated.

Herodotus and Aristotle both draw attention to one respect in which democracies differ from oligarchies: democracies have no party divisions, or rather no factional divisions, the *demos* being politically single-minded.[50] This observation applied generally to fifth-century Athens—in a positive sense as regards the weighty questions bearing upon central interests, and in a negative sense, inasmuch as institutional arrangements and the distribution of power made it impossible for factions to acquire a decisive role at the center of politics. In oligarchies, by contrast, the formation of factions was a normal phenomenon, leading to recurrent dangers, namely when the defeated party mobilized the *demos* in support of its cause.[51]

As a result of the popular harmony that prevailed in a democracy the nobles and the rich were inevitably in the minority when their interests were at variance with those of the *demos*. This in time led to doubts about democratic equality, according to which the individual citizens were equal, but "the rich" and "the poor" were not.[52] Distinctions were made between different kinds of equality (leading to ideas of a mixed constitution and later to the theory of arithmetical or geometrical equality).[53] The nobles and the rich could assert the special interests they shared only by overturning the democracies and curtailing civil rights.[54] This was not, however, an aim that could be pursued all the time, and so it was usually the interests of the nobles and the rich that were restricted. Yet individual members of these classes had a good chance of seeing their interests realized. Athens, being a world power, offered its nobles quite extraordinary prospects of wealth, distinction, and self-realization in the political, diplomatic, and military fields. With the politically ambitious, such possibilities far outweighed any disadvantages they suffered under the rules of the democratic game. And as Pseudo-Xenophon testifies, few complaints were raised about the Athenian constitution until the beginning of the Peloponnesian War.

If doubts arose about what the fundamental interests of the people required in a given situation, or about particular aspects of the more or less important problems that had to be settled, the case could be argued out in the Assembly. The answers were in the ballot box, as it were. There might be a number of conflicting proposals and sharp disagreements between aristocratic politicians.

It was therefore on the one hand not troublesome, and on the other hand vitally important, that, within the political field, basic lines of policy should be subject to the popular will and matters of contention settled by a vote in the Assembly. The specific structure of affiliations ensured that the civic community identified itself with its political order and the policy it endorsed; there was at least a fairly close approximation between those who made the policy and those whom it affected; the citizens were variously committed and could repeatedly make their views heard as each new situation arose (instead of casting their vote—casting away their vote—once every few years). Within this framework, equal rights were guaranteed in the private and the public sphere.

In Euripides' *Suppliant Women* Theseus explains to the people of Attica that in a democracy even the poor man has an equal share. He refers to the laws as the guarantors of equal justice, to the common man's chance of winning a suit against a prominent opponent, and to the free and equal right of all to speak and put motions in the Assembly. Finally he asks: "What greater equality is there than this in any city?"[55]

A precondition for politics of this kind was that everything outside the political sphere be exempt from political control. The economy and society, educational conditions and religion, were quite simply given; they could not be subject to decision making and so provide a focus for the formation of factions. And they remained for the most part unchanged. It followed that all generally relevant change, that is, change that was of importance to everybody, was political. Any change that was perceived as such arose from political actions and events, and from the consequences that flowed from them. It was in politics that the most important and noteworthy events originated; politics was the source of change—and change was essentially political. The history of events and the history of change were virtually coterminous. Whatever happened was determined by action or contingency.

The civic *presence* in the city had a temporal counterpart in a special kind of *present*. Whereas in modern history specialization in synchrony goes hand in hand with specialization in diachrony (and the simultaneous presence of the nonsimultaneous), fifth-century Greece was hardly acquainted with either. A political identity in which "civic" affiliation had no competitors precluded any relativization of the political within a wider context, any relativization of the citizens in time. Politics could not be functionalized and so become a means to an end as it can today[56]—the end being to transform us all into what some would like to imagine we are to become—a New Humanity, for instance. The citizens of Athens wanted above all to be citizens,[57] to be themselves and to work for themselves. Because they politicized themselves, there could be no politicizing of their nonpolitical interests. Besides the *polis* virtually nothing existed except the house.[58]

The Greeks thus knew nothing of state and society as the two are distinguished today—on the one hand the state, originally a separate entity with a great potential for action and change, far exceeding the bounds of the political; on the other hand society, which, having at first been pushed aside by the state, became diversified in specialized activities in the most varied fields, giving birth in modern times to a great, all-embracing process of change, and then finally succeeded, by means of the secondary politicization of social issues, in making the state subservient to itself.[59]

The *polis*, by contrast, became identical with the civic community (the *politeia*).[60] And because the constitution was in all essentials equated with the civic community, *politeia* came to designate both, so that the two senses could not be separated.[61] The civic community *was* the constitution, in a way that it had never been before and has never been since. Aristotle could thus in all seriousness ask whether a *polis* remained the same if its *politeia* changed, say from democracy to aristocracy.[62] He concluded that it did not, since the *politeia* was not just the constitution of the state (which, being a legal person, did not change), but the civic community, and a change in this meant that one community was replaced by another.

Nor was there any overriding national identity such as has evolved in modern times, embracing both rich and poor and affording compensation for numerous inequalities. True, there was a strong sense of cohesion, uniting both high and low, especially in Athens—a proud awareness of belonging to the foremost city in Greece. Such a sense of belonging, in one form or another, is of course implicit in any political identity. The specific difference between the ancient world and the modern consists in the way such a sense of belonging arises. It may come from the practical experience of citizenship, of being a citizen with a voice in the city's affairs, or it may derive from a more abstract identification with lofty ideas and symbols. On the one hand it may be concentrated in the citizens; on the other hand the citizens may be absorbed—taken up, taken care of, taken over—in a national identity. It may give meaning to everyday life, or it may simply be a compensation for it. It is a question of the point at which we begin to feel the need for a "meaning"—of the extent to which we have to identify ourselves either with a whole that is constituted by ourselves and our like, or with "the divine plan," the nation's destiny, or some such.[63]

There is thus only a superficial resemblance between the social identity of Periclean Athens and modern national identity. What made the cohesion of the different classes in Athens so strong were the power and potential of the city, and all the attractiveness it had developed—partly at the expense of the rest of Greece. Athens was exceptional. This was still true in the fourth century, despite all the criticisms that were made of it, and despite the fact that the grandiose pretensions of political theory led some to find fault with democratic practice.[64]

The city that appears to have served as Aristotle's model of extreme democracy only partly bears out his thesis regarding the partisan nature of constitutions. Hence his thesis appears highly theoretical. The Athenian constitution can be understood only if due attention is paid to the content of the city's politics, and above all to its external policy.

Nevertheless, Aristotle's definition remains correct, inasmuch as under democracy "the free and the poor who form the majority hold supreme power" and exercise it for their own ends.[65] Of course, in a city with the potential of Athens, this seldom happened with the degree of partisanship—that is, to the detriment of the rich—that is implied by the definition. But rich and poor, nobles and commoners, were on an equal footing politically, and this had important practical consequences.

The scope of such politics may to us seem very limited, and we may think political equality unimportant. We may be tempted, on grounds of mere numbers, to call the extreme democracy of Athens an oligarchy, since the free and equal who enjoyed full political rights were a small minority beside metics, slaves, and women.[66] But this is to apply modern criteria. In a society that has a political identity, political rights are of central importance, and to this extent the nobles, the rich, and the "educated"—especially outside Athens, and especially if they viewed the matter from a theoretical angle—may have felt themselves to be at a disadvantage and considered the constitution unjust because they were obliged to share political rights and honors with the poor. These rights and honors meant just as much to the poor.[67] Moreover, what is decisively important for world history is the fact that, for the first time ever, the community became a living entity in which, if only among the ranks of the citizens, men "lived in consideration of the greater number"—of the governed, regardless of rank, possessions, and education.

PART III

The Political and Time:
The Political World of the Greeks
and Its Capacity for Change

SEVEN

Changing Politicosocial Concepts
in the Fifth Century B.C.

THERE ARE PERIODS when the entire stock of concepts in the politicosocial field changes.[1] Central concepts are newly formed; important inherited terms undergo a fundamental change of meaning or become peripheral; the whole conceptual world is transformed and takes on new functions—and then, with minor modifications, remains unchanged for a considerable time.

One such period that has recently received a good deal of attention is the "saddle period," as Reinhart Koselleck calls it, between 1750 and 1850. According to Koselleck's hypothesis, which has in all essentials been confirmed, the transformation of the world of concepts that took place during that period can be reduced to a few common denominators.[2]

The place occupied by concepts in society and time is subject to change. The meanings of important concepts become "temporalized" (or are invested with a temporal dimension from the beginning), with the result that the world of concepts incorporates factors involving expectations: the concepts serve to set targets for substantial sections of the population, and their content remains to be realized, if at all, in the future. Any experiential content is thus either reduced or eliminated; the result is a high degree of abstraction, of remoteness from current reality (or, more precisely, from what has been experienced in the past and can still be experienced in the present). The concepts can thus be charged with ideological elements. This is only one aspect of the process; the other is that the concepts acquire a new function in the political struggle, namely that of "organizing the socially dislocated masses under new watchwords."[3] To this extent the concepts not only are indicators of change, but become to a large extent factors of change. As a result, the circle of those who command the language of politicosocial concepts is widened and "democratized"; social barriers inhibiting the use of the concepts are swept away.

Different sides lay claim to the same concepts, which then become controversial and are used in a partisan fashion.

The principal and essentially new element in this transformation of the world of politicosocial concepts is seen by Koselleck as the "relinking of historicophilosophical designs for the future (and the concepts associated with them) with political planning and its control of language. The relation between concept and content is reversed; the content shifts in favor of linguistic anticipations that are designed to shape the future."[4] A rift appears between the space of experience and the horizon of expectation; one becomes aware of the new reality of a comprehensive change running in a certain direction, not least in the world of concepts. Concepts, then, played an important part in the historical process that was in train during the period in question.

Koselleck uses the term *temporalization* to characterize this transformation of the world of concepts. Within the category of temporalization almost everything—the particular species of abstraction, the way the concepts come to function as target concepts and grouping factors, the generation of expectations and all that goes with it—can be reduced to one common denominator. A *new* epoch was beginning, defined by Koselleck with the aid of the categories "experience" and "expectation." "The modern age," he says, "can be viewed as a new epoch only from the point at which expectations became dissociated from all previous experiences" or "detached themselves from everything that all previous experiences had to offer."[5]

If we are to try to distinguish precisely between temporalization and other kinds of change that occur in the world of concepts, other categories seem to be required: temporalization indicates a new species of universally relevant change. Staying for the time being with a rough thesis, we may characterize the perception of history in different periods by stating the kinds of change they envisage. More precisely, we have to ask, first, to what extent changes in general conditions are expected, whom they affect, and in what areas they occur. In this regard there are significant differences between periods. This leads on to a second question: in what configurations are these changes effected? Third, one might ask about the form of participation, the degree of interest in history, and the degree of inner dependence on it.

On the basis of these categories, temporalization can be understood not only as a comprehensive transformation of all the social conditions of human life, going far beyond all previous experience, but also as something that happens within the framework of a broadly based *autonomous process*.[6] The "objective" nature of this process—the confidence with which it is expected (and which is reflected in the world of concepts)—arises from the fact that the motive forces behind it are widely distributed throughout the most diverse areas of society: we could not properly speak of progress unless this progress were taking place in all centers of production and all channels of trade, in the scholar's study, in lecture rooms and schoolrooms, among editors and readers, on the stage and among audiences, among parents and teachers, in societies and states. For unless this were so it would be unable to generate substantial improvements in prosperity, enlightenment, morality, and law. Thus, if change is perceived by those who cause it as something taking place outside them, as it were, and almost without their agency—if it is perceived as the great spontaneous, self-accelerating[7] movement of "the times"—it then appears to be "objectivized." It is therefore an essential feature of temporalization that it gives rise to concepts that "themselves articulate historical time—such concepts as 'development,' endless 'progress,' 'history pure and simple' . . . 'revolution,'" all of which are "characterized by temporal definitions involving clusters of processual meanings and experiences."[8]

These observations on the period 1750–1850 prompt us to ask about other changes in the world of politicosocial concepts. One does not have to be an ancient historian to be reminded of the fifth century B.C., that other period of history in which broad sections of society succeeded in winning and institutionalizing an authoritative share in political government, and which witnessed that other (sophistical) movement of enlightenment (though in this case *after* the emergence of democracy). The fifth century saw a transformation of the world of concepts that, in its rapidity, profundity, and momentum, approximates most closely, though on a far more modest scale, that which occurred in the "saddle period."

Is it possible, for this early period too, to discern a common denominator that will enable us to understand the direction of change and the manner in which it took place? Are there common features in the history of the various concepts? And to what extent can an investigation of these concepts provide an insight into fifth-century politicosocial change as a whole? The questions used by Reinhart Koselleck to supply parameters for the change that took place between 1750 and 1850 are in the main sufficiently formal to serve as a starting point for the fifth century too. They will later be supplemented by a few further questions.

In studying the politicosocial concepts of the fifth century B.C. we must begin with the various constitutional concepts—in the first place "democracy," "oligarchy," "monarchy," and "tyranny," and then "aristocracy." We must also consider "eunomy" and "isonomy," as well as *politeia* (in the sense that is later rendered by *res publica*) and *dynasteia*. In addition to these, important roles were played by such concepts as "freedom" and "equality," "law" and "right," "citizen" and "civic community" (which was synonymous with "constitution," since *politeia* denoted both). On the periphery there are a few other terms that must be mentioned, such as "ancestral constitution," "harmony," "mixture," "rule," and "power." We will not, at present, consider the terms used to designate change itself.

Conceptual change in the fifth century is clearest in the case of the new constitutional terms. The central constitutional concept of the sixth century was eunomy[9]—a just order enjoined by the gods that embraced a certain social and economic structure and political institutions corresponding to them, the whole being governed by ethical principles. To put it more precisely: men arrived at the conviction that such a just order existed; it might or might not be realized in the *poleis,* and so they spoke of either "eunomy" or "dysnomy." It could of course be modified, but no fundamentally different order of a positive kind existed beside it. Eunomy and dysnomy were constitutional concepts only in a very general sense, namely insofar as they designated the proper or improper condition of the *polis.* That this was understood as such an all-embracing set of conditions had to do with contemporary problems. For it was hardly possible to describe the *polis* in any other terms. The way in which power was distributed among the nobles, for instance, with government in the hands of either a whole class or a tyrant, was just one question among several. For many nobles it was a central question, but we may presume that it had no great bearing on the general assessment of a constitution. This assessment (which seems to have been concentrated in a group of political thinkers operating throughout the whole of Greece)[10] focused on the many burning problems of the age. It embraced the whole condition of the *poleis,* including many factors that could not be attributed to the distribution of power within the nobility. Not even the mode of government and jurisdiction was simply a function of the distribution of power. Many political thinkers may in principle have been opposed to tyranny, but this did not mean that it would have been possible, on the basis of the distribution of power, to make a fundamental distinction between different constitutions and thus—in whatever sense—between the conditions obtaining in the different *poleis.*

The concept of eunomy was a great discovery. It was arrived at by extrapolation from the status quo; one examined this in order to identify what was wrong with it and then sought to reconstruct an earlier state that contrasted with the unsatisfactory present. This procedure supplied a criterion for the restoration of the *polis* order and created the conviction that such a restoration was feasible. The very fact that the goal was conceived in conservative terms, as something preexistent or given, made possible an entirely new mode of action: the *polis* could be placed at the disposition of individuals who were endowed with superior insight and authority.[11]

There were many problems to contend with—the hardship suffered by large sections of the population and the causes underlying it, namely the breakdown of the trust that had once existed between nobles and people, the position of superiority occupied by the former, the wide discrepancy between the opportunities for action available to powerful magnates and the weakness of the institutional obstacles to such action. As long as there was no possibility of creating authorities that were capable of keeping the nobles in check, it was immensely difficult to contain injustice and violent factional conflict; given the powerful array of contemporary forces, the divinely enjoined order could hardly be established from a "third position" that had no powerful authority behind it. Hence it was probably only in exceptional circumstances that conditions in the civic communities could be set to rights by direct action.[12] The outcome was usually tyranny, which first suppressed the crisis and then often removed its economic causes. The consolidation that was achieved in this way produced a state of affairs in which democracy became possible, for only when the economic problems were solved could the citizens concentrate their interest on the political sphere. This was the immediate precondition that had to be met if the people were to acquire an authoritative role in the *polis*. Once the rule of the people was established, it was possible to consider different constitutional alternatives. This outcome is reflected in the history of concepts.

The use of constitutional concepts, as it evolved in the fifth century, was determined by democracy, and we can best understand how they were used by considering first the term *demokratia* itself.

From the 460s onward we have securely datable evidence that the orders of different city-states could be distinguished by the criterion of rule.[13] Aeschylus, in a tragedy that was probably performed in 463, proudly reminded the inhabitants of Attica that the people there were the rulers.[14] Presumably such self-confidence was relatively new or had only recently become potent and widespread.

Although the sources available to us are so meager as to preclude any *testimonia e silentio*, there are nevertheless arguments to support such a late dating for the concept of democracy. It must have been exceedingly difficult to recognize such a thing as the rule of the people in the context of a type of thinking that was directed primarily to *nomos* and existing rights within a largely inherited order. The Greeks, after all, had no Greeks as forerunners, from whom they could have learned that such a thing was possible. It was a great advance when the *demos*—that is, the Assembly or the crowd of common citizens who attended it—was granted *arche* or *kratos* (or *archein* or *kratein*)—that is, functions or positions that had formerly been seen as pertaining wholly to individuals. What made it more difficult was the fact that for a long time—until fairly late in the fifth century—politics remained in the hands of the nobles. At first only the rules of the game had changed: the status of the citizens at large had been enhanced, and they had begun to make the nobles dependent on them. It cannot therefore be fortuitous that the order which rested upon wide sections of the community was at first understood as *isonomia* (at the end of the sixth century or the beginning of the fifth). The idea of equality, that is, equality of political rights among the citizens, was grafted onto the old ideal of eunomy.[15] This entailed a redefinition of the relations that existed between the citizens *qua* citizens and hence of the rights that obtained under the existing order. The question of who should govern this order was not, I suspect, one that sprang immediately to mind. And the early terminology for democracy or its pre-forms (besides *isonomia* we find *demos, isegoria,* and *isokratia*) provides clear evidence that it was at first conceived simply as a modification of the inherited order through the introduction of new elements.[16]

The notion of isonomy clearly was directed against the arbitrary rule of tyrants (and no doubt also that of narrow aristocratic cliques), not against the nobles in general, who continued to hold offices and therefore to govern. This is confirmed by the fact that the notion continued to function as a yardstick against which constitutions were measured.[17] For this was obviously an echo of the original notion that equality was equivalent to justice and a guarantee against arbitrary rule. To this extent isonomy remained a modification of the old ideal of eunomy; it was still seen against the background of the one *nomos* and nomistic thinking.[18] In many places, however, equality had consequences for the structure of government, and so *isonomia* provided a link with the new constitutional concepts: its opponents could denounce the "order of equality" as the rule of the "impetuous populace," yet at the same time the people could take a conscious pride in being their own rulers.[19] This led eventually to an entirely new insight: that the people too could hold the reins of government. Hence in time it became possible for the constitutional concepts of *demokratia* and *oligarchia* to develop, and also for *monarchia* and *tyrannis* to be understood as types of constitution.

It is perhaps debatable whether the first occurrence of these terms necessarily indicates a recognition of the fact that they denote three different forms of constitution. It would depend on the extent to which the Greeks had evolved a general concept of "constitution" that could subsume these terms, and this is impossible to determine. We may presume that they were already familiar with the constitutional notions of *kosmos* and *katastasis*,[20] but these were no more than general designations for "order" or "institution."

At all events, the new concepts indicate that fundamental distinctions were beginning to be made between different *polis* orders on the basis of specific forms of government. And it must have become clear fairly soon that the decisive feature of any constitution was the form of government it involved. We can therefore see here at least the results of a twofold process: on the one hand, what can be loosely called a constitution—namely, what constitutes the order of the *polis*—is now centered on the political element or, more precisely, on the political organization of the community and the relations obtaining among the citizens as citizens. Here too isonomy supplied the transitional link in that it too had related chiefly to a political state of affairs. On the other hand, the constitution—in this restricted sense—was placed at the disposition of the citizens (depending on the prevailing power relationships). This change was in large measure determined by democracy and the process by which it emerged. For under democracy the broad mass of the people acquired an entirely new interest in the political sphere. As soon as they had the opportunity to participate in political affairs it became a matter of great importance to them whether or not they actually did so. As a result the question of the political order took on a new complexion for their opponents too, in both theory and practice. Confronted by the rise of democracies, the nobles realized that if their rule was to be preserved it would have to be institutionally reconstituted.[21] It is to this extreme form of aristocratic rule that the term *oligarchia* is applied in the first phase of its history.

It is true that oligarchies do not seem at first to have played a prominent part in the consciousness of the emergent democracies. It is interesting to note that until well into the period of the Peloponnesian War the new constitution was regularly contrasted with tyranny, as though it were a matter of a simple dichotomy.[22] This may reflect the difficulty of providing a legitimation for popular rule, which could carry most conviction if the alternative was tyranny. Above all, democracy was apparently not clearly delimited against the many forms of what might be called moderate oligarchic rule; these seem to have counted as democracies. It may be that they included some element of popular participation, or that the ruling classes could not be identified with a narrow aristocracy, so that they appeared democratic or caused the boundaries of democracy to seem somewhat fluid. How high up the social scale (democratic) equality began was at first far from clear. Even ruling minorities—provided that they were not too narrow—may have made a convincing show of equality, as understood in the context of isonomy. As late as 430 it proved difficult to convince the Athenian nobles that their rule could not be restored by means of slight modifications to Athenian democracy, which had meanwhile become quite radical.[23] At first, then, the notion of democracy embraced a relatively broad spectrum of constitutional forms. Nevertheless, at an early date (ca. 470) we begin to find statements to the effect that there are three kinds of constitution. This idea recurs in the constitutional debate reported by Herodotus, where oligarchy is clearly understood as government by a small circle of nobles.[24]

In this debate it is clearly stated that democracy means placing the political order at the free disposition of the people: "When the people rules, it fills offices by lot, holds the government to account, and brings all matters that are to be resolved before the commonalty" (3.80.6). Only through secondary (that is, intentionally established) institutions could the broad masses acquire—and retain—an effective voice in the community. For the first time in world history it was recognized that the constitution was a matter of institutions. The problems facing the *polis* could scarcely have been overcome in the archaic period—or at least doing so would have involved the most wide-ranging endeavors in many different areas, requiring long and patient effort and very gradual change. These problems could now be mastered through the authoritative intervention of the dominant force in the community.

In the constitutional debate, democracy is recommended with the words *en gar to pollo eni ta panta*. This lapidary formulation has been variously rendered, but nowhere have I found the most obvious translation, namely the literal one: "For in the majority is the whole." "Majority" implies the "greater number," that is, the majority of the *plethos*. This sentence elucidates the preceding one, which advocates giving up monarchy and "exalting the whole" (*to plethos aeksein*). This elucidation therefore supports the principle that the majority is authoritative within the whole.[25] This is the most important institutional consequence of what is expressed in the following words at the start of the voting: one should place affairs (*ta pragmata*) in the midst (*es meson*) of the people.[26] This is also an indirect way of saying that the body politic must have disposal over the civic order. It is taken for granted that it will act in accordance with the "ancestral law."

It emerges, then, that the broad constitutional notions that had formerly been current—embracing economic, social, ethical, and political affairs and grounded in religion and metaphysics—were superseded in the fifth century by others that centered narrowly upon the public order and relations among the citizens as citizens *(politai)*—in other words, on what we would call the political sphere, which now assumed an almost autonomous role within the total structure of social relations. This presupposed that a whole range of extrapolitical conditions, especially the consolidation of the economy, had already been met. Attention now turned to the problem of living together as citizens, ensuring civil rights and popular participation in politics, and safeguarding political equality. This meant creating a new plane of civic life on which the citizens would in future come together and treat with one another, understand one another, call upon one another's good offices, and take concerted action.[27] This plane accommodated an artificially established order that was quite distinct from the social order and consolidated itself in its own institutions. The result was that the ordinary citizens, though powerless as individuals, could join forces to assert their interests. Politics had formerly been the preserve of a small minority, with the majority virtually at its mercy; but now, after a period of transition, this new political order came to occupy a central position in the life of the *polis*.[28] As soon as the problem of the *polis* had shifted to this plane it became a matter for secondary institutions. The constitution (in this restricted sense) could now be framed.

In the democracies, the emergence of this central political plane and the establishment of popular control over constitutional institutions were two sides of the same coin: the new institutions could be built only on the foundation of an existing civic solidarity and a readiness for political commitment, and these could become enduring and effective only in secondary institutions. Now that the new political order was being realized, in varying measure, in the different democracies of Greece, the other constitutions were also to a large extent being placed on a new footing.

The hiving off of the political sphere and the powerful development it now underwent are reflected in the transformation of constitutional concepts. There was a general trend toward *politicization*. This at least is how I would wish to state my thesis. In using this term, however, we incur certain difficulties associated with the subsequent semantic history of the word *political*. For this reason—and for the sake of general clarity—it must be explained more precisely. Politicization is to be understood as a change toward the comprehension of a social world that was constituted by the citizens acting in their capacity as citizens and, to this extent, became political.

Characteristic of the political plane was the vast expenditure of time and energy it required.[29] The Greek democracies could arise only as direct democracies.[30] Whatever "state" organization they created was a matter for the citizens—to a degree that has never been matched since. Up to now they had been first and foremost nobles, farmers or artisans, members of religious communities, heads of families, kinsmen, masters or retainers, townsmen or villagers, while their role as citizens, which involved certain political and military rights and duties, had been negligible. Yet now this role became all-important and was taken so seriously that one can actually speak of a change in the structure of social affiliations. In this way a specifically Greek identity arose—the political identity of the *poleis*. The citizens were expected to act as citizens *(politai)*, that is, "politically" (in the Greek sense of the word), and this expectation was now given institutional form. Political identity was not exposed to any significant competition from group loyalties based on religion, common economic interests, the individual's place in the work process, or the like—from those spheres, in other words, that in modern times are represented by church or society and set themselves up in opposition to the state (though today they may undergo secondary politicization and so be brought into the ambit of politics). Such interests either did not exist or could not give rise to significant groupings.

In devoting themselves to political life, broad sections of the citizenry in the Greek democracies saw themselves primarily as participants in the governance of the *polis*. The *polis* rested essentially on their interests in order and justice, which formed the basis of their solidarity. These had once been only secondary, indirect interests; but now, with the new *polis* in the making, they became central and pervasive. The absence of any powerful organs of state, which had been a precondition for the emergence of Greek democracy, now made it imperative—if the *polis* was to be reconstituted—that the common interest of its citizens engender a solidarity that would ultimately harden into a common identity. In this sense the *polis* and the *politai* could continue to interact. Insofar as the citizens pursued economic interests in politics, these arose from their desire, as partners in the city, to assure themselves of the necessities of life, of remuneration for their political activity, and of a share in the city's revenues; they did not derive from any economic position or activity that might have been of prime concern to them.[31]

Hence, for a fairly large number of citizens, politics became a consuming interest that made up much of the content of their lives: they did not make their originally nonpolitical interests into the content of politics. There was a strict separation between the *polis*, the area in which they acted jointly as citizens, and the house, between politics and the "realm of necessity" *(anankaia)*.

To this extent, the whole of society became politicized, and this process is reflected in the history of concepts—principally, though not exclusively, in the democracies. Another aspect of the same process is that the *polis* could increasingly assert itself against the pretensions of the magnates. Aeschylus depicts this in the *Oresteia*, with the "politicizing" of Zeus.

In this context, "politicization" has a quite precise sense: it denotes the central tendency of a collective change that made politics the very stuff of civic life—in which the community found its collective identity in voting and decision making, in performing public functions, and in supervising and enforcing public order; in which the political was hived off as an autonomous area, not of a society that set its own values against the state, but of a community that was literally identified with the state, a community in which the constitution (in the political sense of the word) was placed at the disposition of the citizens. This specific kind of politicization took place in the isonomies and democracies; at the same time it reshaped men's understanding of the whole politicosocial world. What this implied will presently become clear from a discussion of other concepts, and finally from some notable aspects of men's perception of the events and changes taking place in their society.

First, however, we must say a little more about the term *politicization*. We have said that it denotes a move toward the understanding of a world that was constituted by the citizens among themselves. This tendency is specifically Greek.[32] The word does of course have a general, nonspecific application, denoting a tendency toward a separate political order that is to a limited degree detached from the totality of social relations, to constitutionalism in the modern sense of the word, that is, to gaining control over constitutional affairs in general. In this sense one might use *politicization* to designate part of the process of change that took place in society and the world of politicosocial concepts during the period 1750–1850. This later phase of politicization seems at times to approximate quite closely what we find in the Greek *polis*. In the French Revolution, for example, people were expected not only to regard one another as citizens, but to address one another as such. However, "during the Revolution no work is done."[33] What was to some extent the rule among the Greeks, was the exception in modern history; this later politicization was on the whole just one element of temporalization.[34] When Koselleck uses the term, it denotes not a transformation of social reality reflected in the world of concepts, but the tendency to use concepts in an increasingly partisan manner. There is no escaping the difficulties that arise from the polysemy of the term. But it is indispensable precisely when we are dealing with the Greeks, and there can be no harm in reemphasizing the Greek origins of the word—as both *signifiant* and *signifié*.

Politicization may be observed in the constitutional terms of the earlier period too. These continued in use and later became watchwords (as indeed they had been earlier). They were regarded as general criteria by which constitutions and political intentions could be measured. This presumably gave them a certain propaganda value. Yet at the same time they related to the new constitutions.[35]

The same tendency can be seen very clearly with the terms for freedom and equality. We may surmise that, in the archaic period, "equality" within the *polis* referred above all to the claim that there was an essential similarity among the citizens.[36] The word used to denote this similarity was *homoios*. In the fifth century the central terms are *isos* and its derivatives.[37] *Homoios* and *isos* belong to the same semantic field, in the sense of "equal" and "similar." However, *homoios* tends to denote a qualitative likeness or similarity, while *isos* relates rather to quantitative similarity; it describes something that can be equally distributed, like shares in booty. An illustration of the joint use of the terms is the statement, reported by Herodotus, that citizens who are *homoioi* should not be ruled, but granted *isonomia*.[38]

If the citizens claimed to be *homoioi*, this meant that they wanted to be considered alike in their capacity as citizens, despite any differences between them. This was a way of differentiating themselves from others. But it also implied an internal postulate, a relativization of existing social and economic disparities, as well disparities of education and power. One thought of equality of military obligations, and of certain political consequences associated with it. There might also be a demand for the redistribution of land in equal shares *(isomoiria)*.[39] In most cases this amounted in fact only to modifications within a class structure—even in Sparta, where equality in education and life-style was enforced, though politics continued to be controlled by the kings and the nobles, and the popular assembly had little say. Gregory Vlastos says that "its members, though social 'peers' *(homoioi)* were not political equals."[40] Political equality could in fact become effective only when wide sections of the citizenry broke with the nobility to such an extent that they were able to take over the *polis*—when they had so far detached themselves from the social order as to be able to build up, in opposition to it, a political sphere in which different power relationships prevailed—that is, only after the end of the sixth century. Only when the citizens had gained political equality could they go beyond their claim to be *homoioi* and really become equals, at least in certain respects.

Equality, which then found expression in the term *isonomia* and the associated terms *isokratia* and *isegoria*,[41] related essentially to what was allotted to the citizens—their shares in the community and in political rights (which in principle could be equal, like shares in booty).[42] It was equality in politics and in nothing else. In many respects it was little more than a claim, for the nobles naturally remained superior in education, influence, and bearing. Nevertheless, the repeated assertion that under democracy everyone "had the same" was not wrong. Euripides makes Theseus tell the people of Attica expressly that in a democracy even the poor man has the same *(cho penes echon ison)*.[43] He makes him point to the written laws as guarantees of equal rights and to the common man's chance of winning a lawsuit against a prominent citizen; finally he makes him ask: "What greater equality than this is there in any city?" *(ti touton est' isaiteron polei;)*.[44] What was guaranteed was in fact not personal equality and equality of power, but effectively equal rights in the private and public domain. And equality of suffrage,[45] of access to respected public functions,[46] of the right to speak and submit motions, counted as equality even if in the exercise of this equality one had in some respects to concede precedence to prominent magnates. One can presumably even say that the more the individual became aware of the power and respect he enjoyed, the more he regarded it as equality, in view of his "natural" inequality vis-à-vis the more prominent citizens.[47] And whatever he lacked as an individual was possessed by the *demos* as a whole. When Euripides makes Theseus say: "The people rules by turns, year by year,"[48] this is to be taken in a quite concrete sense: those who rule are the "same citizens" (and hence "equal citizens"). Finally it should be remembered that, given the political identity of *polis* society, equality of political rights ensured that the citizens were equal in the area of their central affiliation. Thus the Athenians, while "socially" far less equal than the Spartans, attained equality in the one respect that was for them decisive. Moreover, when an oligarchic pamphlet dating from about 430 states that in Athens the poor and the *demos* actually have more than the nobles and the rich, this is not untrue. For in many respects the nobles had no chance to assert themselves.[49]

Equality was all the more important because it was seen as closely linked with justice. This was due to the fact that, as Jacob Burckhardt puts it, the Greeks "were never able to combine civic equality with political inequality. The poor man, in order to protect himself against injustice, had to be able to vote and become a judge or magistrate."[50] On the other hand, the idea of equality was closely associated with that of concord *(homonoia)*.[51]

As equality had been largely transferred to the political sphere and could be created by institutional means, the closely related concept of freedom *(eleutheria)* underwent a similar development.[52] The noun is first attested in Pindar. In the archaic period the adjective *eleutheros* had been used chiefly to describe the status of a freeman. Then, after the experience of tyranny, under which farmers were enslaved for debt and their land mortgaged, the meaning of the word was extended. "Freedom" came to be seen as a vital component of eunomy.[53] This idea was reinforced when the Greeks confronted the Persians and became conscious of freedom as their essential attribute and the cause of their victory. Yet for all that they remained bound to traditional law. Freedom, rather like Roman *libertas,* had at first fairly concrete links with quite specific conditions and rights,[54] and the rulers had to be relied on to guarantee it.

This changed when freedom came to be linked with equality. In the isonomies and democracies, equality was a safeguard against tyranny and arbitrary rule, and hence a guarantee of freedom. Once the equality of the citizens was established, an entirely new kind of freedom arose—the freedom to participate in politics, and in particular to vote; to this was later added the freedom to live as one chose. "The city is free, the people rules," we read in Euripides.[55] Freedom was thus realized in popular rule. Thenceforth it was agreed that freedom (together with equality) was the central feature of democracy.

Being linked to equality, freedom was detached from the horizon of nomistic thinking, where it could denote only concrete rights within an inherited order. Through this break with tradition, the concept became sufficiently abstract to embrace the citizens' freedom in political life (and subsequently in private life). Whether freedom had previously been demanded of tyrants can be neither proved nor disproved. In the fifth century, at all events, the concept underwent a distinct shift in the direction of politicization. It no longer had the merely negative sense of freedom from domination by others, but a positive one too: it denoted a primarily political status and primarily political opportunities for all;[56] freedom could of course be ensured only in the political sphere, but here it became a simple matter of institutions (until the private freedom to live as one chose came to the fore).

A particularly characteristic variety of politicization can be observed in connection with terms denoting power.[57] In the fifth century we encounter the notion that in isonomies or democracies it was possible to overcome the old problem of the arbitrary use of power. "Power has been given to the people" (dedemeutai kratos), we read in Euripides.[58] The institutionally regulated alternation of rulers and ruled, we are told, is the best means to guarantee the restriction of power. Both Thucydides and Anonymous Iamblichi criticize "rule that is sought out of a desire for power and honor," which is contrasted with the power that is exercised within the bounds of law and justice.[59] The latter is clearly political power, power that is compatible with the polis. Aristotle later distinguishes between politike arche (political rule/power/government—the Greeks made no clear distinction) and despoteia.[60] The new form of "government that is not domination" could thus be described by the term politikos, which related to the whole body politic and the basic equality of the citizens.[61] This was admittedly not reflected in a change in the actual designations for "power." Neither in the fifth nor in the fourth century did the Greeks succeed in inventing a concept of power that was divorced from persons and situations. They were unable to view the political from the outside or to ignore the huge disparities in the exercise of power; they therefore could not conceive of power in terms sufficiently abstract for it to be understood as an agent in its own right.

The new and extremely important term for "constitution," namely politeia, appears later than the conceptual changes considered so far. It is derived from polites, the old term for one who is affiliated to the polis, that is, the city, or, more precisely, for those of its inhabitants who possessed full civil rights (as distinct from metics and slaves). Politeia first occurs in the last book of Herodotus (9.34.1) as a term for citizenship.[62] It is a fairly logical development that it should later come to denote the civil community and public life. What is harder to explain is why it assumed the sense of "constitution"; indeed, at first—and not infrequently later—it is used in such a way that it can also be translated by "citizenry." The first occurrence of the word in which we find an indication of the new sense dates from around 430.[63] There was no dearth of terms to designate the institutional order in the cities; examples are *katastasis, kosmos,* and probably *taxis;* these continued to be used, becoming uncommon only with Plato and Aristotle.[64]

The coining of this new constitutional term and its continued currency must have stemmed from the realization that the city's constitution was determined not so much by its institutional organization as by the composition and restriction of the body politic. This came at the time when the first component of the term *democracy, demos,* began to be problematical.[65] In the history of concepts this is indicated by a remarkable shift in constitutional terminology, which is expressly attested in Aristotle (*Politics* 1297b24). The wide range of constitutions that were designated as isonomies or democracies, by contrast with "tyranny," was divided up about the year 430 into "democracies" and "oligarchies," each term now being understood in a new sense. Up to this date *oligarchia* is attested only as a designation for a narrow oligarchy; now it applies also to constitutions in which power is held by a bare majority or a substantial minority. Thucydides, for instance, speaks of *oligarchia isonomos.*[66] The real antithesis of democracy is now no longer tyranny, but oligarchy. At the same time some difficulty arose over the precise definition of constitutional types, and this led to numerous modifications of the existing terminology.

We cannot go into the reasons for this development—for instance, the part played by conflicts and by external and internal politics (and the links between them). At all events, the yardstick for democracy was from now on supplied by Athenian democracy, which included the *thetes.* In Athens and elsewhere it was realized that the most effective way to alter a constitution was to enlarge or restrict the number of those enjoying full civil rights, or to link certain political rights to a property qualification or some other requirement.[67] In this way it was possible to ensure that the decisive question was "Who are the citizens?" From then on the determination and apportionment of political rights became highly problematical. The right of citizenship was understood essentially as a right of access to political functions, and this proved controversial. Pursuing this idea, one might conclude that the constitution was not merely a question of institutions, but could also be strongly influenced by the sociological composition of the *polis.* Thus, during the Peloponnesian War, the "middle" strata *(mesoi)* came to enjoy high esteem.[68] At this point the institutionalizing competence of the Greeks reached its limit. In the end everything came down to sociology, and this seemed all the more painful, as it was widely felt that the democracies had failed. However, we do not know to what extent men became conscious of this in the fifth century. There were, for instance, numerous attempts, involving much institutional effort, to design a "middle constitution" or restore the *patrios politeia*.[69] But this amounted to no more than a switch to the opposite direction, as it were; the institutional possibilities were considered to be if anything more important than before. But we cannot pursue these conceptual changes, which in the long run were relatively unimportant.

It should at all events have become clear that the trend toward politicization reached its culmination in the term *politeia,* which established the identity of the *polis* with the civic community. It expresses the concept of the "political community" and at the same time reflects the fact that this was subject to institutional disposal. Hence it is perhaps not surprising that this general constitutional term superseded those that had prevailed hitherto, chiefly as designations for "institution" and "order." From later political writings, especially Aristotle's *Politics,* it becomes evident that the sense of *politeia* generally lies midway between "civic community" and "constitution," and that it means substantially more than the old terms denoting "order."[70]

Aristotle uses *politeia* in various senses. In a formal sense it means "constitution" in general, but can also be restricted to the four nonmonarchical constitutions or to the narrower circle of the three good constitutions, which includes monarchy; finally it denotes the good form of democracy. The concept thus had a normative component, not only in the sense of "civic community" but also in that of "legitimate order."[71] When *politeia* was originally coined it applied to democracies, either to characterize them as the *polis* of the whole community or to denote a democracy that accorded equal rights not to the very humblest citizens, but only to those who "deserved" to possess civil rights. The ambiguity of *polites,* fluctuating as it did between "citizen" and "active citizen,"[72] meant that *politeia* was a particularly problematical but convenient term. The democrats always laid claim to it as a designation for their order.[73] Fourth-century theory—and probably already fifth-century rhetorical practice—restricted the term to good democracy, clearly because this form of government was thought to give proper representation to the community as a whole. This presupposed certain mixtures: Aristotle speaks of a mixture of democracy and oligarchy that is so good that it can be taken for the one or the other.[74] Underlying these ideas is the complex of problems connected with the notion of equality (problems that began to proliferate from the last third of the fifth century onward) and the related problems regarding the totality within which all were deemed equal. Curious formulations in Thucydides and Aristotle indicate that the equality of the parts of the *polis* was played off against the equality of the citizens: when the new conflicts (from the last third of the fifth century onward) inevitably put the nobles and the rich at a disadvantage because of their numerical inferiority, there could be no equality.[75] Certain remedies might be devised; the best solution seems to have been to place the real power in the hands of the *mesoi*, the hoplites, who were deemed to be the ideal citizens. In this way the term *politeia* would have acquired a special sense. We may surmise that these claims were grafted onto the concept of *politeia*. This became the most appropriate term once *demos* and *demokratia* had become semantically restricted. This too demonstrates the centrality of the concept and the high degree of politicization it underwent.

At about the time when the term *politeia* came into use, another term was coined to designate narrow oligarchies, namely *dynasteia* (literally "lordship," from *dynastes*, "lord"). The starting point was the identity existing between those who possessed political rights—that is, the rulers—and the *polis*.[76] Taken together with the older word *basileia*, these terms formed a triad. Plato was later to speak of *stasioteia*, implying that most *poleis* were only "groupings," because in them one part ruled over the other.[77] Here again we are obviously dealing with the consequences of politicization.

Finally, the transformation of the field of legal concepts points in the same direction. We will confine our attention to the most interesting strand, the history of the term *nomos*. This seems originally to have meant "recognized rules," "modes of living and behavior," as well as "order of life" or (in a very general sense) "legal order."[78] In Hesiod, where the word is first encountered, it has both senses, and perhaps also the wide semantic spread from individual customs to a general order.[79] It continues to have this wide semantic range (even today, after frequent revivals). What remains constant is that *nomos* denotes "what(ever) is customary for a group of living creatures."[80]

The word obviously related to the objective world, to concrete conditions, though it allowed of certain distinctions between the real and the ideal, and these became increasingly common. It is far more comprehensive than the grand legal term *dike*,[81] and consequently much better suited to designate the totality of a given order, as well as its individual aspects; for this reason it was the obvious word to express the notion of a binding order within the complex of *polis* life. Hence the earliest constitutional terms, *eunomia* and *dysnomia*, were derived from *nomos* in order to describe conditions in which *nomos* was realized either well or badly. *Nomos* embraces "law" (in the widest sense), "custom," "usage," and "tradition." Individual laws may be subsumed under *nomos* by being equated with tradition, but this was at first only a minor semantic component of the word.

Nomos, like Eunomy, was personified as a divinity, presumably in the Orphic circle. Pindar celebrates "Nomos, lord of all, of mortals and immortals." Heraclitus speaks of "divine Nomos" *(theios nomos)*, from whom all human *nomoi* draw sustenance. The imperious and all-embracing power of this divine order is the reason why the city must adhere to its *nomos*.[82]

These words of Heraclitus, from about 500 B.C., contain the first mention of the *nomos* of the *polis*, and this is placed in parallel with *xynon panton*, that which is common to all—that is, the concern of the whole city (doubtless in contradistinction to that of a tyrant). This is something new: on the one hand, what is customary in the various *poleis* takes on various forms because they have all developed differently and have different laws *(thesmoi)*; awareness of this fact was probably reinforced by the incipient interest in the *nomoi* of foreign peoples. On the other hand, the legal order of the isonomous cities was now acquiring increased importance, and this led in due course to a curious shift in the meaning of *nomos*.

Within this wide semantic field an entirely new sense developed during the fifth century: *nomos* came to mean "law" or "statute." This cannot have happened—as has recently been claimed[83]—through a deliberate act on the part of the Athenians at the time of Cleisthenes. Were this so we would have to suppose that a positively modern consciousness prevailed in Athens at that time—and there is not the slightest ground for such a supposition. It is clear that the new meaning evolved gradually, probably about the middle of the century.[84] We can discern roughly how this happened. In legal texts from Athens, as well as from other cities, we find a curious usage: one and the same law is designated on the one hand, in a formal sense, as a resolution of the legislative body *(psephisma, hados, thethmion)*, and on the other, with reference to its content, as *nomos* or *nomimon*.[85] This can be explained only by assuming that *nomos* meant a law that was valid irrespective of its source, in the sense of a "prescription" or "ordinance." The later statement that Nomos ordains what it is necessary to do and to leave undone[86] can apply to "usage" and "custom" as well as to "law." Obviously no distinction is being made between written and unwritten rules of conduct. What was resolved by the people was directly incorporated into the totality of the *nomoi*.

Given the word's original meaning, it seems to me unequivocal that *nomos*, in this new sense, related first to those laws that laid down what was to be done and left undone.[87] Subsequently the meaning was extended to laws or statutes in general.[88]

For with time *nomoi* increasingly came to mean "laws." In considering what was "binding," one now had to think above all of written laws enacted by the people. This went so far that other customs had to be very specifically distinguished from them by recourse to the term *agraphoi nomoi* (just as the laws of individual cities had to be distinguished from *ta koina ton Hellenon nomima*).[89] Alternatively, a formula such as *nomoi kai ethe* might be used to designate the whole of what had previously been covered by the one word *nomoi*. In this way *nomos* became a legal term, though its wider meaning remained and probably reinforced the binding nature of the laws. As the matters regulated by *nomos* became more and more subject to legislation, the semantic nucleus of the word shifted from the content to the formal aspect of the laws.[90]

The history of democracy played an important part in all this. To the Greeks it was a source of pride that Nomos held sway among them.[91] Whereas under a tyranny or a narrow oligarchy men were dependent upon the goodwill of the rulers, the isonomies were controlled by institutions; Nomos was universal and beyond the control of despots.[92] In a democracy, institutional control (which could also be exercised by *nomoi* in the old sense of the word)[93] gradually increased to the point where "written laws" guaranteed legal security and freedom and became a central feature of the constitution.[94] Before this could happen, however, the whole territory of what was susceptible of normative regulation had to be populated, as it were, by laws.

At the same time the possibility of arbitrary decision making arose;[95] hence there was presumably good reason not only to take institutional measures to prevent it,[96] but also to stress the distinction between *nomoi* and *psephismata*. Yet since Nomos was now subject to arbitrary disposal, the problem arose of setting something against it that was beyond such disposal, and for this and other reasons the relation between *nomos* and *physis* became a burning question.

The shift in the meaning of *nomos* reflects men's growing capacity to control their conditions of life, though it is impossible here to be more precise and devise formulations that might convey—within the horizon of "legal revolution" that has recently been opened up—the true extent of this capacity. Here it must suffice to point out that while in general the social and economic order could not be affected by political action, deep inroads could nevertheless be made, even within the limited contemporary framework, upon the lives of many people.[97] It was not for nothing that the age was full of violent upheavals and conflicts verging on civil war, and that countless citizens fled or were driven into exile.

In the concept of *nomos*, then, we see the interdependence—or rather the unity—of the trends that we have observed in the changing world of concepts: if this word, which originally had nothing to do with a decision or resolution,[98] came to denote a law or statute, it is clear that the realm of Nomos had become subject to political decision making. The significance of this at once becomes clear if one tries to imagine the Roman word *mos* supplanting *lex* in the same sense.[99]

Only when the nomistic basis of thought had been eroded by constitutional and legal organization could *nomos* come to designate a statute and so be transformed from a term expressing something given and preexistent (which could at most be supplemented by regulations) into one denoting a legal disposition.[100] The new constitutions having called the traditional order into question, the civic community was able, indeed obliged, to act in its legislative capacity and so become the real source of *nomos*. Law thus became a matter of institutions, and it was held that even arbitrary legislation could be prevented by establishing what Aristotle called a "rule of laws."[101] Everything in the political sphere was regulated by *nomoi* to such an extent that it was possible to decree that "the authorities shall not apply an unwritten law in a single case."[102]

Our thesis seems to be confirmed by everything we can observe of the changes undergone by the most important concepts during the fifth century: constitution, law, power, equality, freedom, the civic community, all of which are understood as political matters (in both the narrower and wider senses of the word), were susceptible of regulation by political action. Everything implied by these terms is detached from its religious, social, economic, and ethical associations and centered upon the political; everything is seen as capable of being changed or created according to human design. As a result, the terminology of constitutional affairs, equality, freedom, and law is restricted, while the scope for action is vastly enlarged. Constitutions (in the narrow sense) can be established through institutions. Wherever it is a question of institutions, the problem can be solved. This change can be traced in the history of the concepts we have discussed, but change itself does not figure in them. We must now ask how or to what extent change was understood, and how far its uniform tendency was matched by a unified general change.

It is clear that "politicization" was to the conceptual world of the fifth century what "temporalization" was to the period 1750–1850—the common denominator to which everything was reducible. And in the classical age the situation was presumably more clear-cut than in the modern period, when matters were complicated by the fact that certain important concepts underwent not only temporalization but also politicization. We shall presently have to consider what this means, and how these two categories can be related to each other. But first we must discuss certain special features of the change that took place in the ancient world of concepts, using Koselleck's categories as our point of departure.

Most of the concepts arose at about the same time as the realities to which they were meant to refer. The case of "eunomy," however, was somewhat different: the term was intended to denote the proper order of the *polis,* a norm that was thought to lie, as it were, behind the status quo, but at the time it obviously functioned as a target concept (like *dike*),[103] though the targets were near to hand and represented nothing new. Yet they remained generally unattainable. The demand for isonomy too must have been anticipated in some form; otherwise it would have been impossible to generate the broad solidarity that was an essential basis for the reforms of Cleisthenes.[104] One might of course wonder whether the notion of isonomy antedated—or was at least contemporaneous with—Cleisthenes' constitution, to which it was so well suited. In all probability, however, the coining of the cratistic constitutional terms (and the further shifts in the concepts of freedom, equality, and law) were actually prompted by experience of the new reality. One might argue that the *concept* of democracy must have played some part in the emergence of the *phenomenon* of democracy—or at least been contemporaneous with it—but this would be true only insofar as the rule of the people could not really be the rule of the people until it was understood as such. For, in the isonomies at least, the target of democracy could have been reached as soon as it was recognized. When once a right to participation had been won by broad sections of the body politic, it could not have failed to command a majority. Opponents could have thwarted this development only as long as the *demos* did not know the extent of its power and how to consolidate it as the basis of popular rule. Since the emergence of democracy was, as we have said, the starting point for the new understanding of the constitution, based on the criterion of governance, the same applies to "oligarchy" and "monarchy," and also (in a somewhat different way) to "freedom," "equality," and "law." In each of these new concepts, then, an existing state of affairs was recognized, brought into consciousness, formulated, and thereby substantially reinforced. This combined, for the *demos* at least, with a proud awareness of its own role in the governance of the *polis* and an ambition to go on playing it. Using Koselleck's terminology, we may say that the concepts we are dealing with were "experience-registering" rather than "experience-creating."[105] This is not true of the sentences that precede them, of the insights couched in these. On the whole this applies also to the new constitutional concepts based on identity. None of them aims beyond the present.

All remain highly concrete and empirical, encapsulating what was taking place and taking shape among the citizens. The degree of abstraction is slight. True, the constitutional concepts single out from a host of other factors the principle of the forms of rule that characterized them, and then the quite different principle of the identity of civic community and *polis*.[106] Yet they always remain tied to current reality and palpable facts. Admittedly the form of rule in question accorded a certain latitude to the ruling factor. The whole of the political sphere, together with numerous rights that had hitherto been assumed to belong to the nobles, may have been placed at the disposal of the people.[107] But this disposal was limited: it could not encroach upon the social and economic spheres, though it might affect them indirectly. It was only in the later schemes of constitutional theory that the social and economic orders ceased to be taken for granted and were reconstituted from a political viewpoint. However, such schemes aimed far beyond current realities and had hardly any practical effect. In short, the concepts were as abstract as the opposing factions, contemporary controversy, and the resultant knowledge permitted and required them to be. To put it another way: there was as much scope for abstraction as was compatible with political disposal and the political alternative. The alternative was the most fundamental that could face a body of citizens acting together as citizens: namely, whether the nobles or the people should rule—whether the governed should, *de jure et de facto,* have an authoritative voice in government. Whatever was created, disputed, or advocated within this sphere in which the citizens interrelated as citizens could be articulated and raised to the plane of lasting principles by the political concepts of the fifth century. The concepts thus detached themselves from numerous traditional connotations that had formerly been taken for granted, and were no longer tied to the apparently unambiguous meaning of surface phenomena. Yet they could not free themselves from the conditions prevailing outside the political sphere, from the possibilities and limitations that were directly entailed by these, and above all from the basic facts of social stratification, educational conditions, and economic structure. The concepts remained wholly concentrated on and bound up with the political.

This meant also that the Greeks were unable, in their shaping of concepts, to extrapolate from the action of individuals and communities. They could not, for instance, "subjectivize" concepts and view them as active entities generating their own effects (as we do when we speak of, say, "power" or "history," "democracy" or "capitalism").[108] There was obviously neither the wish nor the temptation to fictionalize politicosocial concepts in this way; such fictionalization can occur only after substantial exposure to the autonomous force of great impersonal processes.[109] This was hardly ever the case with the Greeks. The occasional exception proves the rule.[110] There was little occasion for such experience, on the one hand, because such processes were far less powerful in the Greek *poleis* than they are in modern societies, and, on the other, because the Greeks lacked the detachment that would have enabled them to see forces at work (in and behind the actions of the immediate agents) that could have been designated by abstract terms. This was a necessary consequence of their absorption in the political, and it was matched by the extraordinary degree to which events were commensurable with individuals and communities.[111] It was no doubt connected also—as both cause and effect—with the absence of temporalization. For any significant degree of subjectivization in the world of concepts seems to go hand in hand with temporalization. At all events there is good reason to presume that the recognition of autonomous processes—insofar as it becomes a dominant experience and goes beyond isolated observations—presupposes the crossing of a threshold into the realm of temporalization. Such subjectivization is a somewhat different phenomenon from the personification of concepts that we find in the archaic period (such as that of *eunomia*).[112] These still belong wholly within the nomistic horizon and relate to far more than the political order in the narrow sense of the word. They are not really subjectivized concepts, but rather subjects that are at the same time abstractions, or, more precisely, subjects that lose their subjectivity as they gain in abstraction.

All this was consonant with the fact that the concepts current in the fifth century did not open up new expectations for the future: they related primarily to what had already been achieved. Even where democracy developed further, as it did in Athens under Pericles, the possibility of such a development can hardly have been appreciated much before it happened. Only with time did the experience of numerous improvements give rise to the assumption that even better institutions could be found—not necessarily, of course, in terms of democratization, but generally, in terms of growing insight and opportunities for political achievement. [113] A remark made by Theramenes at the end of the century and reported by Xenophon has an unusually modern ring. He spoke of certain men who would not find democracy attractive *(kale)* until a share in it was given to the slaves and those who were so needy that they would betray the city for a drachma.[114] It is not clear whether the men in question derived this idea from the term *demokratia*. At all events, one cannot infer that they envisaged a trend toward further democratization. They simply had a certain view of democracy. Half of what they said did not relate to anything new, for in Athens the needy had long had a share in the city; and as for the other half, relating to the slaves, no one could seriously envisage its realization, even at some future date, as it would have been bound to be resisted, especially by the *demos*. Yet even if these men—who were certainly not numerous—were serious in what they said, they would have seen such an extension of democracy as a function of power and institutions, not as a function of time—of time working steadily toward political participation for the slaves.

Various concepts could of course become ideologically charged and their content controversial. One such was *aristokratia,* which gave expression to oligarchic pretensions; others were *politeia* and *polites,* and also *demos,* as the first component of *demokratia.* This was especially true of key concepts that stood for potent ideals, above all "equality," which could not be divorced from its connotation of justice. Consequently there appears to have been a tendency during the Peloponnesian War toward a new concept of equality that came into competition with the democratic one; then, in the fourth century, a distinction was made between arithmetical and geometrical equality.[115] "Isonomy" too was a useful watchword.[116] One might also recall the ideals of *homonoia* and *philia,* or the attempts that began toward the end of the Peloponnesian War to invest the new ideal of an Ancestral Constitution *(patrios politeia)* with various meanings; finally one might mention general concepts such as *dikaion,* especially those connected with external policy.[117] It is perfectly natural to invest concepts with new contents in this partisan fashion.[118] What is surprising is that the ideological content of the target concepts related essentially to experience, not to a future that would somehow be different and could be read into or deduced from the concepts. Such ideologies involved no time factor. Indeed, the *patrios politeia* explicitly aimed at the restoration of earlier constitutions. The concepts were thus indicators of change, not factors for change.

To sum up: on the whole there was an almost complete identity between experience and expectation. In the archaic period there had been a certain excess of expectation over experience—or rather an excess of demands— and even after the middle of the fifth century men seem to have entertained expectations of improvement by extrapolation from the experience of various successes. Yet these expectations were not pitched very far beyond existing conditions. True, one can cite certain statements that, taken in isolation, have a quite different ring. In Sophocles' *Ajax,* for instance, there is mention of "long immeasurable time," and it is stated that "there is nothing that cannot be expected" *(ouk est' aelpton ouden).*[119] But this refers only to the conduct and ability of individuals, to the unpredictability of future change, not to an incomparable future. When the Athenians were called "innovators" *(neoteropoioi),* this meant above all that they were always embarking upon something new in foreign affairs, thus changing the situation of their city and with it the "interpolitical system."[120] Admittedly it is also emphasized that they were always discovering something new and thus helping to bring about changes in power relationships and conditions of life. Here, then, is another instance of expectations running ahead of experience—as with the improvements expected from institutional innovation—but again to only a relatively modest extent.[121]

It will be asked, on the basis of modern historical experience, how democracy could evolve at all in such circumstances. We may generalize the question and ask what kind of changes we are dealing with here. Earlier we asked whether the uniform trend of conceptual change was matched by a uniform change on the politicosocial scene. Moreover, it remains an open question whether, and to what extent, there was any appreciation of change at all. In many respects these questions go beyond our present theme and take us into a much wider field; hence, in pursuing them to a conclusion, our approach must focus strictly upon our present thesis, which cannot be more than a thesis.

The main Greek word for change was *metabole*, which became the normal term for the overturning of a constitution. *Metabole* does not denote a self-motivated change, but one that is brought about more or less deliberately through political action, producing new power relationships and new institutions. Another term is *kinesis*, which means "movement, changeability, disturbance." [122] The incipient historiography of the period is concerned with *erga* and *pragmata* (meaning primarily "works" and "actions"). From the point of view of the history of concepts, it is interesting to note that both these terms denote the complex of interlocking actions that constitute an event. In a general sense one speaks of *genomena*. Historiography was thus concerned with the actions that took place on the political stage and the changes that resulted from them. This was at the time almost the only kind of change that affected the whole and was universally relevant. [123] Consequently the most significant surviving reflection on the decisive stage in the conflict between the old and the new is Aeschylus' *Eumenides*, which takes as its model the struggle between divine dynasties; this was presumably not dictated solely by the poet's choice or by the rules of tragedy. [124] In general what was perceived here was probably not so much change itself as the intensity of the political conflict, its shattering effects, and the special character of the new constitution.

It is true that other processes were observed—more broadly based processes such as the growth of knowledge, skills, and material resources, or the increase in the size and power of the *poleis*—but these observations seem to have been largely peripheral, and there is no term to designate the processes as such. [125] Whatever change was taking place was not powerful enough to break through the barrier that impeded its perception. Hence no consciousness of processual dynamism could evolve—no concept of progress or history.

There was of course an awareness that men could significantly improve their conditions of life. This awareness existed above all among those endowed with technical knowledge (in the widest sense)—artists, sophists, politicians. It amounted essentially to a consciousness of human ability, an awareness that new things could be invented, especially in such circles, and that new techniques were discoverable in many different areas. The term for such ability was *techne,* which in the fifth century came to designate the ability to achieve great things in the most varied fields by applying the proper methods. Here lay the hope for institutional improvements. Although this consciousness of human ability had a historical dimension in the doctrine of the emergence of culture, it centered upon the abilities themselves, not upon their potential increase. It was therefore confined to the actions and the actors; any perception of the resultant process was merely coincidental, and any expectations of future improvements correspondingly slight.[126]

This kind of perception was determined by the mode of change that shaped the prehistory of democracy and its eventual emergence into history.[127] The preconditions for democracy were created in the course of a protracted crisis in the archaic period. This crisis resulted from the failure of both monarchs and nobles to provide satisfactory solutions to the urgent problems that beset the communities of many Greek city-states. During this period there grew up, all over Greece, a circle of political thinkers who eventually took up a third position between the disputants, fostering an interest in the *polis* as a whole and seeking to tackle the crisis by reflecting on the problems and devising institutions. Their thinking gradually aligned itself with the interests of broad sections of the people, who sought security against the arbitrary actions of the nobles and improvements in their own conditions. Popular discontent was transformed into demands for certain rights of participation, partnership, and control, and these demands finally resulted in the rule of the *demos.*

This produced the alternative that had given unity to the process ever since the archaic period. As far as can be judged, it aimed only at isonomy. At all events, the further development to democracy probably did not take place until after the Persian Wars; possibly it could not have taken place at all had it not been for the conditions that prevailed after the wars. It was at this point that the real change in the world of concepts began (except for *isonomia,* which had come into use earlier). Only now did the shift to democracy find expression in a uniform tendency toward the politicization of concepts. But this historical differentiation is not important here, since we are concerned only with the way in which the Greeks perceived and understood the changes that were taking place.

The single steps along this road were prompted chiefly by certain nobles who wished to assert themselves against their fellow nobles with the help of the populace.[128] However, after the consolidation of economic conditions during the sixth century, they could no longer win the permanent support of the people through material inducements: they now had to offer them political rights.

In this process there are sporadic indications of a spontaneous movement toward the progressive widening of popular influence (which was achieved in the isonomies), but no one really knew where it was leading. Only one step could be taken at a time, with only the vaguest inkling of what came next. The process involved countless *poleis,* all situated in proximity to one another, and this gave it a fairly powerful thrust.

Yet there could be no thought of gradually enlightening the broad mass of the people, of educating or preparing them for a constitution that would guarantee freedom and equality and could be envisaged as an ultimate goal. This was still true in the fifth century. When new possibilities were discovered—for instance the democratic effect of filling offices by lot—they could be put into effect immediately. Their usefulness was obvious and usually answered to concrete interests. Expectations could even now gain no more than a short lead over experience, because they could be realized so easily—as soon as they became conceivable, in fact—and because experience always caught up with them immediately. For a long time any gaps that opened up between experience and expectation could be closed by fresh planning and action. It was only in about the last third of the century, when the democratic alternative was exhausted, that expectations began to run ahead of experience.[129] Yet even these were chiefly expectations of action, entertained by a small section of the body politic; no steady process of change was envisaged. This intensification of expectations was part of the process whereby the intelligentsia detached itself from the *demos:* the excess expectations were absorbed by theory.

The process of preparation could therefore scarcely impinge upon the general consciousness while it was still in train; nor could it be appreciated with hindsight. Consequently men were all the more aware of the possibilities when they were finally achieved—above all the possibility of creating institutions through action and thought. The problems had been pondered for ages, and practical solutions had at last been discovered. The discovery had taken place among the political thinkers—among the experts, in other words—but also, in some way, in the communities in which they lived and to which their thinking was directed. This probably explains why men became conscious above all of their capacity for action—and why this consciousness was matched by such a tremendous surge forward, by the emergence of the political alternative, and by an extraordinary intensification of political life. In the constitutional debate reported by Herodotus it is stated that under democracy the *nomaia patria* are respected. This suggests that, because this old conservative aim had been achieved, there was little awareness—or only an incidental awareness—of the capacity of democracy to bring about change.

There was a further factor. Since the process of democratization led to political identity (and then combined, after the Persian Wars, with the exploitation of the new scope for action in foreign affairs), the forces released by it were largely absorbed into political life and seized upon the undreamt-of problems and opportunities to which it rapidly gave rise. For a number of reasons, then, action and the capacity for action were bound to play an important part in the perception and comprehension of contemporary events.

The changing politicosocial concepts of the fifth century, while pointing to the changes that were taking place in the period, give expression only to the results of these changes, not to the changes themselves. Trends in the sphere of concepts were quite closely paralleled by patterns in the sphere of action, yet the main function of the concepts was to provide orientation; they did not play a prominent part in shaping events.

It is impossible to say where the terms were coined, but although some might have originated with the sophists, this is not very likely. Presumably they arose in the same place as the reality they were intended to express—in the civic communities or among those who guided them and devoted such intense thought to the *polis* and to politics. It is true that there were some sophists among these, but the sophists' real contribution to Greek language and thought consisted rather in creating a gulf between the educated class and the mass of the citizens. This did not exist earlier. If a "democratization" of conceptual language did take place among the Greeks, then it consisted, up to the end of the fifth century, in enlarging the circle of those who had access to such language; this social enlargement went hand in hand with the politicization of the content of the concepts.

To sum up: it appears that an examination of the conditions for action that generates change makes it possible to analyse the relation between politicization and temporalization in categorical terms. The "saddle period" from 1750 to 1850 envisaged an all-embracing change that affected the whole of humanity and took place primarily as a process. Deliberate action directed to particular aims was, so to speak, superimposed on the process, which was for the most part sustained by an infinity of individual actions and changes; it was the accumulation of these that constituted the process. The world as a whole was moving in a predetermined direction. Concomitant with this was the temporalization of concepts and the totality of their content. The Greeks, by contrast, reckoned only with changes occurring in the *poleis*—that is, among themselves—and with a certain growth in men's capacity for action throughout the Greek world. The mode of change was determined by political action, and also by the recognition, invention, and planning of new possibilities by a comparatively small number of "experts" scattered throughout

Greece. The human world as a whole was perceived as static.[130] All this was matched by the politicization of the world of concepts.

Politicization was the central tendency of change in the ancient world, and this precluded temporalization. Temporalization involved an element of politicization, though this was never more than one among a number of components of change, let alone the predominant component. Above all, in a world in which the state was confronted by a powerful society (or underwent a secondary amalgamation with society), and in which rapid changes were taking place in all areas of life, the political was bound to be something fundamentally different from what it had been in the ancient world, where conditions outside the political sphere remained essentially static. In the modern world the political could not remain immune to the all-pervasive process of change, to which it was constantly exposed and constantly had to adapt itself. The political was thus increasingly liable to be viewed as merely functional.

In the context of the question of generally relevant change and the conditions for action within it, the contrast between politicization and temporalization thus becomes evident. They are two fundamentally different modes of historical development that manifest themselves in the corresponding conceptual worlds (and assign to the concepts different roles in the historical process). It follows that in the ancient world men were conscious above all of action and human ability rather than of change, and this is reflected in the whole of their culture. It follows also that structural improvements could be expected to arise only through politics and institutions, and only in the political sphere, whereas we—insofar as we hope for improvements at all—expect them rather to be a function of time and to occur in all spheres of life.

It thus emerges from a consideration of the category of conditions for action that the mode of change specific to the fifth century B.C. can be traced in the transformation of concepts and more especially in the way these lagged behind events. Since the changes were so rapid, this simply indicates that affairs remained *en meso*, in the midst of the citizens, and that actions did not accumulate to produce discernible large-scale processes. Thinking also remained in the midst of the citizens. This meant that what they were able to comprehend was not the movement of history, but the political world in which they lived. The distances separating the different theoretical positions from one another—and from reality— were no greater than those separating the real political oppositions (which related at most to the constitution of the body politic). And so it remained until Socrates and Plato opened up new dimensions.

An Ancient Equivalent of the Concept
of Progress:
The Fifth-Century Consciousness of Ability

W HETHER THE ANCIENT world was acquainted with a concept of progress has long been a matter of controversy.[1] The
question has received a variety of answers, ranging from an
unqualified "yes" to an unqualified "no." Opinion seems to fluctuate,
tending now toward a positive, now toward a negative answer.[2] At present
the former tendency predominates. There has also been unmistakable
progress in research on the subject. In recent years some very cautious
studies have appeared, yet even the most cautious scholars agree in supposing that some notion of progress existed in the fifth century B.C. It is
with the fifth century that we shall be concerned here, though we shall
also have to consider the beginning of the fourth.

The wide differences of opinion are due not least to the categories
underlying the arguments, which start out from differing notions of progress. The really unsatisfactory feature of the debate is that writers tend to
operate with quite general notions of what constitutes a concept of progress.[3] This is just one instance of a procedure that is common in other
areas too: we constantly seize upon questions that arise in our own world
and then project them into remote epochs in the search for equivalents.
This procedure has often proved fruitful, indeed indispensable; yet there
is always a danger that the sharp edges of the modern categories will be
rubbed smooth, and the more they are designed to fit specific modern
conditions, the more likely this is to happen. Imprecise application of the
categories then results in a failure to perceive the special features of
the ancient equivalents precisely enough, or even correctly. To avoid this,
my discussion will proceed from the following general postulates.

Today, any treatment of what may perhaps be called ancient ideas of
progress presupposes a precise knowledge and an explicit exposition of
the modern concept of progress. We all have specifically modern notions

about what the term means, and so whatever is predicated about the ancient world must be explicitly set off against such modern notions.

However, when dealing with so modern a concept, we are likely to find that the comparison with its supposed equivalent inclines us to make negative assertions about the ancient world's lagging behind the modern to a greater or lesser degree in this or that respect. It is doubtful whether this is the right way to do justice to the ancient world. This leads to my second postulate.

In considering what may be called ancient ideas of progress, we should not simply contrast the ancient concepts with the modern, but try to arrive at a third term that will allow us to grasp the special and distinctive features of the ancient concepts.

Here we come up against problems of a general theoretical nature. In recent decades these have been discussed above all with regard to the concept of the state. From the field of ancient history one might also cite recent discussions of economics and social stratification.[4] In any treatment of important problems we should, in my judgment, always have recourse to such third terms of comparison or work them out for ourselves within the framework of a historical theory, for in the absence of such a theory success will elude us.

In the present case this means evolving a concept that will furnish the minimal conditions for asking what may have corresponded, in ancient times, to the modern idea of progress. The modern notion and its putative equivalents will then appear as different species of the construct; moreover, the latter must contain the most important dimensions within which our question has to be accommodated.

At first, however, such general concepts relate only to single elements—in this case to some form of awareness of improvement—and these cannot properly be treated in isolation. Their meanings and probable functions emerge only within the context of the individual period. This leads to my third postulate.

What may be called ancient ideas of progress must be seen and understood explicitly within the context of their age. Periods of history differ above all in that, within each, the individual factors and areas of life stand in a specific relation to one another. There are considerable disparities, for instance, in the importance accorded in different periods to economic affairs and religion within the total structure of conditions. This is no less true of the scope for human action, as well as the specific configurations in which action occurs, and which are crucial in determining stability and change. The specific forms of historical change vary greatly from period to period, as does the relation between change and awareness of change. I use the term *historical* change quite deliberately, because the sociologists' concept of social change is at once too narrow and too specifically modern to comprehend the phenomena under discussion: we should avoid the risk of being drawn too much into the ambit of sociological terminology.

This means that we must not simply transfer to another age a paradigm that represents the whole of our own, and then register the presence of different details in the apparently corresponding sites. We must also work out theories for the individual periods in order to account for the way in which important elements and processes relate both to one another and to the total structure of conditions.

It seems to me that the most important theoretical program for the day-to-day life of the historian consists, on the one hand, in establishing a third term for every universally important element, complex, and movement (including anthropology) and, on the other, in constructing theories appropriate to different periods. This is especially necessary in ancient history and will be of benefit not only to this particular discipline, but also to historical theory. In pleading for unfamiliar or unpopular causes one does well to enlist the support of classical writers: on 14 October 1797 Goethe wrote to Schiller: "On this occasion one learns yet again that an experience, to be complete, must contain a theory. And we are the more certain of meeting at one central point, since we approach the matter from so many sides."[5]

In the present framework this means that the ancient consciousness of improvement must be seen within the particular context of the elements, complexes, and movements with which it is directly linked; in other words we must work toward a theory of the fifth century. This, then, is the ambience of the thesis I wish to propound.

The Modern Concept of Progress

I would formulate the meaning and nature of the modern concept of progress in roughly the following terms, relying in large measure on Reinhart Koselleck's history of historical concepts.[6]

This concept was a distillation of a large number of assumptions about progress that were current about the year 1800. These related to a variety of improvements (in the plural) in many different areas. The general concept of progress (in the singular) not only embraces all these, but subsumes them at a higher level of abstraction. It thus asserts not just the progress of this or that, in this or that respect, but progress per se. According to this concept, the whole of humanity, and especially the most "progressive" parts of it, is engaged in a general advance: with regard not only to knowledge, applied science, economic affairs, and prosperity, but also to enlightenment, law, civilization, equality, and freedom—indeed to the New Man that we, by some wonderful metamorphosis, are destined to become. Only by virtue of its comprehensiveness, interdependence, and uniformity of direction can this movement be viewed so positively, "uniformity of direction" being understood here in the sense of a certain clustering of ideals in which social classes that were new to world history—the bourgeoisie and later the proletariat—thought to find self-realization as an alternative to what had come down from the past and as representatives of true humanity. Were the historical movement to lack such uniformity of direction, the individual instances of progress would be bound to appear ambivalent—as ambivalent indeed as, for the most part, they appear to us today.

According to this notion the forward march of mankind is so powerful, is endowed with such inherent dynamism, and so transcends all individual agents that it can—indeed must—be seen as an objective force. It appears as an autonomous process:[7] quite independently of intentions and events on the political stage, it is bound to prevail everywhere—in the solitude of the scholar's study, in laboratories, seminars, and academies, in sitting rooms and schoolrooms, in discussions, among editors and readers, on the stage and in the audience, among parents and children, and, last but not least, in production centers and channels of trade—in short, in the industry, advancement, enlightenment, and civilization of countless individuals. This means, at the same time, that the mode of change indicated by the concept is processual. Change takes place essentially—according to the concept, at least—in the form of an autodynamic process. To those from whose actions it springs, it presents itself, as it were, from the outside. Although we are all part of the movement,[8] we find ourselves confronted time and again by "the age" or by "history." Change, which was once quantitative, has become qualitative. Society appears and perceives itself in certain essential respects as the embodiment of "history" (so long as things continue in this way, that is, so long as society does not come to feel itself rather to be the sum total of contingencies, colliding processes, or the force of circumstances).

The modern concept of progress thus amounts to a statement about history, namely that all history is essentially progress. It reflects something entirely novel—the change that the new class of the European and North American bourgeoisie saw taking place both in itself and in its position in society and the international world. The change was so all-embracing, so intense, and so rapid as to give rise to an entirely new form of history: not only the actors on the political stage, but culture and society too, seemed to have a history. History was seen as a great process of change. In earlier ages men had hardly been aware that this was so—nor was it so to such an extent that they could have been aware of it.

We must bear in mind that although there is probably always some correspondence between the way in which a society undergoes change and the way in which it perceives it, the connection between the two is not always uniformly close. It appears that there are thresholds of perception, on both sides of which perception gravitates in different directions. (And this is connected with how far—that is, in what social circles—change is observed and experienced.) The gravitations of perception do not easily tend toward the point where change becomes the most conspicuous feature of the world.

It was only in the eighteenth century, then, that the perception of the world gravitated toward change. Men began to understand themselves and the world in terms of history. History could thus be understood as a unity, as the history of mankind, as a current that was generally moving toward a better world, and the enlightened Western bourgeoisie saw itself in the vanguard of history. Within this perspective, past, present, and future were brought into line: history consisted above all in the great process of change that led up to and beyond the present; hence, history came to be identified with this process.

Since progress leads to something entirely new, it opens up a wide gulf between the space of experience and the horizon of expectation.[9] However much the expectations may have been generated by experience, they were directed toward a totally different horizon. This meant that the concept could become a receptacle for ideology. Hence, the notion of the endless march of humanity is always liable to be reoccupied—with the familiar result that those who believe themselves to be absolutely in the right find themselves confronted by others whom they regard as absolutely in the wrong.[10]

However, if history is viewed as a process, this means that the concept of progress is not merely an indicator, but at the same time a factor: it gives additional momentum to the historical movement (though it remains an open question whether what is then done in the name of progress is consonant with what is implied by the concept).

In an age of profound and pervasive change, this concept provided orientation for vast numbers of people. It gave meaning to their lives: the oppressive sense of impermanence, instability, and contingency was transformed into a sense of progress.[11] The modern notion of progress thus performed quite central functions, extending to the numerous identifications with the movement to which it referred. Its function of ensuring identity is extraordinarily important. Goethe recognized the psychological mechanism at work here when he wrote, in his *Maxims and Reflections:* "Man detests whatever he thinks is not his own doing; this is why the party spirit is so zealous. Every dolt thinks he has a hand in what is best, and every nobody becomes a somebody."[12] All that is required is an act of faith (and for others an *auto-da-fé*). Under such pressure, progress is characterized by the fact that, in the words of Johann Nestroy, "it generally appears much greater than it really is."[13]

This, I believe, is the only way to describe the modern concept of progress. It is specific to modern times. Like so much else, it was taken over from the bourgeoisie by the proletariat. Naturally one can express many different views about the nature of progress. Everyone can arrive at his own. One may even question whether there is any such thing as progress. What the notion implies may well be wrong—at least for many periods of history. But, once invested with the semantic content we have just outlined, it became a concept with an unmistakable identity of its own.[14] From then on, no progression toward something bad could be progress. True, one can still measure the concept against the literal meaning of "going forward" or "advancing." Yet however the individual may define progress—or even deny its existence—there is no longer any way of avoiding the notion. Here we have spoken of the concept of progress only in this general sense.

The Third Term: *Auxesis*-Consciousness

If we want a more general concept of progress, which can also be applied to other periods of history, we shall have to work it out for ourselves. In doing so we must be clearly aware of what is involved. Progress, in the sense we have been considering, is patently a form of "generally relevant change," change that is important to a whole society or culture. Such change must obviously take place in essential areas of life, or, to be more precise, in general conditions that are essential to human action, achievements, and modes of living. Hence, if we are to find an equivalent in other periods, we must presume that there was a broadly based process of improvement in essential conditions of life. Moreover, there must have been substantial agreement that this was so.

Nothing that fell short of these minimal conditions would suffice. It is not enough that individuals should entertain such assumptions. Nor can it be a question of just any improvements. The improvements must affect not only conditions in particular areas of life or in a single state, or even the power of a single state (such improvements can be reckoned as, at most, additional symptoms). It may make sense, up to a point, to view this or that reconstruction of historical developments—say, of a literary genre or a branch of learning—as "paradigms of the idea of progress."[15] But this is not what concerns us here. By generally relevant change we mean a very significant improvement in the human situation as a whole and in possibilities for human action. Whether it involves the whole of humanity or all members of a particular culture is another question; so too is the extent to which the consciousness of such improvement is projected into the future.

I should like to call this kind of consciousness of improvement a "consciousness of *auxesis*": the Greek word *auxesis*, which can readily be used as an equivalent of "progress,"[16] is not theoretically encumbered, and so we are free to define how we intend to use it for our own purposes. *Auxesis*-consciousness would thus be the third term, the major term subsuming both the Greek and the modern notions of progress.

This consciousness need not represent the most important way in which generally relevant change is conceived in a given period. It may be in competition with other conceptions; it may even lag behind them. But there must be no contradiction between the different conceptions—at least insofar as the competing terms play a dominant role.

We are operating here within the context of a problem that has hitherto scarcely been appreciated. Are there, in individual periods, specific kinds of generally relevant change? And are there corresponding modes of perceiving change? Contemporaries may have opinions that differ in many respects. However, if there is to be any sense in speaking about modes of perceiving change that are specific to a particular epoch, it must be possible, at least at certain levels, to observe a unified conception of change or a predominance of certain modes of perception. It is within these modes of perception that *auxesis*-consciousness must be accommodated.

At this point many questions arise—about the units that are affected by change, the motive forces that lie behind it (and their configurations), and the speed with which it occurs; about how it is perceived; and, finally, about how all these factors interact. We cannot expatiate on all these questions here.

Nevertheless, one important distinction must be made. The mode of change is determined by the configurations from which it results, that is, the configurations in which change is generated by human action—either directly or indirectly (through the sum of its side effects, for instance).[17] If one finds oneself dealing with a significant improvement in general conditions of life, it at once becomes obvious that this must be due to the ability and achievements of many individuals—however much it may have been favored by political and economic conditions and sanctioned by political authority. One may ask how far change transcends those who have caused it, by detaching itself from them and becoming self-motivating. Roughly speaking, there are two possibilities. The first is that the sum of the impulses behind it may be so great, and the improvements in the different areas so interdependent, that the process of change acquires a dynamism of its own, so that there is a sudden "switch" from a sum total of motive forces to an autonomous movement. How such a switch occurs can hardly be stated in theoretical terms,[18] but its result can be described: within the whole structure one thing is propelled by another; everything is multiplied or raised to a higher power; one is caught up in a current that generates its own momentum; even the most remarkable achievements merely ride the current and are relativized. When this happens a whole structure becomes involved in change. In such a situation concepts may be temporalized and subjectivized, and so become agents of their own effects.

The other possibility is that the various impulses combine only to a limited extent or only in particular areas. There may be cross-fertilization, and many new endeavors may be stimulated by a general awareness of advance, yet on the whole the impulses work in parallel, and the most that can happen is that new inventions, insights, and possibilities are added to the existing stock. There is no universal movement. One is conscious only of the abilities, achievements, and successes of individuals— of numerous individuals, perhaps—but not of a current that sweeps everything along with it. In this situation the structures within which one lives may remain unchanged, or at least appear to do so. Change takes place only in certain parts of the social world. The politicosocial concepts are not temporalized or subjectivized, but remain for the most part descriptive.

In this way, then, two modes of change may be distinguished under the heading of *auxesis*. The second would involve a minimum of change—a sum of improvements in the sense of an accretion of possibilities. The first would embrace far more—an autodynamic change, the elements of which were largely interdependent. Perception of change would also differ. In the second case, the abilities and achievements of many individuals would occupy the foreground; in the first, one would be conscious, additionally or principally, of a process of change, and this might relativize the consciousness of individual ability. The gravitation of perception may also have a part to play. This is not the place to elaborate the distinction between the two modes of change:[19] in what follows we have to demonstrate that the distinction is valid.

The configurations of action are of course embedded in wider social relationships, including those that determine affiliation and identity. Starting from these, one might be able to determine what basic features *auxesis* shares with other contemporaneous forms of change and perception of change.

Evidence of *Auxesis*-Consciousness in the Ancient World

A genuine concept of progress, involving a complex of many different experiences and expectations of improvement, was unknown in the ancient world. The words that can be rendered by our word *progress* were all used purely descriptively to denote the "growth," "increase," or "advance" of something in some respect—and not necessarily for the better.[20] Nevertheless, there is striking evidence from the fifth and early fourth centuries that allows us to posit an *auxesis*-consciousness.

About 390 B.C. a comedy with a highly modern flavor was performed in Athens. This was Aristophanes' *Ecclesiazusae*. In it the women of Athens mount a conspiracy. They plan to go to the Assembly early in the morning, dressed in male attire, and take over the city, because they consider that the men are bad rulers: they are corrupt, pass senseless resolutions, and are satisfied only if they are constantly instituting something new. The women, on the other hand, are experts at running their households. Above all, they do everything as it was done in the days of old. They dye their wools in the ancient style, they bake their honied cheesecakes as of old, they torment their husbands as of old, they entertain admirers as of old, and so on—all of which is proof enough that their policy would be superior to the men's.[21]

The first part of the play shows how they gain power. One of them proposes in the Assembly that the city be handed over to the women. This is greeted with acclaim by the conspirators. The motion is passed. But the reporter through whom we learn of all this is a man. Unaware of the conspiracy, he can explain the Assembly's resolution only by saying that "it appeared that this was the one thing that had never been done before in the city." It seems that if something was totally new, this was an obvious point in its favor. This was how the men thought.[22]

The women of the chorus at once advise their leader to do something that has never been done or spoken of before. It seems as though everyone is forced into certain roles: hardly have the women taken over the role of the men, claiming to be better able to rule the city because they are in favor of tradition, than they begin to plan something entirely new. The leader also has a plan. She hesitates, however, for though the plan is useful, she says, she fears that the audience may be opposed to innovation and prefer to adhere to time-honored tradition (this is presumably intended as a compliment). Her husband at once replies that she need not be apprehensive about innovation, for "progress, innovation, and contempt for time-honored tradition prevail here as the only true wisdom." Whereupon the leader proposes a motion that all property be held in common, that there be absolute equality in conditions of life, and that even the women belong to all.[23] How this works out is shown in the second part of the comedy, with refreshing realism and charm. It is one of the most telling satires on the mixture of logic and illogicality that typifies communism; the only thing Aristophanes did not know about was the role of the functionaries. But we cannot go into this.

What interests us here is that the arguments deployed in the comedy are temporal arguments, arguments about the value of the new. In commending something, it is not enough to say that it is useful. On the contrary, this can be ignored. The decisive point in its favor is that it is new. To advocate the introduction of something new simply because of its newness is temporal argumentation. The opposite also exists—arguing for the preservation of the old because it is old. Such argumentation is pointless unless it strikes a powerful chord and evokes substantially more agreement than dissent. A society may contain groups that favor the old and others that favor the new (just as the Athenian women, unlike the men, are united in their respect for the old). Temporal argumentation fails, however, unless society at large respects only the new or only the old. If a temporal argument is to be accepted as valid, either the old or the new must be presumed to be right, and the burden of proof lies with those who oppose the presumption.[24]

If we could assume that Aristophanes was depicting life under Attic democracy, this would mean that at that time the temporal argument in favor of the new was accepted in Athens—in the political sphere. The particular irony of the switch of roles, whereby the champions of tradition suddenly become the innovators, seems almost to point to the curious modern confusion between politics and reform (which today seems to guarantee that whenever the political appears on the scene it takes us by surprise). At all events, if we were able to interpret Aristophanes' testimony in this way, this would be an unequivocal and significant indication that the Athenians thought in terms of progress. However, it is rare for the majority of a community to hold that the new is good simply because it is new. This is conceivable only if expectations of improvement are so strong as to overcome the customary inertia that favors tradition. The new as such has value only if one believes that whatever is better will be continually overtaken by something still better—in other words, if one believes in the "categorical comparative."[25]

Such an interpretation of Aristophanes would find some support in Thucydides, where Cleon calls the Athenians *douloi aiei atopon, hyperoptai de ton eiothoton* (slaves of the ever unheard-of and despisers of the familiar). "They are always, so to speak, searching for something other than what we live in" *(allo ti hos eipein e en hois zomen)*.[26] This refers chiefly to the fact that the Assembly was at the time about to overturn a foreign policy decision. But the general nature of the formulation seems curiously to point beyond the immediate situation. The same is true of Cleon's remark that the Athenians are always improving the laws (because they imagine that they are wiser than the laws).[27] Finally, the comic poet Plato says that if one has been away from the city for three months one can no longer find one's way about in it. This too—according to Sextus

Empiricus, by whom the passage is quoted—refers to the rapidity with which the laws were changed, and so would be a further pointer to the view that change means improvement [28]—though the majority of the audience to whom the joke was addressed need not have shared this view.

Yet can these passages really be construed as indicating a universal penchant for the new, even in politics? Normally the words for innovation had clear pejorative connotations, both in Greece and in the ancient world generally. To innovate was to cause unrest, to turn things upside down; it was by no means a positive form of change. As Karl Reinhardt puts it, "'New' will not do as a watchword . . . 'New' is a word used by conservative objectors. 'New' is almost the same as 'unheard-of.' One may go along with it, but one does not boast of it. On the contrary, the new likes to justify itself on the ground that it is something old. Even sophistry seeks its legitimation in being ancient (Plato's *Protagoras*)." [29] In this connection the argument between the old and the new gods in Aeschylus' *Eumenides* (written about 460) is instructive: only the old gods speak of the "new law," and they find it outrageous. The young gods clearly do not see the newness of their law and their conception of law as something to commend it, so they keep quiet about it and advance different arguments and different claims. [30] And the young gods belong to the dynasty of Zeus.

On the other hand, we have a good deal of evidence—precisely from the fifth century—that stresses the value of the new in highly positive terms. The citizens of Athens probably really did enjoy hearing something new—new speeches, new arguments, new modes of speaking (even if they were not necessarily enamored of those who employed them). "I always try to say something new," Hippias of Elis is reported to have said, and he had not only the Athenian public in mind. [31] Aristophanes, in the *Clouds*, pours scorn on the expectations that attach to whatever is new and on the longing to be "in the van." [32] The poets attached great importance to writing something new. [33] They were apparently already doing this in the seventh and sixth centuries. But whereas it had then been a matter of variations within established genres—in the sense of Plato's distinction—the novelty that was now being flaunted consisted in the exploitation of a new freedom that exceeded all previous bounds. [34] What this meant in the sphere of sculpture has been described in detail by Tonio Hölscher: the inherited patterns were broken, and it was now entirely within the artist's discretion to decide how to represent the human form. There arose "alternatives affecting not only the detail, but the whole construction of the figure, that is, various possible ways of making the individual parts relate to one another and combine to form a whole." The works that were now created were thus so individual that they became unrepeatable and could at best be copied. Every artist had to make a highly personal choice. It was said of Zeuxis that he invariably created something new, strange, and extraordinary—and he must have been as proud of this as Parrhasius was of his claim to have reached the limits of art.[35]

What is here extolled as the new contrasts basically with the old and the traditional. If anyone were to make a sculpture in the old manner he would be laughed at, say the sculptors. The same view was taken of the old philosophers.[36] Above all, one no longer contrasted oneself only with one's forerunners in the same field:[37] one could now extrapolate from the latest achievements and claim that the present age had surpassed all that had gone before. Among the pronouncements that have come down to us, the most extreme is that of the musician Timotheus (from the late fifth century), who declared proudly: "I do not sing old melodies; my own are far better. Now young Zeus reigns: Cronus is overthrown."[38] Again, as in the *Eumenides,* the contemporary age is seen to correspond to the accession of the new dynasty of Zeus. Yet here we have an unequivocal and one-sided affirmation of the new, bespeaking a positive consciousness of modernity. This would be inconceivable unless it were accompanied by a great and widespread pride in improvements already attained—unless countless perceptions of improvement in different spheres were united in a consciousness of universal advance.

Yet this is precisely what Socrates implies when he says, in Plato's *Hippias Major,* that there has been an advance in the *technai* as a whole (that is, in the ability to treat the most varied subjects in an appropriate and methodical manner)[39]—when for instance physicians think that all previous knowledge can be discarded and that a completely new medical science must be invented. The author of the treatise *On Ancient Medicine* contests this view, though his sole objection is that one should build upon the foundation of the old; then the rest of what had not yet been discovered during the age-long development of medicine would soon be brought to light.[40]

Sophists stressed that they had a new form of education, superior to any other, promising greater success and making virtue teachable.[41] The flood of textbooks that began to appear in the most varied fields strongly suggests that the Greeks were conscious of the great opportunities they now had to master all kinds of scientific and technical problems (taking "technical" in the broadest sense).[42] This applies not least to the institution of rational forensic procedures for the hearing of evidence, which represented a very remarkable increase in human ability and was obviously noted with pride.[43] What tremendous strides had been made in rhetoric—one could now "make the weaker side the stronger"! If men could make such a boast, how highly they must have prized the technical aspect of this![44] Methodical expertise was advancing everywhere. The trained expert began to set himself off from the layman.[45]

According to Democritus, political *techne* was the greatest of all skills. Socrates is said to have called it the finest *arete* and the greatest *techne*. It was embodied in great statesmen such as Pericles. Young men thought to learn it from books. Aeschylus was undoubtedly alluding to *techne* and *arete* when he set the Zeus-given *phronesis* of the youthful Athene against the wisdom of experience possessed by the older divinities: this is the intellectual power that can settle the threatening conflicts between old and new in the city. The fact that *techne* was not to be understood simply as something "technical" was part and parcel of the aims and traditions of Greek political thought: it implied a view of the whole. The great store set by political expertise, and the fact that it was seen to match that of other experts, led Socrates to have doubts about democracy. Protagoras took the contrary view. He taught that Zeus endowed everyone with political *techne* or *arete* (the terms vary); these comprised both the skill of the politician (in guiding the city aright) and the qualities of the good citizen—justice, mutual respect, and mature judgment, which brought order and friendship into the city. In this way, two things that we think of as belonging in separate compartments were united in Protagoras' notion of political skill. Politics was, in essence, an art that embraced all aspects of living together as citizens. Men knew only too well that this was not something that could be taken for granted; it was an achievement of civilization, and this was ascribed to a broad understanding of *techne*. Being the most important skill of all, it was necessary, under democracy, that it should also be the most widely disseminated.[46]

One of the most remarkable manifestations of the consciousness of newfound possibilities, it seems to me, is the assertion that there is no such thing as chance: chance was an excuse, used by those who were unable to plan properly; or at least good planning made it possible so to calculate chance that it could ultimately be neutralized.[47] Sophocles says that man possesses methodical skills exceeding all expectation *(technas hyper elpid')*.[48]

Hence, Thucydides makes the Corinthians say, in objecting to the Spartans' "old-fashioned modes of living and thinking" *(archaiotropa epitedeumata):* "Necessarily the new [literally: that which has come into being after] retains the upper hand, as with all technical skills." This is meant to call into question Sparta's "unalterable customs and laws" *(akineta nomima).* The power of the new, like the *technai*, thus embraced men's whole attitude to the world and the institutions of communal life.[49] Admittedly the speech in which these words occur is concerned principally with the superiority of Athens. No doubt military skill, especially in naval warfare, played a large part in this, for "naval organization is a technical matter like everything else."[50] And it was precisely in the military field that men became aware of the new possibilities.[51] But the Athenians' rich experience *(polypeiria)* led to innovations far beyond these. The fact that they were constantly adding to their stock of methods and techniques *(epitechnesis)* stemmed from their versatility and openness; this, according to the Corinthians, was possible only if one was not, like the Spartans, wedded to the old. This was why they insisted on the superiority of the new—which went far beyond the sphere of *technai*. This testimony is admittedly isolated and remains curiously general, but it does show that there was something fascinating about the Athenians' *neoteropoiia* (their "craze for novelty," which led to disturbance and ever-changing situations) and about their *tolmeron* or audacity. Herein lies their disturbing "brilliance" *(lamprotes)*, which is frequently attested.[52]

Finally it should be mentioned that Hippodamus, in his design for an ideal *polis*, offered prizes to those who could suggest institutional innovations.[53]

Surveying all this evidence, we see clearly that in the fifth century the new was seen as something positive, even in politics, and that there was a widespread consciousness of the advances that were being made in different spheres.

The most grandiose account of what the men of the fifth century were capable of (and believed themselves capable of) occurs in the famous chorus *Polla ta deina* in Sophocles' *Antigone:* "Many things are awesome, but none more awesome than man. He races safely to his destination over the grey sea, before the wintry wind, under the arch of the crashing waves."[54] There had been earlier descriptions of the hardship, toil, and danger to which the seafarer was exposed; now he is pictured coming through them successfully.[55] After this comes praise for agriculture, fowling, hunting, the ability to build houses, and finally the words: "He taught himself language, the airy breath of thoughts, and the disposition to live together in the city. He who everywhere finds ways *[pantoporos]* approaches dauntlessly whatever faces him. Only from death will he find no refuge, yet from the throes of sickness he has devised an escape."

This chorus is often cited as the prime testimony for contemporary notions of progress. And it does indeed contain the most comprehensive and coherent account of the various manifestations of human skill, subsumed under the idea of the awesome. Finally it is stated (in words we have already quoted) that man possesses *technai* exceeding all expectation.

Yet this statement also marks the limits of these so-called ideas of progress, for it occurs within the framework of another: "Being a master in the invention of things unhoped-for, he goes his way, the way of good and evil." Man's consummate skill is not matched by ethical progress. It merely increases his scope for action, albeit to an extraordinary degree. The succeeding chorus tells us that man remains subject to the gods and is deceived by hope.[56]

It is striking too that Sophocles speaks only of man's ability, not of its increasing over the course of time—only of man's awesome nature, not of his progress. Sophocles is thus making an anthropological, not a historical statement. It does of course imply an advance, as is indicated by the fact that man's ability exceeds all expectations. One should note too the tenses used in the passage: it is couched entirely in the present and the preterite, except for the statement that man will find no escape from death; only here is the future employed. Clearly Sophocles envisaged further improvements,[57] but the temporal dimension was not important to him.

This raises the question of how past and future—and the changes brought by time—are represented within the perspective of the consciousness of improvement. Xenophanes wrote, probably about 500 B.C.: "Truly, the gods have not revealed everything to mortals from the beginning, but in time [chrono] they search and find better things."[58] This stands the hitherto prevailing view of history (if it can be called history) on its head: in the beginning there was no golden age, but only indigence and inadequacy. And the emergence of civilization was due not—or at least not only—to the gift of the gods, but essentially to human intelligence and endeavor. In this process, human and divine agencies may have been seen somehow working in tandem: at all events, the one did not necessarily preclude the other.[59] This idea was subsequently elaborated in the fifth-century doctrines of the emergence of civilization, according to which men at first lived like the animals—indeed worse than the animals, being naked, unprotected, and isolated. Then they discovered ways to find food, clothing, and shelter. They domesticated animals, found remedies against sickness, learned navigation, language, counting, writing, music, divination, religion, and law; they also learned to found and live together in cities.[60] In the end, even the gods were explained as the inventions of men.[61]

The emergence of civilization was reconstructed as history. This proceeded from knowledge of historical and ethnic differences, from the deduction that man was originally needy, and from experience of contemporary achievements;[62] all this took place against a background of skepticism about the golden age, about man's having once been endowed with all good things, and about the divine origin of civilization. The myth did not supply an adequate explanation (and there was no religious authority that might have guarded and developed it). If civilization is the work of man, it must have emerged step by step. Hence, the dimension of time became necessary. A good hundred years later the comic poet Philemon stressed the broadly based causes of the process by saying that all *technai* were taught by time, not by the teacher.[63]

It can be shown that the doctrines of the emergence of civilization occupied an important place in contemporary consciousness.[64] They are frequently attested in the relatively rich source material of the fifth century, whereas we do not find a shred of evidence for a belief in the old myth of the golden age, which was at most a matter for jest. Yet, as far as one can see, these doctrines referred only to the basic conditions of civilization (and apparently more to the discoveries themselves than to the process that gave rise to them).[65] True, Aeschylus seems to have reckoned with an increase in mature insight in Athens, continuing up to his own day (see Chapter 5 above). There was also a lively interest in inventions, perhaps even compendia of information on the various inventions and inventors. Yet as far as we know this interest (and similar interests and opinions that may have existed) did not lead to a general doctrine of further change continuing up to the present. People were clearly more interested in the details, and in the advances made in particular areas, than in bringing them all together in a kind of cultural history.[66]

Only Thucydides attempts to bridge the gap between the emergence of the basic conditions of civilization and his own age. When it comes to the narrower question of how political power developed, he constructs what might be called a history of the Greeks from the migration period to his own day. He traces a consistent process of growth, which clearly derives its logic from the tacit assumption that human diligence and inventiveness, given a free rein, always lead to an increase in goods and skills, and thus ultimately to the possibility of ever greater concentrations of power.[67] This applies at least in the case of the Greeks. All that was needed was to overcome, at least in some respects, the original insecurity of life.[68] In the remainder of his history, Thucydides points out more than once that new experience and expertise continually result from the requirements of an expansionist policy and the problems of warfare—roughly according to the pattern of challenge and response. This contributed significantly to the ascendancy of Athens. These examples from the present, however, amount to quite modest improvements.[69]

It was this state of affairs that led Alcibiades to postulate the need for further expansion and for the conquest of Sicily and, if possible, Carthage. He argued that it was necessary to ensure that the city continued to advance; otherwise it would wear itself out and grow old, with an inevitable decline of skill, learning, and expertise in all fields. If it remained true to its customs and traditions *(tois parousi ethesi kai nomois)*—which, in the case of Athens, meant its dynamism (here again we see the

new parading as the old)—it would "continue to gain new experience."[70]
This argumentation might be taken as evidence of a positively modern
pattern of thought: whoever fails to advance is left behind.

Yet for Thucydides too the growth of power and knowledge was not
necessarily accompanied by ethical improvement. A distinction has to be
drawn here. On the one hand he finds that everything points to nature's
remaining constant[71] (nature being the central motive force in man). On
the other hand, there may be great differences in historical and social[72]
conditions, and therefore in the ways in which men's nature plans and
operates. In early times, for instance, they not only discovered economic
resources and political and military skills, but also found a way to civilize
the communities.[73] This is one of the basic conditions of *polis* culture,
manifesting itself—as Thucydides hints—in the restriction of power that
was achieved in the *poleis*.[74] Admittedly, human nature repeatedly asserts
itself in relations between the *poleis*, especially in war, which "educates
men to violence";[75] it then comes under such pressure that its basic
impulses, fear and the desire for power and advantage, are no longer
inhibited. This is what really interests Thucydides, since his thinking proceeds from the exception.

For Thucydides, then, the constancy of human nature did not preclude
advances in civilized conduct. Yet even if he took it for granted that such
advances had occurred in early times, many aspects of civilized conduct
that were achieved in his own century appeared to him precarious (the
more so, perhaps, as men became more civilized). Hence the real change,
which continued up to the Peloponnesian War, was, as he saw it, limited
to an increase in knowledge and power. The greatness of the war, which
was determined by this increase, consisted above all in the magnitude of
the human sufferings it caused.[76] Perhaps only we, who can view the
matter within the horizon of the modern notion of progress, are in a position to see that the recognition of the constancy of human nature might
militate against a sense of *auxesis*.

To Thucydides, on the other hand, this recognition meant an important step forward, for it was the premise and central tenet of the doctrine
that made his history into the *ktema es aiei;* it was possible to reconstruct
and understand past events, to draw from them lessons for the future,
and thus to open up fresh scope for insight and action (and no doubt for
endurance).[77]

There is much to suggest that the stark realism of Thucydides was a
counterblast to other opinions that he regarded as delusions.[78] He may
have had in mind the general readiness to take a complacent view of
everything. He may have been opposed to the educational optimism of
the sophists. Yet although the sophists may have held different views

about the educability of man, this is not to say that any of them envisaged a general improvement in human conduct. It is true that Protagoras, according to Plato, maintained that laws, tribunals, and the mutual education of the citizens constantly engendered political virtue in the cities; but to illustrate this he cited the difference between contemporary Athens and the savages who appeared on the stage in Attic comedy. He was therefore probably alluding to the basic conditions of civilization, which in his opinion had been created when the first cities were founded. How this took place he does not tell us.[79] Although he is referring essentially to democratic conditions, he says nothing about specific advances toward democracy, or about advances due to democracy. All he envisaged was a better education, provided by the sophists, for the children of the rich. So did many others, but none of the sophists reckoned with a general improvement in standards of conduct.[80] How far they differed from Thucydides in their view of basic human motives is by no means clear. Democritus may have said that education created nature by changing human beings,[81] but how much of this secondary nature could be created, and in how many human beings, remained an open question. Pericles and his friend Damon the musician may have thought they could exercise an educative influence on the people of Attica.[82] However, since this would have stemmed from a totally new conception of politics, it would have been primarily an effect of the new opportunities for knowledge and action available to individuals, not a lasting process of improvement. (Even the later designs for ideal constitutions envisaged universal improvement solely as a matter of institutions and leadership.)[83]

The fifth century provides no further evidence of historical reflections on the question of improvements in contemporary conditions. It is striking too that we have no evidence to suggest that the emergence of democracy was seen as part of a general advance.[84] Many people must of course have realized, at least initially, how much better off they were than before, thanks to democracy—and its pre-form, isonomy. But this is never stated in the extant sources, which say only how beneficial democracy is by comparison with other contemporary constitutions.[85] In Aeschylus we can at least discern an awareness of the upheaval that led to the new constitution. In two great trilogies he deals with the establishment of justice on earth (particularly in Athens) and among the gods.[86] Change appears to him as a conflict between an old and a new regime, and he adopts an exceptionally clear stance: the old must be conciliated and, as far as possible, incorporated into the new.[87] He warns against excessive democracy. The city must be neither ungoverned nor subject to tyranny. The confident statement that the Athenians will increase in *sophrosyne,* in considered and moderate thinking, is conditional upon the existence of fear.[88] Emphasis is placed on the improvement brought by democracy, but also on the dangers arising from it. The new power (and the power of the new) implies the need for a new compromise.

It is hard to see how far improvement was expected to continue. We often hear that the high point has been reached. Artists maintained, as has been mentioned already, that they had reached the limits of art; according to a new interpretation, Timanthes even expressed this directly in his sculpture of the sacrifice of Iphigenia. He is said to have intensified the pain from figure to figure; only the last figure, Agamemnon himself, was represented veiled. Hence, in the last figure but one, the ultimate was reached in the representation of pain.[89]

On the other hand—if one proceeds from Thucydides' premises—the increase in goods and knowledge would have been bound to continue, even if it had suffered a setback through the Peloponnesian War and Athenian power had been substantially reduced, or even destroyed.[90] Moreover, it was not only the treatise *On Ancient Medicine* that predicted further advances. Chairemon wrote, for instance, that there was nothing in human affairs that would not eventually be found by dint of seeking.[91] This seems to point clearly to the future. Similar conclusions may be drawn from other statements relating to learning. Democritus would rather have "discovered a single proof than possessed the kingdom of the Persians."[92] And Antiphon's boast that "through method we become masters of that wherein we are defeated by nature"[93] no doubt implies a continuing mastering of the world.

This is roughly what we can discern of the fifth-century consciousness of *auxesis*. The picture that has emerged is assembled from numerous isolated passages. It seems to meet the minimal conditions set out above: there actually was a significant awareness of improvement in important conditions of life. It was concentrated in the "experts." Yet at the same time it found a wide resonance[94] (as we see especially from the evidence contained in tragedy and comedy).

These findings may be regarded as satisfactory. In order to delimit them further and decide what they tell us, we must relate them to others. It would seem obvious, for instance, to compare them with the modern concept of progress. This is a relatively simple procedure, though it has seldom been performed.

The Consciousness of Human Ability

No concept of progress evolved in the fifth century. Perceptions of improvement related to numerous advances that affected several areas of life. The improvements were either experienced directly or—in the case of primitive times—reconstructed on the basis of experience. We are dealing here with the progress of certain things in certain respects. Insofar as the perceptions were generalized, they combined to produce a consciousness of great opportunities for methodical action: an awareness—with regard to the past—that civilization was the work of men and the outcome of a historical process, and—with regard to the present—of a special level of achievement. This generalization marked the point at which the various observations converged, a limit that was hardly ever transcended. Only a few manifestations of ability went beyond what could be empirically observed.

We are dealing essentially with an increase in technical ability, in the Greek sense of *techne*—the expert performance of tasks in such fields as art, craftsmanship, and shipbuilding, as well as in military, political, constitutional, and educational affairs.[95] This was where the real improvements lay. And the consciousness of such improvements was concentrated in the "technicians" (not in a bourgeois public).

The repercussions were of course felt farther afield—in the widening scope for constitutional and legal improvement; in political planning, warfare, and shipping; and in the rapid growth of material resources. However, this did not lead anyone to suppose that some universal process of improvement, involving the whole of humanity, was in train.

Above all, certain important areas were excluded. No improvement was expected, either in the present or in the future, in general morality, general knowledge, or social and economic conditions;[96] if such a notion was entertained at all, it related to improvements in individual *poleis*, arising, perhaps, from good constitutional organization or legislation—in other words, from institutional expertise—or from war and conquest.[97] These were thus for the most part precarious and reversible benefits, not the outcome of regular, objective tendencies, even if this fact was not appreciated by all those involved.

The self-confidence of the experts was inspired above all by the standards they themselves had attained. One might thus claim that one had reached the limits of art, or that perfection was about to be attained in the sciences.[98] Hence, insofar as men thought in temporal terms at all, they were conscious of the progress they themselves had made, not of progress per se. This consciousness related to an ability to do increasingly more (which was evident from a comparison with past achievements) rather than to an increase in ability over time. Not to put too fine a point on it: they were conscious of a progressive mastering of the world, rather than of a world-mastering progress.[99] There was no question of history's being conceived as progress, or even as a comprehensive process of change. This much we can say here, though we shall presently have to ask what importance was attached to the sense of *auxesis* within contemporary perceptions of generally relevant change.

Many aspects of these ancient ideas become clear when they are set against the modern idea of progress. We see how meager they are, measured against their modern equivalents. Even the area of thought to which the concept of progress belongs—the philosophy of history—did not exist. No change was expected in the structure of society. The linking of the various advances in a unified whole was concentrated on manifestations of the high level of human ability. It did not bear upon humanity as a whole. Above all, the temporal dimension in the ancient notions was hardly developed at all. Indeed, the expectation of future improvements was largely absent. And its absence was due to the one conspicuous and distinctive feature of these ancient notions: consciousness of human ability related to the ability of experts. What modern scholarship likes to call "ideas of progress" (a designation that may at first sight appear apposite) is characterized by a curious absence of dynamism within a relatively broad band of present time.

The ancient notions thus differ from the modern concept of progress in every respect, save for the basic fact that they reckoned with a substantial improvement in the conditions for human life and action. This basic fact is highly significant in terms of world history; it is probably to be found nowhere but in the modern age and classical times. It is questionable, however, whether this justifies our speaking of ancient ideas of "progress." Is this not to put the emphasis in the wrong place? Is it not to set these ideas in the wrong context—quite apart from the fact that this formulation evokes obtrusive modern associations?

This difficulty may be avoided by recourse to a third concept such as the one outlined at the beginning of this chapter. If we free the ancient notions in this way from associations with their modern counterparts and inquire about the configurations for action that are manifested here, their positive aspect emerges clearly: the ancient phenomenon we are dealing with is essentially a consciousness of ability (and expertise). This means that men were becoming aware of the enormous opportunities for action, production, and creation. However, when we consider the areas that were affected and the intensity of the innovation, we see that these opportunities were too limited to coalesce in an all-embracing autodynamic change and to make it possible for consciousness of them to develop into a consciousness of progress.

The word *ability* is used here, for want of a better, to cover the semantic field dominated by the Greek terms *techne* and *sophia*.[100] From Aeschylus and Pindar onward,[101] *techne* is the general term for much of what we divide up into art, science, craftsmanship, and so on, namely for that part of the field that comes under the heading of skill or expertise—that is, of ability. The emphasis came to be placed—perhaps not immediately, but before very long—on the aspect of technical, rational, controlled method.

The sophists too evolved a theory of *techne*.[102] This concept came to occupy a central position in the general consciousness of the age. It was believed that through *techne* man could gain control over things. In the invention of this concept, in the consciousness of methodical ability (a consciousness that transcended all specialisms) lay the truly new element that characterizes the fifth-century view of man and his world. The fact that ability was recognized in so many fields and became a matter for experts made it possible for a general consciousness of ability to develop.

Another term that we find used in the same sense as *techne* is *episteme*, which means "knowledge" and "ability," especially with reference to craftsmanly skills. This is the knowledge that masters whatever it takes in hand and understands how things are done. *Phronesis* too is found as a designation for the methodical expertise that overcomes all difficulties. In Euripides we even read in one passage that *phronesis* would fain be more powerful than a god, namely in its claim to control the conditions of human life and break through the limits imposed on men. The consciousness of ability thus drew the various terms for knowledge into its ambit. It represented the culmination of the kind of knowledge that, in the Greek view, generated appropriate action.[103]

Techne and *episteme* also came into close proximity to *arete*, in the general, abstract sense of this word.[104] The sophists having claimed that virtue could be taught, this too became a matter of *techne*. According to Protagoras and others, *techne* and *arete* came together above all in the communal life of the citizens. The terms became interchangeable when they denoted the different aspects of political ability—the skill required to guide the city properly (and to gain influence), and also the virtues of justice, mutual respect, and mature insight.[105]

The concentration of all knowledge in the major concept of *techne* naturally did not prevail universally. When Euripides says that *phronesis* would fain be more powerful than a god, his very use of the word indicates the paradoxical nature of the statement. For even at this time *phronesis* was used largely to denote a different species of knowledge—knowledge of men's limitations and of the need for self-constraint. Moreover, it was soon discovered that the *technai* might sometimes be used in the unbridled pursuit of personal interests; this led to the development of a new concept of *phronesis*[106] (which continued to be associated with the fifth-century consciousness of ability at a more profound level).

The consciousness of human ability entailed certain consequences with regard to the perception of processes, and men were not slow to draw them. However, the way in which they did so makes it clear that these were only secondary and limited effects of the consciousness of ability: men recognized its direct and obvious consequences, yet for the most part continued to adhere to experience.[107] The hypothesis of a comprehensive process of cultural evolution was needed to bridge the gulf between primitive conditions and civilization. The fact that this doctrine generally stopped short at the founding of the *polis* and the creation of the basic conditions of civilization shows that it was essentially concerned only with origins and not with the phenomenon of change as such.[108] Thucydides' archaeology admittedly extends to the present. However, this was dictated by the question of whether the present war was the greatest that had ever been fought. For the archaeology is essentially presented and constructed as an argument.[109] It seeks to bridge the enormous gap between primitive conditions and the contemporary age, with occasional references to intermediate stages.[110]

Where there was no need to review or reconstruct long time spans—partly for the recent past, but in any case for the present and future—there was no awareness of a change in general conditions, but only of the ability of individuals. This does of course imply some advance: for one can hardly become aware of men's potential for action and production without adding to it oneself and trying to outdo others. This often happened on a small scale—when, for instance, besiegers and besieged invented new ways to outwit one another, or when the prolonged practice of war at sea led to ever new experiences.[111] It happened on a large scale too—when attempts were made to design not only constitutions but even societies, to overcome chance, and to create the most daring works of art, even to represent flight in a large-scale sculpture. It was thus possible to envisage new insights and inventions that would arise in the future. However, although men may have been aware of an increase in human ability, the illusion of finality could easily arise—the psychologically potent sense of having reached the consummation of all that is possible.[112] It was thus essentially the same experience that led them to perceive the emergence and immense growth of human ability and to reconstruct an all-embracing change in the past, to become aware of the high level of their own ability in the present, and finally to assume that there would be little progress in the future.[113]

In other words, the content of the Greek consciousness of ability was accrescence, but not change. It remained tied to the experience concentrated in the experts and to what could be directly inferred from it. It was clearly unable to cross the threshold to a perception of comprehensive change in the present and future. (No doubt one of the reasons was that the quantity of change was insufficient: this is a question we shall presently have to consider.) Given the seemingly changeless structure of society, the new possibilities must have been all the more impressive.[114] Be that as it may, everything points to the conclusion that we are dealing here with a minimal consciousness of *auxesis*. This at any rate explains why such enormous claims were made for human ability, yet so little change was envisaged. We thus see the strengths and the weaknesses of the Greek consciousness of *auxesis,* and at the same time its concentration in fairly restricted circles.

Within the context of the consciousness of ability, we begin to understand how even new possibilities of self-assertion, deception, military tactics, and diplomatic calculation could be a central element in the ancient form of *auxesis*-consciousness, though they are not, properly speaking, features that one would choose to associate with the modern notion of progress. In this regard the picture could be substantially enlarged. One of the most striking testimonies to the ancient consciousness would then be Pericles' pride in the fact that in nine months Athens had conquered the foremost and most powerful Ionians, the island of Samos, whereas it had taken Agamemnon ten years to conquer the barbarian city of Troy.[115] One appreciates the significance of this only when one recalls that the Homeric heroes had hitherto been models of matchless achievement. Homer's phrase "as mortals now are" *(hoioi nun brotoi eisi),* once echoed with resignation, could now be understood in a positive sense: men had surpassed the heroes of old.[116] Moreover, Pericles was the first to use the new battering engines[117]—which was an advance of the same kind. Later we find a similar reversal of the relation between past and present in Thucydides' archaeology.[118]

In all this the citizens of the highly successful city of Athens were able to occupy a special place. Thucydides writes that, in everything they planned, hope and having were one. Whatever they expected they looked upon as already theirs, and were sorely disappointed if they did not obtain it.[119] It was in Athens, more than anywhere else, that expectations overshot experience. "What is there that the Athenians cannot do?" a character asks in a comedy by Eupolis. And in the *Ecclesiazusae* of Aristophanes (ca. 390) a supposedly traditional proverb is quoted: "What we resolve wrongly and in ignorance always turns out to our best advantage in the end."[120] Indeed, things so often turned out for the best in Athens that even foolish resolutions of the Attic *demos* could not fail to be improved by circumstance (though this is of course no proof of ability). Euripides contrasts the citizens' attitude of "much wants more"— to him a symptom of monstrous discontent—with the abundant, god-given achievements of civilization; at the same time he links his praise of these achievements with the middle ranks of *polis* society. While the rich and the poor—and the young too—succumb to discontent, unleashing unrest and war, the simple citizens study to preserve the city and its order. This is clearly directed against the Athenian mania for innovation *(neoteropoiia).*[121]

While the city's external success *(eupragia)* would have no place in the modern notion of progress, it could be seen as a symptom of the consciousness of human ability. The victory over the Persians, to which such a decisive contribution was made by Themistocles' clear appreciation of the situation (and by some quite extraordinary and clearly correct decisions on the part of the Athenians), was a surprising demonstration of what could be achieved by political and military calculation.[122] Pericles, thanks to a long series of successes, was able to become the model of the "wise and discerning" *(phronimos)* politician. According to Thucydides, his plan for the war against Sparta was so excellent that its prospects of success were proof against any number of contingencies (including the plague) or a series of capital errors by Attic politicians.[123] Such thinking was entirely consonant with the consciousness of ability; but this could identify itself with Pericles (and the city, which had such enormous resources and opportunities at its disposal). At all events, it received a considerable impetus from the immense dynamism that emanated from Athens in all spheres; it was perhaps only in Athens that it could be generalized. And it was there that it found its greatest resonance. For it must have involved, at least for part of the time, the common citizens who manned the oars.[124] Even Thucydides must at first have been impressed by the immense possibilities available to Periclean Athens. If Herodotus, by contrast, inclined to the traditional view that constant change was the rule in human affairs,[125] his skepticism no doubt related not only to Athenian optimism, but to pretensions to ability in general,[126] of which this optimism was a symptom. Given the preeminence of Athens, with all its dynamism and apparent immunity to contingency, it is not surprising that the general sense of *auxesis* evaporated when Athens was defeated in the Peloponnesian War.[127]

We do not know how widespread the consciousness of human ability was, or how far it met with skepticism or outright rejection. There were naturally many doubts, of which evidence is to be found not only in Herodotus, but also in Sophocles' *Antigone* and *Oedipus Tyrannus* (and many other tragedies), and not least in Thucydides' juxtaposition of the Funeral Oration with the description of the plague. No doubt opinions often fluctuated (as they have done in the history of the modern idea of progress). People also knew that the emergence of the new was counterbalanced by certain losses.[128] To many this was doubtless disturbing. Nevertheless, in some areas at least—and in Athens in its heyday—the evidence pointed to the existence of extraordinary possibilities. Hence there were probably differing views, especially as to the limits of human ability, and we may presume that these were commonest where its pretensions extended to the political.

It is in any case unlikely that the citizens of Attica ever fell for the temporal argument in favor of the new. There is nothing to suggest that the skeptical attitude to innovation, which is reflected in the pejorative use of the word *neoterizein* (to innovate),[129] was ever effectively overcome. Apart from the *Ecclesiazusae,* we have no evidence that novelty was ever a plank in a political platform. One hears only that the citizens of Attica always wanted to have something new served up to them. But a fashion for novelty must not be confused with a craving for innovation. Nor should we conclude, from the pride that artists took in new works and from the esteem in which new techniques were generally held, that when it came to the governance of the *polis* the mass of the citizens expected preference to be given to the new in case of doubt. At most one can say that there may have been phases in Periclean democracy when the many improvements that were introduced gave rise to an excess of expectation (otherwise it was probably only experts such as Hippodamus who attached a positive value to political innovation as such). By the thirties of the fifth century, at the latest, it was all over.[130] From about 411 there was some political capital to be made out of the "ancestral constitution." Even the sophist Hippias, though convinced that his own age was superior to all others, said that he nevertheless praised the ancients more than his contemporaries, "being wary of the disfavor of the living and afraid of the anger of the dead." [131] It seems, then, that Aristophanes was merely mocking certain innovations by presenting them as innovations for innovation's sake.[132]

In any case, the *Ecclesiazusae* contains hardly any of the specific vocabulary of change. The garb in which the new is paraded belongs rather to the fashion for novelty. Aristophanes speaks, for instance, of "doing new things, saying new things, introducing one novelty after another with excessive zeal." [133] The craze for novelty, for changing existing conditions, appears to be symptomatic of this fashion: the real desire is to escape from the routine of constantly dishing up the old familiar fare—and having it dished up. It is directed against boredom rather than against tradition. It thus accords exactly with Cleon's remark about the Athenians, and with much else besides.

Once we have become attentive to these subtle differences, we can appreciate the whole vocabulary of novelty and innovation in the rest of Greek literature: however much we are tempted to read into it our own notions of change, we must refrain from doing so. It relates primarily to new abilities, to the accrescence[134] of possibilities, and only secondarily, if at all, to change. In tragedy the capacity to bring about change is accordingly shown to be above all something that greatly intensifies the problems of action.[135]

Dodds, at the end of his excellent and cautious discussion of the relevant passages, remarks that in the fifth century "the idea of progress was . . . widely accepted by the educated public at large." Either this says too little or it is wrong. The phenomenon to which it refers is no more than an equivalent of the idea of progress.[136]

The Emergence of the Consciousness of Human Ability

How did the consciousness of human ability arise? What place did it occupy in the context of the age? How was change perceived? What were the configurations in which action produced genuine change? And what was the relation between change and the perception of change?

Here we can offer only brief and tentative answers to these questions. If the fifth century understood innovation and advance as ability and action rather than as change, this was in keeping with other contemporary modes of perceiving time and change—or failing to do so.

The incipient historiography of the period—insofar as it addressed itself to change—was concerned essentially with political actions and events. The change that was to be observed here took place in the relationships between the agents—either on a small scale, as in a battle or a war, or on a large scale, as in the gradual rise of Athens. If some of the works now lost to us described the internal history of individual *poleis,* they also probably concentrated on political action and political events; these in turn generated, among other things, changes of constitution.

For Herodotus the world was for the most part unchanging: we read only of the rise and fall of individuals, cities, dynasties, and empires, of leading powers superseded by others. What was fundamentally new here was that Herodotus was able to understand long-term sequences as a complex history created by a multitude of agents and contingent events. This was an immense achievement, for the understanding of such sequences had hitherto been dominated by self-related surmises as to their meaning, in which destiny somehow had a hand. In such a perspective the whole of a given unit would appear to be undergoing change. Now the world as a whole was seen as unchanging, and this made it possible to perceive the changes in the political configurations.[137] Thucydides, it is true, laid more emphasis on certain relatively stable and calculable conjunctions of power; particularly important to him was Pericles' plan of war, which seemed likely to be proof against all vicissitudes and to impose the will of one city on whatever happened throughout Greece over a fairly long period (2.65.10 ff). Thucydides also thought that quite new financial and power relationships had arisen and that an intellectual and technical advance was in train. However, except in the archaeology, he writes chiefly about political actions and events and about the resultant changes in power relationships within and between the city-states (changes for which there were of course certain preconditions and implications extraneous to politics). On the whole, then, his observations are confined, on the one hand, to political events and, on the other, to the increased capacity for political action (which does not, however, greatly alter the character of the events).

This is paralleled by what we can discern of the fifth-century conception of time. Men reflected a great deal on time and arrived at very different conclusions. Of special interest is the development of the sense of time from Aeschylus to Sophocles and, later, Euripides. We will mention only the most important statements, which are to some extent mutually contradictory. Time is personified, and every possible effect is accredited to it: it brings much to light, teaches much, and produces justice. Time is all-powerful, the cause of perpetual change: in the course of time anything can happen, and nothing is predictable. Chance holds sway in time, which Heraclitus likens to a child playing a game, moving the stones back and forth across the board.[138] Yet with all the diversity of views, what is observed is change and interchange within and between subjects—either individuals or groups—and, for the rest, at most the discovery of new insights, never a process that changes human conditions by pointing them in a particular direction, or in which human beings are mediatized as children of a changing time. The social world as a whole remains untouched by time. Hence, apart from a modicum of new insights, time on the whole brings only a constant shifting of the configurations within given social conditions, not a transformation of the conditions themselves. Time is the dimension in which innumerable events occur within a world that is seen as essentially changeless (thanks precisely to the changes that are constantly taking place in it). This view of the world is determined by the structure of society.[139]

We arrive at the same conclusion by a different route if we study the world of politicosocial concepts. This embodies the results of the most incisive change—the shaping of the world of the *polis* by democracy and all that went with it—but not change itself. Change is merely indicated by striking shifts in the concepts.[140]

Hence, in spite of all that was happening, there was scarcely any awareness of change, other than that taking place between the individuals or groups who dominated the political scene. There was certainly no sense that things were moving in a uniform direction. Perception was concentrated upon action (and took in events and changing circumstances). A more or less precise corollary of this is that even where palpable advances were taking place, they were seen to reflect men's capacity for cognition, action, and creation—for increased versatility and achievement in an essentially static world.

It thus seems significant that the principal extant reflection on the most important stage in the struggle between old and new, Aeschylus'

Eumenides of about 460, presents this as a conflict between divine dynasties. What was perceived here was probably above all the conflict between the parties, the shattering of tradition, and the new elements that emerged, rather than the change it involved. As we have said, Attic tragedy in general rehearsed the problems that resulted from the vast new opportunities for action, and especially for change, while treating them as problems of action and decision making.[141] This can presumably be generalized: change was understood as action, and the problems of change remained embedded in those of action. Johann Nestroy, speaking of the modern world, remarked that progress seemed greater than it really was. May it be that we, considering the ancient world, are faced with the contrary phenomenon: that progress was really greater than it seemed? What change actually took place? In the perspective of world history the change to democracy was a revolution. Why were the Greeks unable, as they clearly were, to recognize this immense transformation for what it was?[142]

Let us state our thesis concisely: the consciousness of human ability corresponded precisely to whatever could be seen as improvement in the great process of change—in accordance with the contemporary capacity for perception and the object perceived. If perception lagged behind change, this was not a result of any intellectual shortcoming on the part of the Greeks or of their particular preoccupations (for instance with the history of events): their perspective was the logical outcome of the contemporary form of actual historical change, that is, of the configurations that produced change.

This becomes particularly clear when one considers the central strand in the process, namely the prehistory and emergence of democracy.[143] Modern scholarship has paid curiously little attention to the question of how it was possible for democracy—or for the political generally—to emerge in Greece. These products of historical change tend to be taken just as much for granted by modern scholars as they were by the Greeks themselves (except that in the case of the Greeks the phenomenon was linked, as we shall show, with the social interpretation of reality). How could democracy, the "rule of the people," evolve among a people who had no Greeks as forerunners and hence no knowledge of the possibility of democracy? There must have been at least some anticipation of what lay ahead. For the people had somehow to organize itself, and this implies an awareness of certain objectives. Institutional possibilities had to be prepared, and so on. But where were these to come from?

Here we are confronted by a curious historical process in which a social force, born of hardship and discontent and pressing for improved conditions, came together with a current of early political thought. Insights came into contact with demands, the aims of a small intellectual elite with the power of broad sections of the body politic. Political thought lived and flourished through its contact with reality, thanks to the wide resonance it enjoyed. In the course of a long crisis, during which it proved impossible to create a durable and legitimate new order based on monarchy, a third force had emerged and established a new position above and between the contending parties. This third force, with representatives throughout Greece and with its center at the Delphic oracle, consisted of a circle of men for whom the interest of the *polis* as a whole became their own particular interest. Within this circle, by slow degrees and with only minimal anticipations of what lay ahead, political insights were discovered and institutions devised that eventually led to reconciliation between the contending forces and to the gradual ascendancy and involvement of the middle strata of the body politic (and ultimately of its lower strata). In this way discontent and disaffection were converted into political demands. Step by step, broad sections of the citizenry were set new objectives, until in the end they acquired decisive power in the community.

As we have said, anticipations were minimal; expectations could gain scarcely any lead over experience. As a result it was never possible to set long-term goals for which the citizens could be prepared and toward which they could work over any length of time. This was never considered even remotely possible. On the other hand, the broad mass of the people did not have to be freed from potent traditional conceptions. What mattered was that concrete aims be realized as and when they were conceived, that institutional plans be put into effect as and when they were devised; and doing these things depended solely on the conviction they carried and the degree of power available. All this was achieved by direct action on the part of certain individuals who were able to win over the community at large.[144] Hence, the real change that was taking place in the middle and lower ranks of society was hardly discernible. All the greater, then, was the experience of the possibilities when they were finally realized—above all the possibilities of thought and action that led to the creation of institutions. To put it in broad terms: the most notable feature of this process was the capacity for action that lay with the experts.[145] It seems to me, incidentally, that an extremely important point in favor of political thought is involved here: the legitimacy of its postulates always resided in its own insight, not in some idea of the people, history, or time. Consequently it is hardly possible to differentiate according to the categories "oligarchic" and "democratic."

Finally, whole constitutions became a matter of secondary institutions, and thus of direct, intentional political action. The communities took control of the civic order. In the constitutional debate reported by Herodotus we can still sense the proud awareness—unprecedented in world history—that the realization of law is an institutional problem, and therefore susceptible of solution.[146] Ancient institutions and relations of rank were placed at the disposition of the people. The scope for thought, action, and decision making was enlarged to a huge and alarming extent. Fundamental alternatives opened up. It was in these circumstances, it seems to me, that the Greeks crossed the threshold beyond which they were able to perceive the extraordinary opportunities available to men.

For they had already experienced striking manifestations of human ability in the archaic period. Seafaring and colonization, for instance, depended on a number of quite remarkable insights and inventions, on large-scale planning and feats of organization. Tyranny often depended on new modes of methodical action and represented an extreme form of human power. The scope of human endeavor had been greatly enlarged by the achievements of the lawgivers and *katartisteres* ("those who put things to rights, brought things back into plumb") and by the many social and economic institutions that were devised and introduced at this period; this cannot have gone unremarked.[147] Bold projects were conceived that went beyond the bounds of the possible.[148] At the same time we may note the remarkable progress that was made in military tactics and artistic skills.[149] Yet many of these achievements were either the work of outstanding personalities such as the *katartisteres*[150] or worked chiefly to the advantage of individuals, such as the tyrants; often they actually aggravated the political conflicts and made the practices employed by the rulers even more intolerable, thus increasing the afflictions of the communities and the widespread sense of impotence. Attempts to establish a just order often proved disappointing. Moreover, Delphi's opposition to all excess, and the anxiety and diffidence of large sections of the population, inhibited the full development of the consciousness of human ability.[151] The decisive factor, however, was that men still lived in the ambience of "nomistic" tradition.[152] At all events, the fact that no ideas of "progress" are attested from this period cannot be a result of the inadequacy of the sources.

The fifth century, however, saw not only the emergence of alternative constitutions but also fresh scope for activity in other spheres. The plastic arts freed themselves from the authority of traditional forms. Artists were now free to determine not just the detail, but the total structure of a figure.[153] The difficulty of decision making in certain human situations became a major theme of tragedy.[154] In foreign affairs, temporal and spatial dimensions of planning and action, hitherto undreamt-of, were revealed.[155] Not least significant was the emergence of rational forensic procedures, which started from highly ambitious demands and at the same time left much more than before to the discretion of the judges. All this was compounded by innovations in the fields of technical skill and craftsmanship. The movement was taken up and enthusiastically promoted by the sophists.

This period seems, then, to have seen the creation of a fundamentally new basis for thought and action that, from the perspective of political thinking, should properly be called "cratistic." Just as constitutions were from now on functions of rule or power *(kratos)*, so too, in a very comprehensive sense, everything was placed (or seemed to be placed) in the hands of those possessed of ability. It was as though hitherto invisible bounds had suddenly been breached. How this happened in different areas is hard to determine. It may be presumed that the chief factor was the breakup of the nomistic horizon by the rule of the *demos* (and its preforms). At least there were close and enduring links between the ways in which advances were perceived in the most varied fields. Moreover, everything seems to have happened with amazing rapidity, in a few tempestuous decades—especially in Athens. Men suddenly found themselves in an astonishingly new situation. Traditional rules and concepts were found wanting, or at least no longer had much to offer the liveliest spirits, who had to rely upon their own resources in coping with everything. To put it more precisely: they were obliged (and found themselves able) to mobilize their own efforts and act on their own initiative to such an extent, they were confronted to such an extent by alternatives and able to make such great strides, that they easily forgot the debt they owed to their predecessors. There was a switch in the gravitation of perception. Moreover, the alternatives were so clear and the new scope for action so wide that the leading spirits—and not only they—became far more aware of what lay within the reach of human achievement. Men became conscious of the new possibilities by consciously realizing them. Much was achieved at once, and much else at rapidly succeeding intervals. Men must have been fascinated by the new vistas that opened before their eyes. This seems to me the best way to explain how the consciousness of ability arose.[156]

The fact that none of this led to a perception of comprehensive change was due essentially to the configurations that produced change and determined how it was perceived. If men were aware of the capacity for cognition and action possessed by many individuals, and if such awareness arose above all among the most outstanding among them, this alone would suffice to impede any recognition of the process that was in train. On the other hand, what was essentially new in the *polis*—grounded as it was in the body politic—was the fact that government *(arche)*, affairs *(pragmata)* and decisions *(bouleumata)* were brought into the midst *(meson)* of the citizens.[157] Having been long subject to the arbitrary rule of the nobles and exposed to many socioeconomic pressures, the citizens were at last able to settle the affairs of the community among themselves; this applied especially to Athens, but also, to a lesser degree, to many other city-states. Herein lay the essence of the political: the affairs of the city were in the hands of the citizens. Most of what happened in the *polis* was discussed, resolved, and executed in public; at all events, whatever happened in internal and external affairs stemmed from the actions of identifiable agents. If contingency played a part in this, it arose from conflicts between them.

Other forms of change—economic, social, or educational—were relatively slight. The main obstacle to appreciating such changes was the mode of perception that went with the prevalent form of social identity. It was a feature of this political world that large sections of the body politic were directly and intensively involved in politics. The first democracies in world history could arise only as direct democracies. This meant that a new identity developed in the *poleis*—a political identity,[158] based on a powerful solidarity, the only powerful and universal solidarity that existed at the time, involving mutual acceptance, mutual understanding, and mutual expectations. The one thing that could be taken for granted in the *poleis* was that the citizens saw themselves as citizens. When political identity is the dominant affiliation—indeed the only significant affiliation—in a society, it follows that it has no competition to contend with. It is bound to be specially robust, concrete, and cohesive, admitting little social differentiation, and indeed blocking and relativizing it if it shows signs of developing. Hence, any impulses toward economic and social change within the community are inhibited, because the citizens are, first and foremost, citizens. In the world of the *polis* this meant that political action by individuals and communities was of central importance, the focus of all perception. Moreover, the citizens were constantly faced by new decisions—which were for the most part their own. Everything that happened was seen from the viewpoint of intentional political action and its impact on affairs. Whatever improvements took place in other areas of life were seen as increasing the opportunities for action, and so working to the benefit of politics (and indeed they were often the outcome of politics and war).

Given such an intense form of the political and the identity that was shaped by it, men found themselves occupying a new position in time, or (to put it in terms that are at once more metaphorical and more concrete) in the current of all that was happening, both in reality and in the perception of reality. Within a theory of historical "times" one may say that a "political time" was emerging.[159] When men are so preoccupied with action and when the field of possibilities is limited to the political oppositions, they are hardly able to see any change taking place in themselves. This was matched by a general view of the world as structurally static.

Comprehensive change probably becomes perceptible only through a process of transformation that affects economic, social, and educational conditions and involves a high degree of interdependence—the kind of process, in other words, that was experienced by the bourgeoisie in modern times. Even today it is not easy to perceive processes of change, especially when one is involved in action; one is most likely to be able to do so by identifying oneself with progress—but such identification rests upon quite modern presuppositions.

If everything in the ancient world led to the concentration of perception on actions and events—processes being invoked solely to bridge the gap between the present and a very different past—it follows that the consciousness of human ability and political history (the form in which generally relevant change was perceived) were mutually complementary. These were further complemented by the fifth-century politicization of politicosocial concepts, which was incompatible with temporalization.[160]

The very fact that there was any public perception of change, albeit only in political affairs, was a significant achievement; it required a high degree of tolerance to contingency and opened up a new realm of experience. With it there arose a new and rigorous empiricism, an unusually practical cast of thought, a special closeness to reality. Whatever the Greeks' capacity for abstraction, they never extrapolated from the present to the future. The range of the terms they employed, for instance, extended no further than the distance between the contemporary political oppositions.

Since everything was determined (and perforce appeared to be determined) by intentional action, expectations too remained limited. There was no concept of an abstract entity such as the modern state, of which much is expected, even though today's citizens know that it is *their* state and nothing more; no notion of the abstract power of a process wherein an infinity of impulses (especially the side effects of intentional action) combines to produce unpredictable results; no thought of subjectivizing concepts so that they become effective forces in their own right; no trace of modern-style social identity, which continually has to compensate for imbalances by fostering universal expectations for the benefit of all;[161] and little by way of ideology.

Hence, the general consciousness of ability could not survive beyond the period that inspired it—especially in the sphere of the political. By the end of the fifth century, that is, by the end of the Peloponnesian War, it was played out. It then withdrew into the sphere of academic speculation, where in due course the belief in progress was reinforced.[162] In the grand constitutional designs of the later period, especially Plato's, we find a greater faith in the power of cognition, action, and creation to shape the *polis* than had existed in the fifth century. It was a faith that found its legitimation in the consciousness of human ability, without being obliged to seek it in identifications with higher powers—with God or history, the people or the proletariat. Knowledge and virtue could thus become a justification for rule. Man was the master of his world, confronted neither by an almighty God nor by the power of processes. He therefore did not have to take such deep soundings. To gain control of the constitution was such a feat of political skill as to generate extraordinary pretensions. Hence almost every constitution, especially democracy, was now found wanting. A solution was therefore sought in political theory. Aristotle then observed that in the realm of the political everything had been discovered.[163]

The consciousness of ability is thus an equivalent of the modern idea of progress, though not a *functional* equivalent. It registered achievements and was above all an expression of pride in the possibilities that had been realized. It provided scarcely any orientation. It made no general statements about time. Hence the most varied changes, both for the better and for the worse, could be seen to coexist, without any implied contradiction.[164] Accordingly there were only rudimentary observations on the "simultaneity of the nonsimultaneous."[165] The result was, in short, a combination of

1. political action as the central factor in historical change
2. the consciousness of human ability
3. political identity (as a robust and practical form of social identity realized among the citizens)
4. the strict adherence of thinking to present experience
5. a somewhat inadequate perception of change

These are paralleled in modern times by

1. the process as the principal form of historical change (beside which political action is only ever incidental, being simply carried along by the process)[166]
2. the consciousness of progress
3. a partly national and partly temporal identity (to the latter I would also assign the marked class identities of the lower social strata), which has to span immense disparities and bridge the gaps that are continually opening up between experience and expectation
4. extrapolation of expectations from the present
5. a somewhat exaggerated perception of change

We may presume that only two possible species of *auxesis*-consciousness can develop. One of these relates to the ability of relatively few agents, is restricted in its range, and is concentrated in the realms of cognition and action, and also in the political. The other embraces also social and moral conditions and envisages a broadly based process. Herein lies a crucial difference between the ancient world and our own. But is there not some degree of comparability too? True, change in ancient Greece was restricted in its extent and confined to certain areas. Modern change is so broad and pervasive that our world appears as history, and progress, in accordance with the concept, as an objective force; the activity of countless millions becomes an achievement of time, and social structure becomes temporal structure. In the ancient world men looked for an order that corresponded to what they were: we look for progress toward what we are to become—the New Man, the New Society. Whereas ancient expectations and disappointments were slight, ours are great; and our disappointments require repeated compensations. The ancients evolved a theory of politics, we a philosophy of history, as Hannah Arendt observed.[167] Whereas the ancients were empirical, we favor abstraction and ideology. Whereas the ancient "constitution" meant the civic community *(politeia)*, Karl Marx demanded "that progress be made the *principle of the* constitution and therefore that the real bearer of the constitution, the people, be made the principle of the constitution. Progress itself is then the constitution."[168] The civic community on the one hand, progress on the other—politics there, social change and history here. Then once again we become impatient and expect politics to do everything—to change society. The danger then is that the surface will be planed smooth and the shavings discarded: "Master of things unhoped-for, he goes his way, the way of the good and the bad." To put it briefly: in those respects that we have considered here, as in others, much has changed since the fifth century B.C.—yet at the same time little has changed. The period is at once very close and very remote. The reason for this is that, to quote Uvo Hölscher,[169] it is the nearest point to home in foreign territory. And this calls for a theory that will result in our "meeting at one central point, since we approach the matter from so many sides."

Notes

Introduction

1. On this point see C. Meier, "Handeln und Aushalten," in *Imago Linguae. Festschrift F. Paepcke* (Munich 1976), 359.
2. This is the view of H. G. Kippenberg (ed.), *Seminar: Die Entstehung der antiken Klassengesellschaft* (Frankfurt 1977). See also idem, *Zeitschrift für Politik* 25 (1978) 5 n. 20, 13 n. 46; R. Rilinger, *Historische Zeitschrift* 228 (1979) 387 ff.
3. See H. Lübbe, *Geschichtsbegriff und Geschichtsinteresse* (Basel/Stuttgart 1977), 35 ff.
4. K. Jaspers, *Vom Ursprung und Ziel der Geschichte* (Munich 1949) (*The Origin and Goal of History*, trans. M. Bullock [London 1953]); S. N. Eisenstadt (ed.), *The Origins and Diversity of Axial Age Civilizations* (New York 1986). Cf. B. Nelson, *Der Ursprung der Moderne. Vergleich-ende Studien zum Zivilisationsprozess* (Frankfurt 1977), esp. x ff.
5. C. Schmitt, *Der Begriff des Politischen* (rev. ed. Berlin 1963) (*The Concept of the Political*, trans. G. Schwab [New Brunswick, N.J., 1976]). Cf. H. Meier, *Carl Schmitt, Leo Strauss und "Der Begriff des Politischen." Zu einem Dialog unter Abwesenden* (Stuttgart 1988).
6. For a discussion of this topic see the important book by D. Sternberger, *Drei Wurzeln der Politik* (Frankfurt 1978).
7. See E.-W. Böckenförde in a 1969 article, repr. in *Kirchlicher Auftrag und politische Entscheidung* (Freiburg 1973) and cited with approval by C. Schmitt, *Politische Theologie* II (Berlin 1970), 25 f; more recently, Böcken-förde, *Der Staat als sittlicher Staat* (Berlin 1978), 12 f.
8. This is expressed very appositely in the account of Solon's *stasis* law given in the *Athenaion Politeia*, originating in the school of Aristotle and com-monly attributed to him (8.5). Cf. Chapter 5, note 180, below.
9. Lübbe, *Geschichtsbegriff*, 326.
10. W. Benjamin, *Gesammelte Schriften* I.3 (Frankfurt 1974), 1232. For a de-tailed discussion of Benjamin's theses on the philosophy of history ("Über den Begriff der Geschichte") see G. Kaiser, *Benjamin, Adorno. Zwei Stu-dien* (Frankfurt 1974); also idem, *Neue Antithesen eines Germanisten.*

1974/5 (Kronberg 1976), 99 ff. Benjamin's emphasis on the moment, the present ("arrêter le jour"), the interruption of the continuum, the forcible seizure of possibilities for freedom, decision, and opportunity, the image of "jumping out" of the continuum, of "leaping," of the "tiger-leap," the play on the German word *Ursprung* (normally "origin," but construed etymologically as *Ur-sprung*, "out-leap"), the notion of time coming to a halt (and of being "man enough to break the continuum of history")—all this makes one thing abundantly clear: that action, the real "state of emergency," can bring salvation to the quick and the dead (in accordance with the "weak messianic power" that is given to us). [*Translator's note:* In the German text the word *Ausnahmezustand*, "state of emergency," is hyphenated: *Ausnahme-Zustand*. This draws attention to its literal sense, "exceptional state."] Progress, by contrast, is the "storm" that blows from paradise and forces the "angel of history," against his will, "irresistibly into the future, on which he turns his back, while in front of him the rubble rises sky-high." A "sullen faith in progress" and a "servile submission to an uncontrollable apparatus" (together with "trust in the mass basis") are obviously only different aspects of the same thing. They are "corrupting" because they make us subject to the process and emasculate us. The "political child of the world" is thus chained to thinking in terms of processes (and in thrall to processes) and forced to forgo the present. The theses are reprinted in *Gesammelte Schriften* I.2, 691 ff. Thesis 17a (I.3, 1231) is also of particular importance.

11. E. Auerbach, *Mimesis. Dargestellte Wirklichkeit in der abendländischen Kultur* (3d ed. Bern/Munich 1964), 41.

12. C. Schmitt, *Politische Theologie* (2d ed. Munich/Leipzig 1934), 7 and passim.

13. On another aspect of "preliminary decision making" (what might be called the "warming up" of processes), which often seems to be the only way to set in motion a process that will entail decisions, see C. Meier, in K.-G. Faber and C. Meier (eds.), *Historische Prozesse* (Munich 1978), 16 f. Cf. H. Kissinger, writing in the *New York Times* on 14 March 1979: "the fact that we are in an endless process in which each solution of the foreign policy puzzle is an admission prize to another problem."

14. This does not relate to the regular "decision-making processes," which at least directly envisage a decision, but to the problems posed by the impossibility or difficulty of making decisions, given the disappearance of the differential of influence and the infinite reciprocal dependency (reciprocity and multipolarity) in all relations. See N. Elias, *Was ist Soziologie?* (Munich 1970), 70 ff, 100 f.

15. Cf. O. Marquardt and K. Stierle (eds.), *Identität* (Munich 1979).

16. Cf. D. Jähnig, *Welt-Geschichte: Kunst-Geschichte. Zum Verhältnis von Vergangenheitserkenntnis und Veränderung* (Cologne 1975), 83 ff, 87 ff, 102 f.

17. On this central point I differ from S. C. Humphreys, *Anthropology and the Greeks* (London 1978). Humphreys rightly maintains that the anthropological approach to the ancient world needs to be revived. But in the context of a long-overdue attempt to remedy the isolation of classical research,

one should also try to bring the special features of the classical period more clearly into focus, both in detail and in general. We should see it afresh in the context of world history, rather than rob it of its special character (which is a danger inherent in Humphreys' extremely interesting approach).

18. K.-G. Faber, *Theorie der Geschichtswissenschaft* (Munich 1971), 147 ff.

1. From *Politikos* to the Modern Concept of the Political

1. Or else they endeavored to equate themselves with the *polis,* like certain political groups.

2. Aristotle, *Politics* 1305b; cf. 1273b12 *(politikos* closely linked with *demotikos* and *koinos),* 1293a41, 1298a39. Thucydides 8.89.3; cf. 3.82.8. Aristotle, *Politics* 1255b16; cf. 1252a7, 1254b2, 1277a33 and b9, 1325a27 (countering a widely held view: "to believe that every government *[arche]* is despotic is not correct"), 1333a5. Cf. Plato, *Republic* 303c.

3. Aristotle, *Politics* 1255b20, 1277b7 (cf. 1254b3, 1259b1), 1295b21 (cf. 1296a29). This is most likely to be the case with the good form of democracy, *politeia* (cf. C. Meier, "Demokratie," in W. Conze, R. Koselleck, and O. Brunner (eds.), *Geschichtliche Grundbegriffe* I [Stuttgart 1972], 831). It was in danger of being lost in Aristotle's time (1926a40 f: "It has become a fixed habit no longer to desire equality, but either to seek to rule *[archein]* or to endure being under a master"). Cf. Demosthenes 10.4: only a part of the citizenry wishes "neither to rule by force nor to serve, but to live as citizens in freedom and justice among equals" *(en eleutheria kai nomois ex isou politeuesthai).* See Chapter 7 of this volume and C. Meier, "Macht und Gewalt," in W. Conze, R. Koselleck, and O. Brunner (eds.), *Geschichtliche Grundbegriffe* III (Stuttgart 1982), 820 ff.

4. Isocrates, *Panegyricus* 79, 151. Demosthenes 9.48, 10.74, 18.3, 25.74; Aristotle(?), *Athenaion Politeia* 14.3, 16.2. Cf. *Politics* 1259b1, 1324a37.

5. See V. Sellin, "Politik," in W. Conze, R. Koselleck, and O. Brunner (eds.), *Geschichtliche Grundbegriffe* IV (Stuttgart 1978), 789 ff. Cf. D. Sternberger, *Macchiavellis "Principe" und der Begriff des Politischen* (Wiesbaden 1974); idem, *Drei Wurzeln der Politik* (Frankfurt 1978), 24 ff; G. Bien, *Die Grundlegung der politischen Philosophie bei Aristoteles* (Freiburg 1973), 212 ff.

6. "Testament Politique" (1752), in *Politische Korrespondenz. Ergänzungsband: Die politischen Testamente,* ed. G. B. Volz (Berlin 1920), 27.

7. Cf., e.g., Thucydides 1.138 and Chapter 8.

8. Cf. C. Schmitt, "Inter pacem et bellum nihil medium," *Zeitschrift der Akademie für deutsches Recht* (1939) 593 ff; idem, *Positionen und Begriffe* (Hamburg 1940), 244 ff; idem, *Der Begriff des Politischen* (rev. ed. Berlin 1963), 12 (*The Concept of the Political,* trans. G. Schwab [New Brunswick, N.J., 1976]). (Unless otherwise stated, all citations are to the 1963 edition.)

9. See H. Maier, *Die ältere deutsche Staats- und Verwaltungslehre. Polizeiwissenschaft* (Neuwied 1966).

10. Schmitt, *Begriff des Politischen*, 23; *Politische Theologie* II (Berlin 1970), 24 f.

11. Schmitt, *Begriff des Politischen*, 38.

12. Ibid., 26 ff.

13. Ibid., 37 ff.

14. Ibid., 29.

15. Ibid., 48.

16. Ibid., 9 ff.

17. Cf. J. Julliard, in J. Le Goff and P. Nora (eds.), *Faire de l'histoire* II (Paris 1974), 232.

18. Schmitt, *Politische Theologie* (2d ed. Munich/Leipzig 1934), 7.

19. Cf. the important but not altogether apposite review by L. Strauss (1932), repr. in *Hobbes' politische Wissenschaft* (Neuwied 1965), 161 ff (translated in *The Concept of the Political*; see note 9 above). H. Meier, *Carl Schmitt, Leo Strauss und "Der Begriff des Politischen." Zu einem Dialog unter Abwesenden* (Stuttgart 1988).

20. A. Heuss, *Antike und Abendland* 2 (1946) 38 ff, 53 ff, repr. in F. Gschnitzer (ed.), *Griechische Staatskunde* (Darmstadt 1969), 36 ff. See also Chapter 3.

21. Schmitt, *Begriff des Politischen*, 12, 28 ff; idem, *Theorie des Partisanen* (Berlin 1963), 92. For a general discussion of Schmitt's concept of the enemy see H. Laufer, *Das Kriterium des politischen Handelns* [! C. M.]. *Eine Studie zur Freund-Feind-Doktrin von Carl Schmitt auf der Grundlage der aristotelischen Theorie der Politik* (Munich 1961); K.-M. Kodalle, *Politik als Macht und Mythos* (Stuttgart 1973), 25 ff.

22. Schmitt, *Begriff des Politischen* (1933 ed.), 11. Cf. the anecdote about Themistocles in Plutarch, *Aristides* 2.5 (a different story is related in *Themistocles* 5.6; both in *Moralia* 807A–B).

23. Schmitt, *Begriff des Politischen*, 30.

24. It is not a question of semantic variants, but of the nucleus of what is understood by "political." Cf. Schmitt's formulation in "Staatsethik und pluralistischer Statt," in *Positionen und Begriffe*, 141: "Political unity . . . represents . . . the most intense degree of unity, which in consequence determines the most intense distinction, that between friend and foe." This is "the highest unity, not because it dictates in an all-powerful way or levels all units, but because it makes decisions and, within itself, can prevent all other contrasting groupings from dissociating themselves to the point of extreme enmity (i.e., civil war)." This we may endorse.

25. Schmitt, *Begriff des Politischen*, 30.

26. On this point H. Lübbe, *Theorie und Entscheidung* (Freiburg 1971), 11, has said all that needs to be said.

27. B. Snell, *Die Entdeckung des Geistes* (4th ed. Göttingen 1975), 205. It is true that the word occurs in substantivized form, but only as a designation of the civic community (Herodotus 7.103.1; Thucydides 8.93.3; cf. Xenophon, *Helenica* 5.3.25, 4.4.19) or—in the plural—to denote political affairs (Thucydides 2.40; cf. 6.15, 89). Similarly Aeschylus, *Supplices* 370: *to demion* 689. Cf. Pindar, fr. 109.

28. Steinberger, *Drei Wurzeln*, 19 ff.

29. And it would certainly be improper simply to state that a particular sense of the adjective represented "the political"; were one to do so, one would think one recognized what one was defining and work at a category that then unexpectedly behaved as a phenomenon. There are two quite different ways out of the difficulties outlined here; they should not be confused or allowed to contaminate each other. One is to define expressly what the political is or should be. We are quite free to do this. Such definitions can be sharp and precise, but for this very reason they will often prove inadequate when it comes to dealing with much of what is called political. There will inevitably be many definitions; each will be right, but only by virtue of being a definition of this kind. The only controversy they could provoke would relate to their usefulness. The other way is to find a comprehensive concept that embraces everything expressed by the term itself. One might then argue about whether one had correctly defined "the political" in relation to what is described as "political," especially as the nucleus of the concept would have to be fairly concentrated. But one would have an object that could be clearly circumscribed—not what the political *should be,* but what the word *political means* in its whole semantic spread.

30. Schmitt, *Politische Theologie* II, 25 f.

31. Ibid.; Schmitt, *Begriff des Politischen,* 27, 38.

32. Nothing is so revealing about the present meaning of the word *political* as the fact that certain groups—e.g., terrorists—claim to be "political" (and not criminal), while others—one need not cite examples—describe themselves as nonpolitical (and sometimes use this as a means to gain political power). H. Lübbe, *Merkur* 31 (1977) 822, concurs on the first point. Cf. ibid., 825.

33. Julliard, in Le Goff and Nora, *Faire de l'histoire* II, 243 ff.

34. Ibid.; C. Meier, "Der Alltag des Historikers und die historische Theorie," in H.-M. Baumgartner and J. Rüsen (eds.), *Seminar: Geschichte und Theorie. Umrisse einer Historik* (Frankfurt 1976), 44 ff.

35. This relationship seems to me more important than the simple one between mutability and susceptibility to controversy; on the latter see C. Meier, *Res Publica Amissa* (1966; repr. Frankfurt 1980), 159 f.

2. The Political in Ancient Greece

1. See D. Sternberger, *Ich wünschte ein Bürger zu sein* (Frankfurt 1967), 67 (cf. 54 f, 57, 93 ff).

2. Aristotle, *Nicomachean Ethics* 1094a26 ff; *Politics* 1282b14 ff. Cf. 1252a3 ff, *Eudemian Ethics* 1182b1. See also Chapter 8.

3. Cf. C. Meier and P. Veyne, *Kannten die Griechen die Demokratie?* (Berlin 1988), 48 ff.

4. Plato, *Republic* 422e.

5. Cf. F. Jonas, *Die Institutionenlehre Arnold Gehlens* (Tübingen 1966), 30: "Modern society is fundamentally different from the ancient *polis;* it cannot be understood in terms of the latter—as Montesquieu, for example, saw very clearly—nor is the pathos of the *polis* compatible with the func-

tioning of bourgeois society. Modern societies are not political in the way in which the Greek or Italian city-states were political. The attempt to find in politics the unifying bond that holds modern states together is bound to lead to terror, as the French Revolution demonstrated. . . . Our states are held together neither by a common political will nor by a common faith, but by a third element, which was first recognized in the works of the English economists of the eighteenth century."

6. Because whole communities were ranged against one another in the hoplite armies, a particularly bloody battle could make a city indefensible for many years. In Argos it was necessary on one occasion to resort to slaves in order to provide (temporary) reinforcements for the citizenry until a new generation grew up (Herodotus 6.83). When a city suffered defeat, all the men might be executed and the women and children sold into slavery.

7. O. Marquard, "Kompensation. Überlegungen zu einer Verlaufsfigur geschichtlicher Prozesse," in K.-G. Faber and C. Meier (eds.), *Historische Prozesse* (Munich 1978), 332.

8. Cf. H. Strasburger, *Homer und die griechische Geschichtsschreibung* (Heidelberg 1972), 23 f, 33 ff, and passim.

9. On the spirit of the Delphic oracle already present in Homer, see W. Schadewaldt, *Der Aufbau der Ilias* (Frankfurt 1975), 8. On greatness, see K. Reinhardt, *Von Werken und Formen* (Godesberg 1948), 22 ff.

10. Cf. D. Sternberger's assessment of Hannah Arendt's: "Die versunkene Stadt," *Merkur* 30 (1976) 935 ff.

11. Cf. C. Schmitt, "Die legale Weltrevolution. Politischer Mehrwert als Prämie auf juristische Legalität und Superlegalität," *Der Staat* 17 (1978) 321 ff.

3. The Emergence of the Trend toward Isonomy

1. See C. Meier, in K.-G. Faber and C. Meier (eds.), *Historische Prozesse* (Munich 1978), 221 ff. For a more recent consideration of the topic of this chapter see C. Meier, "Die Griechen. Die politische Revolution der Weltgeschichte," *Saeculum* 33 (1982) 133 ff.

2. Herodotus 1.170.

3. On this term (and the possible occurrence of the phenomenon in ancient Mesopotamia) see T. Jacobsen, in H. Frankfort, H. A. Frankfort, J. A. Wilson, and T. Jacobsen, *Before Philosophy. The Intellectual Adventure of Ancient Man. An Essay on Speculative Thought in the Ancient Near East* (Harmondsworth 1949), 141 ff. On the powerful cult-based cohesion see W. Burkert, "Opfertypen und antike Gesellschaftsstruktur," in G. Stephenson (ed.), *Der Religionswandel unserer Zeit im Spiegel der Religionswissenschaft* (Darmstadt 1976), 184 ff; idem, *Griechische Religion der archaischen und klassischen Epoche* (Stuttgart 1977), 382 ff. Cf. C. Meier, *Die Welt der Geschichte und die Provinz des Historikers* (Berlin 1989).

4. See M. I. Finley, *The World of Odysseus* (Harmondsworth 1962), 33, 89 ff, 105 ff; B. Borecki, in *Geras: Studies Presented to G. Thomson* (Prague 1963), 60.

5. See Meier, in Faber and Meier, *Historische Prozesse*, 51 ff.

6. Cf. H. K. Erben, *Die Entwicklung der Lebewesen. Spielregeln der Evolution* (Munich/Zurich 1975).

7. This is the view of W. F. Otto, *The Homeric Gods*, trans. M. Hadas (London 1955). The same view is taken by H. Lloyd-Jones, *The Justice of Zeus* (Berkeley 1971), 169 n. 45.

8. Cf., e.g., F. Gschnitzer, "Politische Leidenschaft im homerischen Epos," in H. Görgemanns and E. A. Schmidt (eds.), *Studien zum antiken Epos* (Meisenheim 1976), 1 ff. W. Schadewaldt, *Der Aufbau der Ilias, Strukturen und Konzeptionen* (Frankfurt 1975), 91 ff, writes: "The old memories of that prehistoric era combined with a self-confidence that looked boldly into the future to produce a situation that was extraordinarily fruitful for poetry." The memories of a great past were permeated by ideas belonging to contemporary everyday life and its conflicts, creating a picture of an easygoing peasant world that was at the same time a world of public action. Affairs of state took on something of the air of peasant quarrels, as it were. Cf. H. Strasburger, "Der soziologische Aspekt der homerischen Epen," *Gymnasium* 60 (1953) 97 ff; idem, *Homer und die Geschichtsschreibung* (Heidelberg 1972), 22, on the "precise potential reality of the epics." In the *Odyssey* too we already find traces of the new belief in justice, current in the middle and lower classes, of which the work of Hesiod, from the beginning of the seventh century, provides the most important evidence. Much of the character and effect of the epics is thus determined by the fact that they are composed essentially in the spirit of this extremely primitive age, which was at the same time already keenly aware of the power and exposedness of man and took the liberty of reshaping the old epic tradition. It is in this way that poetry already played a part in the emergence of the basic conditions that helped shape the Greek character. For a cautious dating of the epics, see A. Lesky, "Homeros," *RE Suppl.* XI (1967), 7.

9. This can best be seen in the Homeric epics. Cf. Finley, *The World of Odysseus*, 96 ff; A. Heuss, *Antike und Abendland* 2 (1946) 40 ff, repr. in F. Gschnitzer (ed.), *Griechische Staatskunde* (Darmstadt 1969), 36 ff; F. Schachermeyr, *Forschungen zur griechischen und römischen Geschichte* (Vienna 1974), 32.

10. Cf. C. W. Starr, *The Economic and Social Growth of Early Greece, 800–500 B.C.* (New York 1977), 56 ff.

11. Ibid., 61 f.

12. H. A. Ormerod, *Piracy in the Ancient World* (Liverpool 1924).

13. The fact that overpopulation was gradually increasing seems to me quite unmistakable, even if it was not the only reason many Greeks found the homeland restricting; cf. J. N. Coldstream, *The Formation of the Greek Polis* (Rheinisch-Westfälische Akademie, Düsseldorf 1984), 9 f. Starr's arguments *(Economic and Social Growth,* 41 ff), however, do not carry conviction. The analogies with classical Athens do not take into account the enormous losses as a result of war; Hesiod's advice need not have been followed everywhere; fluctuations in the size of the population cannot be ruled out. Above all, one cannot explain away the extraordinary movement of population to the colonies. It also seems very dubious that colonization

was really "the product of prosperity rather than of poverty" (C. A. Roebuck, quoted by Starr, 44). It seems to me to have been promoted simultaneously by poverty and prosperity (which increased with colonization). Cf. also E. Ruschenbusch, *Untersuchungen zur Geschichte des athenischen Strafrechts* (Cologne/Graz 1968), 41.

14. Starr, *Economic and Social Growth*, 49 f.

15. P. Spahn, *Mittelschicht und Polisbildung* (Frankfurt/Bern/Las Vegas 1977), 84 ff. To some extent Argos too is an exception.

16. Heuss, *Antike und Abendland* 2 (1946) 41 ff, 47 ff, 54. Cf. H. Schaefer, *Probleme der Alten Geschichte* (Göttingen 1963), 362 ff, esp. 377 f, who overrates the power of monarchy, as does V. Ehrenberg, *The Greek State* (2d ed. London 1966), 17 f. Cf. Starr, *Economic and Social Growth*, 46 ff, 191 ff.

17. Heuss, *Antike und Abendland* 2 (1946) 37 f, 41 ff 44, 48 ff. Cf. Schaefer, *Probleme*, 283 ff. On what follows here, see also H. Strasburger, "Der Einzelne und die Gemeinschaft im Denken der Griechen," *Historische Zeitschrift* 177 (1954) 227 ff.

18. Schaefer, *Probleme*, 298.

19. The many different attempts at political reform introduced by the nobles (discussed by Heuss, *Antike und Abendland* 2 (1946) 41, 43; Schaefer, *Probleme*, 311, 389; and Ehrenberg, *The Greek State*, 20 f, though with insufficient attention to the extent to which they were prompted by pressure from below) were obviously inadequate to deal with the full magnitude of the difficulties in the more turbulent cities.

20. Cf. esp. J. Hasebroek, *Griechische Wirtschafts- und Gesellschaftsgeschichte bis zur Perserzeit* (Tübingen 1931), 158 ff; E. Will, "La Grèce archaique," in *Deuxième conférence internationale d'histoire économique* (The Hague 1965), 41 ff. I know of no comprehensive analysis of the crisis that assembles and evaluates all the material (including the numerous indications contained in the contemporary lyric). At all events, the crisis went far beyond the economic sphere.

21. In addition there were structural changes resulting from inequalities in the size of families and the allocation of land. See S. C. Humphreys, *Anthropology and the Greeks* (London 1978), 162 f.

22. The latter is attested chiefly in contemporary sources and the archaic lyric (cf. H. Fränkel, *Dichtung und Philosophie des frühen Griechentums* [2d ed. Munich 1962], 610 f [*Early Greek Poetry and Philosophy*, trans. M. Hadas and J. Willis (Oxford 1975), 530]; idem, *Wege und Formen frühgriechischen Denkens* [3d ed. Munich 1968], 23 ff), the former only occasionally (Fränkel, *Early Greek Poetry*, 527 f), though it can be inferred from the way men acted and also—as a mirror image—from observations about the transience of human greatness. Cf. Heuss, *Antike und Abendland* 2 (1946) 58 f: "If man became aware, with the collapse of the old forms, of what lay open to his own initiative, he was bound to realize at the same time that he was exposed to uncertainty, lacking all guidance and, with all his strength, essentially a frail creature." Cf. Starr, *Economic and Social Growth*, 171 f. On the

same ambivalence in the fifth century see J. de Romilly, "Thucydide et l'idée du progrès," *Annali della Scuola normale superiore di Pisa. Lettere, storia e filosofia,* ser. 2 (1966), 158.

23. See H. Berve, *Die Tyrannis bei den Griechen* (Munich 1967). For a cautious account of the spread of tyranny see E. Ruschenbusch, *Untersuchungen zu Staat und Politik in Griechenland vom 7.–4. Jh. v. Chr.* (Bamberg 1978), 18 ff.

24. C. Meier, *Gnomon* 41 (1969) 353 f; idem, *Entstehung des Begriffs Demokratie* (Frankfurt 1970), 32 n. 20. H. W. Pleket, *Talanta* 1 (1970) 140, fails to understand the problem. When one speaks of an absence of "suprapersonal aims" it is not a question of whether the tyrants frequently produced positive results, but of whether they could sufficiently underpin their rule by means of institutions. Cf. D. Lanza, *Il tiranno e il suo pubblico* (Turin 1977), 163 ff.

25. Heuss, *Antike und Abendland* 2 (1946) 45 f; Schaefer, *Probleme,* 215, 314 ff; W. G. Forrest, *The Emergence of Greek Democracy* (London 1966), 104, describes the alternative very well, stating that a harmless statement such as "Tyranny in Greece was brought about by dissatisfaction with aristocratic rule" is false "if we mean by it that men said to each other in the marketplace 'I hate aristocratic rule' as they now might say 'I hate capitalism.' Rather they said 'I hate those men of families *a, b* or *c* who rule us,' and their reason would be not 'because they are aristocrats' but 'because they have done *x* or have not done *y*.'" In every state the men who were hated were different men and the reasons for the hatred were different reasons. Equally different were the politicians who took advantage of this hatred and the methods they used to exploit it." Cf. ibid., 119 ff.

26. The material is presented by Berve, *Die Tyrannis,* 765 ff. For Athens see A. French, *The Growth of the Athenian Economy* (London 1964), 30 ff, 44 ff, 56. See also Schachermeyr, *Forschungen,* 205 ff.

27. Most recently J. Salmon, "Political Hoplites?" *Journal of Hellenic Studies* 71 (1977) 84 ff. See also Pleket, *Talanta* 1 (1970) 19 ff. Salmon cites the most recent literature and makes some important distinctions concerning the political role of hoplite service. Also relevant are the observations of Starr, *Economic and Social Growth,* 33, 127, 178 ff, especially his objections to the postulation of a hoplite class.

28. Aristotle, *Politics* 1297b16ff. Cf. 1305a18. Cf. A. Raubitschek, "Meeresnähe und Volksherrschaft," *Wiener Studien* 71 (1958) 112 ff.

29. If the struggle for legal security had been successful, the way to isonomy might perhaps have been dispensed with, as it was in Rome (where the peasants likewise had to serve).

30. Cf. Humphreys, *Anthropology,* 216 f.

31. See N. Luhmann, *Rechtssoziologie* (Reinbek bei Hamburg 1972), 33 ff, 51 f, 64 ff.

32. Spahn, *Mittelschicht und Polisbildung,* 32, presents some interesting observations on this with the help of the notion of *pistis* (compared with the Roman *fides*).

33. M. Weber, *Ancient Judaism*, trans. and ed. H. H. Gerth and D. Martindale (New York 1967), 206.
34. M. I. Finley, *The Ancient Economy* (London 1973), 96.
35. Ibid., 95.
36. This is an attempt to render the word *katartister* ("one who puts things to rights," "one who brings things back into plumb"); cf. Chapter 4, note 26, below. For the background to this institution see Heuss, *Antike und Abendland* 2 (1946) 60 f; Schaefer, *Probleme*, 286 ff; also the following discussion of the rise of the "third position" in political thought.
37. F. Dornseiff, *Philologus* 89 (1934) 397 ff; *Les sagesses du proche-orient ancien. Colloque de Strasbourg 17–19 mai, 1962* (Paris 1963); G. von Rad, *Wisdom in Israel*, trans. J. D. Martin (Nashville/New York 1972).
38. J. Burckhardt, *Griechische Kulturgeschichte* III (Basel 1957), 280; cf. 296 f, 339 ff; Frankfort et al., *Before Philosophy*, 250 f; J.-P. Vernant, *Les origines de la pensée grecque* (Paris 1969), 46 ff.
39. On what follows see H. Berve, *Gestaltende Kräfte der Antike* (Munich 1949), 9 ff; idem, *Gnomon* 28 (1956) 174 ff; H. W. Parke, *A History of the Delphic Oracle* (1939); M. P. Nilsson, *Geschichte der griechischen Religion* I (3d ed. Munich 1967), 625 ff; Schaefer, *Probleme*, 250 f, 295 f, 367 f; W. G. Forrest, *Historia* 6 (1957) 160 ff.
40. J. Burckhardt, *Weltgeschichtliche Betrachtungen*, ed. R. Stadelmann (Tübingen 1949) (*Reflections on History*, trans. M. D. H. [London 1943]), frequently uses the term *Tauschplatz* ("place of exchange") when speaking of Athens. The English translator renders this as "centre of intellectual exchange," "intellectual mart" (e.g., 106 f).
41. Admittedly there were not necessarily as many as was later believed. The need to corroborate successes by means of a sacred authority may have led many early colonies to invent oracles at a later stage and establish their contacts with Delphi. Nevertheless, there were enough instances of good advice emanating from Delphi to ensure that the oracle had a lead that could later be consolidated.
42. A similar view is expressed by J. Burckhardt, *Griechische Kulturgeschichte* II (Basel 1956), 312 f; IV (Basel 1957), 69 f.
43. Nilsson, *Geschichte der griechischen Religion*, 637 ff; H. H. Rohrbach, *Kolonie und Orakel* (Heidelberg diss. 1960); Forrest, *Historia* 6 (1957) 173 f.
44. It would be interesting to know how much of the importance of the "international" games at Olympia, Isthmia, Delphi, and Nemea was derived from the fact that they provided a kind of public forum for visitors from the entire Greek world. This function of the games undoubtedly aroused great interest and may have contributed to their popularity. At all events there is a connection between the high value attached to sport and the importance of the Panhellenic public (and the relative weakness of the individual *polis* as a point of reference or sounding board) in the thinking of the nobility.
45. Cf. also Schaefer, *Probleme*, 250 f, 286 ff; Heuss, *Antike und Abendland* 2 (1946) 60 f.
46. Cf. the distinction made by Vernant (*Origines*, 210) between transcen-

dental power and transcendental—or immanent—order. See also Humphreys, *Anthropology*, 210.

47. J. Burckhardt, *Griechische Kulturgeschichte* I (Basel 1956), 11.

48. Pindar, *Pythia* 3.59 ff. W. Schadewaldt, *Der Gott von Delphi und die Humanitätsidee* (Frankfurt 1975), 7 ff (the passage quoted occurs on 29). Cf. Heuss, *Antike und Abendland* 2 (1946) 60, who speaks of the "secular policy" of the oracle. See also H. Arendt, *Vita Activa* (Stuttgart 1960), 190 f, 227 (*The Human Condition* [Chicago 1958]). Sophocles, fr. 590 (Pearson); Democritus B191 (*Fragmente der Vorsokratiker* II, 81 ff); Aristotle, *Nicomachean Ethics* 1177b31 ff and passim; P. Aubenque, *La prudence chez Aristote* (Paris 1963), 167. B. Snell, *Die Entdeckung des Geistes* (4th ed. Göttingen 1975), 214, contrasts this with Plato, for whom the good is a goal that always lies beyond the present and the possible.

49. E. R. Dodds, *The Greeks and the Irrational* (Berkeley 1951), 28 ff, 64 ff; G. Vlastos, *Classical Philology* 41 (1946) 76. The practices of purification came from the Orient: see W. Burkert, "Die orientalisierende Epoche in der griechischen Religion und Literatur," *Sitzungsberichte der Heidelberger Akademie* (1984), 57 ff.

50. C. Meier, *Entstehung*, 19 ff.

51. F. Solmsen, *Hesiod and Aeschylus* (Ithaca 1949), 223 f.

52. Cf. Solon 23.19 ff; Berve, *Die Tyrannis*, 769 ("Neuverteilung des Bodens"). Beside this was the program of the cancellation of debts. See Will, "La Grèce archaïque," 72 f, on the political consequences (which were admittedly only negative).

53. This is true at any rate of the archaic period. At that time it was at best a question of confiscating the property of the opponents (Berve, *Die Tyrannis*, 768).

54. See Chapter 5, note 180, below.

55. See Spahn, *Mittelschicht und Polisbildung*.

56. The peasants' political importance in the Greek civic communities at this period was quite exceptional, owing to the link between civic affiliation and land ownership. In some *poleis* this link arose from the settlement of the land after the Doric migration and then colored the thinking of other *poleis*. Everyone who was affiliated with the *polis* was a landowner; no one else was allowed to own land (see Finley, *The Ancient Economy*, 48, 95 f; D. Asheri, *Historia* 12 [1963] 2 ff). This meant that only those who owned land could belong to the *polis*. This last principle was frequently relaxed or breached, in Athens from the time of Solon (Plutarch, *Solon* 24.4); but it remained true that within the community as a whole those engaged in trade and commerce counted for little (cf. M. Weber, *Economy and Society*, ed. G. Roth and C. Wittich (Berkeley 1978), 1346 ff; J. Hasebroek, *Staat und Handel* [Tübingen 1928], 31, 105, and passim), despite their numbers and the wealth that some of them possessed (cf. the literature in note 26 above and A. E. Raubitschek, *Dedications from the Athenian Acropolis* (Cambridge, Mass., 1949), 455 ff. This was not enough to place commercial activity and those who lived by it on a par with land ownership and those who drew their livelihood from the land: the city-states were far too agrar-

ian. This was the basis of the solidarity that existed among broad sections of the population and hence of their politicization. It also meant that the alternative to the existing order was limited.

57. The subject needs to be thoroughly reexamined; after all that has been established about Athens in recent years there is a need for fresh research into parallel changes taking place in other cities, e.g., Corinth, Argos, Aegina, Megara, Chios, and the cities of Ionia. Most of the relevant material is already available in G. Busolt and H. Swoboda, *Griechische Staatskunde* II (Munich 1926). The study by H.-D. Zimmermann, "Frühe Ansätze zur Demokratie in den griechischen Poleis," *Klio* 57 (1975) 293 ff, has unfortunately little to offer.

58. A real "revaluation of values" was taking place. It is notable, for instance, that strong emphasis was placed on certain *polis*-oriented virtues among the aristocratic ideals, largely in opposition to the aristocrats—virtues such as bravery (Tyrtaeus, fr. 9 Diehl), justice (Phocylides, fr. 10; Theognis 145 ff), and wisdom (Xenophanes, fr. 2), to cite only the explicit statements. (One should also mention the whole complex of *eunomia* and other strands in the preparatory phase leading up to the emergence of the "civic"—or "political"—ethic.) Cf. W. Jaeger, "Tyrtaios über die wahre Arete," *Sitzungsberichte der Preussischen Akademie* (1932); idem, *Paideia* I (4th ed. Berlin 1959), 140 ff, 185 ff. See also A. W. H. Adkins, *Moral Values and Political Behaviour in Ancient Greece* (London 1972), 35 ff; G. Steinkopf, *Untersuchungen zur Geschichte des Ruhms bei den Griechen* (Halle diss. 1937), 42 f, 49 f. On *dike* as a popular slogan see V. Ehrenberg, *Die Rechtsidee im frühen Griechentum* (Leipzig 1921), 135.

59. Dodds, *The Greeks and the Irrational*; Heuss, *Antike und Abendland* 2 (1946) 52 f.

60. C. Meier, "Die politische Identität der Griechen," in O. Marquard and K. Stierle (eds.), *Identität* (Munich 1979), 374 f, 381 f.

61. J. Martin, "Von Kleisthenes zu Ephialtes," *Chiron* 4 (1974) 5 ff.

62. But cf. C. Meier and P. Veyne, *Kannten die Griechen die Demokratie?* (Berlin 1988), 67 ff.

63. D. Hume, *Essays, Moral, Political and Literary*, ed. T. H. Green and T. H. Gose, I (1875), 125; M. Weber, "Die Wirtschaftsethik der Weltreligion," in *Gesammelte Aufsätze zur Religionsgeschichte* I (Tübingen 1920), 252. Aristotle later wrote (*Politics* 1261b34): "One attends first and foremost to one's own affairs, less to those of the community or only insofar as these affect individuals." This belongs to a different context but expresses very well the fact that the common interest, to be effective, has to *affect the individual*, to take its place among those things that directly concern him.

64. This topic is treated to some extent by L. Pearson, *Popular Ethics in Ancient Greece* (Stanford 1962); also by A. W. H. Adkins, *Merit and Responsibility* (Oxford 1960). The whole topic calls for a comprehensive and broadly sociohistorical investigation.

65. *Politics*, 1297b24.

66. See Chapter 7. K. Raaflaub, *Die Entdeckung der Freiheit* (Munich 1985), 115 ff.

4. Cleisthenes and the Institutionalizing of the Civic Presence in Athens

1. This chapter is a revised version of a paper given at the Institut de Droit Romain of the University of Paris on 10 March 1972. In view of the complex and somewhat unfamiliar nature of the subject it seemed advisable to retain the character of the investigation, to which the preceding chapter may serve as an introduction.

2. The most recent comprehensive study is that of P. Lévêque and P. Vidal-Naquet, *Clisthène l'Athénien* (Paris 1964). This admirable work has done much "to relate the great reform to the birth of philosophical thought" (p. 11). The geometrical thinking indicates Cleisthenes' lack of bias and characterizes important features of his convictions. But "Cleisthenes was no theorist," as M. I. Finley remarks (*The Ancient Greeks* [London 1963], 70). The concrete problem that Cleisthenes faced and the reason for his success cannot be deduced from the structure of his thought. Nor can the question of how the *polis*, "qui est pluralité," could be made "commune et une" (as P. Vernant puts it, *Annales* 20 [1965] 590 ff) have been more than peripheral. Cleisthenes had quite different concerns. The unity of the city became interesting only when it was in danger of being lost. It arose, on the other hand, as an indirect result of a different endeavor, the aim of which was to secure justice and enable broad sections of the community to participate in politics. See M. Ostwald, *Nomos and the Beginnings of the Athenian Democracy* (Oxford 1969). A synopsis of the relevant literature is provided by E. Will, *Le monde grec et l'orient* (Paris 1972), 63 f. See also J. Martin, "Von Kleisthenes zu Ephialtes," *Chiron* 4 (1974) 5 ff. For a study of the system of demes and tribes on the basis of archaeological and epigraphical evidence see G. R. Stanton, *Chiron* 14 (1984) 1 ff. Cf. C. Meier, *Gnomon* 58 (1986) 504 ff.

3. C. Meier, *Entstehung des Begriffs Demokratie* (Frankfurt 1970), 36 ff, 44 ff.

4. C. Hignett, *A History of the Athenian Constitution* (Oxford 1952), 92 ff; J. Day and M. Chambers, *Aristotle's History of Athenian Democracy* (Berkeley 1962), 200 f. On the historicity of the Council of 400 see P. Cloché, *Revue des études grecques* 37 (1924) 10 ff; H. T. Wade-Gery, *Essays in Greek History* (Oxford 1958), 145 ff; P. J. Rhodes, *The Athenian Boule* (Oxford 1972), 208 ff.

5. E.g., the institution of the prytany and the "political calendar" (cf. Rhodes, *Athenian Boule,* 17 ff, 209 ff, 225 ff; for another view see Lévêque and Vidal-Naquet, *Clisthène l'Athénien,* 22 ff; but see also Plato, *Gorgias* 516d–e for 489, and other passages cited by Rhodes, 17 f; Will, *Le monde grec,* 72), of ostracism (cf. R. Werner, *Athenaeum* 36 [1958] 48 ff; D. Kienast, *Historische Zeitschrift* 200 [1965] 282 n. 1; cited hereafter as Kienast), and of the sumptuary law (cf. C. Karousos, *Aristodikos* [Stuttgart 1961], 26 ff, 93, 97).

6. Hignett, *Athenian Constitution,* 50 ff; and K. Latte, *RE* XX (1941), 747 ff, 994 ff. On the general need to divide the community see Aristotle, *Politics* 1264a6 ff. Cf. recently F. Bourriot, *Recherches sur la nature du genos. Etude d'histoire sociale athénienne* (Lille/Paris 1976); D. Roussel, *Tribu et cité. Etudes sur les groupes sociaux dans les cités grecques aux époques archaïqe et classique* (Paris 1976).

7. Cf. K. Latte, *Kleine Schriften* (Munich 1968), 294 ff, esp. 304 f.

8. Homer, *Iliad* 2.362 f. Cf. Tyrtaeus, fr. 1.51; Latte, *RE* XX (1941), 747, 1006; idem, *Kleine Schriften*, 304 f.

9. *Iliad* 9.63; Latte, *RE* XX (1941), 747; G. de Sanctis, *Atthis* (2d ed. Rome 1964), 45. Cf. the Cretan *apetairos:* de Sanctis, 42.

10. *Inscriptiones Graecae* I², 115.1, 13 ff. Cf. [Demosthenes] 43.57; Latte, *RE* XX (1941), 1006. Cf. Homer, *Odyssey* 15.272 ff; G. Glotz, *La solidarité de la famille* (Paris 1904), 31 ff; Hignett, *Athenian Constitution*, 58; in general, Latte, *Kleine Schriften*, 259.

11. M. P. Nilsson, *Geschichte der griechischen Religion* (3d ed. Munich 1967), 708 ff; de Sanctis, *Atthis*, 45; G. Busolt and H. Swoboda, *Griechische Staatskunde* II (Munich 1926), 958 f; Latte, *RE* XX (1941), 753.

12. Plato, *Laws* 708c; 738d, e; Aristotle, *Politics* 1280b37. Cf. D. Fustel de Coulanges, *La cité antique* (28th ed. Paris 1923), 134 (*The Ancient City* [New York, n.d.]); V. Ehrenberg, *Aristophanes und das Volk von Athen* (Zurich 1968), 218; W. Burkert, *Griechische Religion der archaischen und klassischen Epoche* (Stuttgart 1977), 382 ff. Aristotle (*Nicomachean Ethics* 1161d13) speaks of friendship between members of the *phylai*. Peisistratus' establishment and promotion of public cults seems to have counteracted this solidarity.

13. Busolt and Swoboda, *Griechische Staatskunde* II, 241; Latte, *RE* XX (1941), 749 f, 751 ff; H. J. Wolff, "Die Grundlagen des griechischen Eherechts," in E. Berneker (ed.), *Zur griechischen Rechtsgeschichte* (Darmstadt 1968), 622 f.

14. G. Glotz, *Histoire grecque* I (Paris 1926), 393; "It was admission by the phratry that gave the infant his birth certificate and furnished proof of his legitimacy—so much so that the phratry, the intermediary between the clan and the city, conferred at once the right of inheritance and civic rights."

15. Aristotle, *Politics* 1309a10. Cf. 1305a32.

16. For *phratriai* and *gene* see Hignett, *Athenian Constitution*, 57 ff, 64, with some probability. See note 21 below. For the *phylai* see G. W. Botsford, *The Development of the Athenian Constitution* (New York 1893), 102 ff; Kienast, 274 ff. The best observation is that of de Sanctis, *Atthis*, 54 f: "It is clear in fact that the groups of individuals and phratries gathered together in a single tribe for the common interest (cf. 41 ff) had to be settled close to one another." (Hignett, 55, is less convincing. But in any case much in this area remains very doubtful.)

17. *Politics* 1319b26.

18. Herodotus, 4.161 (cf. Ostwald, *Nomos and Beginnings*, 164 f. But Aristotle, *Politics* 1319b22, cannot refer to Demonax. On the wider historical context see H. Schaefer, *Probleme der Alten Geschichte* [Göttingen 1963], 222–252, esp. 249; however, Schaefer fails to recognize that this really was an innovation, even though it was introduced in a relatively conservative spirit). On the various intentions behind reforms of the *phylai* see W. G. Forrest, *Annual of the British School of Athens* 55 (1960) 172.

19. They could prove very fruitful in competition: cf. Homer, *Iliad* 2.362. On the later period see Glotz, *Histoire grecque* I, 472. Cf. Aristophanes, *Birds* 1403 f; Xenophon, *Hieron* 9.5.

20. Cf. M. I. Finley, *Politics in the Ancient World* (Cambridge 1983), 42 ff. On this book see Meier, *Gnomon* 58 (1986) 496 ff.

21. Hignett, *Athenian Constitution,* 61f; Glotz, *Histoire grecque* I, 392; A. Andrewes, *Journal of Hellenic Studies* 81 (1961) 7 f. They also controlled admission to the rolls; see Andrewes, 6 ff. The *phylobasileus* was always a member of a noble family; Pollux 8.111. W. G. Forrest, *The Emergence of Greek Democracy* (London 1966), 55 f, gives a graphic description: "In 800 B.C., then, life for the ordinary man in Greece was narrow. He was almost certainly a farmer . . . not far away from his farm, in a richer part of the valley was one large estate, one substantial house, and in it lived a man who controlled his life almost as absolutely as if he were a slave. This man was mayor, the police-chief, magistrate, lawyer, the draft-officer, commander, minister of religion, and a dozen other things rolled into one. Those not in his favour did not prosper long. And should the same farmer ever come into contact with the 'State' the same rich neighbour, with others like him, appeared as judge, general, priest, magistrate or senator."

22. Hignett, *Athenian Constitution,* 84 f.

23. Ibid., 87 f. There must have been an uprising. Solon presented a precise program of his social policy (fr. 23.18D: *ha men gar eipa syn theoisin enysa*).

24. H. Berve, *Die Tyrannis bei den Griechen* I (Munich 1967), 51 ff., 74 ff.

25. By contrast, for instance, with their conduct at the time of Cylon's attempted usurpation between 636 and 624. See ibid., 41 f.

26. P. Spahn, *Mittelschicht und Polisbildung* (Frankfurt/Bern/Las Vegas 1977), 121 ff. The expression *katartister*—which occurs in the oldest sources (Herodotus 4.161.2; 5.28 f; Theognis 40) beside *euthynter*—seems to me to correspond precisely to archaic ways of thinking; cf. Solon 3.32; 36; 39; 24.19. It means "one who brings things back into plumb." Aristotle's term *aisymnetes* was presumably a designation for a regular official. Cf. F. Gschnitzer, in *Lexikon der Alten Welt* (Zurich 1965), 85.

27. Herodotus 1.59.4. Aristotle(?), *Athenaion Politeia* 14.1 f. C. Mossé, *L'antiquité classique* 33 (1964) 401 ff (cited hereafter as Mossé), has recently argued persuasively that the archons' compromise of 580/79 really did take place. One should add, however, that it was clearly part of an unusual and temporary situation in which the division of the lower classes according to vocation had to serve as the justification for a solution of parities. Possibly individual peasants and artisans pushed themselves to the fore and could be brought in as archons in the search for a settlement. As the demand for *isomoiria* shows, we presumably have to reckon with many possibilities at this period, though not with the possibility that they produced lasting solutions that tended toward democracy.

28. Herodotus 5.66, 69; Schaefer, *Probleme,* 139, 1; 358; Ostwald, *Nomos and Beginnings,* 143. On the conflict between Cleisthenes and Isagoras see Schaefer, 137 f; R. Sealey, *Historia* 9 (1960) 172.

29. Herodotus 5.66.2; *Athenaion Politeia* 20.1.

30. *Athenaion Politeia* 21.6; Hignett, *Athenian Constitution,* 143.

31. Herodotus 5.69.2; *Athenaion Politeia* 21. Cf. notes 33–36 and 41 below.

32. Herodotus 5.69.2. Cf. B. Haussoullier, in Daremberg-Saglio (ed.), *Diction-*

naire des antiquités II (1892) 89 ff. On the numbers see Polemon in Strabo 9.1.16: 174. For a dissenting opinion see J. S. Traill, "The Political Organization of Attica: A Study of the Demes, Trittyes and Phylai and Their Representation in the Athenian Council," *Hesperia* Suppl. 14 (1975) 75 ff. A different view is taken by Walker, *The Cambridge Ancient History* III (Cambridge 1930), 143. Lévêque and Vidal-Naquet, *Clisthène l'Athénien*, 13, 4: 100. On the size of the demes see A. W. Gomme, *The Population of Athens in the Fifth and Fourth Centuries B.C.* (Oxford 1933), 54 f. (It appears to me doubtful, however, whether Halimous really was overrepresented in the Council; 85 to 90 *demotes* might be the lower limit of the demes with three councillors. This would give three for an average of 100 [80–120] or 110 [90–130]. This would mean that Leontis had between 1,700 and 1,800 citizens. This would certainly have been possible if it belonged to the smaller *phylai*.) On this point see Haussoullier, 83. On Acharnai see most recently W. E. Thompson, *Historia* 13 (1964) 400 ff.

33. *Athenaion Politeia* 21.5; Hignett, *Athenian Constitution*, 136.
34. See note 109 below.
35. De Sanctis, *Atthis*, 339; Hignett, *Athenian Constitution*, 136.
36. *Athenaion Politeia* 62.1. Cf. J. A. O. Larsen, *Representative Government in Greek and Roman History* (Berkeley 1955), 5 ff; idem, *Classical Philology* 57 (1962) 104 ff; Rhodes, *Athenian Boule*, 8 ff, 12 f. Cf. Aristotle, *Politics* 1298b21.
37. *Athenaion Politeia* 21.4; de Sanctis, *Atthis*, 341 f; C. W. J. Eliot, *Coastal Demes of Attica* (Toronto 1962), esp. 136 ff. See also the observations of D. M. Lewis, *Gnomon* 35 (1963) 723 ff.
38. *Athenaion Politeia* 21.4; see also Ostwald, *Nomos and Beginnings*, 154 n. 2. Cf. note 118 below.
39. See note 19 above. We may presume that at this time solidarity could take root in the shared political will of a large number of citizens.
40. Walker, *Cambridge Ancient History* III, 144; D. W. Bradeen, *Transactions of the American Philological Association* 86 (1955) 22 ff (cited hereafter as Bradeen).
41. Glotz, *Histoire grecque* I, 472 (see Herodotus 6.111.1); Latte, *RE* (1941), 1006; de Sanctis, *Atthis*, 344 f.
42. *Athenaion Politeia* 21.3.
43. Ibid., 21.4; Hignett, *Athenian Constitution*, 139 f; Aristotle, *Politics* 1275b34 f; D. Kagan, *Historia* 12 (1963) 41 ff.
44. Plutarch, *Solon* 24.4. Cf. *Athenaion Politeia* 13.5. Harpokration s.v. *diapsephisis;* Hignett, *Athenian Constitution*, 112.
45. Hignett, *Athenian Constitution*, 132 ff; A. Heuss, *Propyläen Weltgeschichte* III (Berlin 1962), 188; Kagan, *Historia* 12 (1963) 46; Lévêque and Vidal-Naquet, *Clisthène l'Athénien*, 43 ff.
46. Admission to the *phratria* remained a prerequisite for civil rights (see note 14 above). It is difficult to see how the old local principle or the new principle of mixing the population could favor the admission of new citizens. If they did have a better chance of asserting themselves in the new units, and if the distinction between the new citizens and those of long standing

became blurred—as is suggested by J. Hasebroek, *Griechische Wirtschafts-und Gesellschaftsgeschichte* (Tübingen 1931), 198—the reason must have been that the latter had recently become integrated, and such integration cannot have been instituted for the benefit of the former. The explanation offered in *Athenaion Politeia* only demonstrates how poorly its author understood the reform. Cf. Forrest, *Emergence of Greek Democracy*, 194 f.

47. Schaefer, *Probleme*, 139 f.

48. Glotz, *Histoire grecque* I, 474.

49. See note 118 and accompanying text.

50. All that is attested is that after the victory over Cleomenes various supporters of Isagoras were executed (Herodotus 5.72.4) or expelled (*Athenaion Politeia* 28.2; scholion to Aristophanes, *Lysistrata* 273). This was thus not the original intention. It may have contributed to the success of the reform, but this is not considered in the literature.

51. The Athenian Assembly, unlike the Roman *comitia*, was not structured into subunits. See Busolt and Swoboda, *Griechische Staatskunde* II, 994 f. On the other hand, the arguments of E. Ruschenbusch, *Athenische Innenpolitik im 5. Jahrhundert v. Chr.* (Bamberg 1979), 50 n. 20, are entirely unconvincing, especially as there is no mention in Philochorus of the *phylai* occupying separate positions in the Assembly, but only of their having separate entrances (and this was clearly an exception that applied in the case of ostracism). Cf. also the cautious commentary of K. Kouroniotes and H. A. Thompson, *Hesperia* 1 (1932) 104 f. There is thus no suggestion of group pressure within the *phylai*. More probably the nobles tried to muster and coerce their retinues. Yet this is precisely what the reform was designed to counteract. See the following discussion.

52. A recent exception is Ostwald, *Nomos and Beginnings*, 147 ff.

53. This is reliably attested only for the period before the tyranny of Peisistratus (Herodotus 1.59.3,61.2; cf. *Athenaion Politeia* 13.4; R. J. Hopper, *Annual of the British School of Athens* 56 [1961] 189 ff; cited hereafter as Hopper).

54. This is the view taken by Sealey, *Historia* 9 (1960) 155 ff; and Kienast, 174 f.

55. There were dynastic groupings within the nobility. The leading families lived in different regions, where they presumably had groups of followers (cf. note 16 above. Hopper, 201, misses this point when he considers only the connections existing within the nobility, which can scarcely have been governed by geography.) To some extent they also took advantage of social differences. However, none of this means that there were permanent regional differences of interest that influenced politics as a whole (as Sealey, *Historia* 9 [1960] 163 f and 167, surmises, contrary to Hopper, 201 ff). The groupings were based largely on personal connections. Before the tyranny this led, whether or not by chance, to a tripartite and later to a bipartite grouping; in both cases the Alcmeonids played a crucial role (cf. Mossé, 410 ff). There is nothing to suggest a link between the four *phylai* and the three factions (cf. also Bradeen, 23 ff). The tripartite grouping of the factions depended on the old order of *phylai* and *phratriai* only insofar as the possibility of conducting a kind of politics based on aristocratic attitudes

depended on the nobles' control over their followers and on the weakness of other sections of society, whose conduct was guided by quite different criteria. To this extent it was frustrated, like every other aristocratic grouping, by Cleisthenes' reform. Modern scholarship has largely failed to recognize the special features of aristocratic politics (but cf. A. Heuss, *Antike und Abendland* 2 [1946] 50 n. 15; repr. in F. Gschnitzer [ed.], *Griechische Staatskunde* [Darmstadt 1969]). Hence Hopper (207 f) throws the baby out with the bathwater and takes refuge in Salamis. There has also been a partial failure to appreciate what limited opportunities there were at the time for a kind of politics that favored particular economic interest groups.

56. To this extent we may agree with H. van Effenterre, *Revue des études grecques* 89 (1976) 2 f. One should not, of course, carry sobriety to the point where the emergence of isonomy becomes incomprehensible.

57. Schaefer, *Probleme*, 139; Wade-Gery, *Essays*, 150 f. (Crucial evidence against the "secular state" and against a general separation of the religious and the political spheres is of course provided by the institution of the *phyle* hero; see *Athenaion Politeia* 21.6. Lévêque and Vidal-Naquet, *Clisthène l'Athénien*, 23, are therefore right to speak of the "creation of an authentically political religion, parallel to the traditional cults."

58. Lévêque and Vidal-Naquet, *Clisthène l'Athénien*, 13 ff. On "temps civique" see note 5 above. One cannot properly speak of "espace civique" solely on the basis of the application of geometry to the map of Attica (which should in any case not be overestimated); such a notion makes sense only when this space is filled by the citizens, and in particular it entails certain presuppositions that are related to the way people thought, to their intentions, the economic situation, modes of communication, and so on.

59. Cf. E. Will, *Revue historique* 262 (1979) 436 ff.

60. Herodotus 5.66, 69. Cf. *Athenaion Politeia* 20.1.

61. The chronological details, none of them certain, are of no relevance here. On this point see F. Schachermeyr, *Forschungen und Betrachtungen zur griechischen und römischen Geschichte* (Vienna 1974), 60 ff; Wade-Gery, *Essays*, 135 ff; H. W. Pleket, *Talanta* 1 (1969) 56 ff.

62. Herodotus 5.70. Cf. *Athenaion Politeia* 20.2.

63. Herodotus 5.72. Cf. *Athenaion Politeia* 20.3; Thucydides 1.126.12. On Cleisthenes' supporters see F. Jacoby, *Atthis* (Oxford 1949), 366 n. 77; Schachermeyr, *Forschungen*, 67, 223 ff.

64. Herodotus 5.72.2, 4; 73.1. Cf. *Athenaion Politeia* 20.3 f. The *boule* can hardly have been the Areopagus, but it may have been the Council of 400. See Glotz, *Histoire grecque* I, 468 n. 203. Kienast, 271 and 273, takes a different view (see note 67 below).

65. Herodotus 5.72.1 *(ou syn megale cheiri)*; *Athenaion Politeia* 20.3. Clearly it was a private undertaking on the part of the king (cf. Herodotus 5.76), yet even so he could have achieved more; cf. Heuss, *Antike und Abendland* 2 (1946) 50 f.

66. Herodotus 5.72.1; *Athenaion Politeia* 20.3.

67. This would also apply to the Council of 400, if it really existed. In that case membership of this council would presumably have been incompatible with

membership of the Areopagus. The councilors thus stood on the periphery of politics, even if they belonged to the nobility. In such circles there may well have been growing indignation at the traditional practices of the leading nobles. Here were the natural leaders of a popular rebellion. Whatever their earlier political stance may have been, the new situation produced new allegiances. (Kienast, 271, believes that the Council was made up of supporters of Isagoras.)

68. This view is shared by de Sanctis, *Atthis*, 347, 358; and by E. Meyer, *Geschichte des Altertums* (3d ed. Darmstadt 1954), 746 f. Thanks to the tyranny these broad sections of the population were now much better off economically (A. E. Raubitschek, *Dedications from the Athenian Acropolis* [Cambridge, Mass., 1949], 455 ff; Schachermeyr, *Forschungen*, 205 ff). On the involvement of artisans see Mossé, 408. The fact that we are dealing essentially with a peasant democracy was recognized by M. Weber, *Economy and Society*, ed. G. Roth and C. Wittich (Berkeley 1978), 1346 ff.

69. V. Ehrenberg, *Polis und Imperium* (Zurich 1965), 132. On the content see G. Vlastos, *American Journal of Philology* 74 (1953) 352, 361 (cited hereafter as Vlastos).

70. Chapter 7 and Meier, *Entstehung*, 36 ff.

71. C. Meier and P. Veyne, *Kannten die Griechen die Demokratie?* (Berlin 1988), 67 ff. Cf. Herodotus 5.78; Latte, *Kleine Schriften*, 294 ff. This interpretation of "isonomy" has nothing to do with the various attempts that have been made to derive the word etymologically from *nemein* or *nomos;* cf. V. Ehrenberg, *RE Suppl.* VII (1940), 293 ff; Vlastos, 348 ff. It seems to me beyond question that *isonomia* is directly connected with earlier words formed with *–nomia,* in the senses in which they were then understood and not in any etymological sense. Cf. P. Frei, *Museum Helveticum* 38 (1981) 205 ff. The term *eunomia,* which was clearly derived from *nomos,* was understood to mean a "well-ordered" polity: see Ehrenberg, *Polis und Imperium,* 152 f; C. Meier, in *Discordia Concors. Festschrift E. Bonjour* (Basel 1968), 6; cf. Pindar, *Pythia* 5.66 f. Isonomy modifies this notion of an ideal order by adding that of equality. Equality always presupposes some form of distribution, whether or not the old sense of *nemein* (to distribute) is involved (cf. C. Schmitt, *Verfassungsrechtliche Aufsätze* [Berlin 1958], 489 ff). At a later stage another semantic component of *nemein* (to rule, to administer) comes more to the fore: Herodotus 1.59.6; 5.29.2, 71.2, 92.1; Aeschylus, *Prometheus* 526; Sophocles, *Oedipus Tyrannus* 201, 237; *Ajax* 1016; Pindar, *Olympia* 13.27.

72. Herodotus 3.142.3.

73. Lévêque and Vidal-Naquet, *Clisthène l'Athénien,* 32. Cf. esp. Bacchylides, *Dithyrambs* 15.53 ff. See Chapter 7, note 26, below.

74. This is the view taken by M. Detienne, *Annales* 20 (1965) 425 ff.

75. I hope to treat this topic in greater detail in future; meanwhile see Chapter 3.

76. Cf. provisionally Meier, *Entstehung,* 15 ff; idem, "Die Griechen. Die politische Revolution der Weltgeschichte," *Saeculum* 33 (1982) 133 ff.

77. Meier, *Entstehung,* 19 f.

78. Cf. note 26 above. On the power that the *demos* could already deploy on occasion see also Solon, *Elegies* 8, 11.
79. Vernant, *Annales* 20 (1965) 577; Wade-Gery, *Essays*, 142 ff; Ostwald, *Nomos and Beginnings*, 158; see also Weber, *Wirtschaft und Gesellschaft*, 782 f.
80. Cf., e.g., Solon, fr. 23.21; W. Donlan, *Historia* 22 (1973) 145 ff.
81. Spahn, *Mittelschicht und Polisbildung*, 98 ff.
82. This had existed formally since the time of Solon (see fr. 24.18–20). Peisistratus did nothing to change it (Thucydides 6.54.6; *Athenaion Politeia* 16.8). To this extent the demand for equality before the law was nothing really new. If this had been all it amounted to, the reform of the *phylai* would be incomprehensible.
83. Meier, *Entstehung*, 41. On the further preconditions see R. Hirzel, *Themis, Dike und Verwandtes* (Leipzig 1907), 228 ff.
84. H. Schaefer, *Staatsform und Politik* (Leipzig 1932), 106.
85. Lévêque and Vidal-Naquet, *Clisthène l'Athénien*, 45. Ostwald, *Nomos and Beginnings*, 153, overestimates the function of the watchword "isonomy," since he clearly fails to appreciate that in the end tyranny became oppressive and was perceived to be undesirable as soon as the people themselves were in a position to safeguard the law.
86. The Athenian region covered approximately 2,550 sq. km. (excluding Oropus). The next largest *polis* was Argos, with approximately 1,400 sq. km.; see Busolt and Swoboda, *Griechische Staatskunde* II, 163 f. For a recent discussion of the sizes, populations and number of the *poleis* see E. Ruschenbusch, *Untersuchungen zu Staat und Politik in Griechenland vom 7.–4. Jahrhundert v. Chr.* (Bamberg 1978), 3 ff.
87. V. Ehrenberg, *Der Staat der Griechen* (Zurich/Stuttgart 1965), 38 (*The Greek State* [2d ed. London 1966]). Herodotus (5.97.2) estimates the population at 30,000 in the year 500. Cf. Thucydides 1.80.3.
88. Even at a later stage it was a good turnout if about one-fifth of the citizens attended the Assembly (6,000 citizens constituted the *demos plethyon;* see Busolt and Swoboda, *Griechische Staatskunde* II 987). Cf. Aristotle, *Politics* 1319a30, 1318b9. However, see Ehrenberg, *Aristophanes*, 92 f.
89. Gomme, *Population of Athens*, 37, 66: approximately one-sixth in the city, a bare third in Cleisthenes' district *asty*. For the end of the fifth century see Thucydides 2.14.2, 15.1, 16.1; Gomme, 47.
90. This view is already found in V. Ehrenberg, *Neugründer des Staates* (Munich 1925), 93.
91. Aristotle, *Politics* 1297b28 with Madvig's conjecture. Cf. 1305a18.
92. See the works cited in Chapter 6, note 48.
93. Aristotle, *Politics* 1317b30 ff; cf. 1299b32 and 38 ff, 1323a9.
94. J. W. Headlam, *Election by Lot at Athens* (2d ed. Cambridge 1933), 26–32, 41–56.
95. Hence we should assume that membership in the Areopagus precluded membership in the Council of 500.
96. Moreover, many members of the Council had to be able to ride to Athens: on this point cf. H. A. Thompson, *Hesperia* 6 (1937) 42. For possible

restrictions on applying for or being admitted to election by lot see Rhodes, *Athenian Boule*, 2 and 4 ff. The numbers available cannot have been very large. This is suggested by considerations arising from the observations of C. W. Starr, *The Economic and Social Growth of Early Greece, 800–500 B.C.* (New York 1977), 122 f; also Ruschenbusch, *Untersuchungen*, 3 ff.

97. This refers to the councils whose membership was representative of the *phylai* and that were in competition with the old councils. The term occurs admittedly only in the charter from Chios: see R. Meiggs and D. Lewis, *A Selection of Greek Historical Inscriptions* (Oxford 1965), no. 8 C 2 f, 5 f. Cf. note 122 below.

98. Cf. the beginning of Chapter 6.

99. Cicero, *De re publica* 2.56; C. Meier, *Res Publica Amissa* (3d ed. Frankfurt 1988), 116 ff.

100. T. Mommsen, *Römisches Staatsrecht* II.1 (3d ed. Leipzig 1887), 291 f.

101. No certain example is known, however. A different view is taken by Hasebroek, *Griechische Wirtschafts- und Gesellschaftsgeschichte*, 212 ff. Certain functions of opposition magistrates were exercised by the Spartan ephors (see Busolt and Swoboda, *Griechische Staatskunde* II, 683 ff) and the Molossian *prostatai* (see H. Schaefer, *RE Suppl.* IX [1962], 1288 f), but these were meant—at least originally—to represent the interests of the nobility against the king.

102. For some observations on the problem of the "civic presence" in Rome see C. Meier, *Historische Zeitschrift* 213 (1971) 398 f, where Roman conditions are compared with those of modern times. The problem was quite different in Rome, since there the civic presence was generally concentrated in much smaller circles—among the senators and the tribunes of the people (insofar as these were not also senators). Wider circles of citizens were brought in only occasionally and to varying degrees, especially after the scope of Roman citizenship had been substantially enlarged.

103. Hignett, *Athenian Constitution*, 155; de Sanctis, *Atthis*, 352; cf. Busolt and Swoboda, *Griechische Staatskunde* II, 992. A different view is taken by Hignett, 150, and Rhodes, *Athenian Boule*, 21 n. 4.

104. See "Cleisthenes' New Order," above.

105. Certain modifications arose later, since affiliation to the deme was hereditary and independent of domicile: see Gomme, *Population of Athens*, 39 ff, who probably overrates the degree of mobility (cf. the evidence he cites on p. 46). But if this was Cleisthenes' intention (A. Aymard, *Peuples et civilisation* I [Paris 1950], 590, argues the contrary), the general rule probably did not change much.

106. The councilors were later chosen by lot (*Athenaion Politeia* 43.2; Rhodes, *Athenian Boule*, 6 f). No one was permitted to serve more than two terms as a councilor (*Athenaion Politeia* 62.3; cf. Hignett, *Athenian Constitution*, 227 f and 231; Rhodes, 3 f and 242 f). This latter rule, which presupposes the payment of expenses, cannot go back to Cleisthenes, while the former might. At least, he might have made regulations along these lines (e.g., *klerosis ek prokriton;* cf. *Athenaion Politeia* 43.2; see Busolt and Swoboda, *Griechische Staatskunde* II, 882; Headlam, *Election by Lot*, 187 f

and 196 f; Will, *Le monde grec,* 68. There is a later rule attested for Erythrae, according to which no one might become a councilor more than once in any period of four years; see Larsen, *Representative Government,* 12 f).

107. Rhodes, *Athenian Boule,* 16 ff; Will, *Le monde grec,* 67 f; Bradeen, 27 f. The new *phylai* were not the only means of making the *prytania* representative (it would have been possible to choose a tenth of the total citizenry by lot). Naturally the growing links among the members of the *phylai* could facilitate collaboration and the performance of such tasks. It was no doubt also in keeping with Greek custom to resort to the *phylai* for these purposes and many others (Larsen, 12 f). The solution was so obvious. Nevertheless, Will takes an unduly restrictive view when he interprets the reform as pertaining solely to the Council of 500. As has been shown, this council needed to be embedded in the civic community and in the autonomy of the citizens vis-à-vis the nobles. This called for a large-scale transformation. Cf. Meier and Veyne, *Kannten die Griechen die Demokratie?* 78 ff.

108. Latte, *Kleine Schriften,* 254 ff. For the later period see Glotz and Cohen, *Histoire grecque* II, 236 ff; Ehrenberg, *Aristophanes,* 219 ff.

109. B. Haussoullier, *La vie municipale en Attique* (Paris 1884); Busolt and Swoboda, *Griechische Staatskunde* II, 964 ff; Headlam, *Election by Lot,* 167; R. J. Hopper, *The Basis of the Athenian Democracy* (Sheffield 1957), 14 f.

110. What this might mean is indicated by Aristotle, *Politics* 1309a11.

111. T. Tarkiainen, *Die athenische Demokratie* (Zurich 1966), 299.

112. J. G. Droysen, *Kleine Schriften zur alten Geschichte* I (Leipzig 1893), 373 ff; Ostwald, *Nomos and Beginnings,* 152 f.

113. Latte, *Kleine Schriften,* 267.

114. Cf. Plutarch, *Cimon* 10.2; Ehrenberg, *Aristophanes,* 220. Here it is a question of the degree of consideration accorded to fellow citizens. Finley, *Politics in the Ancient World,* 45 f, rightly points out that certain patron-client relations were always present. But they had a history, to which his excessively materialistic categories can scarcely do justice.

115. Cf. Glotz and Cohen, *Histoire grecque* II, 241 f.

116. Cf. Plato, *Laws* 738d–e, 771d–e (from a different viewpoint); Aristotle, *Politics* 1319a30, 1326b14 (cf. 1305a32); Thucydides 8.66.3 (on the difficulties still existing a century later); Aristotle, *Politics* 1313a40; 1313b4.

117. Cf. A. Gehlen, *Urmensch und Spätkultur* (2d ed. Frankfurt/Bonn 1964), 60, states: "It is impossible to change the conduct of a society merely by proposing or propagating 'values': the appropriate institutions must be provided as well. If certain norms are to be singled out and stated to be valid, there must be a broad measure of constant, direct interpersonal contact." Cf. Chapter 6, note 12, below.

118. Statements in the modern literature create the impression that Cleisthenes actually resettled the citizens or built walls to separate them: e.g., D. Lewis, *Historia* 12 (1963) 30 ff; Lévêque and Vidal-Naquet, *Clisthène l'Athénien,* 18 (who use the phrase "détruire le contexte géographique"). On Probalinthos cf. Eliot, *Coastal Demes,* 144; idem, *Phoenix* 22 (1968) 11 ff. Cleisthenes was clearly at pains to create geographically coherent *trittyes*

(not *phylai*, however, *pace* Eliot). Yet these must not be too large. This is a fairly obvious assumption and comes closer than anything else to explaining the division he adopted. Thus, the separation of Probalinthos from the Tetrapolis was certainly necessary (and raises no political questions). On the other hand it is striking that—like Halimous—it was not allocated to the contiguous *trittys*, but to one farther away. However, no political reasons for this can be adduced. Clearly we know far too little about the Attica of this period to draw any precise inferences. We have hardly any absolute figures; the numbers of citizens attested throughout several centuries from individual demes are statistically not clear or relevant enough to allow of any extrapolation. (Eliot, *Phoenix* 7 ff, disagrees.) The number of councilors sent to Athens by a given deme does not tell us much, as proportional representation applied only within the *phyle*, not within the community as a whole: see W. E. Thompson, *Historia* 13 (1964) 402 ff; Eliot, *Phoenix* 7. On what follows see Traill, "Political Organization of Attica," 99 ff. Cf. also note 2 above. An example of a real resettlement—actually to get rid of democracy—is supplied by the events that took place in Mantinea in 386: see Finley, *Politics in the Ancient World*, 42.

119. This is the view taken by Lévêque and Vidal-Naquet, *Clisthène l'Athénien*, 16 f.

120. Hignett, *Athenian Constitution*, 156.

121. See Chapter 5, note 7; Rhodes, *Athenian Boule*, 162, 200, 202 f.

122. This includes the function of holding preliminary deliberations. The contention that this was the only significant function of the Council of 500 (Rhodes, *Athenian Boule*, 209) pays scant attention to the constitutional situation, namely the lack of balance between the various organs and the need for regular oversight of what took place in Athens. Oversight of the Assembly was hardly necessary at this period. On the limited role of the Council of 500 see also Martin, "Von Kleisthenes zu Ephialtes," 23. Two councils are attested on Chios (see note 97 above) and in Argos (Thucydides 5.47; M. Wörrle, *Untersuchungen zur Verfassungsgeschichte von Argos im 5. Jahrhundert* [Erlangen diss. 1964], 56 f). Possibly the coexistence of two councils at Ephesus goes back to a similar situation (Dittenberger, *Sylloge Inscriptionum Graecarum* [3d ed.], no. 353; cf. Strabo 14.1.21. D. van Berchem, "La gérousie d'Ephèse," *Museum Helveticum* 37 [1980] 25 ff suggests that the *boule* might have been set up simultaneously with a reform of the *phylai* and the readmission of the citizens by Aristarchus. It may be that it too began as a "council of the *phylai*" and an organ of opposition).

123. Hignett, *Athenian Constitution*, 142; Bradeen, 30; Ehrenberg, *Polis und Imperium*, 283; Schaefer, *Probleme*, 102, 136, 139; Will, *Le monde grec*, 75 f.

124. Mossé, 412 f.

125. A similar view is taken by Martin, "Von Kleisthenes zu Ephialtes," 18. On the (limited) continuance of the old aristocratic politics see W. R. Connor, *The New Politicians of Fifth-Century Athens* (Princeton 1971), 53 ff. Connor rightly discovers the importance of aristocratic thinking and aris-

tocratic connections in the early and mid-fifth century and concludes, somewhat abruptly (and without paying attention to the other factors of democracy), that the aristocratic factions continued to play a central role in politics. He is clearly unaware of the problem of interpreting ancient political groupings (Meier, *Res Publica Amissa*, xxxii ff; C. Meier, *Introduction à l'anthropologie politique de l'antiquité classique* [Paris 1984], 45 ff).

126. Bradeen, 25. Cf. Latte, *Kleine Schriften*, 260, 264 f; Schaefer, *Probleme*, 390.

127. Vernant, *Annales* 20 (1965) 591.

128. I intend to present elsewhere a thorough examination of the political grammar of the period. The *katartisteres* of Paros in Miletus tried to solve similar problems by handing the city over to those who were not involved in the feuds (Herodotus 5.28 ff; a similar idea is found in Isocrates 7.24). Their property was in good order, whereas that of the others had been neglected or laid waste. Cf. Phocylides 12: *polla mesoisin arista. mesos thelo en polei einai*, where *mesos* is to be understood not in a sociological sense, but in the political sense of "neutral, uninvolved."

129. Herodotus 3.82.3 f; Aristotle, *Politics* 1302a8.

130. Schaefer, *Probleme*, 297; H. Strasburger, *Historische Zeitschrift* 177 (1954) 238 f. Cf. esp. Aeschylus, *Eumenides* 984 ff.

131. See the beginning of Chapter 3. M. Kriele, *Einführung in die Staatslehre* (Reinbek bei Hamburg 1975), bases his introduction to political science on a three-stage progression: the first stage is "peace: the state," the second "freedom: the constitutional state," the third "justice: the democratic constitutional state."

132. See Chapter 3.

133. Herodotus 5.78. The practical equality represented by participation in communal affairs also manifested itself as participation in its material profits and surpluses (from customs, duties, mines, etc.), which were distributed among the citizens. See K. Latte, "Kollektivbesitz und Staatsschatz in Griechenland," in *Kleine Schriften*, 294 ff.

134. H. van Effenterre, *Revue des études grecques* 89 (1976) 2 f, draws attention to some of the military consequences of Cleisthenes' reform; it would be wrong, however, to assume that these were its main aims.

135. See note 91 above.

5. The *Eumenides* of Aeschylus and the Rise of the Political

1. J. Burkhardt, *Reflections on History*, trans. M. D. H. (London 1943), 271. Cf. D. Jähnig, *Welt-Geschichte: Kunst-Geschichte. Zum Verhältnis von Vergangenheitserkenntnis und Veränderung* (Cologne 1975), 85 ff, 102 f.

2. But see K. J. Dover, *Journal of Hellenic Studies* 77 (1957) 230 ff; E. R. Dodds, *Proceedings Cambridge Philological Society* 186 (1960) 19 ff; idem, *The Ancient Concept of Progress and Other Essays* (Oxford 1973), 45 ff; S. J. Lurje, *Bibliotheca Classica Orientalia* 5 (1960) 295 (cited hereafter as Lurje); A. J. Podlecki, *The Political Background of Aeschylean Tragedy* (Ann Arbor 1966); A. Lesky, *Die tragische Dichtung der Hellenen*

(3d ed. Göttingen 1972), 133, with further references. All concentrate mainly on allusions to individual events. Cf. now C. Meier, *Die politische Kunst der griechischen Tragödie* (Munich 1988), 117 ff (English translation in preparation).

3. Cf. Dodds, *Ancient Concept of Progress*, 62 n. 4. Reference should be made above all to Bachofen's famous interpretation: J. J. Bachofen, *Gesammelte Werke* II (Basel 1948), 174 ff.

4. Quoted by G. Murray, *Aeschylus, the Creator of Tragedy* (Oxford 1940), 179; and by A. Lesky, *A History of Greek Literature*, trans. J. Willis and C. de Heer (London 1966), 256.

5. The date of performance is given in the hypothesis to the *Agamemnon*: under the archon Philocles in the second year of the Eightieth Olympiad.

6. E. Badian, *Antichthon* 5 (1971) 1 ff; but see J. Martin, "Von Kleisthenes zu Ephialtes," *Chiron* 4 (1974) 27 f. E. Ruschenbusch, *Athenische Innenpolitik im 5. Jahrhundert v. Chr.* (Bamberg 1979), offers no detailed criticism (54 n. 23).

7. Aristotle(?), *Athenaion Politeia* 23.1, 25.1. The author's statement is probably correct, but he seems to underrate the role played by the Areopagus between the time of Cleisthenes and 480 (cf. Chapter 4 above), and so has to resort to a rather forced explanation of the considerable power that this body continued to enjoy until 462. In reality the old council probably remained authoritative even after Cleisthenes (cf., e.g., *Athenaion Politeia* 8.4, admittedly not a very reliable witness; more important are the inferences that can be drawn from the whole structure of the constitution). Certainly the importance of the Areopagus increased when it was invoked in the wars after 480, perhaps partly because Cimon came to occupy a very prominent position: his successes won him great renown, not least with the *demos,* and his power was presumably compounded by that of the Areopagus.

8. This is attested on the one hand by its juridical powers, on the other by somewhat general formulations (cf. C. Hignett, *A History of the Athenian Constitution to the End of the Fifth Century B.C.* [Oxford 1952], 198 ff; Martin, "Von Kleisthenes zu Ephialtes," 29 ff; Ruschenbusch, *Athenische Innenpolitik,* 58; idem, *Historia* 15 [1965] 373 f). Its powers cannot have been solely juridical. Its supposed role as the guardian of the constitution seems to echo later theory rather than early fifth-century reality. At the period in question the influence of this body, whose membership probably still included most of the powerful nobles (Pericles being an exception), can hardly be assessed on the basis of its nominal powers, and certainly not on the basis of those "laid down by law" (Martin, 33). Its de facto superiority in power, experience, and knowledge must have given it substantial control over civic affairs. Cf. now C. Meier, "Der Umbruch zur Demokratie in Athen (462/61 v. Ch.)," in R. Herzog and R. Koselleck (eds.), *Epochenschwelle und Epochenbewusstsein* (Munich 1987), 353 ff; idem, *Die politische Kunst,* 93 ff.

9. Sources cited by G. F. Hill, *Sources for Greek History between the Persian and Peloponnesian Wars,* ed. R. Meiggs and A. Andrewes (rev. ed. Oxford

1951), 350; most recently R. Sealey, "Ephialtes," in *Essays in Greek Politics* (New York 1967), 42 ff; Martin, "Von Kleisthenes zu Ephialtes," 29 ff.

10. Martin, "Von Kleisthenes zu Ephialtes," 36 ff. Ruschenbusch, *Athenische Innenpolitik,* 61 ff, is certainly correct in observing that the political disputes of the fifth century were ideologized in the tradition of the fourth century, but his alternative—"ideology or pragmatism"—fails to do justice to the phenomenon. Whatever aims the politicians may have had, it is surely impossible to dismiss the notion that one of them must have been to reduce the status of the nobles and the Areopagus and increase that of the *demos* (for whatever reason), and that, because of the questions of power and institutions involved, they were able to see differences regarding the constitution in quite fundamental terms (cf. Meier, *Die politische Kunst,* 105 ff).

11. This was supported by the temporal argument in favor of the old (see later in this chapter and Chapter 8). Scholars have recently tended to overlook this aspect of the question.

12. Plutarch, *Pericles* 7.8, with an allusion to Plato, *Republic* 562c–d.

13. On the building of the Long Walls and the conspiracy against it, see Hill, *Sources,* 350 f. It was preceded by the threat of Spartan intervention in the affairs of the Delian League. Athens was thus not solely to blame for the increased tension. How new this policy was can probably be illustrated by a remark that Thucydides attributes to Themistocles regarding the first walls that were built after the Persian Wars (1.91.4 f). He lays very strong emphasis on the *gnome* of Athens, which clearly means the city's ability to take appropriate decisions freely, that is, without being tied merely to traditional courses of action and traditional authorities. In future, he says, it shall be known that the Athenians are well able to recognize *(diagignoskein)* what is of benefit to themselves and the generality. This shows that Athens had acquired a quite new mode of political action, which had first proved its worth at Salamis, with the daring decision *(tolmesai)* to evacuate Athens and board the ships. It is a bold departure from adherence to traditional modes of action and a consensus geared to established rules (and determined especially by Sparta)—a new capacity for a kind of detached analysis that goes to the heart of the matter and is appropriate to a given situation, a kind of action that (not to put too fine a point on it) relies less on tradition than on individual judgment. This is matched by a new kind of politics. This intellectual daring and adventurousness are interestingly adumbrated by the advice given by Hecataeus on how the Ionians might conquer the Persians (Herodotus 5.36.3). We see here how the emergence of opportunities for taking control of the internal order of the city was matched by the emergence of new possibilities of planning and action in external affairs; these began to appear limitless thanks to the victory over the Persians.

14. The new expansionism in foreign policy and war that began at this time— see E. Will, *Le monde grec et l'orient* I (Paris 1972), 150 ff—clearly corresponded to the interests of the *thetes* in particular and was bound to bring them increased participation and power.

15. See Chapter 4.
16. Plutarch, *Cimon* 15.3; Thucydides 1.107.4 f; Plutarch, *Cimon* 17.4 f, *Pericles* 10.1 ff (on 457, but the concern was probably older; see Aeschylus, Eumenides 858 ff, 976 ff, and note 175 below). The murder of Ephialtes probably took place before 458 *(Athenaion Politeia* 25.4; see also F. Wilamowitz, *Aristoteles und Athen* [Berlin 1893], 342).
17. Cf. F. Schachermeyr, *Die frühe Klassik der Griechen* (Stuttgart 1966), 146.
18. Cf. C. Meier, *Entstehung des Begriffs Demokratie* (Frankfurt 1970), 226 ff. At the time of Cleisthenes these questions were only partly settled: as far as we can judge, the problem of who should govern—the nobles or the *demos*—had not yet been posed.
19. See Chapter 7.
20. See Chapter 3.
21. See Chapter 6.
22. Cf. C. Meier, *Die Entstehung des Politischen bie den Griechen* (Frankfurt 1983), 363 f.
23. Cf. Sophocles' famous chorus, *Antigone* 332 ff (see Chapter 8), which has an interesting link with Aeschylus, *Choephoroi* 585 ff.
24. Ever since Homer and Herodotus, Greek descriptions of warfare are remarkable in that they treat enemies (even female enemies, namely the Amazons) with great fairness—essentially as equals. This has often been remarked, but there is to my knowledge no study on the subject. (Ion X. Contiades, *"Echthros" kai "polemios" eis ten synchronon politiken theorian kai ten Helleniken aechaioteta* [Athens 1969], deals only with the use of words, in particular the distinction between *echthros* and *polemios*.) This attitude to the enemy seems to me to be one of the most revealing indications of the special "place in the world" occupied by the Greeks. It is closely linked with the fact that the city-states could not see themselves naively as worlds unto themselves (despite tendencies in this direction: see C. Meier, *Arethusa* 20 [1987] 49 ff). They were confronted by a cosmos that was far greater than any single power (see later in this chapter) and had no ideology to protect them against openly acknowledging the seriousness of political reality. The difference between the Greek and the Oriental views of the enemy becomes quite clear if one compares the Assyrian friezes with the metopes from Bassai in the British Museum in London. I could not discover a single fallen—or even wounded—Assyrian, but only an infinite number of defeated and "disqualified" enemies (mostly of inferior stature). For the Greeks, by contrast, friend and enemy were essentially equals, victory and defeat roughly equally apportioned. For an interesting treatment of this topic in connection with ancient Israel see Lothar Perlitt, "Israel und die Völker," in G. Liedke (ed.), *Frieden—Bibel—Kirche* (Stuttgart/Munich, [after 1970]), 17 ff, esp. 38 ff.
25. See Chapters 2 and 8.
26. Cf. Meier, *Entstehung*, 19 ff.
27. Plutarch, *Cimon* 15.1: *akratos demokratia*. This applies within the framework of the alternative *demos/oligoi*.

28. On this and what follows see A. Pickard-Cambridge, *The Dramatic Festivals of Athens* (2d ed. Oxford 1968), esp. 58 f, 67, 84 ff, 95 ff, 263 ff; see also W. Jaeger, *Paideia* I (4th ed. Berlin 1959), 319 ff.

29. Plato writes (*Gorgias* 502b–c) that the tragedies were intended to please the audience. See V. Ehrenberg, *Aristophanes und das Volk von Athen* (Zurich/Stuttgart 1968), 35. The voting procedure among the jurors is interesting: see Pickard-Cambridge, *Dramatic Festivals*, 95 ff; J. Ferguson, *A Companion to Greek Tragedy* (Austin 1972), 24; Meier, *Die politische Kunst*, 66 ff.

30. There were between 30,000 and 40,000 adult male citizens. However, women and boys were also allowed to attend; so too, on occasion, were foreigners. Cf. Ehrenberg, *Aristophanes*, 24, 395 n. 52.

31. The money was used chiefly to enable the poor to attend without paying for their seats. It is not clear how far it was meant to compensate for loss of earnings; see Pickard-Cambridge, *Dramatic Festivals*, 265 ff.

32. In his surviving plays Aeschylus is not usually so topical.

33. On Aeschylus see Podlecki, *Political Background*.

34. 290 f, 397 ff, 670 ff, 772 ff. See Lurje; J. H. Quincey, *Classical Quarterly* 14 (1964) 191; Dodds, *Ancient Concept of Progress*, 47.

35. See later in this chapter. On the difference between references to internal and external politics see Lurje. An equally clear indication of support for Themistocles is said to be found in *Persians* (see Podlecki, *Political Background*, 8 ff); this seems to me somewhat dubious.

36. Aristophanes, *Frogs* 1009 f, 1054 ff. Cf. Pausanias 1.3.2 on the effect of this doctrine.

37. Cf. Jaeger, *Paedeia* I, 317.

38. See Chapter 3 and discussion later in this chapter.

39. See later in this chapter. Jaeger (*Paedeia* I, 320 f) probably somewhat overstates the contrast between the performances of tragedy and everyday life. On the political factions see W. R. Connor, *The New Politicians of Fifth-Century Athens* (Princeton 1971). Connor does not perceive all the problems inherent in his subject; cf. C. Meier, "Der Alltag des Historikers und die historische Theorie," in H. M. Baumgartner and J. Rüsen (eds.), *Seminar: Geschichte und Theorie. Umrisse einer Historik* (Frankfurt 1976), 39 ff. It is important to realize that the factions of ancient times depended largely on the issues in question and shifted accordingly; disagreements on fundamental constitutional principles were rare. For the sources see Ruschenbusch, *Athenische Innenpolitik*, 3 ff. This topic needs further investigation.

40. *Agamemnon* 1090 ff; cf. 1502 f, 1582 ff; *Choephoroi* 1065 ff; *Eumenides* 175 ff. See G. Grossmann, *Promethie und Orestie. Attischer Geist in der attischen Tragödie* (Heidelberg 1970), 219. Clytemnestra's crime thus appears as just one in a long series.

41. *Choephoroi* 461; cf. *Agamemnon* 1560 f, 1283: "to put the coping-stone upon these infatuate iniquities of his house" (Loeb).

42. *Choephoroi* 269 ff, 940 f, 1030 ff; *Eumenides* 465 ff (cf. *Agamemnon* 1560 f). Orestes naturally accepts the verdict.

43. *Choephoroi* 1030 ff.
44. *Eumenides* 64 ff, 88, 219 ff, 232 ff; *Choephoroi* 1030 f. Cf. note 104 below.
45. See M. P. Nilsson, *Geschichte der griechischen Religion* I (3d ed. Munich 1967), 101.
46. See ibid., 100 f; K. Reinhardt, *Aischylos als Regisseur und Theologe* (Bern 1949), 149; F. Solmsen, *Hesiod and Aeschylus* (Ithaca 1949), 186 f, 198 f; H. Lloyd-Jones, *The Justice of Zeus* (Berkeley 1971), 63 f; Lesky, *Die tragische Dichtung,* 132 f. Apollo had even threatened Orestes that he would be pursued by the Erinyes if he did not avenge his father's death on his mother (*Choephoroi* 283 ff). There is no thought of purification here! The chorus had asked the Moirai, the half-sisters of the Erinyes (*Eumenides* 961), to support the act of vengeance (306 ff). Then, according to the chorus, Erinys leads Orestes too to commit the murder (*Choephoroi* 651) in accordance with the wishes of Dike (646). Cf. 400 ff, 461, 925. Cf. *Agamemnon* 59, 749, 1580.
47. *Eumenides* 69, 321, 416, 745, 845, 1034. See Solmsen, *Hesiod and Aeschylus,* 178 ff. The sharpness of this contrast was unusual: 183 ff; cf. 155.
48. W. Burkert, *Griechische Religion der archaischen und klassischen Epoche* (Stuttgart 1977), 376.
49. There are many inconsistencies here. Cf. Lesky, *Die tragische Dichtung,* 132; idem, *Hermes* 66 (1931) 209 ff. Dodds, *Ancient Concept of Progress,* 50 f, thinks that the role of purification is "deliberately minimized." It seems to me, however, that the apparent effect—the depiction of the factional situation—is intended: Athene is convinced (473 f), but the Erinyes are unimpressed. Cf. also Reinhardt, *Aischylos,* 161 f. The extent to which Aeschylus believed in the value of purification is of little relevance. See G. Thomson, *Aeschylus and Athens. A Study in the Social Origins of Drama* (London 1941), 260 and 272; idem, *The Oresteia of Aeschylus* I (2d ed. Amsterdam/Prague 1966), 45 f, 56. Thomson views the problem of purification within the context of a grand scheme of social development: the Erinyes stand for tribal order and the principle of retribution, Apollo for aristocracy and purification, Athene for democracy and trial by jury. This seems highly unlikely. In the first place, Aeschylus was not a historian, and certainly not a historical materialist; in the second place—even supposing that he had made any such historical distinction—he would have been bound to associate the Areopagus with the aristocracy; in the third place, it is Athene who is convinced by the purification, though she realizes that it does not remove the difficulty with the Erinyes (476 ff). Such historical differentiations create more problems than they solve (see note 113 below). Aeschylus' whole construction can be understood only if we assume that for him the temporal relation between old and new was independent of any absolute chronology and of successive stages of social development— i.e., if we suppose that he was content to draw parallels between the old and the new—of various origins and periods—without attempting to match them up precisely. Thus, on the one hand, the succession of divine dynasties corresponds to the succession of old and new in the poet's present, while at

the same time the old Areopagus is linked with the new forensic procedures. Finally, when it comes to their conceptions of law, Apollo belongs to
the new order no less than Athene; indeed, he is more passionately committed to innovation than the conciliatory goddess. On dynastic unity see
H. D. F. Kitto, *Greek Tragedy* (3d ed. London 1961), 89 n. 52. Cf. Meier,
"Der Umbruch zur Demokratie," 366 ff.

50. On this problem generally see R. Specht, *Innovation und Folgelast* (Stutt-
gart/Bad Cannstatt 1972).

51. See Lesky, *Die tragische Dichtung,* 109 f, 132 f; for a partly differing view
see Wilamowitz, *Aristoteles und Athen,* 333 f. Thomson (*Oresteia* I, 57)
and Reinhardt (*Aischylos,* 154 ff) also believe that it was Aeschylus who
transformed the Erinyes into the Eumenides; the contrary is suggested by
the relief from Argos adduced by Nilsson, *Griechischen Religion* I, 101
(plate 51.2). Thomson considers the possibility of Orphic or Pythagorean
precursors. At all events, the mythical archetype was probably still concerned only with the destinies of great families, whereas Aeschylus places
the city, the threat of civil war, and possible ways of meeting this threat at
the center of interest.

52. *Agamemnon* 757 ff, 1560 ff (a law of Zeus); *Choephoroi* 306 ff (the effect of
Dike, ultimately of Zeus), 400 ff (a *nomos*). See also 910 f (Moira), 935 ff;
Eumenides 175 ff, 808 f (*nomos*); and the passages cited in note 104.

53. Cf. Solmsen, *Hesiod and Aeschylus,* 216. Reinhardt, *Aischylos,* 144, suggests that the institution of the cult of the Eumenides is more significant
than the establishment of the Areopagus; yet the latter is presented in such
a way that it clearly has to be understood politically. Quite apart from this,
Reinhardt's reasoning is hard to follow. Lloyd-Jones, *The Justice of Zeus,*
94 f, doubts whether the "transition from the vendetta to the rule of law" is
the real issue. But these are false alternatives. Lloyd-Jones concentrates on
competences and the sequence of historical events (while underrating the
extent to which historical events can produce change); he therefore fails to
appreciate what takes place in the play—the full extent of the conflict
(which results from the strict prosecution of demands for revenge), the fundamentally new decision that is reached (broadly through the power of
the *polis*), or the new configuration that results from the compromise.
According to Reinhardt, 161, all this is symbolic rather than historical.
One cannot explain away the profound change, as Aeschylus sees it, merely
by reference to the changeless tenets of Greek theology.

54. Cf. the recent observations of U. Hölscher, "Das existentielle Motiv der
frühgriechischen Philosophie," in F. Hoermann (ed.), *Probata-Probanda*
(Munich 1974), 58 ff. On Solon see Solmsen, *Hesiod and Aeschylus,* 117.
On Anaximander see H. Fränkel, *Early Greek Poetry and Philosophy,*
trans. M. Hadas (Oxford 1975), 265 ff.

55. This is the view adopted by Kitto, *Form and Meaning in Drama* (London
1956), 71 ff; see also Ferguson, *Companion,* 110.

56. *Agamemnon* 62 ff, 438 ff, 687 ff, 799 ff; cf. 714 ff, 821 ff, 1455 ff, also
374 ff. These passages are interesting in that they reveal a certain skepticism regarding the desire for war that arises from wealth. The value of

fighting is called in question and set against the value of life and the aims of fighting. Cf. also Aeschylus, *Supplices* 476 f. See B. Daube, *Zu den Rechtsproblemen in Aischylos' Agamemnon* (Zurich/Leipzig 1938), 136 f; Kitto, *Form and Meaning*, 21. (On the identification of Zeus with vengeance: *Agamemnon* 62, 362, 367, 369, 526, 582, 704, 748, 813 f, 1486 f, 1563 f; *Choephoroi* 313).

57. *Agamemnon* 1560 ff; *Choephoroi* 306 ff, 400 ff; *Agamemnon* 1485 ff; cf. 176 ff. See Kitto, *Greek Tragedy*, 70 ff. On the Erinyes see note 46 above. True, Zeus wishes only to punish the violation of law and hospitality. Apollo, on the other hand, seems to punish in his own cause: Cassandra has to die for scorning his love (*Agamemnon* 1080 ff).

58. See Grossmann, *Promethie und Orestie*, 74 ff; Solmsen, *Hesiod and Aeschylus*, 124 ff, 205, 217; Lesky, *Die tragische Dichtung*, 142 f. In the *Prometheus* the idea of learning through suffering is related expressly to Zeus (981 f). This may of course be a partisan statement on the part of the Titan. However, J. de Romilly is probably right in remarking: "time is such an essential feature of Aeschylus' world that he has to go into the evolution and history of the gods in order to grasp the final nature of justice"; *Time in Greek Tragedy* (Ithaca 1968), 68. Cf. Meier, *Die politische Kunst*, 168 ff.

59. Reinhardt, *Aischylos*, 69 ff; W. Kraus, *Gnomon* 23 (1951) 23; Schachermeyr, *Frühe Klassik*, 166. Cf. Heraclitus, fr. 67, and later discussion; also Lloyd-Jones, *The Justice of Zeus*, 95 ff; J.-P. Vernant, *Mythe et société en Grèce ancienne* (Paris 1974), 110. Although it is wrong to read the modern notion of development into Aeschylus' ideas, the Greeks were clearly capable of distinguishing between the old regime and the new.

60. *Agamemnon* 61 f, 362, 704, 748; cf. 525, 973; *Eumenides* 973; Ferguson, *Companion*, 110.

61. Schachermeyr, *Frühe Klassik*, 173 f; Romilly, "Thucydide et l'idée de progrès," *Annali della Scuola normale superiore di Pisa. Letere, storia e filosofia*, ser. 2 (1966) 144 ff; Dodds, *Ancient Concept of Progress*, 6.

62. A third and probably earlier interpretation occurs in the fragment *Oxyrhynchus Papyri* XX, 2256.9a (= fr. 282 Lloyd-Jones-530 Mette), according to which the rule of Zeus was just from the beginning because he defended himself against his father Cronus when attacked.

63. On the other trilogies see Solmsen, *Hesiod and Aeschylus*, 172 ff (who nevertheless fails to bring out sufficiently the special character of the *Prometheia*).

64. The very consistency with which the Prometheus trilogy seems to have depicted the transformation of the rule of Zeus—taken together with stylistic considerations—indicates that it postdates the *Oresteia*. After all, it was probably extremely audacious to depict Zeus as at first a young and tyrannical ruler and so to postulate a protracted process of learning among the gods, corresponding to the gradual politicization of the *polis*. In the *Oresteia* Aeschylus was not yet able or willing to embark on such a bold course. Hence the historically unsatisfactory solution of a sudden shift in earthly affairs. This solution, while in no way detracting from the greatness of the work, clearly represents an earlier stage in Aeschylus' thinking on justice and its temporal dimension. On the dating see Thomson's commen-

tary on lines 640–643; one wonders, however, in what the suffering of Zeus can have consisted. See Solmsen, *Hesiod and Aeschylus*, 167, 189 (with literature), 172 f. (The striking difference between the trilogies and the other plays—which cannot have been composed much earlier—should probably be ascribed not only to an attempt to come to terms with Hesiod's theogony, but also to the political experiences of 462/61, which gave this its topicality. In my view, the very arguments used by Solmsen suggest that the *Prometheia* should be dated later than the *Oresteia;* cf. also ibid., 155.) See also Dodds, *Ancient Concept of Progress*, 37; Schachermeyr, *Frühe Klassik*, 165. On the question of authenticity see Lesky, *Die tragische Dichtung*, 141 ff (with literature); M. Griffith, *The Authenticity of Prometheus Bound* (Cambridge 1977); Dodds, 26 ff, esp. 37.

65. Reinhardt, *Aischylos*, 69, takes a contrary view. But even if this is true of Greek religiosity in general, it still does not determine the limits of what was conceivable at a time of such radical change. On young or new rulers see *Eumenides* 148 f, 170, 310, 439, 942, 955.

66. *Eumenides* 614 ff; cf. 713, 797 f; *Choephoroi* 558 f.

67. What we observe, then, is an essential logic in the handling of the plot and the characters—despite some residual inconsistencies—and not (as Grossmann, *Promethie und Orestie*, 224, would have it) an "archaic juxtaposition of quite disparate meanings attached to the Erinyes."

68. Kitto, *Greek Tragedy*, 91.

69. *Agamemnon* 844 f, 938; cf. 951 ff, 1452, 1489, 1513 (cf. Clytemnestra and Aegisthus: 883 f, 939, 1617 ff, 1638 ff). Cf. already 36, 548, 615 f.

70. *Agamemnon* 1355, 1365, 1633; cf. 1409 ff, 1424 f, 1615 f; also 904 ff, 935 f, with Ferguson, *Companion*, 85.

71. *Choephoroi* 302 ff, 863 f, 973, 1046; cf. 55 ff; Daube, *Rechtsprobleme*, 46 f. Also, with reference to the house, 131 ff, 237, 264, 480, 793 ff, 809 ff, 915, 942 ff; Kitto, *Form and Meaning*, 56.

72. *Choephoroi* 345 ff, 360 ff, 431, 439 ff, 491 ff, 723 f, 980 ff, 1010 ff. Cf. 808 ff, 919, 921, 1071 ff. The sacrifice of Iphigenia, which plays such an important part in the *Agamemnon,* is mentioned only once in the *Choephoroi* (242; cf. 1065 ff), and Clytemnestra refers to his misdeeds only in general terms (918). See Kitto, *Form and Meaning*, 39.

73. Solmsen, *Hesiod and Aeschylus*, 192 f.

74. Kitto, *Form and Meaning*, 71 ff.

75. *Agamemnon* 174 ff; cf. 250 f. Reinhardt, *Aischylos*, 20 ff, states: "Every Greek god, as the embodiment of a particular order of existence, demands a kind of human behavior that is in keeping with his divine nature. What Zeus demands of men is 'wisdom'!"

76. Kitto, *Form and Meaning*, 39, 46 f, 83; Dodds, *Ancient Concept of Progress*, 60 f.

77. Dodds, *Ancient Concept of Progress*, 53, 61 f.f Cf. Romilly, *Time in Greek Tragedy*, 69, although her subsequent remarks should be modified in view of line 521.

78. *Agamemnon* 1425, 1620. Cf. also *Prometheus* 983, 1012, 1035.

79. Dodds, *Ancient Concept of Progress*, 46 f. Cf. the striking formulation

in *Eumenides* 550: the blessing depends on man's being just *without compulsion*.

80. This interpretation arises from the context of the passage. The parallel between the Erinyes and the Areopagus is considered later in this chapter. On the notion of such "internalization" see *Choephoroi* 55 ff, *Eumenides* 691, together with Thomson's textual suggestions, *Oresteia* I, 78.

81. Which Aeschylus obviously regarded as tending toward anarchy: 526, 696, also 506 f. Cf. later in this chapter.

82. The violent revolution that brought the dynasty of Zeus to power is hardly mentioned in the play (*Agamemnon* 171 f. Cf. esp. the account of the legitimate succession at Delphi, *Eumenides* 1 ff. See Kitto, *Greek Tragedy*, 87). The old powers are represented only by the Erinyes, who themselves invoke the Moirai.

83. The *Prometheus* too is steeped in politics and political experience, which dominate the foreground (cf. Reinhardt, *Aischylos*, 42 ff), but the trilogy is set in a wide temporal perspective (*Prometheus* 94 with the scholion: 30,000 years! 189 ff, 982).

84. F. I. Zeitlin, "The Dynamics of Misogyny: Myth and Myth-making in the Oresteia," *Arethusa* 11 (1978) 168 f. Ancient opinion was divided as to whether the children of the Night had a father; cf. G. Ramnoux, *La nuit et les enfants de la nuit dans la tradition grecque* (Paris 1959): Aeschylus' own view is not clear. It is noteworthy that he often identifies people as the children of their mothers (e.g., *Agamemnon* 1040; see Zeitlin, 154; *Choephoroi* 813 f). Is this a tacit refutation of Apollo's argument (see later in this chapter)? For a general discussion of the Erinyes as daughters of the Night see Solmsen, *Hesiod and Aeschylus*, 178 ff.

85. Zeitlin, "Dynamics," 149 ff, esp. 153. Cf. 150: "If Aeschylus is concerned with world-building, the cornerstone of his architecture is the control of woman." When Zeitlin writes (161): "The primary issue in the *Oresteia* is, of course, justice," this must mean that justice consists largely in the subjection of woman. In this connection *Choephoroi* 596 ff is important: the general theme here is not woman's craving for power, but *thelykrates aperotos eros* (the loveless love that controls women).

86. This raises the general question of whether we are justified in crediting Aeschylus with a knowledge of and interest in early history, and, if so, to what extent. On this question cf. Kitto, *Form and Meaning*, 55, 58.

87. Cf. note 46 above.

88. Dodds, *Ancient Concept of Progress*, 6, 43 f.

89. I would now adopt a somewhat different approach to the question: cf. Meier, *Die politische Kunst*, 152.

90. This is not to deny that with the emergence of democracy the role of women became much more restricted than that of men—which was at the same time significantly increasing—just as the development of Greek freedom brought the status of slaves into stronger relief. (Again this is not to say that women were relegated to the status of slaves. When discussing these questions it is unfortunately necessary to guard against any possible misunderstandings. We are concerned only with the correspondences between

different by-products of the emergence of Greek civil liberty.) On the other hand it is highly unlikely that Aeschylus really regarded "the subordination of woman (quite correctly) as an indispensable condition of democracy," as Thomson maintains (*Aeschylus and Athens*, 269). This condition was after all probably taken for granted at that time.

91. *Eumenides* 210–224, 490 ff, 727 f, 778 ff, 808 ff. Cf. Solmsen, *Hesiod and Aeschylus*, 183; Grossmann, *Promethie und Orestie*, 219.

92. Schachermeyr, *Frühe klassik*, 164.

93. This is to be seen in Aeschylus' *Supplices*; cf. later discussion. The idea occurs earlier in Pindar (but perhaps only as an aristocratic judgment).

94. One thinks perhaps of the legal proceedings initiated against Cimon (*Athenaion Politeia* 25.2) and various other Areopagites, of the disputes regarding the despatch of a contingent to Sparta, or of other matters of which we know nothing.

95. Reinhardt, *Aischylos*, 149 f; Solmsen, *Hesiod and Aeschylus*, 178 ff, 183 ff. The fact remains that it did belong together, even if at first there had been contention between the old powers and the new.

96. Solmsen, *Hesiod and Aeschylus*, 184 f, against Thomson, *Oresteía*.

97. Solmsen, *Hesiod and Aeschylus*, 183 f. The force of their claims is also reflected in the outcome of the ballot.

98. Thomson, *Oresteia* I, 50. Solmsen, *Hesiod and Aeschylus*, 184 n. 31, fails to make a sufficiently clear distinction here. There had to be solidarity between Athene and Apollo (as champions of the law of Zeus and his dynasty), yet they had to occupy very different positions (as far as party allegiance and political method were concerned). See later discussion.

99. Reinhardt, *Aischylos*, 149 ff; Kitto, *Form and Meaning*, 58 f; Solmsen, *Hesiod and Aeschylus*, 190 f. (Solmsen, however, fails to bring out the factor of contemporary experience that prompted Aeschylus to develop Hesiod's ideas so radically. Cf. 155, 185.)

100. *Eumenides* 150, 162, 490 (?—see note 102), 731, 778 f, 808 f. Cf. 172, 838, 847 f, 882 f; Reinhardt, *Aischylos*, 158. Only line 69 contains a possible hint of contempt for the old, and it is uttered—significantly—by Apollo.

101. See Chapter 8.

102. *Eumenides* 808; presumably also 490 ff, though here both the text and the sense are disputed. If the received text is correct, the Erinyes are saying that the "new institutions" just established by Athene are "now" (i.e., in the event of an acquittal) "in danger of being overthrown." Dover, *Journal of Hellenic Studies* 77 (1957) 230 f, and Lloyd-Jones, *The Justice of Zeus*, 92, have defended this reading, but in all probability the text is corrupt. For, as Thomson says in his commentary (supported by Solmsen, *Hesiod and Aeschylus*, 183, n. 25): "The attitude of the Furies at this stage is that if the older laws are overthrown the result will be utter lawlessness." An objection to Dover's view is that for the Erinyes an acquittal will undoubtedly overthrow *all* law, and that to restrict their words to the new law would be incomprehensible and arbitrary. Moreover, the term *thesmos* certainly does not apply only to the new law: at 391 ff the Erinyes use it to designate

their traditional function. It is true that the spirits of vengeance agreed to submit to Athene's tribunal, especially as she had treated them with respect (433 ff), but the goddess had meanwhile refused to give judgment herself and had set up a human tribunal (470 ff), of which the Erinyes could hardly become supporters. Finally, in the context of Dover's interpretation, the word *nyn* is hard and meaningless, for it would then have to distinguish very precisely between the danger threatening the new law and its very recent institution. Even before it is fully established it is being put to the test. Thus the word *now* does not relate to a particular moment. A quite different sense emerges if the passage refers to the old law: the word would then relate to the great decision in the history of law (and humanity) in which everything was *now* at stake.

103. See Chapter 8.

104. *Choephoroi* 400 ff; *Eumenides* 75 ff, 175 ff, 225, 230 f, 246 ff, 267 ff, 299 ff, 334 ff, 358 ff, 383 ff, 423, 808 f. Cf. note 52 above.

105. *Eumenides* 429 f, 432 (with Kitto, *Form and Meaning,* 62); also 218 (where Apollo states that marriage is more sacred than the oath) and 621 (where he emphasizes that the oath is not more important than Zeus). On the other hand, of course, oaths are extremely important for all law; there are subsequently two references to the oath of the Areopagites (680, 710; cf. 768). What applies to the oath also applies to Peitho: it is a means that can be employed for very different purposes (cf. note 140 below). On the Erinyes as oath-goddesses see Thomson, *Oresteia* I, 56 f, commentary on 934 ff (with the surmise that they therefore pursue the descendents of perjurers).

106. *Eumenides* 462 ff, 588. An archaic feature of the Erinyes' behavior is their insistence on "honor and office" (208 f, 227, 325, 394, 419 ff, 712, 747, 780, 845, 878 f). There is of course nothing corresponding to this on the opposite side, which is in this respect more generous.

107. *Eumenides* 470 ff, 682; cf. *Choephoroi* 120 (on this passage see Ferguson, *Companion,* 91 f; Grossmann, *Promethie und Orestie,* 247). On the humane character of the Athenian courts see Grossmann, 242 ff.

108. F. Solmsen, *Antiphon-Studien* (Leipzig 1931), 47 ff.

109. Solmsen, *Hesiod and Aeschylus,* 223 f.

110. *Eumenides* 625 ff; cf. *Choephoroi* 345; Grossmann, *Promethie und Orestie,* 225.

111. This has to be, and is, made clear; see Reinhardt, *Aischylos,* 147 ff. The partisanship of the Erinyes is seen in minor details: cf. 340, where we learn that even in death the murderer is not safe from them, though Clytemnestra is (603).

112. Reinhardt, *Aischylos,* 147 (see *Eumenides* 336 f, 421); Lesky, *Die tragische Dichtung,* 132 f; Solmsen, *Hesiod and Aeschylus,* 181 f (except that the reasons are probably not only dramatic). On the textual tradition see Thomson, *Oresteia* I, 56 f. Cf. note 46 above.

113. 658 ff. Cf. Orestes' doubts, 606. See Reinhardt, *Aischylos,* 148. Kitto, *Form and Meaning,* 58 ff, 66: "Nothing but an absurd argument is possible if one has to argue that it is worse to kill a husband than a mother, or vice

versa. Aeschylus may not have had the slightest interest in matriarchal trib-
alism or theories of parentage. The value of these arguments to him here is
purely dramatic. They enable him to present the two parties to the conflict
as utterly one-sided, and irreconcilable" (cf. p. 55). See also A. Lebeck, *The
Oresteia: A Study in Language and Structure* (Cambridge, Mass., 1971),
124 ff; R. Schottländer, *Das Altertum* 16 (1970) 150 f. A different view is
taken by Thomson, *Aeschylus and Athens*, 269 ff; and in his commentary on
657 ff, 741 (see also Solmsen, *Hesiod and Aeschylus*, 192 n. 57). For what
may well have been the poet's own view see *Choephoroi* 421 f (cf. Thomson's commentary and that of P. Groeneboom, *Aeschylus' Choephoroi.
Met Inleiding, critische Noten en Commentar* [Groningen 1949]). Translated literally, the text means "a spirit unsoftenable from the mother."
Hence it may also mean that Electra cannot be softened by her mother. But
the alternative interpretation, namely that Electra has her unsoftenable
spirit from her mother, is at least equally possible. Aeschylus was thus
in any case taking the risk of being misunderstood as implying that he
believed in inheritance from the mother. Cf. also 140 f and *Agamemnon*
727 f, 771. On the possible political background of this argumentation see
Schachermeyr, *Frühe Klassik*, 145 ff; Lurje, 297. On the origin of the
theory see E. Lesky, "Die Zeugungs- und Vererbungslehren der Antike,"
*Abhandlungen Akademie Mainz, Geistes- und Sozialwissenschaftliche
Klasse* 19 (1950) 1278; A. Peretti, *Parola del passato* 11 (1956) 241 ff;
Zeitlin, "Dynamics," 180 n. 22.

114. That the old corresponds to the female may have accorded with some contemporary views. It recurs, e.g., in Aristophanes' *Ecclesiazusae* (though
here it applies only until the women slip into the men's role as citizens;
see Chapter 8).

115. Kitto, *Form and Meaning*, 56 f, speaks of "the very fabric of civilized
society."

116. This is indicated above all by the fact that the Erinyes become one-sided
and partisan only temporarily (when confronting Apollo). Previously they
have served Zeus and the other gods. In court they show themselves greatly
superior to the god of Delphi; this is a superiority enjoyed by the old when
they are faced with the young and impetuous (Kitto, *Form and Meaning*,
67)—and the majority of the Areopagus (made up entirely of men) acknowledges them to be in the right. Athene alone pronounces against them—and
then conciliates them. Is this how an ancient fundamental conflict between
male and female was conducted and resolved?

117. *Eumenides* 46 ff, 68 ff, 192; Ferguson, *Companion*, 103.

118. Kitto, *Form and Meaning*, 54; Nilsson, *Geschichte der griechischen Religion* I, 529 ff. Cf. also *Agamemnon* 522, 1646; *Choephoroi* 808 ff; *Eumenides* 52, 72, 352, 379, 386, 395, 417 (665?), 745 f. In this way Apollo
denies that any honor is due the Erinyes (721 f). Admittedly they have previously called into question his office as a seer (715 f). On the barbarous see
Agamemnon 919.

119. Cf., e.g., Zeitlin, "Dynamics," 171 f.

120. 667 ff, 711 f, 719 f. See Lebeck, *Oresteia*, 135 (the prohibition on their

speaking in the Areopagus on matters extraneous to the case); Reinhardt, *Aischylos*, 146. One should note too the utterly partisan view to which Apollo resorts in order to extricate himself from the pressure of uncomfortable arguments: 725 f and similarly 232 ff.

121. F. Grillparzer, *Sämtliche Werke*, ed. A. Sauer, XVI, 67. On the further problems (including theological problems) of the court scene cf. Solmsen, *Hesiod and Aeschylus*, 194 f, who writes that "it is typical of Aeschylus that while his tragedy has its roots . . . in the realm of primitive religious beliefs . . . he finds the final solution of his problem in the clearer, and at the same time colder, atmosphere of civic institutions, and with the help of dialectical reasoning"—except that it is not the "final solution" of the play. Important arguments are also advanced by K. Schneider, in H. Hommel (ed.), *Wege zu Aischylos* II (Darmstadt 1974), 319 ff.

122. Kitto, in *La notion du divin*. Entretiens Fondation Hardt I (Vandoeuvre 1954), 186.

123. Chapter 7 and Meier, *Entstehung*, 26 ff.

124. Lesky, *Die tragische Dichtung*, 78 ff (certainly between 467 and 459).

125. Cf. Chapter 7. At first these contrasts make only a brief appearance; at a later stage they are conceptualized.

126. Only from this point on can it be maintained that every order is based *on a decision and not on a norm;* see C. Schmitt, *Politische Theologie* (2d ed. Munich/Leipzig 1934), 16.

127. *Eumenides* 435. Kitto, *Form and Meaning*, 62 f.

128. Solmsen, *Hesiod and Aeschylus*, 216, 221. Cf. Reinhardt, *Aischylos*, 160 f, who states that "according to Aeschylus the liberating factor" (of the progress to *polis* jurisdiction) lies in the fact "that the legal jurisdiction of men over men is a divine institution, not one that is designed to serve human expediency."

129. On this and what follows see B. Snell, "Aischylos und das Handeln im Drama," *Philologus* Suppl. 20.1 (1928); Lesky, *Die tragische Dichtung*, 166 f. What is crucial, however, is the public representation of such situations of decision! Cf. also T. Hölscher, *Griechische Historienbilder des 5. und 4. Jahrhunderts vor Christus* (Würzburg 1973), 205 ff.

130. An extremely realistic (though inconclusive) decision-making process, with several persons involved, is to be found in *Agamemnon* 1347 ff. It concerns the age-old problem that arises when one has to take immediate action against a current usurpation, yet feels obliged first to seek clarification.

131. *Eumenides* 711–753, 795; see Kitto, *Form and Meaning*, 65 ff. It has often been denied that the tie results only from Athene's intervention. Even in ancient times the tie was held to have arisen from the ballots of the mortal judges, after which the goddess's vote, the *calculus Minervae*, produced a majority in Orestes' favor (and was then added to the tied vote, as if it turned this into a majority in favor of the accused). Yet the text leaves us in no doubt about the correctness of the above interpretation. Cf. Lesky, *Die tragische Dichtung*, 130 n. 95. This decision has a counterpart in Agamemnon's arrogant remark that the decision of the gods against Troy had been unanimous (*Agamemnon* 813 ff): this is clearly meant to indicate the

unequivocal nature of the chain of revenge and counterrevenge that arises when the gods decide upon punishment (though as a rule there are factional divisions among them, as among mortals). No such certainty is possible if one views the conflicting claims from a third position, which sought to weigh them against each other and break the chain (*Agamemnon* 1560–65); cf. *Choephoroi* 416).

132. 795. Cf. Dodds, *Ancient Concept of Progress,* 59, who nevertheless views the matter rather too narrowly in terms of the work's internal structure. Since the closeness of the outcome subsequently supplies grounds for reconciliation, it becomes almost a consolation—in the context of the hopes and ideals that Aeschylus then proceeds to rehearse.

133. Plutarch, *Cimon* 16.9 f. On the numbers cf. Aristophanes, *Lysistrata* 1143, together with the scholion to the passage; see also Hill, *Sources of Greek History,* 37 (with incorrect dating). Cimon's absence when the vote was taken is attested by Plutarch: "when he had again departed on a campaign" (15.2). That this refers to the campaign against Sparta is suggested by 17.3 and Thucydides 1.102.4 (cf. also Diodorus 11.64.2 f) and is now generally accepted; cf. Will, *Le monde grec,* 146, 150. It may be doubted whether the absence of the 4,000 hoplites was so crucial to Ephialtes' success—rather than that of Cimon or his Pyrrhic victory in the question of the dispatch of the Attic contingent which was then sent home by the Spartans. With regard to numbers, if 6,000 citizens (out of a total of about 35,000) were present the Assembly was clearly considered to be well attended; see Hignett, *Athenian Constitution,* 153, 216, 236.

134. 734 ff; see Reinhardt, *Aischylos,* 148. Kitto, *Form and Meaning,* 85, has a different interpretation: "She votes for the male because she had no mother: that is to say, although she recognises to the full the strength of the Erinyes' case, she recognises too that the authority of the social order is logically prior."

135. *Eumenides* 433, 468, 482 (in the context of the speech beginning at line 470), 612. Cf. Solmsen, *Hesiod and Aeschylus,* 206, on the way in which Aeschylus develops these possibilities.

136. H. Lübbe, "Dezisionismus. Zur Geschichte der politischen Theorie der Entscheidung," in A. Müller (ed.), *Gesellschaftliche Entscheidungsvorgänge* (Basel 1977), 33 ff; idem, *Theorie und Entscheidung. Studien zum Primat der praktischen Vernunft* (Freiburg im Breisgau 1971), 7 ff; idem, *Wissenschaftspolitik* (Zurich 1977), 77 ff. As regards the problem of decisionism and its intellectual prehistory, not enough attention has been paid to C. Schmitt, *Gesetz und Urteil. Eine Untersuchung zum Problem der Rechtspraxis* (2d ed. Munich 1969).

137. Solmsen, *Hesiod and Aeschylus,* 173, 218.

138. It is interesting to note the repetition of the image of being "downridden": 150, 731, 779, 809.

139. See note 16 above.

140. *Eumenides* 885, 970. Cf. Thomson, *Oresteia* I, 50, 65 f; II, 321; Grossmann, *Promethie und Orestie,* 138. Peitho (see also Isocrates 15.254) can also be made to serve quite different ends: *Agamemnon* 106, 385; *Choephoroi*

726. She makes words captivating: *Agamemnon* 886, 900; cf. 81; Voigt, *RE* XIX, 204. See also Solmsen, *Hesiod and Aeschylus*, 176 f. Cf. C. Meier, *Politik und Anmut* (Berlin 1985) (*La politique et la grace*, trans. P. Veyne [Paris 1987]).

141. *Eumenides* 988. Cf. Pindar, *Olympia* 1.110. On finding the way see also 82.

142. Cf. Ferguson, *Companion* 105.

143. Cf. C. Meier, "Macht und Gewalt," in W. Conze, R. Kosselleck, and O. Brunner (eds.), *Geschichtliche Grundbegriffe* III (Stuttgart 1982), 823 n. 24; Aeschylus, fr. 282 (Lloyd-Jones in Loeb = Mette 530).

144. The earliest example of any such suspicion is found in Socrates' remark in Plato's *Protagoras,* relating to the education of the young (310a ff, esp. 314a–b).

145. *Eumenides* 973. Cf. *Supplices* 623 f.

146. *Eumenides* 1041. Cf. 384, 805, 838, 855, 871, 1007, 1023, 1037; Pausanias 1.29.2. Those whom the Areopagus acquitted were supposed to make sacrifices to them. See Thomson, *Oresteia* I, 56 f. As to whether the equation of the Erinyes with the Semnai is Aeschylean see note 51 above.

147. Most recently Lloyd-Jones, *The Justice of Zeus,* 93 f. Solmsen, *Hesiod and Aeschylus,* 201, takes a contrary view. The denial of a transformation in Zeus is based on an objection to the transference of the modern notion of development to classical times. This is partly justified, but it is not so easy to distinguish precisely between ancient and modern notions. Cf. Chapter 8.

148. Cf. 313 ff, where we find a purely negative formulation of what happens to one who does not commit a crime.

149. *Eumenides* 796, 824 f, 833 ff, 854 f, 868, 890 f, 894 ff, 930 f, 992 ff.

150. D. Kaufmann-Bühler, *Begriff und Funktion der Dike in den Tragödien des Aischylos* (Heidelberg diss. 1951), 102 ff.

151. Cf. also the statements about the uniqueness of Athens, 853 ff.

152. This is the view taken by Reinhardt, *Aischylos,* 71 f, 143.

153. Solmsen, *Hesiod and Aeschylus,* 149 n. 116.

154. Cf. 502 (on what will happen if they give up their office). A different and not very convincing view is advanced by Podlecki, *Political Background,* 79.

155. Disagreeing with Lloyd-Jones, *The Justice of Zeus,* 94. In this context it is irrelevant that the *Iliad,* on the one hand, contains instances of feuds' being settled by kings, and that the Athenian penal code, on the other, preserves residual traces of ancient notions of vengeance: Aeschylus does not maintain that the period before 458 was one of revenge, which was then succeeded by a period of civic jurisdiction. He is concerned rather to point a particular contrast and, in doing so, brings together many elements widely separated in time. See also Kitto, *Form and Meaning,* 86.

156. Solmsen, *Hesiod and Aeschylus,* 201 f. This is a survival of an archaic idea, cf. Homer, *Iliad* 16.386 ff, *Odyssey* 19.108 ff; Hesiod, *Works and Days* 225 ff. See G. Vlastos, *Classical Philology* 41 (1946) 65 ff.

157. Although they themselves had said that they must remain apart from the immortals (350 ff, 365 ff). Apollo had declared that they were universally hated and had the respect of neither the young gods nor the old (645, 721 f).

158. Solmsen, *Hesiod and Aeschylus,* 203. Cf. H. J. Wolff, "Die Grundlagen des

griechischen Eherechts," in E. Berneker (ed.), *Zur griechischen Rechts-geschichte* (Darmstadt 1968), 624. A different view is found in Aeschylus, *Seven against Thebes* 200 f (the house as the sole domain of women).

159. Notes 105 and 140 above. Aeschylus is the first to make a similar distinction between healthy and unhealthy fear; see J. de Romilly, *La crainte et l'angoisse dans le théâtre d'Eschyle* (Paris 1958), 107 ff. Cf. also the distinction between two kinds of dispute: *Agamemnon* 698, 1461; *Eumenides* 975.

160. They plead against *hybris* and *dyssebeia*, wholly in the spirit of Zeus; see Solmsen, *Hesiod and Aeschylus*, 198 f.

161. Dodds, *Ancient Concept of Progress*, 50.

162. Kitto, *Form and Meaning*, 63 f.

163. Solmsen, *Hesiod and Aeschylus*, 198 n. 72.

164. Ibid., 200, offers a different interpretation, according to which the audience has to be prepared for the reconciliation, but it seems to me that any such preparation is adequately achieved in what follows.

165. Thomson, *Aeschylus and Athens*, 275.

166. Pindar, *Pythia* 4.291. See Kraus, *Gnomon* 23 (1951) 20 f; Ferguson, *Companion*, 78 f. On the one-sidedness of divine rule see esp. p. 163, together with Thomson's commentary on *Agamemnon* 1026 f. Now, however, the Eumenides call Zeus "all-powerful" (*pankrates* 917).

167. Cf. Chapter 7 and Meier, "Macht und Gewalt," 825, 829.

168. 530 f: *panti meso to kratos theos opasen, all' alla d'ephoreuei.*

169. Cf. Romilly, *La crainte et l'angoisse;* Grossmann, *Promethie und Orestie,* 45 f. On the attribution of the Sisyphus fragment, however, see A. Dihle, *Hermes* 105 (1977) 28 ff. It would be interesting to pursue the links between this idea and the recurring pre-Socratic notion of an equilibrium between opposites; cf. notes 189 and 211. C. Meier, in S. N. Eisenstadt (ed.), *The Origins and Diversity of Axial Age Civilizations* (New York 1986), 87; J.-P. Vernant, *Mythe et pensée,* 2 vols. (Paris 1971), I, 8.

170. Cf. Lloyd-Jones, *The Justice of Zeus,* 94; Dodds, *Ancient Concept of Progress,* 48 ff.

171. Nor can one escape this interpretation by adopting the view of Wilamowitz, *Aristoteles und Athen,* 332 ff—shared, with some differences, by Solmsen, *Hesiod and Aeschylus,* 210, and Lesky, *Die tragische Dichtung,* 143—that the Areopagus represents purely and simply the legal tribunal. The praise accorded to this body can only relate to its activities as a whole.

172. To this extent Solmsen, *Hesiod and Aeschylus,* 210, seems to be justified. Cf. also idem, *Gnomon* 31 (1959) 472 f; Dodds, *Ancient Concept of Progress,* 61 f; Wilamowitz, *Aristoteles und Athen,* 341 (who employs dubious arguments).

173. Cf. Lurje, 296 f; Dodds, *Ancient Concept of Progress,* 48 f; Dover, *Journal of Hellenic Studies* 77 (1957) 232 (who presents a highly improbable case). On the text see Thomson's commentary.

174. Cf. also 706 with 948.

175. *Eumenides* 858 ff; cf. 976 ff. At 861 and 866 Aeschylus uses the image of the cockfight, a popular Athenian sport: see K. Schneider, *RE* VII (1912), 2210 ff. The Erinyes will incite the citizens to fight as men incite cocks. It is

curious that although they make many other threats (780 ff, 810 ff; cf. 477 ff) they do not threaten civil war. We need not suppose with Dodds that Aeschylus added these lines later. Cf. also *Supplices* 661 ff, where the formulation is admittedly more restrained. The idea had been familiar since Solon (*Elegies* 3). Such wishes were presumably part of the ritual prayers in Athens (Solmsen, *Hesiod and Aeschylus*, 213).

176. Precise reasons cannot be given for this. It arises from the formulations contained in his poems and from what can be deduced about the concept of eunomy.

177. 976 ff. Grammatically the sentence is hard to disentangle, but fortunately this does not matter here. The translation is confined to what is essential in the context (neglecting the fascinating image of the "dust that drinks the black blood of the citizens" and sucks in the misfortune of the city). What is important is the parallel between reciprocal murder (cf. *Agamemnon* 1576 f) and the reciprocal giving of joy, mentioned two lines later.

178. This is an obvious reference to civil war and bloody feuds. Uniting the *polis* means putting an end to such ills (cf. *kaka*, 976).

179. Plato later formulated, in general terms, an analogous distinction between friend and foe when he said that the Greeks were "by nature friends" (as associates and relatives), whereas the barbarians, being foreigners and members of alien races, were "by nature enemies." While this did not rule out war among Greeks, any such war should nevertheless be limited. Plato thus distinguished between *polemos* against the barbarians and *stasis* (strife, civil war, among the Greeks): *Republic* 469 f; cf. *Menexenus* 245c. Contiades, *"Echthros" kai "polemios,"* 21 f, is wrong, however, to assert that the distinction between *polemos* and *stasis* corresponds to that between *echthros* and *polemios*. The relation between these latter terms is obscure. Their semantic fields partly coincide. To cite just four examples out of many: *polemios* denoting internal political opposition: *Agamemnon* 608; Anonymus Iamblichi 6.4 (*Fragmente der Vorsokratiker* II, 403); Plato, *Republic* 422e; *echthros* for the opponent in war: Plato, *Timaeus* 18a. *Polemios* relates chiefly to military opposition; *echthros* is more general. Only *echthros* yields a general notion of enmity *(echthra)*. Moreover, enmity as a cause of war, the distinction between friend and enemy in external affairs, is mainly expressed by *echthros* (cf. also note 182). Admittedly, where *polemios* is used by historians and orators, it supplants *echthros* in the meaning of immediate military opposition. Cf. Contiades' conclusion, 26. On the coincidence of the semantic fields see especially Thucydides' usage (Contiades, 19 f).

180. Solon's *statis* law was an interesting attempt to mobilize the whole of the citizenry against the contending factions in the event of a civil war. Anyone who failed to take sides was to be *atimos*, i.e., deprived of protection under the civil law (cf. *Athenaion Politeia* 8.5; Plutarch, *Solon* 20.1. See also P. Spahn, *Mittelschicht und Polisbildung* (Frankfurt/Bern/Las Vegas 1977), 153 f, including the probability that the law is genuine. On the political problem see Spahn, 136 ff and passim. On its subsequent effects, see Cicero, *Ad Atticum*, 10.1.2; *In Verrem* 2.1.34). The intention was obviously to

bring out the majority of the citizens in opposition to the minority who were involved in feuding—an interesting institution, though doomed to fail. According to *Athenaion Politeia* Solon saw that some of the citizens were unconcerned about what happened and "loved to let things take their course" *(agapein to automaton);* there could be no clearer expression of the wish to replace processes by politics (see Solon, *Elegies* 3; Meier, *Entstehung,* 19 ff).

181. Connor, *The New Politicians,* 42 ff. In addition to the passages cited by Connor, cf. Homer, *Odyssey* 6.184 f; Archilochus, in *Oxyrhynchus Papyri* XXII, 2310.14 f; Theognis 869 ff; Sappho, fr. 5 (Lobel-Page); Pindar, *Pythia* 2.83 f; *Nemea* 10.78; Gorgias B11a.25 *(Frag. der Vorsokratiker* II, 294); Plato, *Republic* 332d; Plutarch, *Themistocles* 5.6. See also M. J. O'Brien, *The Socratic Paradoxes and the Greek Mind* (Chapel Hill 1967).

182. *Athenaion Politeia* 23.5. On the various types of association see G. E. M. de Ste. Croix, *The Origins of the Peloponnesian War* (London 1972), 298 ff. Thanks to the discovery of a treaty of ca. 500 B.C., the formula is already attested in the alliances made by Sparta (in the Peloponnesian League); here it denotes a one-sided commitment on the part of the allied city to Sparta's identification of friend and enemy. See W. Peek, "Ein neuer spartanischer Staatsvertrag," *Abhandlungen der sächsischen Akademie, Leipzig, Philologisch-historische Klasse* 65.3 (1974); F. Gschnitzer, *Ein neuer spartanischer Staatsvertrag und die Verfassung des Peloponnesischen Bundes* (Meisenheim 1978), esp. 26, 35 ff.

183. The question of how this was envisaged in the long term arises in particular with regard to the "zeal for good" *(agathon eris,* 974 f). However, it was presumably meant to apply only in a temporary crisis (just as Solon relied on the responsibility of the citizens until a "righter of wrongs" was brought in).

184. Burkert, *Griechische Religion,* 382 ff; cf. Wolff, "Die Grundlagen des griechischen Eherechts," 624 ff, 631.

185. 913 ff. Cf. note 56 above. Similarly Aeschylus, fr. 281 (Lloyd-Jones in Loeb). The suffering that war brings to the soldiers and to those they leave behind is nevertheless described in such vivid detail in *Agamemnon* 428 ff and 555 ff that the negative aspects of war are by no means absent; see Daube, *Rechtsprobleme,* 135.

186. The Athenian policy of expansion and conquest is later called *neoteropoiia* (Thucydides 1.102.3); the very fact that it was an element of unrest meant that contemporaries saw it as an innovation.

187. Plutarch, *Cimon* 17.6 f. This admittedly relates to an impending battle.

188. K. Marx and F. Engels, *Gesamtausgabe (MEGA)* I.2 (Berlin 1982), 34 *(Collected Works* [London 1975–], III, 32).

189. Empedocles B16, 17, 22, 26, 30, 35, 36, 59, 109 *(Frag. der Vorsokratiker* I, 277 ff) and the accounts of his teaching (cf. index, III, 289). See also W. K. C. Guthrie, *A History of Greek Philosophy* II (Cambridge 1965), 152 ff. The relation between the notions of friend and enemy on the one hand and the pre-Socratic doctrine of contrasts on the other has to my knowledge not yet been investigated (see the literature in note 211).

190. E.g., Aristotle, *Politics* 1262b7, 1263a30, 1295b23; *Nicomachean Ethics* 1161a10 ff, 1167b2 ff and passim.

191. An important exception is the great dialogue between Pericles and Alcibiades in Xenophon, *Memorabilia* 1.2.40. For the rest, free disposal was taken for granted, and an attempt was made to find criteria for it and to point it in the right direction.

192. Thucydides 3.38.

193. Ehrenberg, *Aristophanes*, 283 ff, esp. 286.

194. Cf. Antiphanes, fr. 191; Ferguson, *Companion*, 24. More generally Jaeger, *Paideia* I, 319 ff, 324 ff. Cf. Plutarch, *Nicias* 29.2 ff.

195. To anticipate a recurrent objection, it must be added that this did not apply to all the citizens. Perhaps it did not apply to even half of them, but it did apply to a comparatively large number; this meant that there was one overriding interest that affected more or less all the citizens and could hardly be matched by any other. In addition, there were corresponding expectations whose fulfillment generated further expectations.

196. Ehrenberg, *Aristophanes*, 32 f. See also C. Schmitt's remarks on the analogous case of a "shared public" in Shakespearean theater and on the mistakes that result from a modern approach: C. Schmitt, *Hamlet oder Hekuba* (Düsseldorf 1956), 33 f.

197. *Agamemnon* 883 f. The meaning is clearly "overthrow." Cf. Dodds, *Ancient Concept of Progress,* 46. There may be similar allusions to Cimon in the striking description of Agamemnon as leader of the army and the fleet (*Choephoroi* 723, *Eumenides* 637). As has been said, this image of the commander had been predominant since the *Choephoroi.*

198. Just as in *Athenaion Politeia* it is stated to have been the aim of Solon's *stasis* law (see note 180 above).

199. Cf. Dodds, *Ancient Concept of Progress,* 62.

200. See W. Nippel, *Mischverfassungstheorie und Verfassungsrealität in Antike und früher Neuzeit* (Stuttgart 1980).

201. Aristotle, *Politics* 1255b20, 1277b9; cf. 1254b2, 1259b1, 1325a28. In this connection Aeschylus, fr. 381 (Nauck = 209 Loeb), is of interest: "Where might and right are yoked together, what team can be stronger than these?"

202. See the beginning of Chapter 2.

203. See C. Schmitt, *Politische Theologie* and *Politische Theologie* II (Berlin 1970). The reverse formulation "theological politics" is intended to emphasize the fact that Greek concepts of politics are not secularized theological concepts, but that in the reciprocal relations between politics and theology the former tended to have primacy. Presumably, theological concepts could be as productive as they are in modern times only when ancient political concepts (in this case especially, Roman) were absorbed into theology. On the development of political religion see Varro, mentioned by Augustine, *De Civitate Dei* 6.4: this, however, can refer only to cults. As for theology as a whole, the processual interpenetration of the political and the religious would not be recognized, especially for the theology of abstract divinity *(theion)* among the Greeks.

204. See Chapter 3. Of the many trends in early Greek political thought we are concerned here only with the strand in which its real dynamism was finally concentrated. One has to reckon with countless variations. Personal inclinations, temptations, impressions, as well as political positions, could lead

to many different paths. The real force of this thinking nevertheless sprang
from the middle position which it finally institutionalized (and in which it
subsequently allied itself with the middle strata of the *demos*).

205. This is a rendering of the term *Erwartungserwartung,* used by N. Luhmann,
Rechtssoziologie (Reinbek bei Hamburg 1972), 33 ff, 51 f, 64 ff. Expectations are generated and, being fulfilled, give rise to the expectation (and
anticipation) of further expectations.

206. On what follows cf. Meier, *Entstehung,* 19 ff.

207. This becomes clear when one compares the first and third elegies. See
Vlastos, *Classical Philology* 41 (1946) 75 ff (though I cannot endorse the
author's conclusion).

208. See W. Jaeger, *Die Theologie der frühen griechischen Denker* (Darmstadt
1964), esp. 17. On what follows see J. Burckhardt, *Griechische Kulturgeschichte* III (Basel 1957), 280 and 296.

209. E. R. Dodds, *The Greeks and the Irrational* (Berkeley 1966), 28 ff, 64 ff.

210. Cf., e.g., Solon, *Elegies* 8, 9, 10, 23. The opposite view must also have
existed, e.g., in Pittacus, but we do not know whether it was really intended
to provide a legitimation for tyranny as a form of government or only to
justify the temporary practicality of a tyrannical regime).

211. Jaeger, *Paedeia* I, 26; H. Frankfort, H. A. Frankfort, J. A. Wilson, and
T. Jacobsen, *Before Philosophy* (Harmondsworth 1949), 251 ff; Guthrie,
History of Greek Philosophy II, 1, 26 ff, 67 ff, 76 ff, 140 ff, 244 ff, 345 f;
J.-P. Vernant, *Les origines de la pensée grecque* (Paris 1969), 119 ff; Bur-
kert, *Griechische Religion,* 452 ff; see also Chapter 3 above.

212. Jaeger, *Paedeia* I, 30 ff. The same applies to political affairs in the writings
of Solon: see Jaeger, "Eunomia," *Sitzungsberichte der Preussischen Akademie* (1926) 69 ff.

213. On its reflection in literature see H. Fränkel, *Dichtung und Philosophie des
frühen Griechentums* (2d ed. Munich 1962), 150, 160, 267 ff, 479 f, 540 f,
570 (*Early Greek Poetry and Philosophy,* trans. M. Hadas [Oxford 1975]);
see also *Eumenides* 650 f, together with Thomson's commentary. Meier,
Entstehung des Politischen, 343 f, 411 f. In general too little attention has
been paid to the (probable) function of this view for the (evident) reinforce-
ment of the belief in justice among wide sections of society.

214. See Meier, *Arethusa* 20 (1987) 49 ff.

215. Cf., e.g., Solon, *Elegies* 1; Bruno Snell, *Die Entdeckung des Geistes* (4th
ed. Göttingen 1975), 167 f.

216. Heraclitus, fr. 94. Cf. Homer, *Iliad* 19.418. On the world as cosmos see
Guthrie, *History of Greek Philosophy* II, 110 f, 131 n. 1, 208 f, 246 ff;
Jaeger, *Paedeia* I, 134 f; see also note 211 above.

217. This will be demonstrated in my forthcoming book, *Die Anfänge des politischen Denkens.* On the particular aspect of the problem that concerns us
here see especially G. Vlastos, "Equality and Justice in Early Greek Cosmologies," *Classical Philology* 42 (1947) 156 ff.

218. Aristotle, *Politics* 1318b4.

219. Cf. Aeschylus, *Persae;* and Herodotus (see Meier, *Entstehung des Politischen,* 409 f); Lloyd-Jones, *The Justice of Zeus,* 88 f.

220. Solmsen, *Hesiod and Aeschylus*, 117 n. 51.

221. Ibid., 220, 222 f. Cf. Herodotus 3.80.6, with G. Vlastos, *American Journal of Philology* 74 (1953) 358 f.

222. *Agamemnon* 281 ff. See W. Riepl, *Das Nachrichtenwesen des Altertums* (Leipzig/Berlin 1913), 50 ff, where earlier examples are cited (e.g., Herodotus 7.183.1, 9.3.1). Such an extensive organization seems to have been new to the Greeks. Who—apart from the Athenians at the time of the Delian League—would have been able to set up such an organization or determine the—scarcely differentiated—questions to which the fires supplied the answers? The novelty of the method seems to be attested by the skepticism of the elders about the reliability of the sign (475 ff, 489 ff, 583 f, 590 ff). If the sign in the *Agamemnon* came from Troy—like Athene in the *Eumenides*—this may also point to some contemporary event (see the literature listed in note 34 above). At a later date Polybius illustrates the high degree of contemporary technical expertise by citing the ways in which news was relayed (10.43 ff, 47.12). It is also one of the important inventions listed by Gorgias B11a.30 (*Frag. der Vorsokratiker* II, 294 ff).

223. Cf. note 13 above and Chapter 8; also Hölscher, *Griechische Historienbilder;* similarly Sophocles, *Antigone* 726 ff. For a general discussion of the subject see Romilly, *Time in Greek Tragedy*, 143 ff.

224. Democritus B2 (*Frag. der Vorsokratiker* II, 81 ff): Athene as *phronesis*. *Phronein* is to calculate correctly, to speak correctly, and to do what is necessary. B119: *phronesis* as calculating understanding that can compete with chance; cf. 193. Euripides, *Suppliant Women* 216 ff (*phronesis*, which would be more powerful than the god; given the normal usage, the formulation verges on the paradoxical, but only if the domain of *phronesis* takes in the area of methodical knowledge that is directed to controlling circumstances). Plato, *Alcibiades* 1, 125a; *Laches* 192d–193. Pericles' *phronesis*, too, must have included a considerable element of political skill (Aristotle, *Nicomachean Ethics* 1141b15; Thucydides 1.139 ff, 2.65. Cf. P. Aubenque, *La prudence chez Aristote* [Paris 1963], 54, 56); similarly that of the bees (ibid., 159).

225. *Agamemnon* 927 f; cf. 175 f; Heraclitus, fr. 112; Sophocles, *Antigone* 1347 ff. See B. Gladigow, "Aischylos und Heraklit," in H. Hommel (ed.), *Wege zu Aischylos* I (Darmstadt 1974), 321 ff: "In a religion that knows no negative demonic power a theodicy can occur only through a confrontation of the true, divine order with one that is created by limited human insight"; see also Dodds, *Ancient Concept of Progress*, 59 ff.

226. On the contemporary sense of *phronein* and *phronesis* see Aubenque, *La prudence chez Aristote*, 23 ff, 53 ff, 56 ff (Pericles was commonly held to be the model of the *phronimos*), 155 ff. On the link between insight and its consequences for action see Jaeger, *Theologie*, 131 ff. (Jaeger's remarks concern Heraclitus but apply equally to Aeschylus; see Gladigow, "Aischylos und Heraklit," 322 f.) See also Schachermeyr, *Frühe Klassik*, 160, and the literature cited by O'Brien, *Socratic Paradoxes* 23 f. (O'Brien's critical reservations seem to me convincing, though they do not affect Aeschylus.) The compromise accorded with the sense of limitation and equilibrium that is

generally thought to be connoted by *phronein* (Aubenque, 156 ff). Cf. the similar antithesis in *Prometheus* 1011 ff: *sophisma,* which in this passage denotes both one-sidedness and cunning (O'Brien, 38), is set against *phronein.*

227. Solon, *Elegies* 3.1 ff, esp. 30: "My mind bade me teach this to the Athenians."

228. See Kitto, *Form and Meaning,* 79 ff; idem, *La notion du divin,* 169 ff; C. Meier, in H. R. Jauss (ed.), *Die nicht mehr schönen Künste* (Munich 1968), 91 ff. The doctrine of the emergence of culture is therefore not to be understood simply to mean that culture is solely the work of man (cf. also Jaeger, *Paedeia* I, 50 ff; and most recently Dihle, *Hermes* 105 [1977], against the exaggerated conception of fifth-century atheism). Cf. Chapter 8, note 108, below.

229. See Chapter 8, note 60, below, with references to the literature.

230. The myth of Protagoras (Plato, *Protagoras* 320c) represents a later development of this idea. See Chapter 8.

231. Cf. Aristotle, *Politics* 1279a39, with Meier, *Entstehung,* 63 n. 78.

232. Whereas Cleisthenes brought a new force into existence, Ephialtes deprived an existing force of its political organ.

233. See Chapter 8.

234. On the parallel to this on the divine plane see Reinhardt, *Aischylos,* 74 f.

235. *all' alla d'ephoreuei.* The translation is that of Smyth (Loeb).

236. Pindar, *Pythia* 2.87 f.

237. Dodds, *Ancient Concept of Progress,* 52.

238. *Eumenides* 171. Cf. Grossmann, *Promethie und Orestie,* 250 ff.

239. *Prometheus* 28 ff. Prometheus admittedly goes much further; cf. his *authadia:* 79, 1011, 1034, 1037.

240. Thucydides 1.102.3 (similarly Plutarch, *Cimon* 17.3). Cf. 1.70.3, 74.2, 4, 90.1, 144.4; 2.43.1; 6.33.4. On "audacity" in art and in other spheres see T. Hölscher, *Jahrbuch des deutschen Archäologischen Instituts* 89 (1974) 100 f.

241. On the portrayal of Apollo, cf. Kitto, *Greek Tragedy,* 89; idem, *Form and Meaning,* 55.

242. Perhaps there is a special significance in the construction of the *Prometheus* in that there is something titanic, immoderate, and elemental about innovation, whereas the Olympian dynasty is actually characterized by its moderation; see Jaeger, *Paedeia* I, 338 f.

243. Kraus, *Gnomon* 23 (1951) 69 ff (though I cannot agree with everything that follows this observation).

244. Kitto, *Form and Meaning,* 14, 36.

245. *Agamemnon* 160 f. The meaning of these words in Aeschylus is by no means confined to what the formula had earlier served to express (see E. Fränkel's commentary on the passage; also Lloyd-Jones, *The Justice of Zeus,* 85 f).

246. In the postscript to the edition of *Prometheus Bound* in the Reclam series (Stuttgart 1965), p. 46.

247. Aeschylus, fr. 105 (Mette = 70 Nauck, 34 Loeb). Cf. *Supplices* 92 ff, 1057

f; Heraclitus, frs. 2, 89, 102, 113; Gladigow, "Aischylos und Heraklit," 325 ff. On Heraclitus 67 see H. Fränkel, *Wege und Formen frühgriechischen Denkens* (3d ed. Munich 1968), 237 ff.

248. According to J. de Romilly (*Time in Greek Tragedy*, 31 and 35), tragedy arose when the Greeks became conscious of the significance of time and the problems associated with it. "Yet, it arose when this consciousness was still recent, and among people who never allowed time to be the perpetual and all-pervading movement that modern authors like to declare they are caught in."

249. See Meier, *Entstehung des Politischen*, 340 f, 343 f.

250. See Vlastos, "Equality and Justice," 156 ff.

251. It is true that the clarity of relations within Greek society, which was so strongly concentrated in the political, gave the positions their decisive character: the nobility was either recognized within society or seen as a dangerous extraneous force. It could not easily be deflected from its aims; nor could it, in the absence of a powerful state apparatus, be easily held in check. If, in such a situation, control of the political order is there for the taking, the establishment of a new order of civic life involves clear oppositions and obvious problems (which were soon solved in Athens on the basis of the city's successes in external affairs).

252. Vernant, *Les origines*, 42, 99, 125. See Chapter 6, note 25, below.

253. On this question see H. Lübbe, *Geschichtsbegriff und Geschichtsinteresse* (Basel 1977), 287.

254. It would be wrong to say that from now on Greek political thought took a conservative turn. True, the repeatedly successful tendency to extend the political rights of the middle and lower strata of society came to a halt: whatever was possible in this direction was quickly realized. Future solutions had to be sought in other directions. However, this could have been a conservative development only if things had moved only in the dimension nobility vs. *demos*, i.e., if this dimension had been equated with history. This did not happen, however (even if at times it may have appeared to happen, in the dispute over the *patrios politeia*).

255. This basic temporal antithesis seems to me conceivable only when two fundamentally different constitutional possibilities are consciously contrasted with each other. This is what distinguishes the situation in question from the one that faced Cleisthenes.

256. Solmsen, *Hesiod and Aeschylus*, 154 f.

257. Reinhardt, *Aischylos*, 161.

258. Ibid.

259. W. Benjamin, *Gesammelte Schriften* I (Frankfurt 1974), 243 ff.

260. This is Benjamin's program (ibid., 886). He himself tells us that its conception was inspired by Alois Riegl and "the contemporary experiments of Carl Schmitt . . . who makes an analogous attempt, in his analysis of political structures, to integrate phenomena that appear to be isolable only in particular areas." Cf. ibid., 887. There is hardly any mention here of economic trends. This is because, in keeping with Greek conditions, they are included in the political in a specific way. The satisfaction of material needs

too was—at least in Athens—largely a political matter, and not only (in fact to some extent not even essentially) a matter of economics.

6. The Political Identity of the Athenians and the Workings of Periclean Democracy

1. Plutarch, *Pericles* 7.5 ff.
2. Before Pericles, Cimon had for years occupied a similar position, though under a less advanced form of democracy and mainly by virtue of his successes in war and foreign policy. On the problem and circumstances of his fall see Chapter 5, "The Situation around 458 B.C." Cf. C. Meier, "Der Umbruch zur Demokratie in Athen (462/61 v. Ch.)," in R. Herzog and R. Koselleck (eds.), *Epochenschwelle und Epochenbewusstsein* (Munich 1987), 353 ff. According to Thucydides 2.65 things changed after Pericles.
3. See the sketch in O. Marquard and K. Stierle (eds.), *Identität* (Munich 1979), 385 ff. (with references to the literature). In this article, however, there is too little differentiation according to time and space. Cf. C. Meier and P. Veyne, *Kannten die Griechen die Demokratie?* (Berlin 1988).
4. E. H. Erikson, *Dimensions of a New Identity* (New York 1974), 36.
5. Cf. C. Schmitt, *Positionen und Begriffe* (Hamburg 1940), 134, 136, 138. An interesting problem would be the history of social identity in the "age of neutralizations and depoliticizations," with their "steps from one central area to another" (C. Schmitt, *Der Begriff des Politischen* [rev. ed. Berlin 1963], 79 ff; *The Concept of the Political,* trans. G. Schwab [New Brunswick, N.J., 1976]).
6. Fustel de Coulanges, *La cité antique* (28th ed. Paris 1923), rightly notes, though with some exaggeration, that this was one of the foundations of the ancient form of affiliation, of the mutual isolation of the *poleis,* and of other features of antiquity (see esp. 237 ff) that we find so strange (cf. ibid. 1 f). But these foundations form an integral part of political life and change with it. They can therefore explain neither the move to democracy nor the special character of Greek political identity. Religion and politics could not be divorced. However, the accent lay clearly on the political. Cf. also J. Burckhardt, *Griechische Kulturgeschichte* I (Basel 1956), 80; V. Ehrenberg, *The Greek State* (2d ed. London 1966), 14, 74 ff; W. Burkert, *Griechische Religion der archaischen und klassischen Epoche* (Stuttgart 1977), 382 ff.
7. Justified objections to a strictly value-oriented approach are raised by S. C. Humphreys, *Anthropology and the Greeks* (London 1978), 74, 157 f, 201, although, as indicated earlier, I would not seek a way out of these problems solely along the lines she suggests.
8. Cf. J.-P. Vernant, *Mythe et pensée chez les Grecs* II (Paris 1971), 28 f.
9. The most important evidence for this is contained in the speeches of Pericles in Thucydides and the comedies of Aristophanes, especially *Wasps* and *Birds.* Cf. K. Reinhardt, *Tradition und Geist* (Göttingen 1960), 261 = *Von Werken und Formen* (Bad Godesberg 1948), 291.
10. A. H. M. Jones, *Athenian Democracy* (Oxford 1966), 17 f, 49 f, 80 ff. One

would, however, have to consider whether, even if the expenses amounted to less than what they earned at work, they were nevertheless sufficient for some citizens, especially in view of the fact that politics had a certain attraction and that they could after all have their wives and children working for them (Aristotle, *Politics* 1323a5 ff). Politics went with a way of life that was relatively free of material needs; see P. Von der Mühll, *Ausgewählte Schriften* (Basel 1975), 525 f.

11. For the sources see C. Hignett, *A History of the Athenian Constitution* (Oxford 1957), 396 f.

12. On this process see A. Gehlen, *Studien zur Anthropologie und Soziologie* (Neuwied/Berlin 1963), 196 ff; idem, *Urmensch und Spätkultur* (2d ed. Frankfurt/Bonn 1964), 74; C. Meier, in K.-G. Faber and C. Meier (eds.), *Historische Prozesse* (Munich 1978), 30 ff.

13. On the relevant Aristotelian theory see J. Ritter, *Metaphysik und Politik* (Frankfurt 1969), 57 ff, esp. 71 ff.

14. Thucydides 7.77.7. As it stands, this much-quoted formulation admittedly means something quite different (the men are the city, not walls and ships). For Nicias cannot have meant to distinguish the men from the state, because he had no conception of the state. Nevertheless the sentence expresses very appositely the character of the *polis*, which was identical with its citizens, but only in the context of our language and our way of thinking. Cf. Aristotle, *Politics* 1274b41; see also Ritter, *Metaphysik und Politik*, 93 f.

15. Whereas Burckhardt (*Griechische Kulturgeschichte* I, 240) explains the "desire of those who do not rule to acquire a full share in this state" by reference to its unlimited power, this power arises, conversely, from the same urge, though admittedly in the special circumstances created by Athenian military and foreign policy in the fifth century.

16. This process has remote parallels with the French Revolution, except that the latter soon passed and the Greeks did not have to call themselves *citoyens*. Nevertheless, Cleisthenes is said to have caused a change (suggesting a kind of politicization) as far as personal names were concerned (Aristotle[?], *Athenaion Politeia* 21.4): the name of the individual was followed officially (and largely for practical reasons) not by the name of the father, but by that of the *demos*, i.e., of the local community to which the individual belonged and in which he was registered. (I am grateful to J. Starobinski for drawing my attention to the parallel between ancient citizenship and the revolutionary use of *citoyen* as a form of address.)

17. To be more precise, state and society were not mutually distinguished and centered in different circles of people. Later there were only two separate planes with no correspondence between them. On the political plane the nobles and the ordinary citizens (as members of a cohesive group) did not carry the same weight as they did on the social plane. This led to the disappearance of the dependence that resulted from primarily social links.

18. This can be seen particularly clearly in Aristophanes, *Wasps* 519 f, 548 ff; cf. 508 ff, 575, 627, 638; also Euripides, *Suppliant Women* 403 f, 429 ff (spoken before the people of Attica); Thucydides 2.37.1. See Vernant, *Mythe et pensée*.

19. There is some discussion of this in L. Pearson, *Popular Ethics in Ancient Greece* (Stanford 1962); A. W. H. Adkins, *Moral Values and Political Behaviour in Ancient Greece* (London 1972); idem, *Merit and Responsibility* (Oxford 1960). The whole question calls for a more comprehensive, sociohistorical investigation.

20. This question is discussed by A. Heuss, *Propyläen Weltgeschichte* III (Berlin 1962), 275 f.

21. H. Arendt, *The Human Condition* (Chicago 1958), 33. Cf. C. Meier, "Arbeit, Politik, Identität," in V. Schubert (ed.), *Der Mensch und seine Arbeit* (St. Ottilien 1986), 47 ff.

22. Meier, "Arbeit, Politik, Identität," 48: "Since the bitter imperative of keeping oneself alive drove men to work, excellence was the last thing they could expect of it."

23. 2.40.1. Cfl. Aristophanes, *Clouds* 53, 316, 334; *Plutus* 903 ff and passim. On the following see V. Ehrenberg, *Aristophanes und das Volk von Athen* (Zurich/Stuttgart 1968), 169, 339 f; Jones, *Athenian Democracy;* M. I. Finley, *The Ancient Economy* (London 1973), 61 ff (q.v. Xenophon, *Memorabilia* 3.7.5 f, 4.2.37; Jones, 109 f). Here one must distinguish clearly among periods, places, and classes. The material calls for a new and thorough treatment. Cf., e.g., the high esteem enjoyed by the *autourgoi* in Euripides' *Orestes* and *Electra;* Plutarch, *Cimon* 11; Anonymus Iamblichi 7.3–5 (*Frag. der Vorsokratiker* II, 400 ff); Plato, *Republic* 565a; Aristotle, *Politics* 1318b13 ff (also 1292b27, 1308b32 ff, 1320a27 f and 35 ff, 1320b8).
    See also J. Hasebroek, *Griechische Wirtschafts- und Gesellschaftsgeschichte* (Tübingen 1931), 265 ff; and the somewhat different view of S. Lauffer, "Die Bedeutung des Standesunterschiedes im klassischen Athen," *Historische Zeitschrift* 185 (1958) 497 ff (though Lauffer oversimplifies the connection between work and social status). See also Vernant, *Mythe et pensée* II, 5 ff, 16 ff (with references to the older literature).

24. A quite different question is how the individual saw it in practical terms. One may do something and think highly of the results, yet make little of it in public because certain social barriers prevent one from doing so. It is of these barriers that we are speaking here; Finley, *The Ancient Economy*, 60, speaks of "overriding values." The views of Heuss, *Propyläen Weltgeschichte* III, should be modified in this direction.

25. See Hasebroek, *Griechische Wirtschafts- und Gesellschaftsgeschichte.* Jones, *Athenian Democracy*, 6 f, points out that even after the collapse of the Attic empire there was still enough money available for expenses. Nevertheless, as he himself says, it remains true that in the fifth century a greater number of citizens lived to a larger extent by politics and military service than in the fourth. The basis for this (and also for Pericles' building program, which was partly designed to provide work for an unusually large number of citizens who had been discharged from the forces) was provided by the city's revenues. Cf. Plutarch, *Cimon* 11; Thucydides 6.24.3. On the revenue produced by the taxing of foreign residents see Lauffer, "Bedeutung," 511.

26. M. I. Finley, *Talanta* 7 (1976) 8. Cf. idem, *Politics in the Ancient World* (Cambridge 1983), 97; C. Meier, *Gnomon* 58 (1986) 504 ff.

27. M. Weber, *Economy and Society*, ed. G. Roth and C. Wittich (Berkeley 1978), 1346 ff.

28. K. Marx and F. Engels, *Gesamtausgabe (MEGA)* I.2 (Berlin 1982), 33 f; K. Marx, *Grundrisse der Kritik der politischen Ökonomie* (2d ed. Berlin 1974), 380 (*Collected Works* [London 1975–], III, 32; XXVIII, 403 f). On the concept of embedding see K. Polányi, *The Great Transformation* (Boston 1957). Cf. W. G. Forrest, *Yale Classical Studies* 24 (1975) 37 ff.

29. Humphreys, *Anthropology*, 147, speaks of "state pay" as a "basis of subsistence and symbol of political identity."

30. Burckhardt, *Griechische Kulturgeschichte* I, 206. On Syracuse see Plutarch, *Dion* 37.5. See also A. Fuks, *Classical Quarterly* 18 (1968) 218 ff. On the following see C. Meier, "Freiheit," in W. Conze, R. Koselleck, and O. Brunner (eds.), *Geschichtliche Grundbegriffe* II (Stuttgart 1976), 427 f (where χεε should be corrected to χεζ'). Cf. K. Raaflaub, *Die Entstehung der Freiheit* (Munich 1985).

31. A vivid sketch is provided by M. Gelzer, *Kleine Schriften* III (Wiesbaden 1964), 13 ff.

32 On the effect see J. W. Headlam, *Election by Lot at Athens* (2d ed. Oxford 1931), 26 ff and 41 ff; Hignett, *Athenian Constitution*, 232 ff.

33. Jones, *Athenian Democracy*, 4 f and 105. For a different view see P. J. Rhodes, *The Athenian Boule* (Oxford 1972), 1 ff.

34. G. Busolt and H. Swoboda, *Griechische Staatskunde* II (Munich 1926), 1028 ff; Hignett, *Athenian Constitution*, 237.

35. Reinhardt, *Tradition und Geist*, 256 (= *Von Werken und Formen*, 286 f).

36. Pseudo-Xenophon, *Athenaion Politeia* 1.3 ff; Busolt and Swoboda, *Griechische Staatskunde* II, 1054 ff, 1081 ff; Hignett, *Athenian Constitution*, 221 ff, 244. Aristotle even writes at one point (*Politics* 1308a14) that it is a democratic institution to fill the offices for only six months.

37. Euripides, *Suppliant Women* 406 ff, *Phoenissae* 543 ff. See Chapter 7, note 48. Cf. Aristotle, *Politics* 1317b2, 14, 19 (also 1274b40, 1277a27, b12, 1283b42, 1288a12); Vernant, *Mythe et pensée*.

38. Herodotus 3.80, 142.3; 4.161.3; 7.164.1; Euripides, *Cyclops* 119; Herodotus 5.78; *On Airs, Waters, Places* 16, 23 (*Corpus Hippocraticum*); K. Latte, *Kleine Schriften* (Munich 1968), 294 ff; Lauffer, "Bedeutung," 502 ff. Thucydides 3.62.4; 4.63.2, 64.

39. Chapter 7, note 59, below.

40. Cf. Aristotle, *Politics* 1305a33 generally.

41. The circles of friends and the objectives of the nobility have been studied by W. R. Connor, *The New Politicians of Fifth-Century Athens* (Princeton 1971), who thus emphasizes a much-neglected feature. When he goes on to draw conclusions relating to the whole of politics he often goes astray through disregarding certain theoretical premises for his statements; cf. C. Meier, "Der Alltag des Historikers und die historische Theorie," in H. M. Baumgartner and J. Rüsen (eds.), *Seminar: Geschichte und Theorie. Umrisse einer Historik* (Frankfurt 1976), 40 ff. What follows is a prelimi-

nary attempt to correct this. A. F. Bentley, *The Process of Government* (Chicago 1908), 412 and 419, distinguishes between "leadership mainly on the discussion plane" and "leadership mainly on the organization plane."

42. Cf. Aristotle, *Politics* 1284a20, b27, 1293a30, 1295b14; Connor, *The New Politicians*, 3 ff, 35 ff.

43. E.g., Plutarch, *Pericles* 11, *Nicias* 11, *Alcibiades* 13.

44. Hignett, *Athenian Constitution*, 159 ff, 164 ff, 185 f. On the new finds see R. Thomsen, *The Origin of Ostracism: A Synthesis* (Copenhagen 1972).

45. Thucydides 2.65.10 ff. These were among others the "new politicians" whom Connor discusses in the second part of his book.

46. Busolt and Swoboda, *Griechische Staatskunde* II, 987.

47. For a useful corrective see M. I. Finley, *Democracy Ancient and Modern* (London 1973). (However, in seeking a topical parallel Finley seriously neglects the special character of the ancient world, which he is at pains to stress in relation to the economy. Cf. *The Ancient Economy*, 21 ff.) Independently of this, Attic democracy had for a long time been favored by external conditions, thanks to the extraordinary power of Athens. In Aristophanes we find the words (quoted as an old proverb): "Whatever we resolve foolishly and wrongly is nevertheless turned to our advantage in the end" (*Ecclesiazusae* 474 f). This, however, seems to have referred primarily to a particular situation; see Chapter 8, note 120, below.

48. Jones, *Athenian Democracy*, 111 ff; A. Andrewes, *Probouleusis* (Oxford 1954); R. Delaix, *Probouleusis at Athens: A Study of Political Decision-Making* (Berkeley 1973).

49. Cf. W. Nippel, *Mischverfassungstheorie und Verfassungsrealität in Antike und früher Neuzeit* (Stuttgart 1980).

50. Herodotus 3.82.4. Aristotle, Politics 1302a8. Cf. Thucydides 8.89.3. See Meier and Veyne, *Kannten die Griechen die Demokratie?* 78 f.

51. Herodotus 3.82.3; Aristotle, *Politics* 1302a8, 1303b17 ff, 1305a37 ff.

52. Cf., e.g., Thucydides 4.86.4; also Aristotle, *Politics* 1291b30 ff and 1297b 24; Thucydides 6.18.6, 39.1 f.

53. Chapter 7, note 115.

54. E.g., in Athens in 411.

55. Euripides, *Suppliant Women* 429 ff. See note 18 above.

56. Arendt, *The Human Condition*, 33; D. Sternberger, *Drei Wurzeln der Politik* (Frankfurt 1978).

57. This begins to change after the end of the fifth century; cf. most recently Humphreys, *Anthropology*, 252 f.

58. Aristotle, *Politics* 1255b16, 1261a17, 29 and passim. This is shown especially by Hannah Arendt in *The Human Condition*. Particularly delightful in this connection is Praxagora's promise, in Aristophanes' *Ecclesiazusae* 673 f, that she wants to "make the city into a single house by collapsing everything into one." Equally comic, though unintentionally so, was the announcement made in Rostock in 1934 by the local *Gauleiter* Hildebrand that the new government would markedly improve the depressing living conditions throughout the country by building "houses of joy." (This is

attested by someone who took part in the public rally, which the university students were commanded to attend; at this point the students applauded loudly.) On the modern confusion of house and *polis* in a different totalitarian context see R. Aron, *Fortschritt ohne Ende?* (Gütersloh 1970), 128.

59. Cf. R. Koselleck, *Kritik und Krise* (1958; rept. Frankfurt 1973).
60. Ehrenberg, *Der Staat der Griechen* (Zurich/Stuttgart 1965), 107 f. But see also C. Meier, *Gnomon* 41 (1969) 374 f.
61. See C. Meier, *Entstehung des Begriffs Demokratie* (Frankfurt 1970), 49 ff.
62. Aristotle, *Politics* 1276a17, b 4.
63. On the whole complex of national identity interesting examples are to be found in O. Vossler, *Der Nationalgedanke von Rousseau bis Ranke* (Leipzig 1937). The numerous invocations of the "whole," exemplified by exhortations such as "Always strive toward the whole, and if you yourself cannot become a whole, attach yourself to a whole and serve it as a part," which occur from Rousseau and Schiller to Hegel, Ranke, and Hofmann von Fallersleben, typify the compensatory function of national identity. The problems of identity in history deserve a more detailed investigation with a comparative component. Of particular interest in this connection is Erikson, *Dimensions.*
64. On this and what follows see Nippel, *Mischverfassungstheorie.*
65. Aristotle, *Politics,* 1290b17; cf. 1279b8 and 1317b8. Precursors of this view from the late fifth century are Pseudo-Xenophon and the author of *Athenaion Politeia.*
66. Ehrenberg, *The Greek State,* 30 ff and 50.
67. On the motives for political action and the importance attached to "rights and honors" cf. Aristotle's *Politics,* where admittedly only material motives are (erroneously) ascribed to the poor.

7. Changing Politicosocial Concepts in the Fifth Century B.C.

1. This chapter is a revised and expanded version of an article first published in *Archiv für Begriffsgeschichte* 21 (1977) 7–41 and later, in modified form, in R. Koselleck (ed.), *Historische Semantik und Begriffsgeschichte* (Stuttgart 1979), 193–227.
2. R. Koselleck, Introduction, in W. Conze, R. Koselleck, and O. Brunner (eds.), *Geschichtliche Grundbegriffe* I (Stuttgart 1972), xiv ff; see also idem, *Futures Past,* trans. K. Tribe (Cambridge, Mass., 1985), 73 ff, 267 ff; idem, "Fortschritt" and "Geschichte," in Conze, Koselleck, and Brunner (eds.), *Geschichtliche Grundbegriffe* II (Stuttgart 1975), 363 ff, 625 ff.
3. Koselleck, *Futures Past,* 288.
4. Koselleck, Introduction, in *Geschichtliche Grundbegriffe* I, xviii. Concepts become authoritative; see H. Günther, in Koselleck, *Historische Semantik und Begriffsgeschichte,* 111 f.
5. Koselleck, *Futures Past,* 231 ff, 276, 279; cf. 284.
6. See C. Meier, in K. G. Faber and C. Meier (eds.), *Historische Prozesse* (Munich 1978), 28 ff.

7. Koselleck, *Futures Past,* 283; idem, "Fortschritt," 400 ff.
8. Koselleck, Introduction, in *Geschichtliche Grundbegriffe* I, xvii.
9. C. Meier, *Entstehung des Begriffs Demokratie* (Frankfurt 1970), 15 ff, 26 ff. I intend soon to treat the theme at greater length. See note 10.
10. This and what follows are considered more fully in a forthcoming book titled *Die Anfänge des politischen Denkens bei den Griechen.* Cf. Chapter 3 above.
11. On Solon see Meier, *Entstehung,* 15 ff. In addition to the basic question of the temporal perspective from which the most effective changes are implemented, the following points should be briefly noted here: those who were discontented or suffering hardship were specifically peasants who were in debt, dispossessed, and threatened with slavery. They were concerned to have their former rights restored. This could be incorporated into the wider program of restoring the good order that had once existed. The legitimation of these demands could thus be best achieved by a "conservative" approach. Moreover, all contemporary conceptions of order were involved in an interplay of cosmic and political notions that frequently confirmed one another (an example being the relations between Solon's thinking and that of Anaximander). Here too there was progress (cf. note 48 below), though it was perceived rather as a growing understanding of a changeless order: the existing state of affairs was viewed in more abstract terms, and this then led to increasing freedom of action.
12. The only significant exception, namely the new order in Sparta, proves the rule: see P. Spahn, *Mittelschicht und Polisbildung* (Frankfurt/Bern/Las Vegas 1977), 87 ff.
13. On what follows cf. C. Meier, "Demokratie," in Conze, Koselleck, and Brunner, *Geschichtliche Grundbegriffe* I, 821 f. We first encounter the idea in Pindar, *Pythia* 2.86 ff. See C. Meier, "Drei Bemerkungen zur Vor- und Frühgeschichte des Begriffs Demokratie," in *Discordia Concors. Festschrift E. Bonjour* (Basel 1968), 11 f. Pindar distinguishes three kinds of *nomos:* "tyranny; when the impetuous people rule the city; and when it is ruled by the wise." What determines the order of the city is thus the form of rule to which it is subject. *Nomos* is also used by Heraclitus (B44.114) as a term for the order of an individual city. From here it would have been but a short step to using the term to denote types of order, but this step was not taken, and Pindar's usage remains isolated. To avoid misunderstanding, we should remark here that the words *monarchia* and *tyrannis* are attested from the sixth century (ibid. 9), and that a term indicating the "rule of the few" occurs already in Homer (*Iliad* 2.204), though the word in question, used within the horizon of monarchy, is *polykoiranie* ("rule of many"). Here, however, it applies merely to the division of rule among nobles, not to a form of constitution. See above in the text.
14. Aeschylus, *Supplices* 604, 699. (On the dating see A. J. Podlecki, *The Political Background of Aeschylean Tragedy* [Ann Arbor 1966], 42 f.) Taken in isolation, these passages cannot of course prove that the form of rule was seen as the decisive element in the total order, but in view of the passage from Pindar just cited we may presume this to have been so. See now C.

Meier, *Die politische Kunst der griechischen Tragödie* (Munich 1988), 188 ff. A different interpretation of the passage is offered by R. Sealey, "The Origins of *Demokratia*," *California Studies in Classical Antiquity* 6 (1973) 253 ff. This article, though containing some very remarkable observations, seems on the whole to miss the point. When emphasizing the partisan use of political terms, one should bear in mind that they may sound positive to one side. How were the people of Athens to take a negative view of their own rule? Even if the same words are used to designate the authoritative role of a majority in oligarchies and democracies, this role may have varied greatly—and perceptibly. The Greeks made no terminological distinction either among government, power, and rule or among different types of these. They perceived any distinctions as deriving from the differences between those who held power, between the institutions, and between the ways in which power was exercised. In general Sealey pays no attention to the shifts in the meanings of "isonomy," "democracy," and "oligarchy" (see note 65 below); he totally misunderstands the peculiarities inherent in the generalizing designation of political factions; and there is much question-begging in some of his interpretations.

15. Cf. H. Schaefer, *Staatsform und Politik* (Leipzig 1932), 106; Meier, *Entstehung*, 36 ff; idem, "Drei Bemerkungen," 10 f. On the content see G. Vlastos, *American Journal of Philology* 74 (1953) 352, 361 (cited hereafter as Vlastos).

16. Meier, *Entstehung*, 38 ff. On *isokratia* see note 41 below.

17. G. Vlastos, "*Isonomia politike*," in J. Mau and E. G. Schmidt (eds.), *Isonomia* (Berlin 1964), 9; V. Ehrenberg, *RE Suppl.* VII (1940), 297; H. Schaefer, *Probleme der Alten Geschichte* (Göttingen 1963), 152.

18. On this term cf. Meier, "Drei Bemerkungen," 14 ff; idem, *Entstehung*, 35 f; and Chapter 8, note 152, below. More detailed reasons are adduced in the first chapter of *Die Anfänge des politischen Denkens*.

19. See Meier, "Demokratie," 823 f (with Pindar, *Pythia* 2.87; idem, "Drei Bemerkungen," 12).

20. On the attestation of the terms see note 64, below.

21. Cf., e.g., the oligarchic reform plans in Athens prompted by the "isonomy" introduced or proposed by Cleisthenes (Herodotus 5.72).

22. Meier, "Drei Bemerkungen," 13; idem, *Entstehung*, 40 f. A number of political allusions in Aeschylus' *Prometheus* might be added: see Podlecki, *Political Background*, 115 ff. Cf. Aristotle, *Politics* 1297b24 and discussion later in this chapter. See Herodotus 5.92a on Sparta, Corinth, and Athens as "isocracies."

23. This is the occasion for the polemical work of Pseudo-Xenophon, *Athenaion Politeia*.

24. Herodotus 3.81; Pindar, *Pythia* 2.88 (cf. 10.71 f), *Olympia* 9.29. See Meier, "Drei Bemerkungen," 12, where Heraclitus B104 should be added: *hoi polloi kakoi, oligoi d'agathoi*.

25. On *plethos* in the sense of "totality" see Meier, "Drei Bemerkungen," 25 ff. Naturally the majority principle applied in oligarchies too; this is not what is meant here.

26. Cf. J.-P. Vernant, *Les origines de la pensée grecque* (Paris 1969), 42, 99, 125; idem, *Mythe et pensée chez les Grecs* I (Paris 1971), 185 ff, 207 ff; P. Lévêque and P. Vidal-Naquet, *Clisthène l'Athénien* (Paris 1964); M. Detienne, *Annales* 20 (1965) 425 ff. In these important studies the treatment of the subject is too abstract and insufficiently historical, no distinction being made between the nomistic and cratistic periods. The Greek terms are handled very freely, and there is a striking lack of consistency in the treatment of the history of the concepts. On the central problem of the Cleisthenian reform see Chapter 4 above, where an attempt is made to explain it in concrete terms on the basis of appropriate categories.

27. On this and what follows cf. the beginning of Chapter 6 and C. Meier, "Die politische Identität der Griechen," in O. Marquard and K. H. Stierle (eds.), *Identität* (Munich 1979), 371 ff. On the emergence of a public domain "in which the Athenians counted as citizens irrespective of descent or possessions," cf. Schaefer, *Probleme,* 139. See now C. Meier and P. Veyne, *Kannten die Griechen die Demokratie?* (Berlin 1988).

28. N. Luhmann, *Soziologische Aufklärung* I (2d ed. Cologne 1971), 226 f., speaks of the "functional primacy" of the political order; cf. idem, "Identitätsgebrauch in selbstsubstitutiven Ordnungen, besonders Gesellschaften," in Marquard and Stierle, *Identität,* 315 ff.

29. Cf. J. Burckhardt, *Griechische Kulturgeschichte* I (Basel 1956), 206. For the special problems of the "civic presence" see the beginning of Chapter 4, above.

30. Cf. C. Meier, "Entstehung und Besonderheit der griechischen Demokratie," *Zeitschrift für Politik* 25 (1978) 18 ff.

31. In Athens one's subsistence was ensured partly in the economic sphere, but otherwise in the political. Cf. also K. Marx, *Die Frühschriften,* ed. S. Landshut (Stuttgart 1964), 51.

32. This understanding was preceded by a revaluation of virtues, which can also, in a certain sense, be seen as politicization: in the archaic lyric the ideals of bravery, wisdom, and justice are related to the *polis;* cf. Meier, "Entstehung und Besonderheit," 16 n. 55. But here it is a matter of a simple orientation of thinking and concepts to the city rather than to the earlier individualistic ambitions.

33. D. Sternberger, *Merkur* 30 (1976) 944.

34. See, e.g., Koselleck, "Demokratie," in Conze, Koselleck, and Brunner, *Geschichtliche Grundbegriffe* I, 848 ff.

35. This is particularly well illustrated for *eunomia* by Pseudo-Xenophon, *Athenaion Politeia* 1.8. Cf. M. Ostwald, *Nomos and the Beginnings of the Athenian Democracy* (Oxford 1969), 83 f; on the survival of the old constitutional terms in general, see ibid., 62 ff; G. Grossmann, *Politische Schlagwörter aus der Zeit des Peloponnesischen Krieges* (Basel diss. 1945), 30 ff. Similarly, *sophrosyne* becomes a political term (ibid., 85 f). In the myth of Protagoras *aidos* and *dike* (cf. Hesiod, *Works and Days* 192 f; *Tyrataeus* 9.39 f) become necessary virtues for all citizens (Plato, *Protagoras* 322c; cf. Chapter 8); they are, so to speak, democratized and acquire a legitimating function. These and many other concepts have received far too little atten-

tion. Classical scholarship has still to discover how fruitful the investigation of conceptual history can be as part of historical study.

36. There is no direct evidence for this. However, we may presume that at least the Spartans came to see themselves as *homoioi* as early as the sixth century. See V. Ehrenberg, *Polis und Imperium* (Stuttgart 1965), 218 f. For the facts see Spahn, *Mittelschicht und Polisbildung*, 101 ff.

37. *Isotes* is first attested in Euripides, *Phoenissae* 536, 542. On *isos* and *homoios* cf. Aristotle, *Metaphysics* 1021a11, *Topics* 6a26. See R. Hirzel, *Themis, Dike und Verwandtes* (Leipzig 1907), 251 ff, 421 ff; C. W. Müller, *Gleiches zu Gleichem* (Wiesbaden 1965), 165, n. 42.

38. Herodotus 3.142.3. Cf. Thucydides 6.38.5; Aristotle, *Politics* 1287a10, 1308a11.

39. Solon, *Elegies* 23, 21D. Cf. Vlastos, 356 ff. In any case this demand did not arise until some time after Solon had begun to issue his warnings (cf. Solon 25.1–3). On this demand see E. Will, "La Grèce archaïque," in *Deuxième conférence internationale d'histoire économique* (The Hague 1965), 72 f.

40. Vlastos, 351; Ehrenberg, *Polis und Imperium*, 172 f; most recently Spahn, *Mittelschicht und Polisbildung*, 101 ff.

41. For *isegoria* see Herodotus 5.78. Cf. Euripides, *Suppliant Women* 438 ff; Eupolis, fr. 291 (Kock); Demosthenes 21.121; Ps.-Dem. 60.28. *Isokratia* (Herodotus 5.92a1) strikes me as particularly interesting: it points to the equal division of power, power being thought of as divided equally among all, just as it is thought of as gathered together under *demokratia* (though here too participation by all is implied). The two notions are complementary. Perhaps *isokratia* was an easier concept than *demokratia*. It should be noted incidentally that the verb *nemein* too (of which there was a perceptible echo in *isonomia*) contains the notion of "governing" and "ruling"; cf. above, Chapter 4, note 71. Later the notion of freedom of speech *(parrhesia)* appears in competition with *isegoria*: see Democritus B21; Euripides, *Ion 672, Hippolytus 421*; Demosthenes, fr. 21 (Sauppe); Plato, *Republic* 557b; also Aristophanes, *Frogs 952*.

42. Vlastos, 352. Hirzel, *Themis, Dike und Verwandtes*, 248. K. Latte, "Kollektivbesitz und Staatsschatz in Griechenland," *Nachrichten der Göttinger Akademie der Wissenschaften* (1946/47), 64 ff.

43. Euripides, *Suppliant Women* 408.

44. Ibid., 429 ff. Cf. *Phoenissae* 538 ff; Thucydides 2.37.1; Lysias 2.56; Demosthenes 24.59, 51.11; Plato, *Republic* 557a. On the problems posed by this equality cf. later in this chapter. On the laws as guarantors of equality see Thucydides 2.37.1, Demosthenes 21.188, Aeschines 1.5.

45. Cf. Euripides, *Suppliant Women* 353 *(isopsephos)*. The noun is first attested in the imperial age.

46. Pseudo-Xenophon 1.2. Significantly, the offices are sometimes called *timai* (cf. G. Gottlieb, "Timuchen," *Sitzungsberichte der Akademie Heidelberger* [1967], 10 f). *Isotimia* occurs first in Strabo 8.4.4.

47. Cf. Aristophanes, *Wasps* 548 (also 508 ff, 575, 627, 638). See F. Schachermeyr, *Perikles* (Stuttgart 1969), 63. On the other hand see Thucydides 2.37.1.

48. Euripides, *Suppliant Women* 406 ff. This notion was also introduced into medicine and applied to the cosmos: *Phoenissae* 543 ff, Empedocles B17.27 (*Fragmente der Vorsokratiker* I, 317). See F. Dümmler, *Kleine Schriften* I (Leipzig 1901), 164 ff; Vlastos, "Equality and Justice in Early Greek Cosmologies," *Classical Philology* 42 (1947) 156 ff; J. de Romilly, *Time in Greek Tragedy* (Ithaca 1968), 90 ff.

49. Pseudo-Xenophon 1.2. Cf. Aristotle, Politics 1317b8, and Chapter 6 above.

50. Cf. Ehrenberg, *RE Suppl.* VII (1940), 298 ff; Burckhardt, *Griechische Kulturgeschichte* I, 206.

51. W. K. C. Guthrie, *A History of Greek Philosophy* III (Cambridge 1969), 148 ff.

52. On this and what follows cf. C. Meier, "Freiheit," in Conze, Koselleck, and Brunner, *Geschichtliche Grundbegriffe* II, 426 ff; K. Raaflaub, "Zum Freiheitsbegriff der Griechen," in E. C. Welskopf (ed.), *Soziale Typenbegriffe im Alten Griechenland und ihr Nachleben bis in die modernen Sprachen* (Berlin 1981). See now idem, *Die Entstehung der Freiheit* (Munich 1985).

53. Cf. Schaefer, *Probleme*, 313. Solon even attributes the concept of freedom to the earth goddess Ge (24.3 ff).

54. J. Bleicken, in his important work *Staatliche Ordnung und Freiheit in der römischen Republik* (Kallmünz 1972), unfortunately contrasts *libertas* only with the modern notion of freedom and not with the Greek, thus forfeiting the opportunity to give a sharper profile to the concept within the possibilities and limits of the classical world.

55. Euripides, *Suppliant Women* 405; cf. 352 f, 438; Pseudo-Xenophon 1.8.

56. This is doubtless why Aristotle saw democratic equality as determined by freedom, since he found a criterion for it only in freedom, not in wealth or descent (see Meier, "Demokratie," 832; idem, "Freiheit," 429). However, since he linked the notion of citizenship to political rights—which varied from constitution to constitution (*Politics* 1275a22, 1275b18)—he could not define democratic equality simply by reference to the citizen's right in the sense of his belonging to the civic community in the general sense of the word (which would have been the most straightforward definition, since the metics too were free, though they had no part in the democratic system).

57. On this and what follows cf. C. Meier, "Macht und Gewalt," in W. Conze, R. Koselleck, and O. Brunner (eds.), *Geschichtliche Grundbegriffe* III (Stuttgart 1982).

58. Euripides, *Cyclops* 119.

59. Anonymus Iamblichi 6 (*Frag. der Vorsokratiker* II, 400 ff); Thucydides 3.82.8. Cf. 2.65.8, 6.39.1 f; Democritus 252 (*Frag. der Vorsokratiker* II, 195 f); Aristotle, *Politics* 1284a 20. For the contrary view see Plato, *Gorgias* 483c ff. Similar views are already found in Aeschylus' *Eumenides*. Cf. Chapter 5.

60. Aristotle, *Politics* 1252a7 ff, 1255b16 ff, 1261a10 ff, 1277a29 ff, 1295b25 ff; cf. 1324a3.

61. Cf. Meier, "Entstehung und Besonderheit," 2.

62. On this topic see H. Reinau, *Die Entstehung des Bürgerbegriffs bei den Griechen* (Basel 1981).

63. The earliest attestations are: Pseudo-Xenophon 1.1, 3.1, 9; Antiphon, *Metast.*fr. 2; Thucydides 1.18.1, 115.2, 2.36.4, 37.1, 4.76.5, 126.2, 5.31.6, 6.17.2, 7.55.2, 8.53.3, 89.2. The term *patrios politeia* appears before the end of the Peloponnesian War: Thrasymachus B1 (*Frag. der Vorsokratiker* II, 324). It appears in the sense of "public life," "nature of civic (communal) life" in Thucydides 1.68.1, 2.16.2, 5.68.2. The title *peri politeias* given to various books probably dates from the fourth century: cf. E. Nachmanson, *Der griechische Buchtitel* (Gothenburg 1941).

64. Cf. Meier, "Entstehung und Besonderheit," 50 n. 44; H. Diller, "Der vorphilosophische Gebrauch von *kosmos und kosmein*," in *Festschrift für Bruno Snell* (Munich 1956), 47 ff.

65. Cf. note 115 below. In this connection we have to understand the caution with which Thucydides (2.37.1, 65.9) defines the concept of democracy: see G. P. Landmann, *Museum Helveticum* 31 (1974) 80. What he says is uttered, as it were, *sub specie aeternitatis* and addressed to a Panhellenic public; we learn nothing about how the term was understood by the broad mass of Athenians. Cf. note 14 above. Given the new vogue for intellectual debates and the increasing sharpness of political oppositions, it may be that this kind of definition is typical only of its period: see W. R. Connor, *The New Politicians of Fifth-Century Athens* (Princeton 1971).

66. C. Meier, "Entstehung und Besonderheit," 54 f. Thucydides 3.62.3, together with 4.78.3, where *oligarchia isonomos* and *demokratia* are clearly subsumed under the major term *isonomia* and contrasted with *dynasteia*. See Vlastos, *"Isonomia politike,"* 13 ff (who unaccountably insists on translating the term as "democratic oligarchy"); the term *isonomos* here solves the difficulty that arose after the shift of the borderline between oligarchy and democracy. For a similar contrast with *demos* as the major term see Thucydides 6.89.4 and, from a different viewpoint, 6.60.1. On the new meaning of *hoi oligoi* see Burckhardt, *Griechische Kulturgeschichte* I, 247.

67. For Athens cf. G. de Ste. Croix, *Historia* 5 (1956) 1 ff; Vlastos, *"Isonomia politike,"* 20 n. 6. For the period after 404: Lysias 26.2, 12.35; Isocrates 7.67.

68. Euripides, *Suppliant Women* 238 ff; cf. *Orestes* 917 ff. See R. Goossens, "La république des paysans," *Revue internationale des droits de l'antiquité*, ser 4, 3 (1950) 551 ff; Grossmann, *Politische Schlagwörter*, 12 ff. One should recall the important part played by the *mesoi* in Aristotle's constitutional theory. In Aristotle one also finds the realization that they are seldom strong and that in general constitutions are largely dependent on the social structure (*Politics* 1293a41; 1296a22, 37; 1318b6 ff).

69. Cf. M. I. Finley, "The Ancestral Constitution," in *The Use and Abuse of History* (London 1975), 34 ff; W. Nippel, *Mischverfassungstheorie und Verfassungsrealität in Antike und früher Neuzeit* (Stuttgart 1980).

70. Meier, *Entstehung*, 64 ff.

71. Ibid., 59 f. This certainly also reflects the relationship (already emerging in

the fifth century) between *politikos* and what the *polis* should be (*politikos* being additionally qualified by *isos*). This relationship inevitably arises from the fact that *politikos* stands for the whole of the civic community. Cf., e.g., Thucydides 3.82.8, 8.89.3; Demosthenes 9.48, 10.74; Isocrates, *Panegyricus* 79, 151; Aristotle, *Politics* 1254b4, 1273b12, 1298a39, 1305b10; *Athenaion Politeia* 14.3, 16.2. For a general treatment of the topic see J. Ritter, *Metaphysik und Politik* (Frankfurt 1969), 71 ff.

72. Meier, *Entstehung*, 62 n. 74. See Isocrates 4.105: distinction between *physei politas einai* and *nomo tes politeias [metechein]*. Neither excludes the other: one can be a citizen simply *physei*, or *physei* and *nomo*, or simply *nomo*. *Politeia* as active citizenship is already found in Thucydides 8.76.5, Isocrates 16.17. On this whole complex cf. V. Ehrenberg, *The Greek State* (2d ed. London 1966), 41.

73. Meier, "Demokratie," 828 and 830 n. 69.

74. Ibid., 831 f. This relates in particular to the hoplites.

75. Esp. Thucydides 6.39.1 f: the advocate of democracy counters the assertion that it is not *ison* with the proposition that in it the rich, the wise, and the general populace *kai kata mere kai xympanta . . . isomoirein*. Demos, he says, is the name for the whole. A similar assertion of wholeness is found at 6.18.6 and Aristotle, *Politics* 1291b30 ff (which is reminiscent of the traditional constitution of the Acanthians, in which "neither the majority was subject to the few, nor the minority to the whole": Thucydides 4.86.4. Cf. also Aristotle, *Politics* 1297b24). On this topic see A. Raubold, *Untersuchungen zur politischen Sprache der Demokraten bei den älteren attischen Rednern* (Munich diss. 1971), 46 ff. On the general context see Meier, "Demokratie," 828. On the prehistory of the idea of equilibrium see C. Meier, in S. N. Eisenstadt (ed.), *The Origins and Diversity of Axial Civilizations* (New York 1986), 87.

76. The earliest attestation (still in the general sense of "rule") is found in Sophocles, *Oedipus Tyrannus* 593 (before 425). Later Andocides 2.27; Lysias 2.18; Thucydides 3.62.3, 4.78.2, 126.2, 6.38.3.

77. Plato, *Laws* 832c. *Basileia* occurs from Heraclitus (B52) on.

78. The etymology must be left out of account here. For a recent discussion of the question see F. Quass, *Nomos und Psephisma* (Munich 1971), 14 n. 83; but also C. Schmitt, *Nomos der Erde* (Cologne 1950), 36 ff; idem, *Verfassungsrechtliche Aufsätze* (Berlin 1958), 489 ff.

79. J. de Romilly, *La loi dans la pensée grecque* (Paris 1971), 23 f.

80. F. Heinimann, *Nomos und Physis* (Basel 1945), 65.

81. Hesiod, *Works and Days* 276 ff, admittedly considers *dike* to be what characterizes human *nomos*, but this simply confirms the word's wide semantic spread. Cf. Heinimann, *Nomos und Physis*, 61 f.

82. Pindar, fr. 169. Heraclitus B114. On these see Heinimann, *Nomos und Physis*, 65 f (who differs from Reinhardt); Romilly, *La loi*, 62 ff.

83. Ostwald, *Nomos and Beginnings*, 160. For a contrary view see also E. Ruschenbusch, *Gnomon* 43 (1971) 415; H. W. Pleket, *Mnemosyne* 25

(1970) 457; Quass, *Nomos und Psephisma,* 17 f. Also C. Meier, *Historische Zeitschrift* 218 (1974) 372 ff.

84. Although one may think one discerns earlier hints of this sense, the first certain occurrence of the meaning "law" is Antigone's appeal to the "unwritten laws" (datable to the year 441). On the attestations cf. Ostwald, *Nomos and Beginnings,* 43 ff; Romilly, *La loi,* 13 ff. A quite different question is considered, apparently unwittingly, by Vlastos, 349 n. 40, namely, that even before the end of the sixth century *nomos* subsumed written laws *(thesmoi).* This is altogether probable, but all it means is that these formed part of the law in the general sense. What concerns us here is to determine when *nomos* took on the sense of a "law" or "statute."

85. Quass, *Nomos und Psephisma,* 18 f, 29; cf. 13.

86. Xenophon, *Memorabilia* 1.2.42, 4.4.13.

87. This is another reason why it is quite improbable that at the time of Cleisthenes it would have been decided to use *nomoi* as a designation for laws. For at that time the sole concern was with questions of organization, i.e., with *psephismata* designed to produce eunomy or isonomy, however it was understood at the time.

88. Cf. Quass, *Nomos und Psephisma,* 28 f, 34 ff; H. J. Wolff, " 'Normenkontrolle' und Gesetzesbegriff in der attischen Demokratie," *Sitzungsberichte der Heidelberger Akademie* (1970) 39 n. Notwithstanding this evidence, it remains true that it was not possible until 403, on the basis of the process of *nomosthesia* that was then introduced, to make a clear legal distinction between *nomoi* and *psephismata.* Cf. also F. Gschnitzer, *Anzeiger für die Altertumswissenschaft* 28 (1975) 206 ff.

89. See Romilly, *La loi,* 24 ff; Grossmann, *Politische Schlagwörter,* 86 f.

90. This is not to say that *nomos* simply replaced *thesmos. Thesmoi* are attested only for Draco and Solon (Quass, *Nomos und Psephisma,* 11 f). In the fifth century they can have competed only with the *psephismata.*

91. Herodotus 7.104.4. Cf. Heinimann, *Nomos und Physis,* 29 ff.

92. Romilly, *La loi,* 1, 20 ff; esp. Herodotus 3.80; Demosthenes 6.25, 21.188, 24.75 ff; Aeschines 1.4, 3.5 f; Aeschylus, *Prometheus* 187. Euripides, *Suppliant Women* 432; Anonymus Iamblichi 7.15.

93. Herodotus 3.80.

94. First encountered in Euripides, *Suppliant Women* 433. Cf. Isocrates 7.40. See also the passages cited in note 92.

95. Particularly impressive in this connection is the enlightening dialogue between Pericles and Alcibiades in Xenophon, *Memorabilia* 1.2.40 ff; cf. ibid., 4.4.14.

96. On this point cf. Wolff, " 'Normenkontrolle' und Gesetzesbegriff."

97. See, e.g., Schaefer, *Staatsform und Politik,* 394 f.

98. Romilly, *La loi,* 23.

99. On *lex* and *mos* see J. Bleicken, *Lex Publica* (Berlin 1975); C. Meier, *Savigny Zeitschrift für Rechtsgeschichte. Romanistische Abteilung* 95 (1978) 378 ff.

100. As such it was then translated by the quite different Latin word *lex*. On this see Schmitt, *Verfassungsrechtliche Aufsätze*, 427, 502: except that Cicero had hardly any option but to translate the word in the sense that it took on essentially—though not solely—in the fifth century.

101. Aristotle, *Politics* 1286a8 ff, 1287a19 ff, 12924 ff, 1293a20 ff and passim. Previously found in Antiphon 3.1.1. Cf. H. Kleinknecht, in *Theologisches Wörterbuch zum Neuen Testament* IV, 1024.

102. Andocides 1.85. Wolff, "'Normenkontrolle' und Gesetzesbegriff," 70 f.

103. V. Ehrenberg, *Die Rechtsidee im frühen Griechentum* (Leipzig 1921), 135.

104. See Chapter 4, "The Attic *Demos* at the Time of Cleisthenes' Reform."

105. Koselleck, *Futures Past*, 285 f.

106. On this achievement cf. Meier, *Entstehung*, 10 f.

107. This can be clearly demonstrated from Aeschylus' *Eumenides* (especially if a comparison is made with Solon). Cf. Chapter 5.

108. Cf. E. Auerbach, *Mimesis. Dargestellte Wirklichkeit in der abendländischen Kultur* (3d ed. Bern/Munich 1964), 41 f.

109. See Meier, in Faber and Meier, *Historische Prozesse*, 19 ff.

110. For instance, the "subjectivizing" of the notion of war in Thucydides 1.122.1, 3.82.2. An extreme example is the notion of monarchy as a corrupting force in Herodotus 3.80.3.

111. See Chapters 2 and 8; C. Meier, *Arethusa* 20 (1987) 55.

112. Solon, *Elegies* 3. On this problem see Meier, *Entstehung*, 17 ff, esp. 22 f; Ostwald, *Nomos and Beginnings*, 63 ff, 71 ff.

113. Cf. the decree of Hippodamus (Aristotle, *Politics* 1268b22 ff).

114. Xenophon, *Hellenica* 2.3.48. As far as the slaves are concerned it is possible that Xenophon (but not Theramenes) is alluding to (and grossly oversimplifying) plans such as those attested by *Athenaion Politeia* 40.2. Cf. also Aristophanes, *Frogs* 693 f. It is true that some sophists spoke of the equality of all men, including slaves, but they are not known to have drawn any political consequences.

115. Doubts about democratic equality toward the end of the fifth century (equality among individual citizens, but not between "the rich" and "the poor") are found in, e.g., Thucydides 4.86.4 (cf. Aristotle, *Politics* 1291b30), 6.18.6, 39.1 f (see Chapter 8, note 121, below); Plato, *Laws* 757; Aristotle, *Politics* 1301b26 ff; cf. 1282b18 ff, 1301a27 ff, 1303b3 ff, 1307a26 ff, 1318a4 ff; *Nicomachean Ethics* 1131a22 ff, 1158b31 ff.

116. Herodotus 3.80.6; Thucydides 3.82.8.

117. Cf., e.g., H. Kramer, *Quid valeat homonoia in litteris Graecis* (Göttingen diss. 1915); J. de Romilly, "Vocabulaire et propaganda ou les premiers emplois du mot *homonoia*," in *Mélanges P. Chantraine* (Paris 1972), 199 ff; A. Moulakis, *Homonoia* (Munich 1973); B. Keil, *EIRHNH, Sitzungsberichte Leipzig* 68 (1916) 4 ff; A. Fuks, *The Ancestral Constitution* (2d ed. Westport, Conn., 1971). See also Finley, "The Athenian Constitution"; Nippel, *Mischverfassungstheorie*. Further detail is given in Grossman, *Politische Schlagwörter*; Raubold, *Untersuchungen zur politischen Sprache*; Connor, *The New Politicians*, 99 ff. All this material should be thoroughly

examined from a historical point of view, with special reference to the conceptual worlds of each particular period taken as a whole. This should include the functions of the terms and the relations between them, the problems posed by the conspicuous occurrence of some concepts and the absence of others (insofar as this can be established), the presence or absence of semantic changes, political perspectives, etc.; and all this should be set against the political and constitutional background of the age.

118. The only point of interest is to know what was controversial and what was not. This reveals the extent of the oppositions and—presumably—the modified survival and tenacity of old ideals with which the new states of affairs were brought into relation.

119. 646 ff. This comes in the "deception speech." But here Ajax was all the more obliged to refer to general experiences (known to Sophocles' own age). One cannot of course entirely ignore the fact that this formulation is informed by the experience of the shocks and upheavals of the age and that what is stated here therefore transcends the immediate context. Even so, the statement remains within the context of "vicissitudes." As in the chorus *Polla ta deina*, in *Antigone*, a new experience is formulated and understood as something timeless: there is no expectation that things will be different in future.

120. Thucydides 1.70 f, 6.18.6 f. Cf. Chapter 8.

121. See the beginning of Chapter 8.

122. Cf. H. Ryffel, *Metabole Politeion* (Bern 1949); A. Heuss, *Historische Zeitschrift* 216 (1973) 4 ff; H. Strasburger, *Die Wesensbestimmung der Geschichte durch die antike Geschichtsschreibung* (Wiesbaden 1966). Cf. also Demosthenes 9.47.

123. C. Meier, "Geschichte," in Conze, Koselleck, and Brunner, *Geschichtliche Grundbegriffe* II, 595 ff. On this topic see H. Arendt, *Between Past and Future* (London 1961), 41 ff.

124. See Chapter 5, "The *Eumenides* as Evidence of Early Political Thought." This invites comparison with the poet's roughly contemporaneous treatment of the overthrow of a divine dynasty in the *Prometheus*. Cf. C. Meier, *Die politische Kunst der griechischen Tragödie* (Munich 1988), 156 ff.

125. Chapter 8 and C. Meier, "'Fortschritt' in der Antike," in Conze, Koselleck, and Brunner, *Geschichtliche Grundbegriffe* II, 353 f.

126. Cf. Chapter 8.

127. See note 10; Meier, "Entstehung und Besonderheit," 8 ff, 11 ff.

128. See J. Martin, "Von Kleisthenes zu Ephialtes," *Chiron* 4 (1974) 5 ff. Martin fails to see, however, that such results depended on the existence of effective popular pressure for greater participation in politics, even though there may have been no clear awareness of the ultimate destination.

129. Cf., e.g., B. Snell, *Dichtung und Gesellschaft* (Hamburg 1965), 165, 174. Of some interest, for example, are the claims articulated in the word *eleutherios*: see Meier, "Freiheit," 429; G. Grossman, *Promethie und Orestie* (Heidelberg 1970), 178 ff.

130. Cf. C. Meier, *Die Entstehung des Politischen bei den Griechen* (Frankfurt

1983), 408 ff. On constancy and change see Chapter 8, "The Emergence of the Consciousness of Human Ability." Thucydides (1.2 ff) saw it somewhat differently, but for him too the framework remained essentially static.

8. An Ancient Equivalent of the Concept of Progress

1. This chapter is a revised version of my inaugural lecture at the University of Basel on 23 May 1975. The lecture was subsequently delivered at the universities of Bielefeld, Munich, Marburg, and Tel Aviv. It owes a great deal to discussions held in the Basel Seminar for Ancient History. I dedicate it to my friends in Basel in grateful remembrance of a period of my career in which teaching and research in ancient history led to a high degree of cross-fertilization. Extensive discussions with Tonio Hölscher enabled me to formulate my questions more precisely and to find some of the answers (see note 2). The exposition has deliberately been kept fairly brief. It was not possible to consider the question of whether the classical quotations always represent the opinions of the authors (e.g., in tragedy and comedy).

2. A survey of the relevant research and the best synopsis of what is contained in the sources are provided by L. Edelstein, *The Idea of Progress in Classical Antiquity* (Baltimore 1967). The subject is discussed, with additional literature, by E. R. Dodds, *Journal of the History of Ideas* 29 (1968) 453 ff. See also S. Lauffer, "Der antike Fortschrittsgedanke," *Actes du XIème Congrès international de philosophie* 12 (1953) 37 ff; idem, "Die Lehre des Thukydides von der Zunahme geschichtlicher Größenverhältnisse," in *Spengler-Studien. Festgabe M. Schröter* (Munich 1965), 177 ff. More recent studies are J. de Romilly, "Thucydide et l'idée de progrès," *Annali della Scuola normale superiore di Pisa. Lettere, storia e filosofia,* ser. 2 (1966) 143 ff; E. R. Dodds, *The Ancient Concept of Progress and Other Essays* (Oxford 1973); C. Meier, "'Fortschritt' in der Antike," in W. Conze, R. Koselleck, and O. Brunner (eds.), *Geschichtliche Grundbegriffe* II (Stuttgart 1975), 353 ff. See also A. Momigliano, "Time in Ancient Historiography," *History and Theory* Suppl. 6 (1966), repr. in *Quarto contributo alla storia degli studi classici* (Rome 1969); T. Hölscher, "Die Nike der Messenier und Naupaktier in Olympia. Kunst und Geschichte im späten 5. Jahrhundert vor Christus," *Jahrbücher des Deutschen Archäologischen Instituts* 89 (1974) 70 ff. Similar conclusions were reached simultaneously by W. den Boer, "Progress in the Greece of Thucydides," *Mededelingen der Koninglijke Nederlandse Akademie* 1977. See also R. Müller, "Die Konzeption des Fortschritts in der Antike," *Sitzungsberichte Akademie der DDR* (Berlin 1983).

3. The prize for this has to go to K. Thraede's article "Fortschritt," in *Reallexikon für Antike und Christentum* VIII (1972), 141 ff, which treats every occurrence of any word that might conceivably be rendered by our word *progress* as evidence of a classical "idea of progress" (so that we can count ourselves lucky that no letters written by young mothers have come down to us from ancient times). According to this view, it also counts as progress if there is an improvement in the fortune of corrupt politicians, in the welfare

of a city under the rule of a tyrant, or after the conclusion of peace—even
when there is none (see the misuse that is made of passages from Isocrates in
cols. 147 and 151). This article must be read with extreme caution.

4. Cf. M. I. Finley, *The Ancient Economy* (London 1973); E. Will, *Annales*
9 (1954) 7 ff; S. C. Humphreys, *Anthopology and the Greeks* (London
1978). For a brief synopsis see M. Austin and P. Vidal-Naquet, *Economies et
sociétés en Grèce ancienne* (Paris 1972), 11 ff. See also the important study
by P. Veyne, *Le pain et le cirque* (Paris 1976).

5. Adapted from *Correspondence between Schiller and Goethe from 1794
to 1805,* trans. L. D. Schmitz, 2 vols. (London 1877–1879), I, 414. See
C. Meier, "Der Alltag des Historikers und die historische Theorie," in
H. M. Baumgartner and J. Rüsen (eds.), *Seminar: Geschichte und Theorie.
Umrisse einer Historik* (Frankfurt 1976), 36 ff.

6. R. Koselleck, "Fortschritt," in Conze, Koselleck, and Brunner, *Geschichtliche Grundbegriffe* II, 371 ff; cf. idem, "Geschichte," ibid., 647 ff.

7. See C. Meier, "Fragen und Thesen zu einer Theorie historischer Prozesse,"
in K. G. Faber and C. Meier (eds.), *Historische Prozesse* (Munich 1978),
28 ff.

8. J. Burckhardt, *Historische Fragmente* (Stuttgart/Berlin 1942), 200: "We
would like to know the wave on which we are borne along in the ocean, but
we ourselves are the wave." See also ibid. 207, 250.

9. Cf. R. Koselleck, *Futures Past,* trans. K. Tribe (Cambridge, Mass., 1985),
267 ff.

10. O. Marquard, *Schwierigkeiten mit der Geschichtsphilosophie* (Frankfurt
1973), 18 f. Cf. R. Koselleck, *Futures Past,* 159 ff.

11. Cf. H. Lübbe, *Fortschritt als Orientierungsproblem* (Frieburg 1975); idem,
Geschichtsbegriff und Geschichtsinteresse (Basel 1977), 254 ff; M. Weber,
Wissenschaftslehre (3d ed. Tübingen 1968), 33 n. 2.

12. Heinemann (ed.) no. 659 (= von Loeper 868). It follows from this that the
perception of powerful processual sequences represents a constant potential for the revival of the idea of progress, for these are obviously hard to
endure. Improvements in one area or another must therefore serve to revive
the concept itself.

13. J. Nestroy, "Der Schützling," in *Gesammelte Werke,* ed. O. Rommel (Vienna 1949) IV, 695: "Progress is like a newly discovered country— with a
flourishing colonial system on the coast, but an interior that is still desert,
steppe, prairie. Altogether it looks much greater than it really is."

14. On this procedure generally cf. R. Koselleck, Introduction, in W. Conze, R.
Koselleck, and O. Brunner (eds.), *Geschichtliche Grundbegriffe* I (Stuttgart
1972); xxii f; idem, *Futures Past,* 84 ff.

15. See, e.g., M. Fuhrmann, *Einführung in die antike Dichtungstheorie* (Darmstadt 1973), 12.

16. Cf. Edelstein, *Idea of Progress,* 92 n. 79. Instead of *auxesis* one could of
course use the commoner term *epidosis,* but this would seem less appropriate in view of the use to which it has been put in philosophy and of its
later semantic history.

17. Cf. Meier, "Fragen und Thesen."

18. On the particular form of process represented by an institution cf. A. Gehlen, *Studien zur Anthropologie und Soziologie* (Neuwied/Berlin 1963), 197.

19. One ought for instance to ask how far particular areas of life can or must be involved in change in certain cases (or alternatively need not), and how far particular activities, ways of life, different forms of expectation and social identity are to be assigned to the one type or the other. Cf. later in the chapter.

20. See Koselleck, "Fortschritt," 353 f; Dodds, *Ancient Concept of Progress;* 1 f. The words are of no further interest here.

21. Aristophanes, *Ecclesiazusae* 1 ff, esp. 137 ff, 206 ff, 214 ff. It is hard to decide where the boundary between "of old" and "now" lies. It seems to me that the former does not—as in, e.g., Cratinus, fr. 238 (Kock)—refer to a golden age; if it did there would not be so much talk of work (cf. Romilly, "Thucydide et l'idée du progrès," 189). A more comparable usage is found in *Frogs* 977.

22. Aristophanes, *Ecclesiazusae* 376 ff, esp. 430 ff, 455 ff. Only the people from the country disagree. They are also wedded to the old (276 ff).

23. Ibid., 577 ff. Further examples are given by Edelstein, *Idea of Progress*, 38.

24. An ancient debate about whether it is good or bad to alter traditional laws and rules is attested by Aristotle, *Politics* 1268b26 ff. But this is not concerned with argumentation. A quite different question is whether the burden of proof should lie with those who wish for change (good reasons in favor are adduced by R. Spaemann, *Wort und Wahrheit* 24 [1969] 463 ff; H. Lübbe, *Wolfenbütteler Studien zur Aufklärung* 1 (1974) 18 f).

25. As far as I know the expression was coined by Christian Morgenstern in his poem "Die Nähe." It was then applied in 1975 by the "Düsseldorfer Kom(m)ödchen" to today's unshakable expectation of endless improvement.

26. Thucydides 3.38.5, 7. The sentence continues: "but they do not reflect sufficiently even about what meets their eyes."

27. Ibid., 3.37.3 f.

28. Plato (comicus), fr. 220 (Kock). In the middle of the century, on the other hand, both Herodotus (3.80.5 f) and Protagoras (in Plato 326d), when commending democracy, speak of old laws and customs. On the problems of legislation see Chapter 7, above.

29. K. Reinhardt, *Aischylos als Regisseur und Theologe* (Bern 1949), 158. Cf. B. A. van Groningen, *In the Grip of the Past* (1953). Cf. note 129 below.

30. Aeschylus, *Eumenides* 162 f, 171 f, 393 ff, 693 f, 727 f, 731, 808 f, 848 ff, 881 ff. See J. de Romilly, *Time in Greek Tragedy* (Ithaca 1968), 149 f.

31. Quoted in Xenophon, *Memorabilia*, 4.4.6. Cf. also Aristophanes, *Birds* 255 ff, *Wasps* 527 f, *Clouds* 1031; Euripides, *Cyclops* 250 f.

32. *Clouds* 479 f, 889 ff (esp. 896, 935 ff, 943 f), 1031 ff, 1369 f, 1397 f, 1421 ff. For the old, on the other hand, see 398, 821, 915, 929, 961 ff, 985 ff, 1356 ff, 1468, and, not least, 547. Also *Birds* 255 ff; Edelstein, *Idea of Progress*, 37 f.

33. Aristophanes, *Clouds* 547, *Wasps* 1536; cf. *Frogs* 971 ff.

34. B. Snell, *Dichtung und Gesellschaft* (Hamburg 1965), 127 f, 171 f. See Plato, *Republic* 424b, c; cf. *Laws* 700d ff, also 656b, e.
35. Hölscher, "Die Nike der Messenier," 95 f, 98 ff.
36. Plato, *Hippias Major* 282a.
37. The inscription on a vase by Euthymides ("Euthymides decorated [it], the son of Polios, as never Euphronios"), quoted by Hölscher, "Die Nike der Messenier," 102, clearly cannot serve as an example, since the two artists were contemporaries.
38. Timotheus, fr. 7 (Diehl), *Persae* 219 ff. See Edelstein, *Idea of Progress,* 35 f. Cf. Pherecrates, fr. 144B (Kock); P. Maas, *RE* VI A, 1331 ff; Xenophon, *Cyropaedia* 1.6.38 ff.
39. *Hippias Major* 281b. Cf. *Gorgias* 448c. See F. Heinimann, *Museum Helveticum* 18 (1961) 105 ff.
40. *On Ancient Medicine* 2, 12 *(Corpus Hippocraticum).* Cf. Edelstein, *Idea of Progress,* 38; H. Herter, *Maia* 15 (1963) 464 ff. On the dating of the treatise see M. J. O'Brien, *The Socratic Paradoxes and the Greek Mind* (Chapel Hill 1967), 65 f.
41. Plato, *Protagoras,* esp. 316c ff, 318e–319a, 323c ff; Aristophanes, *Clouds* 479 f. See W. K. C. Guthrie, *A History of Greek Philosophy* III (Cambridge 1969), 25, 38 f, 250 ff; O'Brien, *Socratic Paradoxes,* 76 ff.
42. Xenophon, *Memorabilia* 4.2.8 ff, etc. See A. Dihle, *Griechische. Literaturgeschichte* (Stuttgart 1967), 202 ff; Guthrie, *History of Greek Philosophy* III, 44 ff; A. Lesky, *Geschichte der griechischen Literatur* (3d ed. Bern 1971), 544 ff (*A History of Greek Literature,* trans. J. Willis and C. de Heer [2d ed. New York 1963]); O'Brien, *Socratic Paradoxes,* 66 f; G. Gruben, *Die Tempel der Griechen* (2d ed. Munich 1976), 172, 174.
43. Aeschylus, *Eumenides* 428 ff, 619 ff. See F. Solmsen, *Antiphon-Studien* (Leipzig 1931), 47 ff.
44. Protagoras, fr. 6b (*Fragmente der Vorsokratiker* II, 266). On rhetoric generally see Plato, *Gorgias* 452d: "The greatest good by virtue of which men are both free themselves and also rule over others"; 452e; 457a, b; *Theaetetus* 167c, 172c (for the good of the *polis*); *Phaedrus* 268a; *Gorgias* A25, B11.8 (*Frag. der Vorsokratiker* II, 277, 290); Thrasymachus B6 (ibid., 325). See J. Burckhardt, *Griechische Kulturgeschichte* IV (Basel 1957), 246 f.
45. Cf. Hölscher, "Die Nike der Messenier," 105 ff; K. Thraede, *Rheinisches Museum* 105 (1962) 159.
46. Democritus, fr. 157 (*Frag. der Vorsokratiker* II, 175); Socrates in Xenophon, *Memorabilia* 4.2.8 ff. Aeschylus, *Eumenides* 847 ff; cf. Chapter 5 above, note 224 ff. Plato, *Protagoras* 319a, e; 322b ff. (*Aidos* is only approximately rendered by "mutual respect." Guthrie, *History of Greek Philosophy* III, 66, paraphrases it at 325a as "a . . . quality combining roughly a sense of shame, modesty, and respect for others"). At 321d it appears as a synonym of *sophia.* Cf. *Theaetetus* 167c. Similarly Anonymus Iamblichi 6.1, 7 (*Frag. der Vorsokratiker* II, 400 ff); Euripides, *Suppliant Women* 433 ff. See O'Brien, *Socratic Paradoxes,* 57, 67 f. Cf. discussion later in this chapter. Aristotle later sees the *phronesis* of Pericles as a com-

bination of craftsmanly skill in detail and knowledge of what is good for the city (*Nicomachean Ethics* 1140a24 ff, b8; 1141b14 ff). Plato makes an interesting distinction between political and tyrannical *techne* (*Republic* 276e).—There are significant contrasts with the Italian Renaissance: see C. Schmitt, *Die Diktatur* (3d ed. Berlin 1964), 8 ff, 14 f. See also J. Reinhardt, "Thukydides und Macchiavelli," in *Vermächtnis der Antike* (2d ed. Göttingen 1966), 184 ff.

47. O. Regenbogen, in H. Herter (ed.), *Thukydides* (Darmstadt 1968), 51, 56 f; W. Müri, ibid., 139 ff; C. Meier, in H. R. Jauss (ed.), *Die nicht mehr schönen Künste* (Munich 1968), 108 f. See also Herodotus 8.60 (but cf. 7.10d.2 for a different view); Plutarch, *Pericles* 4.6, with V. Ehrenberg, *Sophokles und Perikles* (Munich 1956), 116 f; Thrasymachus B1 (*Frag. der Vorsokratiker* II, 322); Plato, *Gorgias* 448c; Aristotle, *Metaphysics* 981a3 ff. See F. Heinimann, *Museum Helveticum* 18 (1961) 108 f.

48. Sophocles, *Antigone* 365.

49. 1.70 f. Cf. Edelstein, *Idea of Progress*, 31 n. 22. Xenophon, *Cyropaedia* 1.6.38. See Romilly, "Thucydide et l'idée du progrès," 171. The Corinthians' opinion accorded largely with Thucydides' own; cf. 8.96.5, 6.18.6 f, 6.36.3. On the other hand there are substantial divergences between his account and that of Pericles (2.35 ff).

50. Thucydides 1.142.9 (on the translation see A. W. Gomme's commentary).

51. Romilly, "Thucydide et l'idée du progrès," 167 ff.

52. Thucydides 1.70, 102.3. On Athenian audacity see also the important passage in the speech of Pericles, 2.40.3, and also 7.21.3, 28.3. See Hölscher, "Die Nike der Messenier," 100 f; G. Grossmann, *Politische Schlagwörter aus der Zeit des Peloponnesischen Krieges* (Basel diss. 1945), 117. Plutarch, *Cimon* 17.3, reports that in the fight against the helots the Spartans feared the *tolma* and *lamprotes* of the Athenians and sent them home secretly *hos neoteristas*. On this cf. Thucydides 1.102.3, 2.64.5, 7.31.6, 75.6. See also Euripides, *Suppliant Women* 902, where *lampros* collocates with *deinos*. Probably also Democritus, fr. 157. On the "change of all conditions" among the Greeks generally as a spur to thought see *On Airs, Waters, Places* 16 (*Corpus Hippocraticum*). Iamblichus, *De mysteriis* 7.5.

53. Aristotle, *Politics* 1268a6 ff.

54. 332 ff. Cf. Euripides, *Hippolytus* 916 ff, *Suppliant Women* 195 ff (with A. Lesky, *Die tragische Dichtung der Hellenen* [3d ed. Göttingen 1972], 360). On *to deinon* cf. Guthrie, *History of Greek Philosophy* III, 32 f. See also Aeschylus, *Eumenides* 517, 698; *Choephoroi* 585; Thucydides 6.36.3; Euripides, *Hippolytus* 921. Gorgias links the qualities *techneeis, deinos,* and *porimos* as characteristics of *sophia* (B11a. 21, *Frag. der Vorsokratiker* II, 300). See also Aristotle, *Nicomachean Ethics* 1144a23 f, 1152a11. Cf. G. Bornkamm, *Mensch und Gott in der Antike* (Bremen 1950), 15.

55. Cf. the early evidence in Hesiod, *Works and Days* 641 ff; Solon, *Elegies* 1.43 ff. The translation "safely to his destination" is not literal, but captures the idea of his "coming through."

56. Sophocles, *Antigone* 604 ff. Dodds, *Ancient Concept of Progress*, 8.

57. Cf. Romilly, "Thucydide et l'idée du progrès," 179.

·58. Xenophanes, B18 (*Frag. der Vorsokratiker* I, 133). Cf. the more detailed account given by Edelstein, *Idea of Progress*, 3 ff, 10 ff (whose interpretation, however, goes too far).

59. Cf. A. Dihle, *Hermes* 105 (1977) 38 ff. On the myth of Protagoras see E. Will, *Le monde grec et l'orient* I (paris 1972), 482 f, and note 108 below.

60. We are not concerned here with the detail of these doctrines or with their history. An admirable survey, with additional literature, is given by Romilly, "Thucydide et l'idée du progrès," 142 ff; see also Edelstein, *Idea of Progress*, 21 ff; Dodds, *Ancient Concept of Progress*, 4 ff. On Archelaus see esp. F. Heinimann, *Nomos und Physis* (Basel 1945), 111 ff. It is interesting to note the very close parallel with the corresponding doctrines in modern thought, e.g., in Samuel Pufendorf: see H. Medick, *Naturzustand und Naturgeschichte der bürgerlichen Gesellschaft* (Göttingen 1973), 52 ff. The key concept of *imbecillitas* corresponds to *chreia*; see Romilly, 154 ff; cf. Herodotus 7.102; O'Brien, *Socratic Paradoxes*, 64 ff. The Greek doctrines are "conjectural history" but had no long-term consequences. Naturally the Greeks were unaware of the wide gap between the presumable intentions of those concerned and the result, which gave Vico and the Scots so much food for speculation. They were not yet able, more than four centuries before the birth of Christ, to form such a poor opinion of the understanding of individuals and their desire to improve general conditions. They approached the matter more from a technical viewpoint and saw the results as the fruits of action that was designed to produce them. They therefore remained unaware of the complex of side effects, of "private vices and public virtues," of the "establishments that are indeed the result of human action, but not the execution of any human design" (cf. F. A. von Hayek, *Freiburger Studien* [Tübingen 1969], 97 ff). Hence they paid more attention to the individual inventors than to the process as a whole (cf. note 145 below).

61. Critias(?) B25 (*Frag. der Vorsokratiker* II, 387 f). The attribution of the fragment to Critias is dubious; there is more reason to believe that Euripides was the author of *Sisyphus:* see Dihle, *Hermes* 105 (1977) 38 ff. See also Prodicus B5 (*Frag. der Vorsokratiker* II, 317); P. Vidal-Naquet, *Revue de l'histoire des religions* 157 (1960) 66.

62. Edelstein, *Idea of Progress*, 11 ff; Dodds, *Ancient Concept of Progress*, 4 ff. It should be noted that the magnitude of men's capacity for achievement could be appreciated only when there was an awareness of their initial indigence (cf. Romilly, "Thucydide et l'idée du progrès," 154 ff). Similarly the Delphic doctrine of man's frailty and limitations made an essential contribution to the discovery of the immense potential of political thought, which led ultimately to democracy. Cf. note 143 below.

63. Philemon, fr. 56 (Kock). See Guthrie, *History of Greek Philosophy* III, 82. The length of time involved is stressed elsewhere too: *On Ancient Medicine* 3 (*Corpus Hippocraticum); Moschion, fr. 6 (Nauck).

64. On this and what follows see Romilly, "Thucydide et l'idée du progrès," 146, 189. For a somewhat different view see Edelstein, *Idea of Progress*, 25, 42 f, 49 ff.

65. On Protagoras cf. Herter, *Maia* 15 (1963) 470 ff; more generally, Romilly, "Thucydide et l'idée du progrès," 148; idem, *Time in Greek Tragedy,* 31 n. 35.

66. A. Kleingünther, *"Protos Heuretes," Philologus* Suppl. 26 (1933); K. Thraede, "Erfinder II," in *Reallexikon für Antike und Christentum* V (1962) 1191 ff. On constant progress in medicine see *On Ancient Medicine* 2. Laufer, "Der antike Fortschrittsgedanke," 39, speaks of "cultural history"; this seems to me greatly exaggerated.

67. For Athens at a later stage see Isocrates 8.20. Cf. 140, 4.103; Diodorus 11.72.

68. Thucydides 1.2 ff. Cf. Romilly, "Thucydide et l'idée du progrès," esp. 160; Lauffer, "Die Lehre des Thukydides," 184 f.

69. See note 111 below; also Romilly, "Thucydide et l'idée du progrès," 167 ff. On the experience of Athens see Thucydides 1.71.3; 2.11.1, 84.3, 85.2, 87.2 ff, 89.3; 6.63.4, 72.3.

70. Thucydides 6.18.6 f. Cf. Euripides, *Suppliant Women* 323 ff. On expansion as far as Carthage: Thucydides 6.15.2. Cf. Aristophanes, *Knights* 1303; Plutarch, *Pericles* 20.4, *Nicias* 12.1, *Alcibiades* 17.3. The same viewpoint underlies the dialogue with the Melians (Thucydides 5.85 ff): they must either expand or lose what they already possess. Only to this extent can the neutrality of Melos be a proof of their weakness. Alcibiades was to some extent taking up an old argument; cf. Aeschylus, *Eumenides* 984 ff. See also Herodotus 7.8a.1.

71. Thucydides 1.22.4, 3.82.2 (where admittedly the words are "as long as human nature remains constant"). For a more precise statement see 1.76.2 f, 3.45.4, 5.105.2. Cf. 1.75.3, 2.65.7, 3.82.8, 4.61.4. On this topic see C. Meier, "Macht und Gewalt," in W. Conze, R. Koselleck, and O. Brunner (eds.), *Geschichtliche Grundbegriffe* III (Stuttgart 1982), 826 ff.

72. Cf., e.g., the description of the differences between Athens and Sparta by H. Gundert, in Herter, *Thukydides,* 114 ff.

73. Thucydides 1.5 ff.

74. Thucydides 3.82.2. Cf. 8 on the exceptional nature of *arche he dia pleonexian kai philotimian.* See also Anoynmus Iamblichi (*Frag. der Vorsokratiker* II, 402 f): Thucydides 2.65.8, 6.39.1 f. Cf. Chapter 7 above.

75. Thucydides 3.82.2. To judge by the way in which this is expressed, Thucydides did not view these conditions as part of a continuous change, but as an interruption of peaceful life (or at least of life without war on the present scale). A different view is taken by Romilly, "Thucydide et l'idée du progrès," 177 f.

76. Thucydides 1.23. Cf. Lauffer, "Die Lehre des Thukydides," 191; see also Herodotus 6.98. In a similar way P. Valéry in 1929 spoke of the First World War within the framework of his *Propos sur le progrès:* "L'étendue, la durée, l'intensité, et même l'atrocité de cette guerre répondirent à l'ordre de grandeur de nos puissances. Elle fut à l'échelle de nos ressources et de nos industries du temps de paix (*Regards sur le monde actuel* [Paris 1945], 148).

77. Thucydides 1.22.4. Romilly, "Thucydide et l'idée du progrès," 165 f.

78. What Guthrie, *History of Greek Philosophy* III, 88 ff, says of Thrasymachus applies equally to Thucydides.

79. Plato, *Protagoras* 323c ff, 325b ff, 326c ff, 327c ff. Describing the emergence of civilization, Protagoras chooses the form of the myth: the predisposition to political (civic) virtue and art came from Zeus. This is of course not to be taken literally (Guthrie, *History of Greek Philosophy* III, 64 ff), yet it does seem significant in that it avoids the difficulty of reconstructing what actually happened. It is not necessary here to discuss the problem of how accurately Plato reproduces the opinion—or indeed a work—of Protagoras. On this question see Dodds, *Ancient Concept of Progress*, 9 f.

80. Plato, *Protagoras* 326c; 328a, b. Cf. J. Martin, *Saeculum* 27 (1976) 145 ff. Protagoras claimed that the art of education was old, but that no one had previously acknowledged it (316d ff); however, this is probably to underrate the claim of the sophists.

81. B33 Democritus (*Frag. der Vorsokratiker* II, 153). Cf. F. Lämmli, *Homo Faber: Triumph, Schuld, Verhängnis* (Basel 1968), 63 f. For a general treatment see Heinimann, *Nomos und Physis*, 101.

82. F. Schachermeyr, *Forschungen und Betrachtungen zur griechischen und römischen Geschichte* (Vienna 1974), 199 ff. Cf. Aristophanes, *Frogs* 1009, 1054 ff, on tragedy as a means of educating adults. In some sense this must also be seen as the reason for subsidizing theatergoing.

83. Edelstein, *Idea of Progress*, 30. Cf. Koselleck, "Fortschritt," 357.

84. Aristotle later sees the prehistory of democracy at least within the framework of a process of comprehensive change (*Politics* 1286b17 ff, 1297b22 ff).

85. The earliest instance is Herodotus 3.80. Cf. C. Meier, in *Discordia Concors. Festschrift E. Bonjour* (Basel 1968), 13; idem, *Entstehung des Begriffs Demokratie* (Frankfurt 1970), 40 ff, 49 ff, 54 f.

86. Dodds, *Ancient Concept of Progress*, 6, 43 f. (However, if there was any hope of combining might and right, Aeschylus tempered it with a good deal of skepticism. His works have an admonitory ring.) See G. Grossmann, *Promethie und Orestie* (Heidelberg 1970), 85 ff, 216 ff. Cf. the beginning and end of Chapter 5.

87. C. Meier, "Der Umbruch zur Demokratie in Athen (462/61 v. Ch.)," in R. Herzog and R. Koselleck (eds.), *Epochenschwelle und Epochenbewusstsein* (Munich 1987), 366 ff.

88. *Eumenides* 526 ff, 696 ff (the idea is put in very similar terms by both the Erinyes and Athene, the former expressing themselves with unusual moderation), 1000 (with 521). See Dodds, *Ancient Concept of Progress*, 53, 61; Romilly, *Time in Greek Tragedy*, 69. *Sophrosyne* recurs in Protagoras (Plato 325a) beside *dikaiosyne* as a universal virtue.

89. Hölscher, "Die Nike der Messenier," 95 f; cf. 108; Edelstein, *Idea of Progress*, 26 ff, esp. 29.

90. Pericles speaks of this; Thucydides 2.64.3. The above assertion is valid according to Lauffer (see note 127 below) despite the cogent observations of Romilly, "Thucydide et l'idée du progrès," 179 ff. A further increase is implied also by the use of "always" at 1.71.3.

91. Chairemon, Fr. 21 (Nauck). He puts this remark into the mouth of one of his characters. A quite different opinion is found in fr. 2. Cf. Alexis, fr. 30

(Kock). Similar views concerning the "progress" of scientific and technical ability become very common in the fourth century. See Koselleck, "Fortschritt," 358 f; Edelstein, *Idea of Progress*, 57 ff.

92. Democritus B118 (*Frag. der Vorsokratiker* V, 166).

93. Antiphon, fr. 4 (Nauck), in Aristotle, *Mechanics* 847a20 f. Cf. Plato, *Gorgias* 448c; Aristotle, *Politics* 1258b36; later Polybius 9.2.5.

94. Cf. also K. Reinhardt, *Von Werken und Formen* (Bad Godesberg 1948), 293 ff, repr. in *Tradition und Geist* (Göttingen 1960).

95. Cf. note 102 below.

96. This remains true. When Aristotle says (*Politics* 1332a28 ff) that everyone should be educated to virtue he is thinking of only a limited circle of citizens (cf. 1329a). In a wider circle the martial virtues are most likely to be widespread (1279a39. Cf. Meier, *Entstehung*, 63 n. 78).

97. Thus, in later historical reflections the "progress" that took place in the fifth century is ascribed to the victories over the Persians (Diodorus 12.1 ff; Aristotle, *Politics* 1341a28 ff). Cf. note 67 above; Isocrates 3.32, etc.

98. *On Ancient Medicine* 2. Herter, *Maia* 15 (1963) 481, remarks that "the object of cognition does not move into the infinite." See Aristotle, fr. 53 (Rose). In the fourth century different views gain ground. See Edelstein, *Idea of Progress*, 57 ff, 188 ff (on Aristotle).

99. Cf. Antiphon, fr. 4 (Nauck), in Aristotle, *Mechanics* 847a20 f.

100. The word *sophos* is used by Aristophanes in *Clouds* 520. A particularly good characterization of ability is found in the caricature in Plato's *Hippias Major* 282b ff. Art is seen as achievement: Hölscher, "Die Nike der Messenier," 102; Edelstein, *Idea of Progress*, 49. On a different aspect of the question cf. the interesting remark by J. Burckhardt, *Weltgeschichtliche Betrachtungen*, ed. R. Stadelmann (Tübingen 1949), 122: "Culture, conditioned by civic duty, fostered ability (in an infinitely wide and intense sense) rather than knowledge, which grows by leisurely addition." Burckhardt also emphasizes "ability" (*Können*) in *Geschichte der griechischen Kultur* I, 12.

101. Aeschylus, *Prometheus* 477, 506; Pindar, *Olympia* 7.50 ff, 13.16 f; *Pythia* 1.41 f. Cf. Snell, *Dichtung und Gesellschaft*, 128. The word is already found in Homer and Hesiod.

102. Heinimann, *Museum Helveticum* 18 (1961) 105 ff. *Technai* are defined by the fact that they prove "useful, life-enchancing, or even life-preserving," each having its particular aim and being able to attain it.

103. Euripides, *Suppliant Women* 216. Snell, *Philologische Untersuchungen*, 29, 83 ff; idem, *Entdeckung des Geistes* (4th ed. Göttingen 1975), 174. (This removes the difficulties raised by Guthrie, *History of Greek Philosophy* III, 66 n. 1.) See Chapter 5, note 224, above. O'Brien, *Socratic Paradoxes*, 23 ff.

104. See Guthrie, *History of Greek Philosophy* III, 252 f.

105. See note 46 above.

106. See Chapter 5, note 226, above. Cf. Euripides, *Hippolytus* 916 ff. See O'Brien, *Socratic Paradoxes*, 22 ff, 57 f.

107. Cf. Lauffer, "Der antike Fortschrittsgedanke," 41; Edelstein, *Idea of Progress*, 27 ff.

108. Cf. Dodds, *Ancient Concept of Progress*, 5. This is quite clear in the myth

of Protagoras. It is a question of the gap between the present state of civilization and primitive conditions (which is not even bridged here: 327c). This leads to the inference that a "long time" has intervened: see Romilly, "Thucydide et l'idée du progrès," 147, 149; Plato, *Laws* 676a f, 678b, and passim. For the same reason the consciousness of the enormous achievements of human civilization often did not go beyond cataloguing them and ascribing them to Prometheus (cf. J. Ferguson, *A Companion to Greek Tragedy* [Austin 1972], 120 f) or Palamedes. This was nothing new, at least where isolated inventions were concerned: see Kleingünther, *Philologus* Suppl. 26 (1933); O'Brien, *Socratic Paradoxes*, 58 ff. What was presumably new was the compilation of long lists of inventions, or at least the widespread interest they demonstrate: people were becoming aware of the many different elements that went to make up civilization, and now thought of them as having been acquired over the course of time. It is another question whether they believed them to be the work of man—with or without the aid of the gods—or the product of a divine purpose. Referring to Aeschylus, whose *Prometheus* contains extensive lists of these elements at a relatively early date, Dodds is surely right when he states (7): "The belief that man's achievements are not purely his own but are the outcome and the expression of a divine purpose was to Aeschylus . . . a basic religious postulate" (cf. note 59 above). The question of how they were acquired (cf. Reinhardt, *Aischylos*, 50 f) might be important for various reasons, but it could also be ignored. Cf. also Romilly, *Time in Greek Tragedy*, 31.

109. A careful interpretation reveals that the train of thought repeatedly ends in the "not yet" of the earlier period—in order to demonstrate that the present war is the greatest there has ever been. This is complemented by the mention of everything that "still" had to develop: yet even here the chief interest often lies more in the difficulty of the advance than in the advance itself—despite the fact that the forces that impel man to acquire ability and power are taken for granted and at times dominate the picture. (It is interesting to note that this happens when Thucydides is describing peaceful times, though in his actual account of events he tends to emphasize the challenge that arises from unrest: cf. discussion above). For Thucydides, of course, the ways and means by which the increase took place were interesting in themselves: cf. Lauffer, "Die Lehre des Thukydides," 187; Romilly, "Thucydide et l'idée du progrès," 159 ff.

110. The same is true in a different way when Protagoras describes the education of the citizens to political virtue as a broad process that is promoted variously by parents, fellow citizens, and *polis* institutions (Plato 324b ff, 327a ff). What is meant is admittedly not a process of change, but one which constantly reproduces the same conditions. Nevertheless, this insight is quite unusual for the period. Yet it too is bound to arise as soon as the general participation of the citizens in a democracy is traced back to its ethical prerequisites. One then becomes aware of an experience that is so obvious as to escape attention: just as all citizens are brought up to speak the language (327e), so too they are educated to political virtue.

111. E.g., Thucydides 4.26 (cf. Aristotle, *Politics* 1331a12 ff); 7.62, 65; 3.82.3

ff. The same must have been true of improvements in the building and fitting out of ships, given the many tasks to be performed, the high degree of competition, and the large number of metics flocking to Athens from all over Greece. Cf. also Xenophon, *Hieron* 9.7 ff; see Edelstein, *Idea of Progress*, 98 ff (who exaggerates the scale of this activity). Cf. note 69 above.

112. Edelstein, *Idea of Progress*, 6; Hölscher, "Die Nike der Messenier," 108.

113. Edelstein, *Idea of Progress*, 34: "Such progress was still understood in additive terms." This applies to the fifth century generally.

114. They could not be relativized by being measured against aims that were pitched beyond the present (especially as comparisons could not be made—as they can in modern times—with earlier cultures that were considered worthy of emulation). It is true that in the course of time the ideals became higher, thanks precisely to the consciousness of ability; cf., e.g., Snell, *Dichtung und Gesellschaft*, 165, 174; Grossmann, *Promethie und Orestie*, 178 ff. One might also think of the demands that Socrates made of political *techne*, of Plato's *Seventh Letter* (324 ff), of the excessive expectations that were linked to the concept of freedom (cf. C. Meier, "Freiheit," in Conze, Koselleck, and Brunner, *Geschichtliche Grundbegriffe* II, 429, etc.). Many achievements proved questionable, for instance in the constitutional sphere: see Dodds, *Ancient Concept of Progress*, 13; Meier, *Entstehung*, 52 ff. This was all the more palpable, as the demands had increased. But these are already symptoms of the crisis in the general consciousness of ability (which even more ambitious conceptions of ability—Plato's constitutional designs, for instance—were meant to remedy). Yet even then there was no resort to expectations whose fulfillment lay in the future: this was prevented by the threshold of which we have spoken.

115. Plutarch, *Pericles* 28.7 f (according to Ion of Chios). See Lauffer, "Die Lehre des Thukydides," 186 n. On the threat from Samos see Thucydides 8.76.4. On the importance that Pericles attached to Homer and to surpassing the great days of old see also 2.41.4 (with Romilly, "Thucydide et l'idée du progrès," 183). It is true that in the sixth century Ibycus compared Polycrates with the Homeric heroes, but Polycrates was just one exceptionally powerful figure, and he is seen only as the equal of the heroes: fr. 3 (Diehl); Snell, *Dichtung und Gesellschaft*, 119 ff.

116. *Iliad* 1.271; 5.304; 12.383, 449; 20.287; *Odyssey* 8.222. Cf. H. Fränkel, *Dichtung und Philosophie des frühen Griechentums* (2d ed. Munich 1962), 38 f.

117. Diodorus 12.28.3. Cf. 46.2; Plutarch, *Pericles* 27.3. See also Diodorus 14.42.1 ff.

118. K. Reinhardt, *Vermächtnis der Antike* (2d ed. Göttingen 1960), 189 f; Lauffer, "Die Lehre des Thukydides," 177; Romilly, "Thucydide et l'idée du progrès," 160.

119. 1.70 f, esp. 70.7. Cf. 3.38.3 ff; 4.55.2, 65.4; 5.84 ff; 6.9.3; 7.34.7. Cf. note 70 above. Euripides, *Suppliant Women* 323 ff. In Aristophanes' *Birds* (414 B.C.) two Athenians have themselves transformed into birds because they are tired of the city. No sooner has this happened than one of them suggests founding an empire: as Reinhardt, *Vermächtnis der Antike*, 307 f, puts it,

"the spirit of audacious activity that is peculiar to Attica celebrates its airiest triumphs in the heroes." Cf. Aristophanes, *Knights* 1087 ff. See Gomme on Thucydides 1.70.8.

120. Eupolis, fr. 217 (Kock); Aristophanes, *Ecclesiazusae* 473 ff; cf. *Clouds* (423 B.C.) 587 ff. Here it has not yet become a proverb, but perhaps expresses a very recent insight: because the Athenians, in electing Cleon, really had more luck than understanding (cf. ibid. 186, with the allusion to the successful storming of Sphacteria; Thucydides 4.27 ff, esp. 39.3 f). It cannot be ruled out that the "proverb" had its genesis in this affair. On the possibilities open to Athens cf. Thucydides 2.38.

121. Euripides, *Suppliant Women* 195 ff, 238 ff. Similarly Democritus B191. Other instances of parallels' being drawn between ages and social groupings occur in Thucydides 6.18.6 (with 12.2), 38.5–39.1. On this point cf. the significant but probably exaggerated observations of W. G. Forrest, *Yale Classical Studies* 24 (1975) 37 ff; Romilly, "Thucydide et l'idée du progrès," 167 ff; idem, *Wiener Studien* (1976). On *neoteropoiia* see note 52 above.

122. Formulated briefly and probably *ex eventu* by Thucydides 1.91.4 f (on this see Chapter 5, note 13, above). Cf. also Herodotus 7.139; H. Kleinknecht, *Hermes* 75 (1940) 241 ff (repr. in W. Marg [ed.], *Herodot* [Darmstadt 1965], 541 ff); Meier, in Jauss, *Die nicht mehr schönen Künste*, 98 f.

123. Aristotle, *Nicomachean Ethics* 1140a24 ff, b8, 1141b14 (see Chapter 5, note 226, above). Thucydides 1.140 ff, 2.65. The way in which Thucydides blames the defeat on the politicians who came after Pericles is comprehensible only if he is basically reckoning with extraordinary possibilities of political ability.

124. Thanks especially to the successes in foreign policy that brought concrete benefits to all; cf., e.g., Pseudo-Xenophon, *Athenaion Politeia* 1 ff. See also Reinhardt, *Von Werken und Formen*, 291. Aeschylus, *Eumenides* 853 f, 915.

125. Herodotus 1.5.3 f, 207.2. See C. Meier, *Die Entstehung des Politischen bei den Griechen* (Frankfurt 1983), 360 ff, esp. 408 ff, 430 ff, 433 n. 96. It is only because these claims also related to external policy that they could be called in question by a history like that of Herodotus.

126. Herodotus himself was keenly interested in inventions (see Edelstein, *Idea of Progress*, 32 ff; Kleingünther, *Philologus* Suppl. 26 (1933), 46 ff; Lauffer, "Der antike Fortschrittsgedanke," 39, but in any case excessive claims, whether of a "technical" or of a political nature, no doubt appeared to him as hubris. Cf. Euripides, *Suppliant Women* 216 ff. See O'Brien, *Socratic Paradoxes*, 70 ff.

127. This is true despite the fact that logically the decline of Athens as a great power did not preclude an increase in the size and power of the *poleis*: see Lauffer, "Die Lehre des Thukydides," 181, n. 10. In the fourth century Isocrates saw Athens as having a cultural mission (4.25 ff, 34 ff, 38 ff, 43 ff; cf. 103; Diodorus 13.26.3): this meant that its rule had a justification similar to that which is urged, within the framework of the modern consciousness of progress, by those claiming to help others towards progress. There

is, however, no trace of this idea in the fifth century. At this period the cultural efflorescence of Athens and the exemplary quality of its laws were associated at most with its political and military achievements as additional evidence of its power, greatness and ability (cf. Thucydides 2.36 ff).

128. Aeschylus in Porphyry, *De abstinentia* 2.18. See Hölscher, "Die Nike der Messenier," 103 f. Timotheus, *Persae* 219 ff. Edelstein, *Idea of Progress,* 35 f. Lesky, *Geschichte der griechischen Literatur,* 476. Cf. Aubenque, *La prudence chez Aristote* (Paris 1963). O'Brien, *Socratic Paradoxes,* 70 ff. Reinhardt, *Vermächtnis der Antike,* 184 ff, 212 ff (on Thucydides and Macchiavelli).

129. E.g., Thucydides 1.58.1, 97.1, 102.3, 115.2; 3.75.5; 4.108.3. Cf. also Aeschylus, *Persae* 782; Herodotus 5.19.2; Democritus B191 (*Frag. der Vorsokratiker* II, 184); Lysias 13.6; Xenophon, *Hellenica* 5.2.9. See note 29 above.

130. F. Schachermeyr, *Perikles* (Stuttgart 1969), 188 ff, 201 ff.

131. A. Fuks, *The Ancestral Constitution* (London 1953); M. I. Finley, *The Use and Abuse of History* (London 1975), 34 ff. See also Plato, *Hippias Major* 282a. Cf. *Protagoras* 316d, e; Thucydides 2.35.2.

132. The issue was obviously the recent increase in expenses for attendance at the Assembly (*Ecclesiazusae* 185 ff, 282 f, 292, 300 ff, 392; *Plutus* 329). J. Beloch, *Die attische Politik seit Perikles* (1884), 120 f. Though it proves nothing, it is interesting to note in this connection that, with regard to innovations, Aristotle acknowledges only a limited similarity between the technical and the political fields (*Politics* 1268b22–1269a28). Cf. Plato, *Laws* 797c. For Aristophanes' audience see T. Gelzer, *RE Suppl.* XII (1971), 1535 ff.

133. *Ecclesiazusae* 220, 338, 456 f, 578 ff, 586 f.

134. Characteristically Thucydides writes *ta epigignomena.* Xenophanes speaks of *epheuriskein,* B18; see note 58. One should note the accumulation of compounds with *epi* in Thucydides 1.70.2 (which is certainly intentional, like that of compounds with *pro* in 3.38.6), 3.82.3.

135. B. Snell, "Aischylos und das Handeln im Drama," *Philologus* Suppl. 20 (1928) 12 ff; idem, *Philologus* 85 (1930) 141 ff; idem, *Dichtung und Gesellschaft,* 147 ff, 170 f; idem, *Die Entdeckung des Geistes,* 103 ff. Cf. C. Meier, *Poetica* 8 (1976) 439 f.

136. Dodds, *Ancient Concept of Progress,* 24. It would be interesting (though the point cannot be pursued here) to show how modern research repeatedly runs into difficulties and contradictions by letting itself be drawn by its discoveries about the ancient world into the ambit of the modern notion of progress, however generally this is understood. Cf., e.g., the motley assortment of correct and incorrect observations in Romilly, "Thucydide et l'idée du progrès," 159, 173 ff, 175 ff. I believe that one can avoid this, as I have attempted to do here, through a precise, theoretically based analysis.

137. Cf. Meier, *Entstehung des Politischen,* 360 ff.

138. Romilly, *Time in Greek Tragedy;* the quotation from Heraclitus occurs in B52 (*Frag. der Vorsokratiker* I, 162). Cf. Thraede, "Fortschritt," 146; Guthrie, *History of Greek Philosophy* III, 82.

139. Cf. Meier, *Entstehung des Politischen*, 408 ff, 419 n. 79. The alternation of rulers and ruled is also characteristic of democracy, where equality among the citizens corresponds to equality in time. On the "social construction of reality" see P. Berger and T. Luckmann, *The Social Construction of Reality* (Garden City, N.Y., 1966).

140. Cf. the beginning of Chapter 7.

141. Snell, *Die Entdeckung des Geistes*, 106.

142. Meier, "Umbruch zur Demokratie."

143. Here follow conclusions that I hope to justify more fully in a forthcoming book titled *Die Anfänge des politischen Denkens bei den Griechen*. Cf. the beginning of Chapter 3 above.

144. Cf. the beginning of Chapter 4.

145. In this connection cf., e.g., the attribution of technical achievements to individual inventors (see Kleingünther, *Philologus* Suppl. 26 [1933]), of cities to individual founders (e.g., Aristotle, *Politics* 1253a31), and even of unwritten norms to originators (H. J. Wolff, "'Normenkontrolle' und Gesetzesbegriff in der attischen Demokratie," *Sitzungsberichte der Heidelberger Akademie* [1970], 70). See also note 60 above.

146. 3.80.6 Cf. G. Vlastos, *American Journal of Philology* 74 (1953) 358. This was the consciousness of the broad sections of the citizenry who now held power, who gave reality to the civic order and opened up new opportunities for the community: O'Brien, *Socratic Paradoxes*, 70.

147. Cf. the certainty with which Solon, in *Elegies* 3 (Diehl), speaks of the kindness of the gods, which clearly reveals itself in his new insights.

148. Cf., e.g., Herodotus 1.170, 5.36.

149. Edelstein, *Idea of Progress*, 11 ff; Kleingünther, *Philologus* Suppl. 26 (1933) 21 ff. Cf. U. Hölscher, *Griechische Historienbilder des 5. und 4. Jahrhunderts vor Christus* (Würzburg 1973), 35 ff, 200.

150. P. Vernant, *Annales* 20 (1965) 577. On the term see Chapter 4, note 26, above.

151. Cf. H. Berve, "Das delphische Orakel," in *Gestaltende Kräfte der Antike* (Munich 1949), 9 ff; M. P. Nilsson, *Geschichte der griechischen Religion* I (3d ed. Munich 1967), 625 ff; E. R. Dodds, *The Greeks and the Irrational* (Berkeley 1951), 43 ff, 64 ff.

152. Hölscher, *Griechische Historienbilder*, 205 f; idem, "Die Nike der Messenier," 98 ff, esp. 101 n. 142. A more precise justification for the distinction between the nomistic and cratistic basis of the constitution and thought is given in Meier, *Die Anfänge des politischen Denkens*. On the attendant problems of source criticism see P. Spahn, *Mittelschicht und Polisbildung* (Frankfurt/Bern/Las Vegas 1977), 15 ff.

153. Hölscher, "Die Nike der Messenier," 99, 103. In architecture things take a somewhat different course. The radical reversal of early classicism is hardly perceptible, but comparable changes occur a generation later. See G. Gruben, *Die Tempel der Griechen* (2d ed. Munich 1976), 120 f, 164 ff, 184 ff, 226 f. Gruben describes Ictinus as a "matchless avant-gardist." It is also difficult to assess the extent to which the "political buildings" in Athens (all probably erected after about 460) are innovations.

154. C. Meier, *Die politische Kunst der griechischen Tragödie* (Munich 1988).
155. Cf. Chapter 5, note 13, above.
156. Cf. Hölscher, "Die Nike der Messenier," 91 (on "brilliant bravura achievements"), 98 ff, esp. 99, 103. We seldom hear of any debt to forerunners, though one exception is *On Ancient Medicine;* Thucydides 2.36.
157. These are the vivid terms used by Herodotus (3.82.2, 6.142.3). Cf. Chapter 7, note 26, above.
158. Cf. C. Meier, "Die politische Identität der Griechen," in O. Marquard and K. H. Stierle (eds.), *Identität* (Munich 1979), 371 ff; C. Meier and P. Veyne, *Kannten die Griechen die Demokratie?* (Berlin 1988).
159. Cf. Meier, *Entstehung des Politischen,* 421. This is matched by the "new quality" of "what we call 'development'" (Hölscher, "Die Nike der Messenier," 104).
160. Cf. Chapter 7.
161. This whole complex is still essentially unexplored; any exploration would probably have to be based on a theory of identity. Some of the relevant problems are discussed by Marquard, *Schwierigkeiten mit der Geschichtsphilosophie,* 73 ff, others by E. Erikson, *Dimensions of a New Identity* (New York 1974). Erikson considers quite different forms of identity that arose in America and were largely based on the initiative of individuals and social groups.
162. See Koselleck, "Fortschritt," 358 ff (with further literature).
163. Aristotle, *Politics* 1264a3.
164. This is found in Sophocles and Thucydides, and subsequently in Plato, *Laws* 676a, 679b; Demosthenes 9.47 ff. See Dodds's review of Edelstein, *Journal of the History of Ideas* 29 (1968) 454; A. Dihle, *Gnomon* 41 (1969) 435 f.
165. Cf. Koselleck, *Futures Past,* 168 f. But when backward peoples were cited as evidence of how the Greeks had once lived, this did not lead to the conclusion that they, like the Greeks, were advancing and would one day reach an equally high level of development. Cf., e.g., the treatise *On Airs, Waters, Places (Corpus Hippocraticum).*
166. This is connected with the "désindividualisation and dépersonnalisation des événements modernes" noted by R. Aron, *Dimensions de la conscience historique* (Paris 1961), 182 ff. The notion of the process remains, even if "progress" is limited to the scientific, technical, and mechanical fields, and action remains in the more narrowly defined sphere of the "feasible." This leaves a "consciousness of expertise" that is restricted at best to certain areas, since the element of action in the political sphere is, by comparison, too weak.
167. H. Arendt, *Between Past and Future* (London 1961), 76 ff, 85 f.
168. K. Marx and F. Engels, *Gesamtausgabe (MEGA),* I.2 (Berlin 1982), 61 (*Collected Works* [London 1975–], 57). (Translator's note: The English translation cited renders the word *Fortschritt* as "advance"; here, as elsewhere in this chapter, I have rendered it as "progress.")
169. U. Hölscher, *Die Chance des Unbehagens* (Göttingen 1965), 81.

Index